The Life of a Patron

The Life of a Patron

ZHOU LIANGGONG (1612–1672) AND THE PAINTERS OF SEVENTEENTH-CENTURY CHINA

HONGNAM KIM

China Institute in America · New York · 1996

This catalogue was produced to accompany the exhibition "The Life of a Patron: Zhou Lianggong (1612–1672) and the Painters of Seventeenth-Century China" held at China Institute Gallery, October 23 – December 21, 1996.

China Institute Gallery
125 East 65th Street, New York, NY 10021
(212) 744–8181

Library of Congress Catalog Card Number: 96–86267

ISBN 0–9654270–0–5

General Editor and Coordinator: D. Page Shaver
Editor: Marilyn Wong Gleysteen
Consulting Editors: Willow Weilan Hai, Freeman Keith
Cartographer: Carolann Barrett
Chinese typesetting: Dawn Carelli
Printed by Pressroom, Hong Kong
Design: Christopher Kuntze

Chinese is romanized in the *pinyin* system throughout the text and bibliography except for the names of Chinese authors writing in Western languages. Chinese terms cited in Western-language titles remain in their original form and have not been converted.

China Institute was founded in 1926 by American philosopher John Dewey and Chinese educator Hu Shih, together with other prominent educators. It is the oldest bicultural and educational organization in the United States with an exclusive focus on China, and is dedicated to introducing Chinese culture to American audiences and fostering international understanding between Chinese and Americans.

Cover illustration (cat. no. 17, Leaf F): "Zhongshan," (detail). Hu Yukun (fl. 1640 –1672). From an album of 12 leaves, "Historic Spots in Nanjing." Ink and color on paper; 25.5 cm x 18.1 cm. Guan Lu Yuan collection.

Frontispiece illustration: "Scholar in a Boat," (detail). Chen Hongshou (1599–1652). Album leaf, ink and color on paper. The Freer Gallery of Art, Washington, D.C.

Contents

LIST OF MAPS

Map 1
Places Relevant to Zhou Lianggong and the *Du Hua Lu* Artists

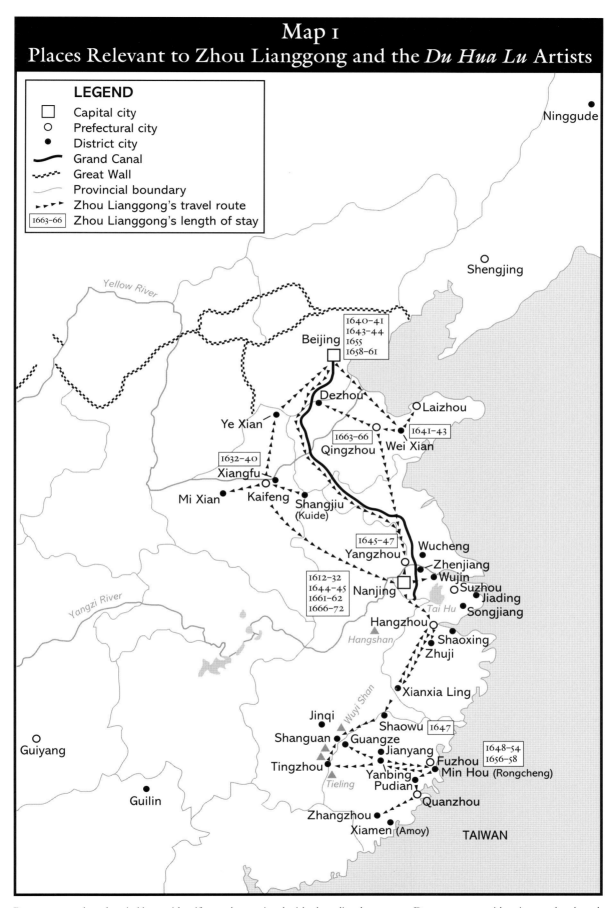

LEGEND
- ☐ Capital city
- ○ Prefectural city
- ● District city
- ▬ Grand Canal
- ⌁ Great Wall
- ～ Provincial boundary
- ►►► Zhou Lianggong's travel route
- 1663–66 Zhou Lianggong's length of stay

Ninggude

Shengjing

Yellow River

Beijing
1640–41
1643–44
1655
1658–61

Dezhou

Laizhou

Ye Xian

Qingzhou   1663–66

Wei Xian   1641–43

Xiangfu   1632–40

Kaifeng

Mi Xian

Shangjiu (Kuide)

Wucheng

Yangzhou   1645–47

Zhenjiang

Wujin

Nanjing
1612–32
1644–45
1661–62
1666–72

Suzhou

Jiading

Songjiang

Tai Hu

Yangzi River

Hangzhou

Shaoxing

Zhuji

Hangshan

Wuyi Shan

Xianxia Ling

Guiyang

Jinqi

Shaowu   1647

Shanguan

Guangze

1648–54
1656–58

Tingzhou

Jianyang

Fuzhou

Min Hou (Rongcheng)

Yanbing

Pudian

Quanzhou

Guilin

Tieling

Zhangzhou

Xiamen (Amoy)

TAIWAN

Roman numerals and capital letters identify people associated with places listed on page 9. Due to space considerations, only selected places are romanized. Maps 2 and 3 are not drawn to scale.

Map 2
Reconstructed Map of Nanjing in the Seventeenth Century

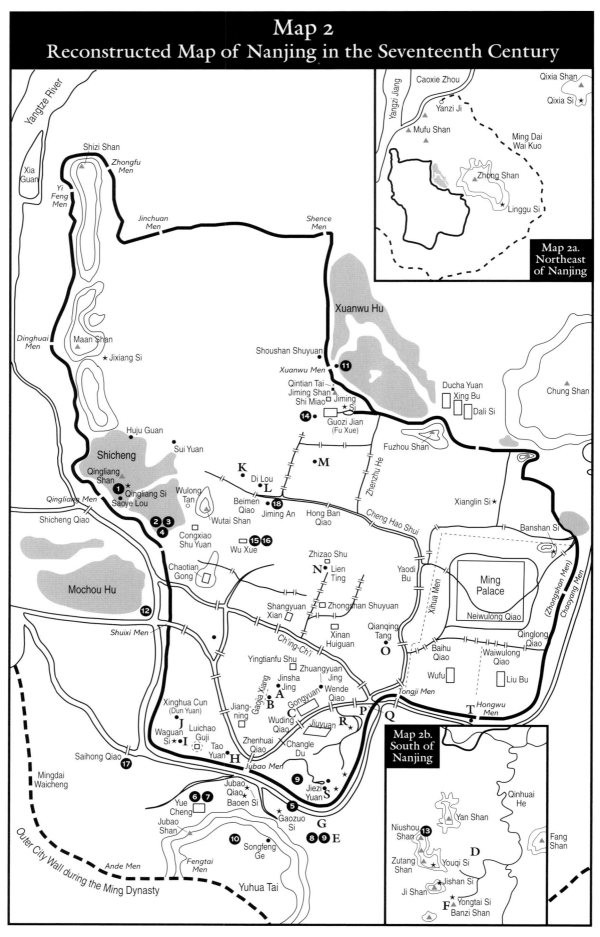

Map 2a.
Northeast
of Nanjing

Map 2b.
South of
Nanjing

Map 3
The Qinhuai Area in Nanjing

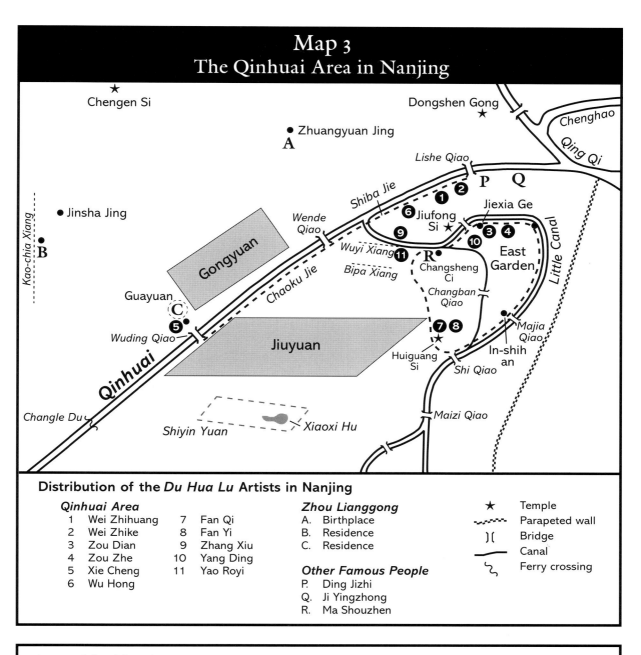

Distribution of the *Du Hua Lu* Artists in Nanjing

Qinhuai Area
1. Wei Zhihuang
2. Wei Zhike
3. Zou Dian
4. Zou Zhe
5. Xie Cheng
6. Wu Hong
7. Fan Qi
8. Fan Yi
9. Zhang Xiu
10. Yang Ding
11. Yao Royi

Zhou Lianggong
A. Birthplace
B. Residence
C. Residence

Other Famous People
P. Ding Jizhi
Q. Ji Yingzhong
R. Ma Shouzhen

★ Temple
⌁ Parapeted wall
)(Bridge
— Canal
〜 Ferry crossing

Legend for Map 2

Qingliang Shan/Shicheng Area
1. Gong Xian
2. Gao Cen and Gao Fu
3. Gao Yu
4. Wu Hong

Yuha Tai Area
5. Chen Danzhong
6. Zhu Ruiwu
7. Zhu Zhiqiao
8. Fang Yizhi
9. Zhang Feng and Zhang Yi
10. Chen Shu

Xuanwu Hu Area
11. Fang Hengxian

Mochou Hu Area
12. Wang Kai

Niushou Shan Area (Map 2b)
13. Kuncan

Other Areas
14. Wu Weiye
15. Hu Zongren
16. Hu Yukun
17. Yang Wencong
18. Ma Shiying

Zhou Lianggong
A. Birthplace
B. Residence
C. Residence
D. Temporary residence
E. Temporary residence
F. Ancestral graveyard

Other Famous People
G. Daoji
H. Ruan Dacheng
I. Fang Wen
J. Ku Qiyuan
K. Jiao Hong
L. Hou Fangyu
M. Du Jun
N. Cao Yin
O. Huang Yuji
P. Ding Jizhi
Q. Ji Yingzhong
R. Ma Shouzhen
S. Li Liweng
T. Matteo Ricci

GLOSSARY FOR MAP 1

Beijing	北京
Dezhou	德州
Fuzhou	福州
Guangze	光澤
Guilin	桂林
Guiyang	貴陽
Hangzhou	杭州
Huangshan	黃山
Jiading	嘉定
Jianyang	建陽
Jinqi	金溪
Kaifeng	開封
Laizhou	萊州
Mi Xian	密縣
Min Hou (Rongcheng)	閩侯 (榕城)
Nanjing	南京
Ningguta	寧古塔
Putian	莆田
Qingzhou	青州
Quanzhou	泉州
Shangqiu (Guide)	商丘 (歸德)
Shanguan	杉關
Shaowu	邵武
Shaoxing	紹興
Shengjing	盛京
Songjiang	淞江
Suzhou	蘇州
Tai Hu	太湖
Tieling	鐵嶺
Tingzhou	汀州
Wei Xian	濰縣
Wucheng	吳城
Wujin	武進
Wuyi Shan	武夷山
Xiamen (Amoy)	廈門
Xiangfu	祥符
Xianxia Ling	仙霞嶺
Yangzhou	揚州
Yangzi River	揚子江
Yanping	延平
Ye Xian	鄞縣
Zhangzhou	漳州
Zhenjiang	鎮江
Zhuji	諸暨

GLOSSARY FOR MAP 2

Ande Men	安德門
Baihu Qiao	白虎橋
Banshan Si	半山寺
Banzi Shan	半子山
Baoen Si	寶恩寺
Beimen Qiao	北門橋
Caoxie Zhou	草鞋州
Changle Du	長樂渡
Chaotian Gong	朝天宮
Chaoyang Men	朝陽門
Cheng Hao Shui	城濠水
Congxiao Shuyuan	叢霄書院
Dali Si	大理寺
Di Lou	地樓
Dinghuai Men	定淮門
Dong Ting	棟亭
Ducha Yuan	都察院
Fang Shan	方山
Fengtai Men	鳳台門
Fuzhou Shan	覆舟山
Gaojia Xiang	高家巷
Gaozuo Si	高座寺
Gongyuan	貢院
Guozi Jian (Fu Xue)	國子監 (府學)
Hong Ban Qiao	紅板橋
Hongwu Men	洪武門
Huju Guan	虎踞關
Ji Shan	吉山
Jiangning	江寧
Jiezi Yuan	芥子園
Jiming An	雞鳴菴
Jiming Shan	雞鳴山
Jiming Si	雞鳴寺
Jinchuan Men	金川門
Jinsha Jing	金沙井
Jishan Si	吉山寺
Jiuyuan	舊院
Jixiang Si	吉祥寺
Jubao	聚寶
Jubao Men	聚寶門
Jubao Qiao	聚寶橋
Linggu Si	靈谷寺
Liu Bu	六部
Liuchao Guji	六朝古蹟
Maan Shan	馬鞍山

Mingdai Wai Kuo	明代外廓	Yi Feng Men	儀鳳門
Mingdai Waicheng	明代外城	Yingtianfu Shu	應天府署
Mufu Shan	幕府山	Yongtai Si	永泰寺
Neiwulong Qiao	內五龍橋	Youqi Si	幽棲寺
Niushou Shan	牛首山	Yue Cheng	越城
Qianqing Tang	千頃堂	Zhenhuai Qiao	鎮淮橋
Qingliang Men	清涼門	Zhenzhu He	珍珠河
Qingliang Shan	清涼山	Zhizao Shu	織造署
Qingliang Si	清涼寺	Zhong Shan	鐘山
Qinglong Qiao	青龍橋	Zhongfu Men	鐘阜門
Qinhuai He	秦淮河	Zhongshan Men	中山門
Qintian Tai	欽天台	Zhongshan Shuyuan	鐘山書院
Qixia Shan	棲霞山	Zhuangyuan Jing	狀元境
Qixia Si	棲霞寺	Zutang Shan	祖堂山
Saihong Qiao	賽虹橋		
Saoye Lou	掃葉樓		
Shangyuan Xian	上元縣	GLOSSARY FOR MAP 3	
Shence Men	神策門		
Shi Miao	十廟	Changban Qiao	長板橋
Shicheng	石城	Changle Du	長樂渡
Shicheng Qiao	石城橋	Changsheng Ci	長生祠
Shizi Shan	獅子山	Chaoku Jie	鈔庫街
Shoushan Shuyuan	首善書院	Chengen Si	承恩寺
Shuixi Men	水西門	Chenghao	城濠
Songfeng Ge	松風閣	Dongshen Gong	洞神宮
Sui Yuan	隨園	Gongyuan	貢院
Tao Yuan	桃園	Guayuan	栝園
Tongji Men	通濟門	Huiguang Si	迴光寺
Waguan Si	瓦官寺	Jiexia Ge	節霞閣
Waiwulong Qiao	外五龍橋	Jinsha Jing	金沙井
Wende Qiao	文德橋	Jiufeng Si	鷲峰寺
Wu Xue	武學	Jiuyuan	舊院
Wuding Qiao	武定橋	Lishe Qiao	利涉橋
Wufu	五府	Maizi Qiao	麥子橋
Wulong Tan	烏龍潭	Majia Qiao	馬家橋
Wutai Shan	五台山	Nanjing	南京
Xia Guan	下關	Pipa Xiang	琵琶巷
Xianglin Si	香林寺	Qing Qi	青溪
Xihua Men	西華門	Qinhuai	秦淮
Xinan Huiguan	新安會館	Shi Qiao	石橋
Xing Bu	刑部	Shiba Jie	石壩街
Xinghua Cun (Dun Yuan)	杏花村 (遯園)	Shiyin Yuan	市隱園
Xuanwu Men	玄武門	Wende Qiao	文德橋
Yan Shan	嚴山	Wuding Qiao	武定橋
Yangzi Jiang	揚子江	Wuyi Xiang	烏衣巷
Yanzi Ji	燕子磯	Xiaoxi Hu	小西湖
Yaodi Bu	邀笛步	Zhuangyuan Jing	狀元境

Summary in Chinese

十七世紀，對漢民族而言，是一個充滿恐怖與恥辱的時代。在異民族滿清王朝的征服下，國破家亡，生靈塗炭，中國文人的命運一變於旦夕。民族的苦難，激發了藝術家的創造性，繪畫藝術於茲取得多元化的成就。周亮工，作為一個政治家，藝術收藏家，鑑賞家，評論家，是當時令人矚目的社會中堅之士。

周亮工字元亮，一字減齋，又字櫟園，學者稱櫟下先生。河南開封人，明萬歷四十年（一六一二）生於金陵，舉崇禎十三年（一六四零）進士。初任濰縣知縣，行取浙江道試御史。明亡，避居南京。清師下江南，迎降，歷任兩淮鹽運史，福建按察使，布政史，戶部右侍郎等職。亮工入清後，官位雖顯，然數有起躓，飽經宦海風霜。康熙十一年（一六七二）逝世。儘管周亮工臣於滿清，遺人話柄，但從政的一席之地卻給與他以衛護漢族民眾，保護和弘揚傳統文化的機會。籍其所享俸祿，他亦有可能收藏藝術品，獎掖藝術家。

從一六四一年為朝廷之命官始，至其病逝的三十年中，周亮工從未中斷過收藏。其所藏各家的作品雖多寡不一，為其所識的畫家卻達一百四十五人之眾。這一畫家的名單恰如十七世紀中期的中國藝術家名人大辭典。除了繪畫作品外，他還鍾愛印章銅器等。他如醉如痴的收藏熱忱，足以證明他是一個與生俱來的收藏家。在其所撰的《印人傳》中曾有一段自我寫照："僕沉湎於印章者蓋三十年，於茲矣，自矜從流溯源得其正變者，海內無僕若間。"又曰："子生平好圖章，見秦漢篆刻及名賢手製，則愛玩撫弄終日不去手，至廢餐寢以求騁其欲，不啻如時花美女。"

周亮工的大宗珍藏，常被載於他的聞名的畫舫，隨其因公私之故往返於北京至福州的途中，供人觀賞研習，甚而延攬畫家至其畫舫及宅邸作畫。他對藝術的巨大影響，令畫家們趨之若鶩，尋求其贊許和呵護。一六六九年，龔賢曾在一幅冊頁的題跋中寫道："…詩人周櫟園先生有畫癖，來官茲土，結讀畫樓，樓頭萬軸千箱，集古勿論，凡寓內以畫鳴者，聞先生之風，星流電激，惟恐遲至，而況先生以書召以幣迎乎，故載几盈床…"

作為一個傳統文人，周亮工堅信藝以載道的美學觀念，把藝術作為修身養性陶冶情操的利器，故將山水畫奉為最高的藝術形式。在是否承襲傳統繪畫風格與弘揚個人風格的藝術評論中，周亮工反對在文學和繪畫中因循守舊，但主張在既不完全棄絕傳統的藝術風格，又不使藝術脫離儒家道德規範的基礎上，發揚繪畫的個人風格。

當時，無論是傳統派畫家或個性派畫家，其畫藝均臻於高妙。周亮工早年偏愛個性畫家，故能激賞具有強烈個人風格的畫家如陳洪綬，龔賢，甚至當時還不甚負名的畫家如髡殘與弘仁。及其晚年，醉心正統畫家王翬的作品，將之奉為徹悟古典繪畫精神和形式，並將之薪傳於世的大家。終其一生，周亮工與其家鄉南京及其地的畫家關係密切，他們的藝術作品亦構成了他收藏的主流。

周亮工又是明末清初的著名學者，才氣高逸，記聞淹博，生平著述甚富，除詩文集外，《讀畫錄》是一部傳記式的畫家筆記，所錄畫家大多活躍於周之同時，自一六七三年刊印始，便被公認為了解十七世紀中國繪畫的經典。其所著《印人傳》，除了將著名篆刻家的豐富資料留給後世以外，還奠定了周亮工作為大散文家的歷史地位。

當年曾由周亮工聚其熱忱與財力，目睹手撫，親自收藏的許多畫作，輾轉易主，留傳于今，構成這一展覽的核心。縱觀周亮工的生平和思想，細咀《讀畫錄》所載畫家之小傳，將使我們如聞其聲，如見其人，引發接近其畫作的親切感受，從而增進我們對中國繪畫的理解。

海蔚藍據Hongnam Kim的英文簡介侈譯並編寫

This exhibition and catalogue have been made possible in part through the generous support of

E. RHODES AND LEONA B. CARPENTER FOUNDATION

NATIONAL ENDOWMENT FOR THE HUMANITIES

NATIONAL ENDOWMENT FOR THE ARTS

JOHN AND JULIA CURTIS

CHINA INSTITUTE GALLERY PATRONS AND SPONSORS

We are also grateful for the continuing support to China Institute from

THE HENRY LUCE FOUNDATION

THE STARR FOUNDATION

We gratefully acknowledge the following Lenders to the Exhibition

THE ART INSTITUTE OF CHICAGO

THE ART MUSEUM, PRINCETON UNIVERSITY

ASIAN ART MUSEUM OF SAN FRANCISCO

THE BRITISH MUSEUM

THE FREER GALLERY OF ART, SMITHSONIAN INSTITUTION

GUAN LU YUAN COLLECTION

THE HONOLULU ACADEMY OF ARTS

HONGNAM KIM

THE LIBRARY OF CONGRESS

H. CHRISTOPHER LUCE

THE METROPOLITAN MUSEUM OF ART

THE NELSON-ATKINS MUSEUM OF ART

A PRIVATE COLLECTION

C. C. WANG

WANG FANGYU

Foreword

China Institute is proud to present the exhibition "The Life of a Patron: Zhou Lianggong (1612–1672) and the Painters of Seventeenth-Century China" which examines the art and artists of one of the most dynamic periods in Chinese painting: that engendered by the collapse of the native Ming dynasty under the military weight of the Manchus invading from the north. While the transition to the new alien dynasty transpired with relative ease, subjugation by a foreign ruler aroused feelings of nationalist pride, resentment, and often despair that served to intensify the tumult that naturally attends periods of dynastic change.

Not surprisingly, these feelings found expression through dynamic, evolutionary developments in the arts, of which contemporary documents offer vivid accounts. In the writings of the great seventeenth-century art patron and connoisseur Zhou Lianggong, we find intimate descriptions of the lives and struggles of many artists who worked in the Jiangnan area during this period. Moreover, his massive, personal art collection, a portion of which is reassembled in this exhibition, preserved for us works by not only most of the greatest masters of the time, but by other fine painters who might otherwise have fallen into obscurity.

A high government official, Zhou Lianggong was in many ways a typical scholar-connoisseur. He collected antiques — bronzes and seals — and cultivated in himself the Confucian "polite arts" of poetry and calligraphy. However, unlike the typical scholar-connoisseur who sought out works by the great artists of the past, Zhou focused on contemporary painters, both individualist and orthodox, as well as seal carvers. Further, concerned with preserving their names in history, he recorded their biographies which he compiled in his books *Du Hua Lu* (Lives of Painters) and *Yinren zhuan* (Lives of Seal Carvers).

This exhibition celebrates Zhou Lianggong's legacy to the study of seventeenth-century Chinese painting. His writings continue to be definitive sources for information, and his accounts of personal encounters and friendships with most of the artists give us an immediate, familiar glimpse into the art world of his time. Most of this knowledge would remain inaccessible to the West, however, were it not for the exhaustive efforts of Dr. Hongnam Kim. Through years of painstaking research and exacting scholarship, Dr. Kim has compiled valuable information about Zhou Lianggong's life and writings, many of which she has translated into English for the first time. China Institute Gallery is delighted and honored to have worked with Dr. Kim during the organization of this exhibition. Her expertise, guidance, and creativity inspired everyone involved.

We are grateful to the many people who gave of their time and talent to make this exhibition a reality. Thanks especially to Candace Lewis, former director of the gallery, for her efforts during the early stages of organization, and to Nancy Jervis, Vice President, and Sarah Stack who guided the exhibition through its subsequent stages of development. President Alan Wachman and members of the Gallery Committee, co-chaired by Marie-Hélène Weill and Millie Chan, gave generously of their support, for which we are very grateful. Gwynne Tuan, Director of Development, and Kimberly Benou enthusiastically supported the project and its promotion. Carl Nardiello, as always, beautifully designed the installation, and catalogue designer Christopher Kuntze graciously met the demands of the production schedule while maintaining good humor and the highest professional standards. We are also grateful to Carolann Barrett who worked tirelessly in creating and refining the maps for the catalogue. We are especially grateful to Dr. Marilyn Wong Gleysteen for editing the manuscript, and offering many helpful suggestions for its improvement.

Many others who gave countless hours of their time to the production of the catalogue deserve our gratitude. Willow Hai Chang, Curator, not only worked diligently to organize the installation, but served generously as a consulting editor for the manuscript. Thanks are also due to Dr. Bai Qianshen of Western Michigan University for his assistance with the bibliography. Freeman Keith served expertly as copy editor and Dawn Carelli assisted with the Chinese typesetting. For their timely help we are thankful. Gallery Assistant Kerrie Lorenzo helped with all aspects of the exhibition and catalogue, and kept track of countless details with aplomb. The generosity and commitment of these people has been exemplary.

Others without whose support this exhibition and catalogue could not have been realized warrant a special word of thanks. I am personally grateful to Maxwell Hearn and Robert Mowry for giving of their time, advice, and assistance with unstinting generosity and good will. Thanks are also due to James Cahill, Jonathan Chaves, and Jerome Silbergeld who served as advisors to the exhibition and supported the project from the beginning. Assistance also came from members of the Art Committee, chaired by Dr. Annette Juliano. Coordination of art transport was arranged by Alix Brown with the Technical Assistance Program of the American Federation of Arts. We are especially grateful to all the lenders, both private and insitutional, who so generously loaned their works to ensure not only the high aesthetic appeal of the exhibition, but its scholarly import as well.

China Institute acknowledges with sincere appreciation its trustees and members whose support continually allows us to offer projects such as this. We are immensely grateful for funding received specifically for this exhibition from the E. Rhodes and Leona B. Carpenter Foundation, The National Endowment for the Humanities, The National Endowment for the Arts, and the China Institute Gallery Patrons and Sponsors. In particular, we owe a debt of gratitude to John and Julia Curtis who generously supported the exhibition and catalogue, and helped in numerous ways to secure their funding. This exhibition was also made possible through the continuing support to China Institute of The Henry Luce Foundation and The Starr Foundation. To them we are most grateful.

D. Page Shaver
Director
China Institute Gallery

Acknowledgments

This exhibition and catalogue mark the culmination of a project that began over a decade ago. My early days of research on the life and times of Zhou Lianggong instilled in me an abiding dedication to biography as a rich venue for the study of Chinese art and culture. Since that time, I have had the pleasure and honor of meeting and talking with Chinese art collectors, connoisseurs, and historians who have owned and enjoyed works once held in Zhou's personal collection. As we talked, I was gratified to see these new friends absorb some of my enthusiasm for Zhou Lianggong as we explored together Zhou's personal life and connection with the artists whose works they so admired.

My own study of Zhou has been guided and enriched by many teachers and colleagues to whom I am deeply indebted. In particular, I would like to thank my graduate school advisor at Yale, Shen C. Y. Fu, and other members of the art history department during my days there, especially Marilyn Wong Gleysteen and Richard Barnhart. Jonathan D. Spence of the history department was particularly instrumental in shaping my approach to art historiography, and to him I would like to offer a special word of thanks. Though space does not allow a complete list, there are numerous others with whom I subsequently worked whose advice and support proved invaluable, especially James Cahill, Wen Fong, and Thomas Lawton, to whom I am very grateful.

To my great delight, several of these friends and colleagues joined in the effort to bring about this exhibition and catalogue. Marilyn Gleysteen graciously edited the manuscript and added many improvements, while James Cahill served generously as a special advisor. I am grateful to China Institute for hosting the exhibition, and for the support of the trustees and members of the art committee. I feel especially grateful to Annette Juliano, Nancy Jervis, and Sarah Stack for their tireless efforts during the early organization of the exhibition. To all of these people, for their support and commitment to the project, I am deeply thankful.

Many others should be acknowledged whose work and expertise have made the project a reality. I am most grateful to Alan M. Wachman, president of China Institute, for his support, to D. Page Shaver, director of the gallery, for keeping the project on course through its final stages, and to Willow Hai Chang, curator, for her invaluable suggestions, advice, and personal warmth. Carl Nardiello's installation design beautifully communicates the exhibition's intimate focus on Zhou's life and personality. I am also grateful to Christopher Kuntze, whose enthusiasm for the art resulted in a sensitive and beautiful catalogue design. In particular, I am indebted to Maxwell K. Hearn, curator of Chinese art at the Metropolitan Museum of Art, for his professional advice and invaluable assistance in procuring the loan of a number of objects in the exhibition.

I am also indebted to all of the institutions and private lenders whose works, here joined together, offer a stunning, yet intimate view of Zhou Lianggong and the Chinese art world of the mid-17th century. And finally, my deepest thanks go to John and Julia Curtis for their unfailing belief in the importance of the project, and their constant support and encouragement. Without their efforts, this exhibition and catalogue could not have been realized.

Hongnam Kim

Fig. 1. Yu Zhiding (1647 – d. after 1701). "Portrait of Zhou Lianggong." Album leaf mounted as hanging scroll, ink and color on paper, 31.8 cm x 34.3 cm. Wang Chi-ch'ien collection, New York. (Cat. no. 2)

Fig. 2. Gong Xian (c. 1620–1689). Colophon dated 1669 to accompany Cheng Zhengkui's painting in an album dedicated to Zhou Lianggong. Album leaf, ink on paper, 27.1 cm x 17.6 cm. National Palace Museum, Taipei. (Cat. no. 6, leaf FF)

This is one of the most frequently quoted colophons of the period. As an important member of the Nanjing art circle, Gong Xian notes Nanjing's prominence as the center of culture and art and pays tribute to Zhou Lianggong's patronage and cultural leadership.

Introduction

The seventeenth century was an age of extraordinary achievements in the visual arts in China. The array of creative energies was as remarkable for diversity as for fruitfulness. It was also an age of terror and disgrace for native Chinese who watched their country collapsing under the Manchu conquest. This crucial historical event fatefully altered and transformed the lives of many important and influential people in politics, culture, and art. Zhou Lianggong (1612–1672) stood in the midst of it all. He served both the fallen Ming dynasty and the new Manchu regime. He became the central figure of the age in the field of contemporary art as patron collector, commentator, and critic. Zhou Lianggong's life and art patronage are intertwined against this historical setting (fig. 1).

Zhou's devotion to contemporary art with all its intensity was perhaps unique in traditional China. He traveled extensively in office and in leisure and often took along his massive collection of contemporary paintings while visiting all cities en route from Beijing to Fujian. Zhou's collection of paintings and seals was unrivaled in his day and his extensive influence within the art world led artists to seek his endorsement (fig. 2):

> The poet Master Zhou Lianggong has a propensity for painting. He is a government official in this place [Nanjing]. He built the *Du Hua* [Viewing Painting] pavilion where he stored his cases of [album] paintings, not to mention his collection of antiques. All painters of renown in this country, upon learning of his reputation, come fast like shooting stars or lightning, only being afraid to arrive late. How much more so when he summons them in writing and welcomes them with money. Therefore [their paintings] fill his desk and bed . . . .
>
> One day, I visited him by chance. He took out this album for me to see. I have carefully viewed it four times. They [the leaves in the album] are all in the class of divine and untrammeled. Among them, I especially liked the one leaf by Vice-president Cheng Zhengkui. Therefore I noted down several words. Luckily this album already has many writings by others [in which they expressed their admiration for him], otherwise, my writing would have been criticized as mere flattery.
>
> (Colophon by Gong Xian, 1669, to an album)

From 1641, the first year of his government service, until his death in 1672, Zhou Lianggong zealously collected contemporary paintings. The number of painters Zhou knew personally exceeded the one hundred and forty-five artists known to have contributed to his collection. Many of these artists spent some time working at Zhou's

Fig. 3. Chen Hongshou (1599–1652). "Scholar in a Boat." Album leaf, ink and color on paper. The Freer Gallery of Art, Washington, D.C. (61.10B)

Canals and waterways were the main means of traveling through Jiangnan, south of the Yangzi River. Zhou's "Jiuyuan" boat was a moving gallery where artists and friends viewed his collection and often painted for him. Many of Chen Hongshou's works in Zhou's collection were begun on this boat.

residence or on his famous gallery boat (fig. 3). The list of artists who contributed to his collection is truly a "Who's Who" of the mid-seventeenth-century art world. The number of works he acquired from each artist varied from a few occasional pieces to massive collections.

Zhou's collection of paintings was so extensive that some must have criticized it as excessive and imprudent. Wang Shimin (1592–1680) defended Zhou against such criticism by arguing that each individual artistic personality and each different painting of a single artist offer something different (fig. 61, cat. no. 20):[1]

> But some people would say that it would be sufficient to have just several paintings for one's emotional outlet and that one does not need so many paintings to appreciate art. I do not agree with them. Although painting is only a minor branch of art, it is there where both the nature-endowed forms and the artist's inspiration truly converge together. Whether they be paintings on pieces of silk

or paper, they represent ten thousand different personalities and schools; every single artist has his own thought, every single painting has different taste and flavor. Furthermore one's mind can not be completely exhausted. [In order to further develop your mind] you should select from [others' merits] and amalgamate them into one; you should discard [their] shortcomings and take [their] merits, carefully single out the best and discard the unimportant . . . .

(Colphon by Wang Shimin to a landscape handscroll by Wang Hui)

Zhou, it seems, was a born collector. His enthusiasm for collecting art extended to seals and other areas as well as painting, and was such that he himself recognized it as an unshakable addiction:[2]

I have been crazy about seals for the last 30 years. I am proud of my having traced their origins and evolutions and the changes in this art. In the whole country there is no one like me.

I have loved seals all my life. When I see seals from the Qin and Han and seals carved by famous masters, I fondle them with love and appreciation all day. I refuse to let them leave my hands. To satisfy my desire I even forget to eat and to sleep. They are to me just like flowers of the seasons and beautiful ladies.

A man of classical culture and taste, in his aesthetic outlook, however, Zhou maintained the typical Chinese literati view — an amalgam of moralistic and pragmatic concepts — that art manifests the *Dao* (the Moral Way), and thereby is an aid to self-cultivation and spiritual enlightenment. For such purposes, he was also no different from the rest of the literati in regarding landscape as the most worthy subject matter for painting. In art criticism, Zhou Lianggong joined the ongoing literary debate of personal expression vs. formal style and advocated the former. His individualism was grounded in an opposition to the blind adherence to rules and models. But typically, both in literature and painting, it points neither to a total rejection of stylistic traditions and artistry nor to the autonomy of the arts divorced from questions of Confucian morality.

The extraordinary array of creative energies in the visual arts during the seventeenth century is best seen in the very different achievements of orthodox masters and individualist artists. In his early years, Zhou's chief emphasis on individuality helped him appreciate the highly personalized expression found in such individual geniuses as Chen Hongshou (1599–1652, DHL 1/15), Gong Xian (ca. 1620–1689, DHL 2/15), and in many less famous contemporaries such as Kuncan (1612–1673, DHL 2/8) and Hongren (1610–1664, DHL 2/9) . In his later years, he became a great admirer of the renowned formalist painter Wang Hui (1632–1717, DHL 2/11), whom he considered an enlightened transmitter of the spirit and form of the great masters from the past. Throughout his life, however, his hometown of Nanjing and its artists remained closest to his heart and central to his collection.

His book *Du Hua Lu* (Lives of Painters) is a collection of biographical notes on seventy-eight painters, most of them active in his time, and is considered the authoritative source on seventeenth-century Chinese painting ever since its publication in 1673. Originally entitled *Huaren zhuan* (lit. Lives of Painters) by Zhou himself, the new title reflects the fact that the biographies were compiled at his private Du Hua Lou (Viewing Painting Pavilion) painting gallery. In addition to the lives of painters, Zhou also devoted much time to the study and collection of seals and left a renowned collection of biographies of seal carvers, *Yinren zhuan*. With this book, it is said, Zhou firmly distinguished himself as a master of prose. A serious poet and essayist, he left collections of his own writings, as well as anthologies of contemporary letters.

Zhou Lianggong led an active political career. Unlike many former Ming officials and intellectuals, he chose to serve the new Qing dynasty established in 1644 by the alien Manchus. He held a number of high posts, but eventually became a victim of the Chinese-Manchu tensions of the day and suffered eight years of trial and imprisonment. Although Zhou Lianggong's collaboration with the Manchus left him open to certain condemnation in life and after death, it placed him in a position to defend the native Chinese populace — including his many loyalist friends — and to preserve and nurture Chinese tradition. This gave added incentive and meaning to his patronage of art, for which his official position provided him the means.

Zhou Lianggong serves as a focus for this thematic exploration of Chinese painting of this extraordinary era. The works of his contemporaries extant from his original collection form the core of this exhibition. Placed in contextual relation to Zhou's life and thought, as well as to the lives of artists themselves in the *Du Hua Lu*, these works enable us to experience the time more directly with unprecedented intimacy and a new sensibility, and thus to reshape our perceptions of Chinese painting.

CHAPTER I

The Making of an Art Patron

FAMILY[3]

ZHOU LIANGGONG was brought up within a cultured literati milieu and it is no surprise that he should have absorbed its ideals, participated in its trends and currents, and adopted its idiosyncrasies. What was unusual was the seriousness with which he approached art and culture in his youth and his early effort to excel in the polite arts.

Zhou was born on the 7th day of the 4th month in the year of *renzi* (1612) in Nanjing at Zhuangyuan jing (see map 3) near the Qinhuai canal. He was the eldest son of Zhou Wenwei (d. 1659), a student at the Imperial Academy of Nanjing and holder of the *shengyuan* (government student) degree.[4] Zhou Lianggong's grandfather, Zhou Tinghuai, had moved from Jiangxi to Xiangfu (modern Kaifeng), Henan. Retaining the family registry at Xiangfu, Zhou Lianggong's father moved his family to Nanjing before Zhou was born. While Zhou Lianggong grew up in Nanjing, he was registered in Henan and considered himself a native of Xiangfu (popularly called Daliang).

Despite the fact that no clan members had entered high officialdom since the Song period, the clan appears to have maintained the status of educated lower "gentry." Although Zhou's father failed to advance beyond the *shengyuan* degree, he managed to provide his sons with sufficient education to prepare for the government examinations. In 1623, when Zhou was twelve, his father finally gave up the pursuit of a higher degree than the *shengyuan* and took up the ninth-rank official post of Zhupu (registrar, also known as the second deputy magistrate) in Zhuji, Zhejiang. He explained his decision in the following way:[5]

> How can a man stick strictly to literary work? Even if I take a minor official post,
> I can still help people, even though the number may be small. Is it necessary for
> me to receive a high academic degree to glorify myself?

Zhou Wenwei's biography, which is found under the section of "Famous Officials" in the local history of Zhuji[6] — a rare distinction for a man of his rank — suggests that he was a highly capable administrator and respected by the local people. He is celebrated in the biography as an upright man full of public spirit, who constantly confronted his superiors in defense of the people. However, his zeal apparently did not please local officials and led to his demotion after two years of service. This in turn prompted his resignation and put an end to a brief career of government service.

Zhou Wenwei's stern Confucian character and his emphasis on family discipline are illustrated in his Family Instruction. Like many literati of his time, the elder Zhou was interested in art and had artist friends like the Nanjing scholar-artist Chen Danzhong (*jinshi* of 1643, DHL 1/8),[7] Yao Yunzai (act. ca. 1600, DHL 2/2), and Chen Hongshou (DHL 1/15) from Hangzhou.[8] He was also friendly with several seal carvers and had a large collection of seals and some old paintings.[9]

Zhou Wenwei was naturally the earliest role model for his eldest son, Zhou Lianggong. The elder Zhou's interest in art, while not unusual for a Confucian scholar, probably exerted an important early influence on Zhou Lianggong. Zhou Wenwei's philosophy of public service and devotion to the interest of the populace also seems to have been adopted by his son and helps to explain some of his future political and social activities.

Little information about other family members is extant. Zhou's younger brother Liangjie (*zi,* or style name, Qinggong), eleven years his junior, was a slow learner and showed signs of weak character. Together with the rest of his family, Liangjie would depend on Zhou for support his entire life.[10]

Given his own failure in the examinations and his family's rather precarious position, Zhou Wenwei must have placed considerable hope in his eldest son, particularly after he showed such precocity and promise in his youth. The pressure to provide for his family and to recover the honor and status the clan once enjoyed during the Song must have weighed heavily upon the youth. As Zhou Lianggong approached puberty and applied himself to examination study, it became apparent that he took his responsibility very seriously. Before age sixteen, Zhou had begun to prepare in earnest for the *shengyuan* degree.

NANJING, THE SOUTHERN CAPITAL, AND THE LITERATI WORLD[11]

DURING HIS YOUTH, while studying for the government examinations, Zhou Lianggong began to show a sensitive appreciation of the cultural world around him and to aspire to become an active participant in the world of the literati. In a broad sense, the literati (*wenren,* lit. "men of culture" or "men of letters") included not only any holder of one of the academic degrees from the lowest *shengyuan* to the highest *jinshi* degree, but also any member of a scholar-family or even a commoner who was erudite and well versed in literature. The ideal literatus was a man who, in addition to the above qualifications, also had a Confucian moral character, a refined manner, and elegant taste. He was often an antiquarian, such as a connoisseur-collector of ancient objects (ranging from bronzes to calligraphy and paintings), an amateur practitioner of one of the "polite arts" such as calligraphy, painting, drama, or music, a connoisseur of tea and wine, or a combination of these. Since the Song period, the practice of the polite arts had become an important form of expression and cultivation of Neo-Confucian ideals and spirit. Confucius noted the beneficial aspect of aesthetic activity upon man's spiritual growth, but gave it a decidedly secondary role. (He mainly talked about it in connection to music and dance.) Confucius said, "A young man's duty is to be filial to his parents at home and respectful to his elders abroad, to be circumspect and truthful, and while overflowing with love for all men, to associate himself with humanity. If, when all that is done, he has any energy to spare, then let him study the polite arts." During the Northern Song period, however, the role of aesthetic activity was redefined and expanded. The literati theory of painting, one important element of the new aesthetic theory developed during the Northern Song, had become the orthodoxy by Zhou's time.[12] Examples of exceptional "men of culture" who preceded Zhou Lianggong and who served as models included Ouyang Xiu (1007–1072) and Su Shi (1037–1101) of the Northern Song, and Dong Qichang (1555–1636, DHL 1/2) of the Ming. All of these men were *jinshi*, prominent statesmen, poets, calligraphers, painters, connoisseurs, and members of a great circle of "men of culture."

Zhou Lianggong sought not only to preserve his family's social status through success in the civil service examinations, but also to acquire the skills of a poet and connoisseur and to live the life of a genuine literatus. This desire was undoubtedly influenced by his father's scholarly bent and interests in art and culture, and was also fanned by the lively cosmopolitan cultural environment of Nanjing where he was raised.

Nanjing was an important center of the Jiangnan[13] literati culture and enjoyed an abundance of eminent "men of culture." As the "Southern Capital" under the Ming, it boasted the presence of the imperial palace, its own complement of court officialdom including high civil and military offices and the Six Boards, and the imperial tombs.[14] Since these offices carried no real power, they were often taken as "a delightful alternative," as one contemporary scholar puts it, by "those scholar-officials who had no taste for the brutal political infighting so typical of Beijing."[15] Nanjing was the capital of Jiangsu province as well as the site of the prefectural and two district governments. It had long been an important educational center for the south and was the site of one of the two imperial academies. As the site of the triennial provincial examinations [for the *juren* (provincial graduate) degree] for both Jiangsu and neighboring Anhui, it attracted numerous scholars, some of whom remained for long periods of time to study. Nanjing was an important regional cultural center of the south known for its famous book stores and libraries. Great monasteries such as Baoen and Gaozuo attracted eminent monks. It was an important historical city with ancient remains from the time of the First Emperor of the Qin. Nanjing was also a city of entertainment and leisurely pursuits. Luxurious pleasure boats sailed day and night along the scenic Qinhuai canal which flowed through the city, while along the bank of the canal renowned prostitutes, singers, musicians, and painters provided all manner of sensuous pleasures and entertainment.[16]

By the late 1620s Nanjing had achieved a new prominence as both a political and cultural center. Young members of the Fushe (Revival Society), which was formally founded in 1629 and by the end of the Ming was the most powerful political and literary society in the country, began to congregate in the city and made it their political base. In 1630, the city hosted a great Fushe meeting which was attended by thousands of scholars from all parts of the empire.[17] Due to the unstable conditions in the North, many prominent northern families, such as the Fang clan members from Tongcheng, Anhui, took up residence in Nanjing.[18] In recognition of the city's strategic importance and its history, some officials during the late Ming, who feared the vulnerability of Beijing under the threat of northern rebellions and Manchu invasions, discussed a proposal to move the entire court to Nanjing.[19]

Among the high officials posted in Nanjing at this time were the president of the Board of Ceremonies of Nanjing, Dong Qichang (served 1625–1627), and the acting head of the Hanlin Academy of Nanjing, Wang Duo (1591–1652, served 1624–1637).[20] Among the city's residents were representatives of numerous prominent families of wealth, influence, and culture.[21] Noted sojourners in Nanjing at this time included the "Four Sons of Eminent Men"—Fang Yizhi (1611–1671, DHL 2/7), Hu Fangyu (1618–1655), Mao Xiang (1611–1693), and Chen Zhenhui (1605–1656) — and such famous scholar-poet-painters as Wu Weiye (1609–1672, DHL 1/3), Yang Wencong (1597–1645, DHL 3/7), and Gong Dingzi (1616–1673).[22] The confluence of such an array of notables provided a catalyst to the social life of the city. Lavish banquets and poetry gatherings were common occurrences. Such activities were the talk of the town and were jealously watched by local young men like Zhou Lianggong who lacked the status to be included. (See Zhou's autobiographical letter to Gong Dingzi, below.)

The bustlings and frivolity of the temporary residents and eminent local elites in the city also were a source of distraction and disillusionment for local families. This was especially true for the Zhou family, which lived in the area along the Qinhuai canal in the southeastern corner of the city next to the Gongyuan, where the triennial provincial examinations (for *juren* degree) were held, and right across the canal from the famous Jiuyuan (Old Courtesan Compound) pleasure quarter (see map 3).[23] Zhou Lianggong's father warned his sons not to get disillusioned, and Zhou issued the same warning to his own sons.[24] Even Fang Yizhi, one of the most active participants in Nanjing social and cultural life, felt discouraged about the way he spent his time in Nanjing. He wrote at the time:[25]

> We have all been living in Nanjing. The whole of our time is for banqueting and enjoying ourselves with our friends. For the most part our scholarship really does not come up to what it should.

The Zhou family's contact with high culture and the perquisites of power and social prestige, even if only on the periphery, must help to explain Zhou's early ambition and his struggle to develop the polite arts and become a "man of culture." One of the most important qualifications for examination success and for recognition as a "man of culture" was an ability to compose poetry. By age seventeen, Zhou Lianggong had established a reputation as a local talent and a poet. His poetry facilitated his recognition by the local literati and his partial admission into their elite circle. He joined a local society for the revival of ancient literature (*gu wen*) that was under the influence of the famous scholar Ai Nanying (1583–1646).[26] Ai, who advocated the return to Han and Wei literature through Tang and Song masters, reportedly spoke highly of Zhou's writings and exerted a powerful influence over the development of Zhou's literary theory and criticism.[27]

The limited local recognition which Zhou received, however, probably only heightened his feelings of inadequacy. Zhou recalled his frustration in a letter dated 1664 to the eminent scholar-poet Gong Dingzi, written to celebrate Gong's 50th birthday:[28]

> I remember when I was a beginning student I could recite your examination essays which were [clear and powerful] as if carved out of metal and stone. Thereafter I regretted that I had no opportunity to meet you. I imagined you would look like a [divine] man from Heaven. I grew up by the Qingji [Nanjing], seeing the remains of the Six Dynasties. I liked to write poems and recited them to myself. I lamented that there was no one who would recognize [my literary talent] and criticize my composition.
>
> Later whenever I heard you had come to Nanjing and were surrounded by

people, I was so envious of those people and regretted that I could not take part. I still had no opportunity to be introduced to you. It was only when I passed the examination and was posted in Yangzhou as a low official that you humbled yourself to make my acquaintance. Thereupon I was able to present some of my poems asking for your instruction. You provided encouragement for my writing. We both felt we should have met earlier . . . .

This recollection of the frustration over the anonymity of his youth in Nanjing provides an insight into one of the psychological motives behind Zhou's unflagging ambition and his drive to make a name in the literati world.

THE QINHUAI PAINTERS

THE MANY ARTISTS active in Nanjing in Zhou's time are indicated in the following passage by Gong Xian:[29]

> Nowadays, Jiangnan is the most important center of painting. Among its fourteen counties, however, the capital city of Nanjing is the most prominent. It has several tens of eminent painters. But if we count all those who can paint, the number exceeds one thousand. . . . Among the Jinling painters, the "able class" painters are most numerous. But the divine and the untrammeled classes also have several artists each . . . .

From the late twenties Nanjing (also known as Jinling) boasted a great number of artists from many different regions. Many took up residence in the Qinhuai area where Zhou Lianggong's family lived (map 3). As noted above, this area, which was often simply referred to as Qinhuai (fig. 4), included Nanjing's famous pleasure quarter and the Gongyuan, the site of the triennial examination ground.[30] Just as the glittering elite literati world of Nanjing helps account for the youthful Zhou's self-consciousness and ambition, his coming of age in the center of the Qinhuai art community helps to explain his early attraction to art.

The gathering together of artists from diverse social and regional backgrounds in Nanjing, many of them living in the Qinhuai quarter, promoted a cross fertilization of regional styles. The overwhelming majority of the artists were not natives of Nanjing. Many were from Fujian, Suzhou, Hangzhou, and Anhui, and therefore came to the city with stylistic backgrounds and tastes peculiar to their native places. Almost all of them were attracted to the city because of its dynamic, cosmopolitan cultural environment. The concentration of scholar-officials and examination candidates made it a natural center for literati painters, while professional painters no doubt were attracted by the abundance of wealthy patrons and connoisseurs. Only in a city as impersonal and competitive as Nanjing could regional and social prejudices be forgotten.

Because of the relative newness of the city as an artistic center and the diversity of the artists in residence, no single dominating stylistic focus or artistic personality developed at this time. Diverse aesthetic and stylistic movements coexisted.[31] Nanjing differed in this respect from Huating under the leadership of Dong Qichang, Taicang under Wang Shimin (DHL/SL) and Wang Jian (1598–1677, DHL/SL), or Suzhou under the descendants of Wen Zhengming (1470–1559).

Fig. 4. Hu Yukun (fl. 1640–1672). "Qinhuai." From an album of twelve leaves, "Historic Spots in Nanjing." Album leaf, ink and color on paper, 25.5 cm x 18.1 cm. Guan Lu Yuan collection. (Cat. no. 17, leaf H)

Zhou Lianggong was born in the Qinhuai area and raised in a neighborhood of many painter families. Several of the painters Zhou grew up with have biographies recorded in the Du Hua Lu.

By the 1620s, the style of the Zhe school, which was once dominant among such Nanjing-based artists as Wu Wei (1459–1508), Shi Zhong (1437–1517), and Jiang Song (act. ca. 1500), seems to have disappeared. The only evidence of vestigial Zhe school influence that remained among later artists was the more generous use of ink. The influence of the Suzhou-based Wu school was also strong on major artists of the city such as Hu Zongren (fl. 1590–1630, DHL 2/4), Wei Zhihuang (b. 1568, DHL 1/9), Wei Zhike (b. ca. 1570, DHL 1/10), Zou Dian (DHL 1/11), Zou Zhe (b. 1636, DHL 1/12), and Zhu Ruiwu (DHL 1/13), all of whom painted landscapes in the *xieyi* (lit. writing ideas) manner in the literati tradition (figs 5–10).[32] The influence of Zhao Zuo (DHL 1/5) from Huating is traceable in works by Zou Dian, who was originally from Suzhou. Such scholar-amateur painters as Yang Wencong, Fang Yizhi, and Zou Zhilin (*jinshi* 1610, DHL 1/18) followed the Yuan tradition either independently or under the influence of Dong Qichang (figs. 11, 12).

Another landscape tradition represented in Nanjing at the time was the late Ming interpretations of the Northern Song tradition practiced by such sojourners from Fujian

Fig. 5. Hu Zongren (fl. ca. 1590–1640). "Landscape." Hanging scroll, ink on paper, 162.6 cm x 75.0 cm. Bei Shan Tang collection, Hong Kong.

Fig. 6. Wei Zhihuang (1568–after 1647). "Forest and Mountains in Hazy Mist." Hanging scroll, ink on paper, 133.5 cm x 55.5 cm. Taitsu Hashimoto collection.

as the two court painters Wu Bin (fl. ca. 1568–1621) and Wang Jianzhang (fl. 1628–1644), who painted monumental landscapes in a finished *gongbi* manner. Of the two, Wu was far more original and developed his own "fantastic mode."[33] This Fujian style persisted in the works of such painters as Gao Yang and Zheng Zhong (1565–1630, *zi* Qianli), who were younger associates of Wu Bin (fig. 13).[34] All four were highly professional and excelled in painting various subjects including religious figures and bird-and-flower paintings.

Although they occasionally painted in the literati mode of the Wen school, none of these painters had literary inclinations; they were at their best with either the revival or the "fantastic" interpretation of the old tradition, especially that of the Northern Song. In their time, they appear to have attracted some scholar-official patrons such as Mi Wanzhong (d. after 1628) and Xu Hongji(act. 1595–1641). But they seem to have been completely ignored by Gu Qiyuan (1565–1628, *jinshi* of 1598), the eminent Hanlin scholar and Nanjing's leading art patron and chronicler of art in his time. Gu authored the

Fig. 8. Zou Dian. "Landscape." Album leaf, ink on silk, 29.8 cm x 21.6 cm. Ching Yuan Chai collection.

Fig. 9. Zou Zhe (b. 1636). "Landscape." Album leaf, ink and color on silk, 28.4 cm x 31.8 cm. L. Prectorious collection.

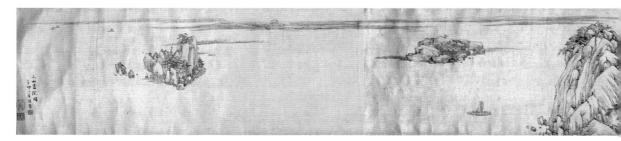

Fig. 10. Zhu Ruiwu. "The Sanshan Academy." Collaborative work with Chen Shu, handscroll. The Shoto Museum collection, Tokyo.

famous book about Nanjing titled *Kezi juiyu* and was a friend and patron of the painters Hu Zongren, Wei Zhihuang, Wei Zhike, and Yao Lushi, all of whom were known for their calligraphy and literary inclinations. Of these artists, Gu had the highest esteem for Hu Zongren:[35]

> [Hu was] the only Nanjing painter since the modern age whose paintings were lofty, placid, and far-reaching; he is not one of those vulgar artists and has attained the essence of the Southern School.

The above passage significantly points to a new development in the Nanjing art world by 1628, when Gu finished the book. It shows that Gu already had been influenced by Dong Qichang's orthodox theory and had made it the basis of his critical judgment of painters.

The extant paintings of Hu reveal that he followed the Yuan models, especially Wang Meng (1308–1385), as interpreted through Wen Zhengming and the late Ming painters. In this respect, Hu was like two other painters, Zhu Ruiwu and Zou Dian, who were active about the same time as Hu. Zhu's extant works suggest that he was more creative than Zou, and had a stronger literati approach. There is some indication that this shift of interest towards the emulation of classic models, with an interest in Yuan style, represented a response to the new vigor of the Huating school of Dong Qichang. This is suggested by Gu Qiyuan's criticism, which follows the terminology and ideas of Dong Qichang's Northern and Southern School theory. Thus in Hu's paintings, Gu sought "the essence of the Southern School," that is, the "lofty, placid, and far-reaching" formal and spiritual mode.

Gu Qiyuan's statement thus suggests that there was another trend emerging in the Nanjing art world in addition to the conservative provincial styles (represented by the professional artists Wu Bin, Wang Jianzang, Gao Yang, and Zheng Zhong) — a stylistic tradition which absorbed the Wu School *xieyi* manner of the literati mode and began to reflect the influence of the new orthodox movement from Huating in its emulation of the Southern School masters with a preference for the Yuan period. Gu clearly preferred the latter trend. The fact that Zhou Lianggong, who later succeeded Gu Qiyuan as the foremost patron-critic from Nanjing, greatly esteemed Gu's opinions of art[36] and completely ignored Wu Bin and the three others[37] indicates that their professional art mode was rapidly falling out of fashion. The strong literati taste of the two successive generations of art patrons represented by Gu and Zhou made it inevitable for such painters to respond to the change.

According to Zhou Lianggong, the most recognized artists residing in Nanjing during the early half of the seventeenth century were the aforementioned Wei Zhihuang and

The emergence of Zhu Ruiwu, a Buddhist priest-painter of Ming imperial descent and of strong literati bent, marked the decline of the Wei brothers' popularity and influence in the city.

Fig. 11. Yang Wencong (1597–1645). "Distant Peaks Beyond an Autumn Forest." Hanging scroll. The Osaka Museum of Art collection.

Fig. 12. Fang Yizhi (1611–1671). "Landscape." Hanging scroll. Bei Shan Tang collection, Hong Kong.

his brother Wei Zhike, Zhu Ruiwu, and Hu Zongren. Zhou specifically singles out the Wei brothers and Zhu Ruiwu:[38]

> The monk Qiqu is Zhu Ruiwu, [zi] Hanzhi. He has been famous for his painting in Jiangnan for the last sixty years. As for Nanjing painting, people had regarded Wei Kaoxu [Wei Zhihuang] and his brother [Wei Zhike] first and best till Hanzhi emerged. He brought a transformation to Nanjing painting. There were no scholars or monks who did not follow him.

Zhu seems to have become an active painter before the 1620s, since Zhu's son Zhu Zhiqiao (DHL 1/14), a classmate of Zhou during this period, had already started to paint. A descendant of the Ming imperial family, Zhu was highly educated and painted in the Ming Wu School interpretation of the literati mode of the Yuan dynasty masters, especially that of Ni Zan (1301–1373) and Huang Gongwang (1269–1354).[39] A number of works Zhu later painted for Zhou in the mid-1640s are extant. Zhu's works exhibit sensitive brushwork and convey a refined, scholarly atmosphere. By contrast, the extant works of the Wei brothers show that they followed a contemporary local style established by a succession of professional artists but with a certain literati pretense and hybrid artistic sources. The Wei brothers seem to have had no interest in recreating ancient models, and their works fail to convey the calligraphic quality of brushwork and placid mode of expression which Zhu managed to express in his works. The literati bent of Zhu set him apart from the Wei brothers and seems to have attracted scholar-connoisseurs and painters of the city such as Chen Danzhong, Fang Yizhi, Fang Hengxian (still act. 1666, DHL 2/12), Zheng Yuanxun (1598–1645, *zi* Chaozong), Chen Shu (act. 1687, DHL 4/10), and Jiang Chengzong (*zi* Kaixien).

A number of scholar and professional painters — as well as several of the artists cited above — excelled in other than landscape subjects, such as bamboo, flowers, birds, and rocks; they include Zhao Bei (famous for bamboo), Yao Lushi (noted for plum), Xie Daoling, Xia Sen, Wu Shiguan, and Hu Zhengyan (ca. 1590 – d. after 1671). Among the women flower painters active in Nanjing at this time were Xue Wu (1564 – ca. 1637) and the poetess-painter Ma Shouzhen, who lived in Qinhuai (map 3, R). The popularity of these subjects eventually led to the compilation of the famous manual of model paintings of bird and flower subjects, the *Ten Bamboo Studio Painting Manual* (cat. no. 3), which was undertaken by the aforementioned Hu Zhengyan and had a preface (dated 1627) by Yang Wencong (figs. 14, 15). Hu was the famous Anhui wood engraver and seal carver living in the city.

Several of the above painters, as well as numerous other painters who have not been mentioned, lived in the Qinhuai area. Among them were Wu Hong (act. 1670–1680, DHL 3/13) and such families of painters as the Xie family (Xie Daoling and Xie Cheng), the Wei family (Wei Zhihuang and Wei Zhike), the Zou family (Zou Dian and Zou Zhe), the Zhu family (Zhu Ruiwu and Zhu Zhichao), and probably the Gao family (Gao Yang and Gao Yu). The Wei, the Gao, and the Xie families all participated in the production of the *Ten Bamboo Studio Painting Manual*, which was a tremendous success in Nanjing and beyond.

Zhou Lianggong grew up with the sons of the painter families of Qinhuai. The Xie family's compound was directly next to Zhou's. Xie Cheng (DHL 3/12) was born in the same year and month as Zhou, and the two grew up together. Xie Cheng from his youth appears to have sought to carry on his family tradition of professional painting. There is no record of his having tried to pass any government examination. In his biography of Xie Cheng, Zhou recalls:

> Xie Cheng's [*zi* Zhongmei] father Daoling, *zi* Bintai, was originally from Wu [Suzhou]. He moved his family to Qinhuai across from my house. . . . Zhongmei was poor. But his generosity, graciousness, and filiality was something people of his own time could not match. Zhongmei and I were born in the same year [i.e., in 1612]. When I just came back from the north [in 1666] it was his birthday. I presented to him a poem which read: "I have lived next to you and your father in Qinhuai; Leaning over the red balustrade, we set out fishing poles together; After many orioles and flowers [many years] we have now grown old . . . .

Zhou's best friend from his boyhood was Gao Fu, an amateur painter of orchids who was a brother of Gao Cen (fl. 1650–1679, DHL 3/14) and father of the painter Gao Yu (DHL 3/15), whose family also appears to have lived in the Qinhuai area. Later Gao Yu married a daughter of Zhou's cousin.[40] Zhou attended a school opened at Yuguoan with

Fig. 13. Wu Bin (fl. ca. 1568–1621), Hu Zongren (1590–1630), and Gao Yang. "Marvelous Views of Rivers and Mountains." Collaborative handscroll, ink on paper, H 23.3 cm. Bei Shan Tang collection, Hong Kong.

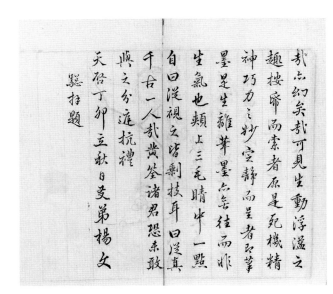

Fig. 14. Yang Wencong (1597–1645). Preface dated 1627 to "Ten Bamboo Studio Painting Manual." (Cat. no. 3)

The production of this painting manual put China in the forefront of book publishing and color printing technology. It became a great source of creative energy in Nanjing and engaged many of the Qinhuai circle of painters. Yang Wencong, a literatus of great means and influence, died in the tumult of the dynastic change.

Fig. 15. Gao Yang. "Banana and Rock." Leaf from "Ten Bamboo Studio Painting Manual," woodblock print, 25 cm x 15.3 cm. Guan Lu Yuan collection. (Cat. no. 3)

other youths from the same area, including Zhu Zhichao, Wei Baizhi, Gao Fu, Le Yao, and his cousin Zhou Minqiu, all of whom were to remain his lifelong friends.[41] Wei Baizhi was from a painter family that had produced at least three painters: his grandfather, his uncle Wei Zhihuang, and his father Wei Zhike. Zhu Zhichao was the son of Zhu Ruiwu. Zhou later entrusted the education of his sons to both Gao Fu and Le Yao.[42]

Growing up among painters, many of whom were his close boyhood friends, Zhou learned to look at objects with the eye of an artist and the visual interests of a poet. He developed a passionate love for things visual and tangible. By the age of seventeen Zhou had already begun to collect paintings by the Qinhuai artists, as documented by an album of paintings and calligraphy executed in 1628–1629 (figs. 16–19). This album (present collection unknown) includes paintings by Wei Zhihuang, Wei Zhike, Gao Yang, Gao Yu, and others. The leaves by Gao Yang and Gao Yu are closely related to their works

Fig. 16. Wei Zhihuang (1568 – after 1647). "Landscape." Dated 1628.

Fig. 17. Wei Zhike (b. ca. 1570). "Narcissus." Dated 1628.

Figs. 16–19 are album leaves originally in the King Kwei collection. Present collection unknown. From Chen Rentao, Jinkui canghua ji, Kyoto: Benrido, 1956.

Fig. 18. Gao Yang. "Tree and Rock." Dated 1629.

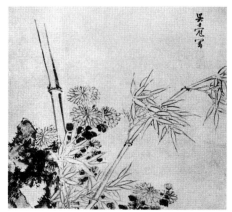

Fig. 19. Wu Shiguan. "Bamboo, Chrysanthemum and Rock." Dated 1629.

in the *Ten Bamboo Studio Painting Manual*. None of the works, however, are particularly impressive. In 1630, at nineteen, Zhou also obtained a painting from a certain Zhu Zhiqiao, whose works are otherwise obscure. As a youth, Zhou Lianggong was clearly a keen observer of the Nanjing art scene.

In addition to Zhou's intimate association with many Qinhuai artists in his youth, he also had the opportunity to befriend one of the great seventeenth-century artists from Zhuji, Chen Hongshou. While Zhou was visiting his father in Zhuji, Zhejiang, at age thirteen he befriended Chen "by means of literature."[43] Chen was a *shengyuan* and already a painter of considerable renown. Zhou accompanied Chen on several tours to Mount Wuxie. It is uncertain how the two met, but given Zhou's age it is likely that Zhou met Chen through his father.[44] Zhou's meeting with Chen left a strong mark and Zhou later became a lifelong friend, admirer, and patron of the painter. There is no evidence that Zhou owned any of Chen's paintings until fifteen years later when they were reunited in Beijing.

In addition to paintings, Zhou also began to demonstrate an interest in seals at an early age,[45] and collected both with enthusiasm. Given his family's limited means, Zhou's early collection must have been largely limited to works that he was able to acquire through friendship.

Later in life, Zhou began to acquire for his collection two additional items from the "Four Treasures of a Scholars' Studio": brushes and ink-sticks. In fact, his collection of ink-sticks and his yearly sacrifice to ink-sticks on the New Year's eve were well known throughout the literati world during Zhou's lifetime and later. At one point he even tried his hand at making ink-sticks and brushes himself.[46] Like many scholars of his day, he also tried his hand at painting but does not seem to have had any obvious talent. Three paintings which bear his name reveal scarcely more than mediocre talent.[47] He did, however, become quite well known for his calligraphy (figs. 20–25; cat. nos. 4, 5).[48]

His enthusiastic activity as collector may in part reflect the restless curiosity and frustration of an amateur who knew that he could never be a painter himself. His insatiable desire to own paintings and to get to know painters may have provided some compensation for his own inability to develop a visual idea into a work of art.

All of Zhou's painter-friends cited above were educated people who, despite their literary attainment, failed to receive the social recognition that only a government career could bring. Most had to make a living by their painting. The lives of all these artists are recorded with great intimacy in the biographical notes on painters he knew and admired, published one year after his death as *Du Hua Lu*.

Fig. 20. Zhou Lianggong (1612–1672). Calligraphy couplet. Hanging scrolls, ink on paper; 114.6 cm x 25.2 cm each. Guan Lu Yuan collection. (Cat. no. 4)

The couplet poem reads: "I use my own method; I also cherish my hut."

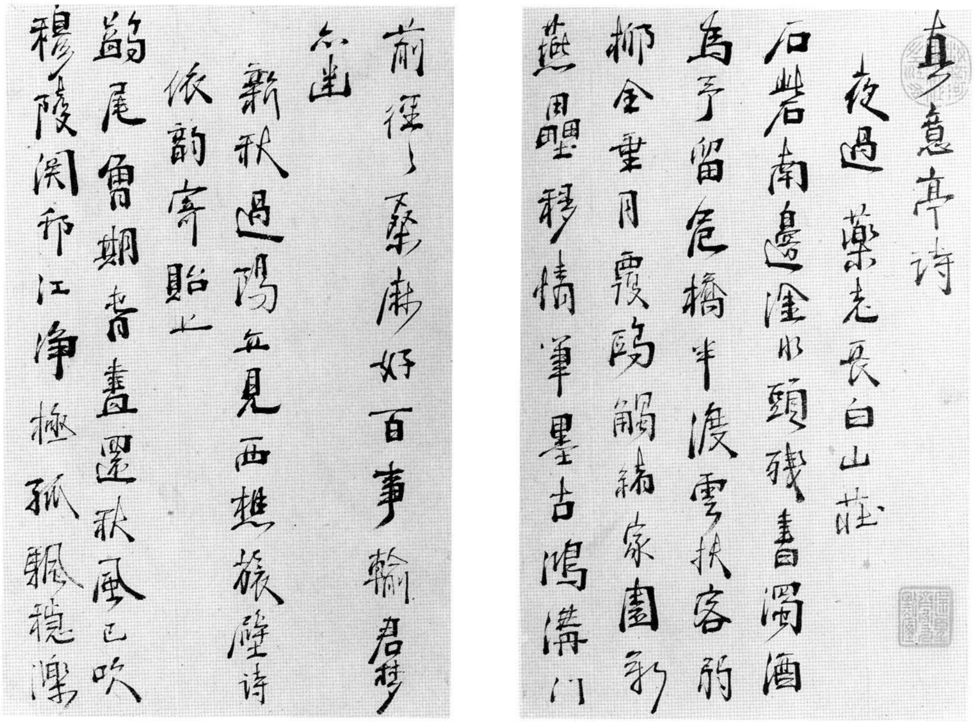

Fig. 21

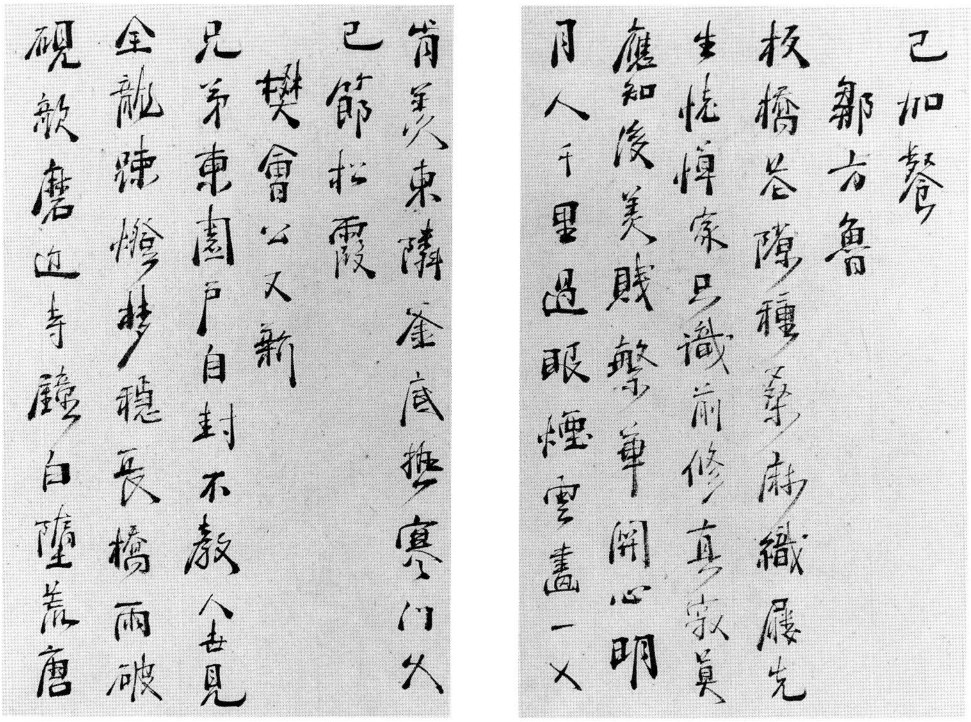

Fig. 22

Figs. 21–25. Zhou Lianggong (1612–1672). "Poems from the Zhenyi Studio." Poems appearing here were written for Zou Dian, Fan Qi, Wu Hong, Hu Yukun, and Gao Cen. Album leaves, ink on paper, 26.5 cm x 16 cm. Guan Lu Yuan collection. (Cat. no. 5)

While posted in Shandong in the mid-1660s, Zhou selected some poems he had written for his painter friends and transcribed them in his archaic xing-kai script. Most of the poems appear in the artists' Du Hua Lu entries.

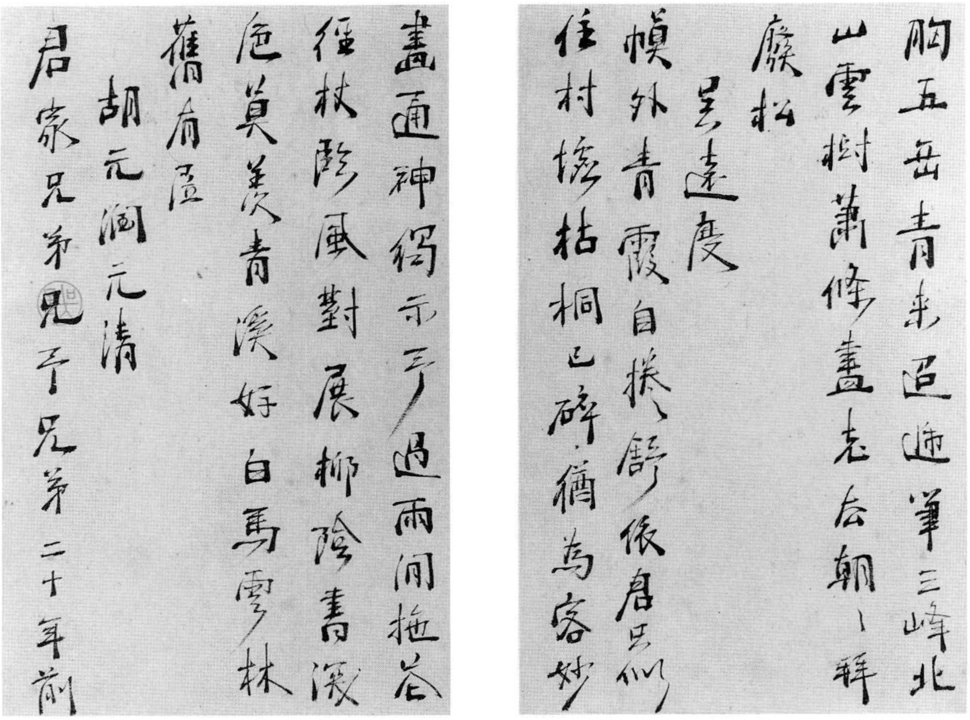

Fig. 23

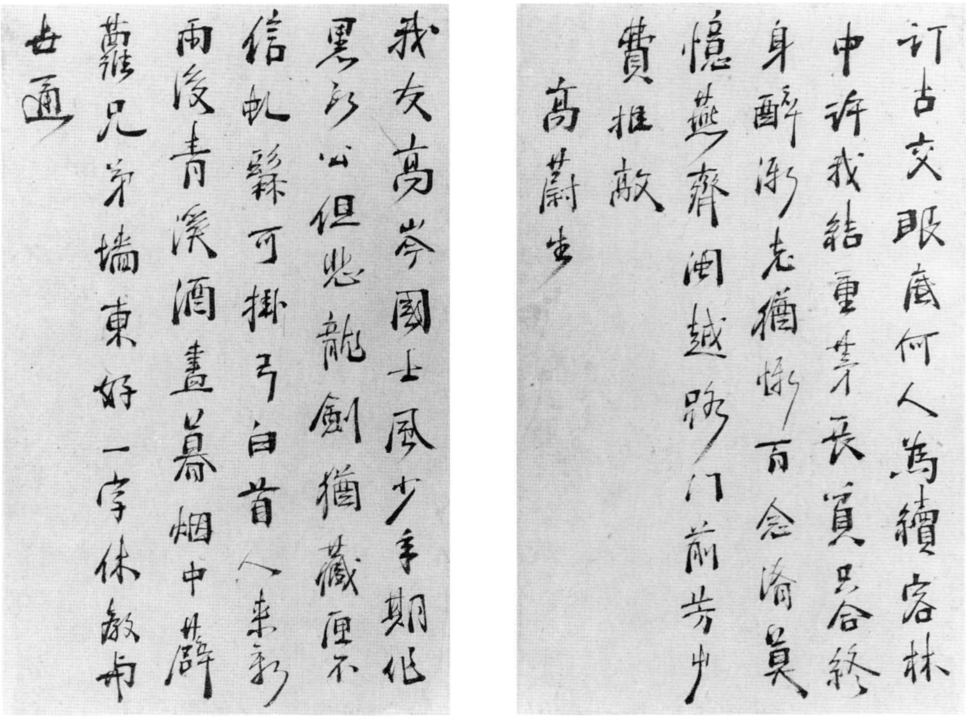

Fig. 24

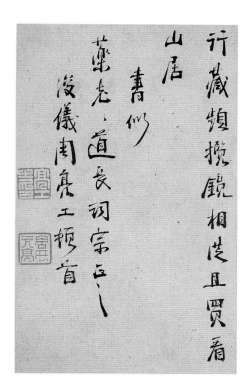
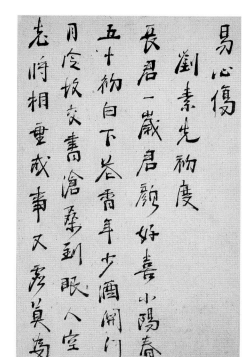

Fig. 25

The failure of these artists to obtain the social status that could accompany the attainment of the *juren* and *jinshi* degrees stood in striking contrast to Zhou's own later successful career. Zhou's sympathetic understanding of the struggles of these masters and his sense of responsibility as a selected man among numerous fellow literati found expression in the form of patronage and in a number of compassionate biographies found in the *Du Hua Lu* devoted to these fellow literati, who were forced by social and political conditions to become painters. Zhou's sense of loyalty to his boyhood artist friends and his compassion for them in similar circumstances were no less important a motivation for his patronage than was his ambition for fame, his poetic sensitivity, and his passion for art and collecting. But what made him an extraordinary patron was the strong sense of purpose and mission embodied in his philosophy of patronage. This philosophy was partly nurtured and influenced by the ideals of patronage espoused by the political group that Zhou joined at age nineteen.

ZHOU LIANGGONG AND THE FUSHE

IN 1630 Zhou joined the Xingshe, which was almost certainly an affiliation of the Fushe, as soon as it was opened at the Gaozuo temple in southern Nanjing.[49] The Xingshe members included such men of reputation as the *shengyuan* Huang Zongxi (1610–1695) and the Dongcheng scholar Wu Daoning.[50] Probably due to his affiliation with the Fushe, Zhou began to widen his circle of friends. He befriended the famous scholar-painter Wan Shouqi (1603–1652), the famous poet-critic Chen Zilong, the young scholar-poet-painter Wu Weiye, and the celebrated *juren* Yang Tingxu(act. 1628–1644), all of whom passed the

1630 provincial examination together with twenty-six other Fushe members, making "a moment of great triumph for the Society."[51]

Zhou later recalled his first meeting with Wan Shouqi, who became a monk after the fall of Ming, and others, at a party held by another famous Fushe member, Shen Shoumin:[52]

> The monk Huishou is my friend Wan Shouqi, [*zi*] Nianshou, from Pengcheng.
> . . . In 1630, when Ro [Wan Shouqi's *zi*] passed the provincial examination, Shen Meisheng [Shen Shoumin], *zi* Zhixian, and his brother invited Weidou [Yang Tingxu], Wozi [Chen Zilong], Jungong [Wu Weiye], and other gentlemen to drink. [At this party] I first met Ro, who at the time was a real celebrity. He loved to visit the courtesan quarter. He was especially good at painting beauties. Courtesans at parties all requested him to paint for them and he immediately complied. Therefore all the famous courtesans liked him. A man of elegant manner and style and of manly character, he was quite an exciting figure at that time and none of his friends could match him.[53]

The Fushe was formally founded in 1628 or 1629 by Zhang Pu (1602–1641), a scholar from Taicang, with his sworn brother Zhang Cai. It aimed at "the regeneration of society" by promoting the literary and moral revival of the ancients. According to Zhang, the society sought to stop the current decline in education as well as to correct the wrongs of contemporary society.[54]

The fundamentalist yet practical-minded Fushe leaders sought to achieve their goals by the recruitment of present and future leaders of society who shared their ideals. Ultimately Fushe sought to implant its followers in government offices so that they could put their ideals into practice. They thus expanded membership by "making friends by means of literature," helping to prepare members for the civil examinations and promoting their official careers. The society demonstrated its social commitment by actively supporting famine relief, tax reform, public projects, the removal of rapacious officials, and the education of poor students and the lower classes. As a result, the movement began to take on certain liberal characteristics, such as the blurring of class lines and a deepening social consciousness.

Another aspect of the group was its strong emphasis on the heroic spirit of camaraderie among its members. Fushe became a nationwide socio-political movement of great significance beginning in 1629 as it won over an increasing number of established scholar-officials and as its membership expanded into the thousands. The society's influence and prestige continued to grow with its young members' remarkable success at both provincial and metropolitan level exams along with their growing presence in officialdom.

While many of the original Fushe ideals were a reassertion of very basic Confucian principles, the movement, like the Donglin movement before it, fostered division and partisanship within the government and the scholar-official class. This partisanship seems to have been reflected in the art world. Since the leading figures in the art world were also scholars and were mostly active in the south, which was the center of the Fushe, it was natural that many of them became embroiled in the Fushe movement — either as active participants and sympathizers or as antagonists.

Fushe provided critical support to ambitious scholars of limited means like Zhou and also offered valuable literati contacts. It seems clear that Zhou sincerely shared the Fushe's social commitment to using "humanitarianism and pragmatic ideals" and to solve contemporary problems. These ideals were consistent with those of his father, and Zhou appeared to abide by them throughout his official career.[55]

NORTHERN PATRONS: KAIFENG

IN 1631, one year after joining Fushe, Zhou passed the district examination and placed first on the list of successful candidates. His entry into the Imperial Academy in Nanjing, which would have provided stipends and access to library facilities and lectures by eminent scholars, however, was blocked by jealous local families who objected to Zhou's Henan registry.[56] With his name removed from the list of successful candidates, Zhou was thus forced to leave Nanjing in 1632 at age twenty-one and to take up residency in his registered hometown, Xiangfu (Kaifeng), Henan, for the next eight years.

After his father resigned from office in Zhuji when Zhou was thirteen, evidently his family's financial difficulties worsened. Therefore Zhou took a tutoring position to support himself and perhaps to provide some money for his family back in Nanjing. The tutoring position had been arranged at the home of Zhang Minbiao (d. 1642), an eminent scholar of Henan and a friend for whom Zhou would hold a lifelong debt. This temporary setback actually turned out to be a mixed blessing. If he had remained in Nanjing, he might have been more deeply involved in the increasingly dangerous Fushe politics.[57]

In the final decade of the Ming many of the provincial areas in both the south and the north were subject to marauding bandits, rebels, and unruly Ming armies. Although the province of Henan was attacked by the rebel armies of Zhang Xianzhong (1605–1647) and Li Zicheng (ca. 1605–1645), the city of Kaifeng, where Zhou lived, was relatively safe and did not fall to Li's army until 1642, after Zhou had departed. Zhou's eight-year stay in Henan turned out to be fruitful for his career: his tutoring job left ample time for study, the examination competition was not as fierce as in Nanjing, and he had a much better opportunity to be recognized by local government officials.

Zhang Minbiao,[58] the man who chose Zhou Lianggong as a family tutor for his sons, was an old friend of Zhou's father. A *juren* and one of the most respected scholars in Henan in his day, Zhang had a famous library and attracted a large number of talented students to study with him. Zhou not only gained access to the library but had an opportunity to associate with Zhang's students and prominent family guests. Although Zhang was not an official, he had enough influence in Henan to promote Zhou's interests. Zhang was Zhou's first real patron and clearly exerted an important influence over the struggling scholar in his formative years.

Zhou describes Zhang as an unusual man who was an ardent Buddhist and took a religious name, Fachuang. Zhang had a keen knowledge of military strategy and was active in organizing the local militia.[59] Much of Zhou's military skill and knowledge of strategy, which served him so well in his official career, was probably gained while staying with Zhang Minbiao in Xiangfu.

Zhang studied in Nanjing as a young man, and his wide circle of friends included Qian Qianyi (1582–1664). Qian was a literatus of artistic cultivation, and his home was a gathering place for artists. Through Zhang, Zhou met three painters whom he would include in the *Du Hua Lu*: Zhao Cheng (1581 – after 1654, DHL 3/9), who was best known for his skill in copying antique paintings; the bamboo painter Feng Yujiang (DHL 4/1); and an eccentric painter Liu Jiu (Liu the Wine) (DHL 4/20). He also met several seal carvers such as Cheng Lin (YRZ 1/12), who practiced medicine and also painted flowers. Cheng became Zhou's lifelong friend and contributed the largest number of seals to Zhou's collection over the course of the next twenty years.

The painter Liu Jiu was living in a house attached to Zhang Minbiao's, and Zhou thus became close to him. As his name suggests, Liu was a heavy drinker. His paintings were likened to those of Zhang Lu (1464–1538), the well-known Zhe School master who was originally from Kaifeng. When Liu died without family or heirs, Zhou buried him. Obscure even in his own time, and unknown to subsequent generations, it is doubtful that any of his works will ever surface. Zhou's inclusion of Liu Jiu in the *Du Hua Lu* may well be no more than an expression of his compassion toward this unsuccessful painter rather than a statement about the quality of his work.

Perhaps the most important contact that Zhou made in Henan was Sun Chengze (1593–1675), a famous connoisseur-collector who is best remembered for his catalogue of paintings and calligraphy called *Gengzi xiaoxia ji* (Notes written idling away the summer of 1660) (fig. 26).[60] Sun came to Xiangfu as a new magistrate in 1635. When Sun read Zhou's essay, he said, "This is certainly not by a man from Kaifeng," and inquired about Zhou. Sun was moved by the story of Zhou's life and his reason for leaving Nanjing.[61]

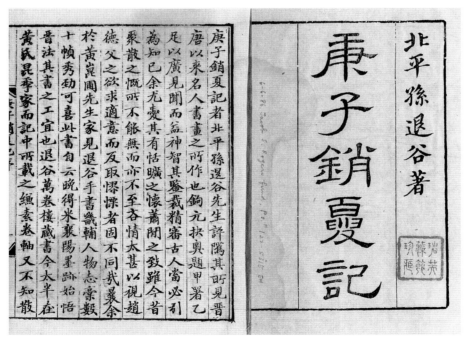

Fig. 26. Sun Chengze (1593–1675). Gengzi xiaoxia ji, *published 1755. Woodblock print. In* Zhibuzu zhai cong-shu, *compiled by Bao Tingbo (1728–1814).*

A scholar-official, connoisseur, and collector, Sun was a member of the Xueyuan circle, a leading cultural society in the north. This book is a compilation of his notes on works in his own and others' collections. While living in Kaifeng, Zhou befriended Sun and was much impressed by the older man. One of Zhou's seals reads, "Student of Sun Tuigu [Sun Chengze]."

Sun Chengze was a scholar-official from Beijing. His Donglin/Fushe sympathies are indicated in his narration of the origin of the Donglin shuyuan, which is recorded by Zhou in the *Yinren zhuan*.[62] They are also evident in his close friendship with Chen Mingxia (d. 1654) and his unfavorable relationship with the opposition of the Donglin and Fushe at the court. Zhou's previous Fushe involvement probably facilitated the friendship that soon developed between the two. Sun must have been pleasantly surprised to meet a Fushe scholar from cosmopolitan Nanjing in such a provincial area. Moreover, Zhou was acquainted with many celebrated Nanjing scholars, some of whom Sun might have known. Their mutual affinity was most likely strengthened by their shared interest in art.[63] An established man, about twenty years Zhou's senior, Sun probably nurtured his youthful commitment to art. Sun became Zhou's lifelong mentor-protector and friend. Zhou later said that he felt indebted to both Sun and Zhang Minbiao throughout his life.[64]

As chief examiner, Sun listed Zhou as the top *shengyuan* candidate in 1635. He even bought Zhou a farm in order to help him financially.[65] Sun also assisted Zhou in passing the qualifying examination for entrance into the Xiangfu Academy in 1635, though he did not supervise the examination himself. Later, in 1654, when Zhou was tied to official posts in the remote, dangerous Fujian province for an unusually long period of eight years, Sun Chengze took the initiative to get Zhou a position at court.

The year Zhou entered the prefectural school, at age twenty-four, he married a girl from a scholar-official family. She was a younger sister of the magistrate of Liyang, Jiangsu, and a daughter of an Imperial Academy student, Feng Yumin.

In the autumn of 1636, Zhou took the provincial examination to obtain a *juren* degree, which would have qualified him to sit for the metropolitan examination the following year. But Zhou failed this examination and had to wait another three years until the autumn of 1639 to take it again. Living off his salary as a tutor, his stipend as a student at the prefectural academy, and the harvest from the farm Sun Chengze bought for him, Zhou managed to survive three more years of diligent study. Finally, in 1639, he passed the examination with distinction. The essay he wrote for the examination was widely circulated in Henan.[66] The passage of the *juren* examination was a significant step. Although Zhou, like most of the other successful candidates, would go on to take the *jinshi* examination, the *juren* degree made him eligible for certain government positions such as district magistrate and thereby marked a significant improvement in both his social status and career prospects.

THE XUEYUAN CIRCLE

IN HENAN, Zhou also became acquainted with some of the eminent collector-connoisseurs in the North who frequently gathered at the Xueyuan (Snow Garden) of Hu Fangyu. Since so little has been recorded about painters in the north during this period, Zhou's accounts shed some welcome light on their activities. Hu was a famous *juren* and one of the Four Sons of Eminent Men along with Fang Yizhi, Mao Xiang, and Chen Zhenhui.[67] All four spent many years in Nanjing. Hu's love affair with a Qinhuai courtesan is featured in Kong Shangren's (1648–1718) drama, *Taohua shan* (Peach Blossom Fan).

Hu joined the Fushe while in Nanjing and, after returning to his hometown, in 1640 organized a branch of Fushe called the Xueyuan Society after the famous garden estate that his family owned. He was regarded as the leading essayist of his day. The Xueyuan served as a center of art, culture, and politics in the north at the end of the Ming and the early Qing. The Xueyuan circle included such important northern connoisseur-collectors as Song Quan (1598–1652), his son Song Lao (1634–1713), Sun Chengze, and Liang Qing-biao (1620-1691). Another possible member of this circle was the northern scholar-official Wang Duo a famous calligrapher, painter, and collector, who was friends with all of these men[68] (fig. 27). The Xueyuan attracted not only artists of the north, such as Zhao Cheng, but also those from the south, including Yao Yunzai and Wu Hong, who was later regarded as one of the Eight Nanjing Masters.

Zhou Lianggong seems to have already known Hu Fangyu and his brother Hu Fangxia for some time before 1639, when he went to Shangqiu to visit the Xueyuan.[69] The painter Yao Yunzai from Nanjing happened to be staying as guest of the Hus at the time. He also went to Kuide to visit Song Quan in 1637.[70] Song Lao was then a boy. Song Lao later became Zhou's lifelong friend and regarded Zhou as one of the two best con-noisseurs of his time, the other being Cao Rong (1613–1685) from Xiushui, Zhejiang.[71]

The Songs and the Hus were two of the most prominent families north of the Yangzi. Both families had rich collections of paintings and calligraphy. Hu Fangyu's father, Hu Ke (*jinshi* 1616), was a respected Donglin member and a well-known cultural figure. Hu Fangyu followed his father's footsteps and in many ways excelled him. Anoth-er member of the Xueyuan circle, Liang Qingbiao, was one of the foremost collectors of the Qing period.[72]

The collections of these northern connoisseurs had one distinctive characteristic — a strong preference for the monumental landscape paintings of the Northern Song tra-dition. The association of such southern painters as Yao Yunzai and Wu Hong with the Xueyuan circle provided an important channel through which some southern artists received the influence of northern collections. In fact, Wu Hong is recorded to have stud-ied Song Quan's collection and also to have been commissioned by Liang Qingbiao to copy the original paintings in his collection. Because of his Xueyuan connection, Wu was one of the most popular painters from the south in his time. Song Lao and Liang Qing-biao remained important patrons of Wu's.[73] The importance of the Xueyuan on Wu Hong's stylistic development was recognized by both Song Lao and Zhou Lianggong. Zhou notes in the *Du Hua Lu*:[74]

> In the years of *guisi* [1653] and *jiawu* [1654] he [Wu Hong] crossed the Yellow River and visited Xueyuan. . . . When he came back, his paintings had been transformed. Free, luxuriant, and refined, his paintings thoroughly assimilated the best of various old masters and further made them into his own ideas.

Zhou's association with Sun Chengze and the Xueyuan circle during his Kaifeng period undoubtedly was a stimulating experience. During his stay in Henan, Zhou broadened his contact with eminent contemporary collector-connoisseurs and artists and gained exposure to the late Ming artistic trends of the north. But he was still a rela-tively unknown man with no influence or economic means. In fact, he later described this eight-year period in Xiangfu to his sons as one of the harshest times of his life:[75]

> When I was twenty-two or twenty-three, my father took me with him to Pianliang (Xiangfu, i.e., Kaifeng]. Thereupon I was hired as tutor to the Zhang

family [which lasted for] eight years. Every day, late at night when people became quiet, I alone faced the lamplight. With my bed cold and hard as iron I could not sleep; I thought of my parents in Nanjing and of my getting old with no accomplishment at all. Whenever these thoughts occurred to me, I unconsciously threw aside my books and wept bitterly. Then I would try to contain my emotions and after a while I would wipe my tears and start studying again. It was like this day after day.

When the spring of 1640 arrived, Zhou went to Beijing to take the metropolitan examination held on the 9th day of the 3rd month. Zhang Minbiao went with him, probably to participate in the same examination.[76] Zhou passed the examination, but Zhang's name was not included on the list of successful candidates. Among the successful candidates was Fang Yizhi, whom Zhou had regarded enviously from afar in Nanjing when he was growing up.[77]

Subsequently Zhou passed the palace examination and received the *jinshi* degree. This marked the beginning of Zhou's scholar-official career and the end of twenty-odd years of hardship and preparation for examinations. It was also the realization of the highest dream of his *shengyuan* father, Zhou Wenwei, who probably had been preparing and waiting for his son's "triumph" ever since his birth. Another happy event which took place in the same year was the birth of Zhou's first son, Zhou Zaijun (b. 1640).

Fig. 27. Wang Duo (1592–1652). "Mountain Landscape." Dated 1651. Hanging scroll, ink on paper, 117.1 cm x 54.9 cm. The Metropolitan Museum of Art, New York. Gift of Ernest Erickson Foundation, Inc. (1985.214.149).

A scholar-official from the north, a distinguished calligrapher and collector, and an accomplished landscape painter, Wang Duo viewed Zhou's collection of contemporary paintings in 1650 during one of Zhou's journeys to Beijing.

CHAPTER 2

A Ming Scholar-Official

BEIJING ARTISTS AND FRIENDS

ZHOU HAD RETURNED to Beijing by 1641 for a palace interview and received an appointment. While waiting for it, Zhou was able to enjoy for the first time since his childhood, freedom from the pressures of the examinations. As a new *jinshi*, Zhou met many eminent men of his day, as well as re-established ties with old friends. Sun Chengze, Zhou's patron and friend from his days in Henan, was now serving as a senior metropolitan censor in Beijing.

Zhou also renewed his acquaintance with Chen Hongshou, who had been in Beijing since 1640.[78] It had been more than fifteen years since Zhou, as a thirteen-year-old boy, first met Chen at Zhuji. The reunion must have been a poignant one for both men. At their first meeting, Chen Hongshou was a twenty-six-year-old *shengyuan* with a considerable reputation as a scholar-painter, who eventually hoped to become a scholar-official. But by the time the two met again in 1641, Chen had given up trying to pass the provincial examination and had decided to purchase a fellowship at the Imperial Academy of Beijing which he hoped would bring him an eventual government appointment.[79] Despite Chen's failure and Zhou's success, the two made this reunion the starting point of a profound friendship. In his *Du Hua Lu*, Zhou recalls their activities together in Beijing at this time:

> In the year of *xinsi* [1641], the year I presented myself as a candidate at the court, I saw him [Chen Hongshou] again at the capital. Together with Jin Daoyin [Jin Bao], Wu Tieshan [Wu Ruilong, 1585–1673], and other scholars, we formed a poetry society. Changhou [Chen Hongshou] liked my poetry. Thereafter we became intimate friends.[80]

Zhou also formed a close friendship in Beijing with his *jinshi* classmate Fang Yizhi.[81] Fang Yizhi's father, the eminent scholar-official Fang Kongzhao, had been in a Beijing jail since 1639 after being blamed for a defeat in a campaign against a bandit army. Although his father had been sentenced to death, Fang's desperate attempts to save him and his display of filial devotion so moved the emperor that his father's life was spared, and by 1641 the sentence had been reduced to banishment to Shaoxing.[82] This long ordeal seems to have greatly affected Fang. Zhou later recalled in his biography of him that he who "led a frivolous life before the age of thirty" had become a serious and introspective man.

A close contact of Fang's, who gathered together with Zhou and Fang at this time in Beijing, was Zhang Yi, a battalion commander in the Imperial Palace Guard. Zhang, a *shengyuan* from Nanjing, had received this post in recognition of the noble death of his father, the famous general Zhang Keda from Nanjing. Zhang Yi probably introduced Zhou to his brother, the *Du Hua Lu* painter Zhang Feng (d. 1662, DHL 3/4), later in Nanjing. Zhang Yi became a lifelong friend of Zhou and contributed the second preface to the *Du Hua Lu* after Zhou's death.

All the aforementioned acquaintances, except perhaps Jin Bao, painted. Zhang Yi, Fang Yizhi, and Wu Ruijong were all amateur artists. Zhang and Fang painted landscapes while Wu did peonies. Until this time Chen Hongshou was of a different caliber both in terms of commitment and talent from all the painters Zhou Lianggong had ever met in Nanjing, Kaifeng, or Beijing. Chen and Cui Zizhong (d. 1644), who also was active in Beijing at the time, were considered the two great figure painters of their day and were often grouped together as "Chen of the South and Cui of the North." Unfortunately Zhou evidently failed to meet the reclusive Cui . But his interest in Cui led him to include his biography in his *Yinshuwu Shuying*, largely based on what he had heard from Qian Qianyi, who, while in Beijing, lived close to Cui 's home and had befriended the painter.[83]

After waiting several months in Beijing, Zhou was appointed magistrate of Wei Xian in Laizhou, Shandong, in 1641.[84] Fang Yizhi, accompanied by their mutual friend Zhang Yi, came to bid farewell to Zhou. They exchanged farewell poems.[85] Chen Hongshou presented to Zhou a painting illustrating Tao Qian's (372–427 A.D.) ode, *"Gui qu lai ci"* (Returning Home) as a farewell gift (fig. 37). Zhou, who appreciated the eremitic ideals of Tao Qian despite his own determination to serve, found the painting moving. The message that Chen seemed to convey — that Zhou should consider retiring to avoid the dangerous politics of his day — must have been particularly poignant to Zhou as he took up his difficult new assignment.

OFFICIAL DUTIES AND ARTISTIC PURSUITS

THE ATTAINMENT of an official position not only marked the fulfillment of his life-long ambition to enter the ranks of the scholar-official class, but also provided adequate means and the proper status with which to pursue his passion for the arts and collecting. But Zhou's assignment to the northern coastal district of Wei Xian in Shandong must not have been taken favorably. Shandong province, which bordered the increasingly aggressive new Manchu state, was inadequately protected by Ming troops and suffered frequent Manchu incursions, the most recent of which had occurred in 1639. The coastal areas of Shandong, including Wei Xian, also had to cope with pirates. The region was badly despoiled, and the local people were weary of constant warfare, economic dislocation, accumulated delinquent taxes, and corrupt local administration.[86] In 1640, Shandong suffered a famine.

Upon his arrival, Zhou swiftly confronted these local problems with considerable administrative skill, amiability, and integrity and won the hearts of the people. According to Song Wan (1614–1673), a famous scholar from Laizhou, Shandong, Zhou was respected for his uprightness and honesty during his tenure in the province.[87]

Zhou also began to promote local education in Wei Xian. He founded a literary society called "Weishe" to promote ancient learning and literature and, at the same time, to prepare its members for the government examinations. Fa Rozhen (1613–1696, DHL/SL), the future *jinshi* and scholar-painter, was among its members. The society was remarkably successful and twelve out of sixteen members Zhou supported obtained the *jinshi* degree.[88] The character of the society's activities strongly suggests that it was probably a Fushe branch.[89] Even if the Weishe was not formally aligned with Fushe, Zhou clearly seems to have been inspired by Fushe ideals and to have sought to offer the same kind of support to struggling scholars that he himself gained from Fushe.

Zhou was selected as one of the examiners for the provincial examinations of Shandong in the autumn of 1642. This undoubtedly increased his influence among the Shandong literati and led to the creation of strong bonds of friendship with successful candidates.[90]

Zhou was especially attentive to his everyday official duties and according to his eldest son, started work each day before dawn.[91] Like many Neo-Confucian scholars of his period, Zhou apparently had begun practicing "quiet sitting" (*jingzuo*) in an effort to set his mind in the state of quiescence, that is, the state of *wushi* ("without affairs" or "not busying the mind with anything").[92] Zhou even named his office hall in Wei Xian *Wushi* and had the name carved on wood and hung in front of the hall.[93]

Wushi, an important concept in Neo-Confucian thought from the Song period onwards, represents a state of concentration or seriousness in which the mind is empty of all selfishness and completely receptive and responsive to the principles of heaven-and-earth and *Dao*, the Confucian Way. As much as Zhou was committed to social and political activity, he also seems to have been deeply concerned that his mind "could be carried away by events as well as by its own persistent egotism, thus losing the equilibrium and self-control that keep it in accord with the Mean (*zhongyong*)."[94] While Zhou was never a serious Neo-Confucian thinker, he was a faithful practitioner who strove to put Neo-Confucian ideals into practice. The search to find a practical means to attain enlightenment seems to have been an everyday concern.

Zhou Lianggong also whole-heartedly accepted the literati view of art as a means for self-cultivation. In his leisure time, Zhou frequently occupied himself in the enjoyment of art — mainly seals and painting — accompanied by his amateur poet concubine née Wang, or by visiting friends, painters, and seal carvers. While in Wei Xian he met a painter from Nanjing, Hu Yukun (DHL 2/5), whose works apparently for the first time enabled Zhou to experience a form of enlightenment or self-cultivation through art. Throughout his writings on Hu, Zhou expressed his elation over having found an artist who could inspire lofty thoughts and the recognition of high principles. The experience marked an important turning point in Zhou's life and was at least partially responsible for turning him into a serious collector of contemporary paintings. His meeting with Hu Yukun was also an important event in that Zhou, for the first time played scholar-official host to an artist guest — a practice he would continue throughout the rest of his life.

Hu Yukun visited Zhou at Wei Xian in the winter of 1641 as a travel companion of Zhou's friend Fang Yizhi.[95] When Zhou later recalled his first meeting with Hu, he commented on the significance of the event in his life as a collector:[96]

It is with him [Hu] that I started collecting albums of paintings. At the very beginning, what I acquired was a *moni* pearl [wish-gratifying pearl, i.e., Hu's painting]. Then I found that pieces of gems or jade [i.e., lesser paintings by others] were no longer pleasing to my eyes. I met him through Fang Mizhi [Fang Yizhi]. Mizhi came to see me at Wei Xian [in Shandong] in the winter of the *xin-si* year [1641], accompanied by him. After Mizhi left for the south, he alone stayed on. Thereafter we visited each other several times. During the period of turmoil [1644-1645], we again saw each other. This is why I have more of his paintings than anyone else's and why I especially have a lot of poems that I presented to him. I have recorded all of them on albums except for the long poems. This is to repay him for his distinguished service as a pioneer [in initiating my collection of albums].

As suggested in the above account, from this point onwards Zhou became Hu's enthusiastic patron, while Hu became Zhou's frequent traveling companion and live-in guest for more than twenty years.

Before taking a closer look at Hu and attempting to see just what Zhou found appealing in the painter, we should pause to consider Zhou's commitment to patronage, which dates from this period. Given Zhou's early interest in paintings and seals, his drive for recognition in the literati world, his compassion for the artist friends of his youth at Qinhuai, and his commitment to Fushe ideals, since he had achieved the status and wealth of a scholar-official, his growing patronage activities were only natural. But his patronage also should be viewed within the context of the growing popularity of various forms of patronage during the late Ming and early Qing.

THE ISSUE OF PATRONAGE

IN TRADITIONAL China, patronage, which involves a reciprocal relationship between the successful and the needy, was an important channel through which successful men could manifest their humanity and virtue, and at the same time establish a reputation and strengthen their influence by their widened associations. Talented men without official positions or of limited means, on the other hand, sought the psychological comfort, economic support, recognition, and career advancement that patronage could bring. Patronage was so popular, no doubt, because this pinion-like relationship established between the patron and the patronized was so mutually beneficial. The expansion of patronage activities in the late Ming-early Qing was, in part, probably due to demographic factors. The population explosion and the expansion of literacy had swelled the ranks of the educated elite well beyond what could be absorbed by government officialdom.[97] Those who were fortunate enough to achieve official posts were relied upon as patrons to support the many who failed the examinations. The political instability and the establishment of an alien dynasty which many refused to serve probably also contributed to the development of mutually beneficial private associations. The Fushe movement, too, appears to have played a role in encouraging the fad of "associating with like-minded men."

The "host-and-guest" relationship, which Zhou formed with Hu and later with others, was part of a tradition that goes back to the 5th–4th centuries B.C.[98] In the early seventeenth century, during the raging conflict between the Donglin and the Fushe and their opposition, this "guest" tradition was revived with a new popularity. The practice abetted the development of factionalism, which at times reached the point of perversity satirized by Fang Yizhi through the words of Baoshuzi in his "Seven Solutions:"[99]

> Sir Brazen stood up and, in an imposing, braggartly manner, said, "A real man, having been born in the world, is going to be of use in this world. Why so constricted?... A man who has integrity and is noble-spirited but who is unable to make himself known because of his poverty and low standing goes to make the acquaintance of a person of rank in order to achieve repute....You just want to crouch hugging your knees and moan and sing while waiting for the time when there will be someone who understands you, someone who adapts his standards and befriends you. In today's world who makes it his business to understand others and esteem talent!" Baoshuzi replied, "I understand that all too well....By depending on others to do things for me, and by using my connections to avenge myself on my enemies, I could have wealthy men provide me with benefits; I could have villages in awe of me; I could have inconstant literati, insincere in their commitments, as my adherents. How grand! . . . I would rather live in a humble lane and find contentment in being 'useless.' "

The "guest" practice was also criticized by the renowned contemporary scholar Gu Yanwu (1613–1682) in his admonition to a young scholar against becoming a guest of his famous nephew Xu Qianxue (1631–1694)[100] and later in the eighteenth century by Wu Jingzi in his novel *The Scholars* (*Rulin waishi*).

All the satire and criticism directed against "guest-host" associations suggest how widely accepted the practice had become. Whatever its excesses, the practice was an important form of patronage. Throughout his career Zhou Lianggong would play host to numerous worthy scholars and artists and, as Fang Yizhi puts it in the above excerpt, made it "his business to understand others and esteem [their] talents." In fact, Sir Brazen's advice to Baoshuzi echoes one of Zhou's statements regarding the importance of patronage:[101]

> Whenever a literatus wants to have his poems and essays known by later generations, he'd better make a plan when he is still alive. He might say, "There must be someone who will understand my work." But do not rely on it.

Thus patronage for Zhou was an almost indispensable means to insure that an artist's work would be "known by later generations." Although Zhou fails to mention it in this passage, certain forms of patronage, such as the compilation of biographies or anthologies, assured both the patron and the beneficiary that their names would not be forgotten by posterity. Zhou, as we will see, was acutely sensitive of his place in history and hence was particularly attracted to this form of patronage.

AESTHETIC ENLIGHTENMENT
AND HU YUKUN

THE FIRST real recipient of Zhou's patronage, Hu Yukun, was from a prominent local painter family in Nanjing which produced at least six painters, the most prominent of whom was Hu Yukun's uncle, Hu Zongren. Extant works suggest that Hu Zongren was a rather conservative painter who followed the Yuan landscape tradition, often through the Wu School interpretation.[102] Towards the final decade of the Ming, Nanjing landscape painters were still very much under the influence of the Wu School, especially Wen Zhengming and Wen Boren (1502–1575). Hu Yukun, instead of closely following the Wen family tradition, experimented with basically two types of landscape painting. One type was an atmospheric landscape painting in a boneless manner with colors as the main medium. This is exemplified by an album leaf datable to the mid-1640s that was dedicated to Zhou Lianggong (fig. 28, cat. no. 17). The other type was executed in ink and terse brush mode. It often depicted Nanjing and the surrounding area as the subject (fig. 29; cat. no. 1, leaf A).

Hu's expressionistic brush manner is reminiscent of the late Ming painters Shen Shichong (act. 1610–40) and Sheng Maoye (act. 1594–1637).[103] Fellow Nanjing painters had mixed reactions to his art. For example, Gong Xian was rather negative about Hu's accomplishments as a painter, while Cheng Zhengkui (1604–1676, DHL 2/6) was favorable.[104] It was largely through Zhou's patronage that Hu was known to contemporary connoisseurs. Others probably did not esteem his works as much as Zhou, whose appraisal was influenced by their close personal friendship and Zhou's own artistic taste during this formative period. While Hu's paintings were not uniformly appreciated by contemporaries, it should be noted that his unwillingness to completely follow in the footsteps of the orthodox masters and his experimental spirit certainly were to become the core thrust of the Nanjing painters in ensuing years.

Fig. 28. Hu Yukun. "Misty Landscape." Album leaf, colors on paper, 24.3 cm x 32 cm. The Art Museum, Princeton University, Gift of Wen C. Fong and Constance Tang Fong, y1962-110. (Cat. no. 7)

Greatly influenced by Hu Yukun, Zhou wrote in his biography of the artist, "He is solitary by nature and so is his painting. In his brushwork and use of colors he loves to depict impressionistic and formless voids. . . . It is with him that I started collecting albums of paintings."

Fig. 29. Hu Yukun (fl. ca. 1630–1670). "Mount Qi." From an album of sixteen leaves, "Album of Landscapes by Famous Mastes Collected by Zhou Lianggong." Album leaf, colors on paper, 24.8 cm x 32.3 cm. Collection of The British Museum, London. (Cat. no. 1, leaf A)

Since Hu's works were once so enthusiastically admired by Zhou and played such an important role in his early aesthetic development, we will pause here to review Zhou's critical comments on Hu and to examine his underlying philosophy of art. In his biography of the artist Zhou notes:[105]

> Li Junshi [Li Rihua, 1565–1635] once said: "The most difficult thing in painting is the area of empty space." As far as I have seen, the only painter good at using empty space is Husan [Hu the Third], [*zi*] Sangong. . . . He is solitary by nature and so is his painting. In his brushwork and use of colors he loves to depict impressionistic and formless voids. As a result, within a fraction of a foot, one can imagine a distance of a myriad *li*.

Zhou thus appreciated the suggestive quality of Hu's paintings and the artist's execution of impressions that were forceful, yet broken and formless. In a colophon on one of Hu's works, Zhou placed Hu's landscape art in the "untrammeled" class: "Whenever he paints he treats ink as if it were gold. He is the so-called 'man who illustrates the case of *yipin* [untrammeled] above the level of *shenpin* [divine class]'. . . ."[106]

Zhou was genuinely moved by the vacuous mood of Hu's landscapes. Through the quietistic, untrammeled expression found in Hu's painting, Zhou thus seems to have had a transforming experience which we might call an "aesthetic enlightenment." This aesthetic experience must have been very special to Zhou in this formative period. It reaffirmed for him the Neo-Confucian value of painting as a means of self-cultivation, which in turn gave him an important rationale for his patronage and collecting.

In one of his letters to Hu Yukun he explained the importance of art as a means of cultivation:[107]

> Paintings of one streak of water and one small rock [i.e., landscapes in general] are the means for us to cultivate our *xingqing* [personal disposition and emotion]. But contemporary paintings offer us only pleasure, and induce us to recklessness. Therefore they have nothing to do with *xingqing*.

The letter goes on to explain that while he has rarely been moved by others' works, he is moved right away by the slightest touch of the brush by Hu. Zhou believed that a work of art could not be successful if it failed to move its viewers: "The reason why some of the art cannot be transmitted to posterity has no other explanation but that the works sit there and do not inspire people. . . ."[108]

THE CRITICAL STANDARDS: *XINGQING* AND "A SCHOLARLY SPIRIT"

THE TERM *xingqing* — personal disposition and emotion — which Zhou uses in the above letter was one of the key critical concepts in his art and literary criticism. It was particularly prominent in his poetry criticism. The term was used to refer not only to the viewer as above, but also to the creative process of artists. Art was viewed as a means for the artist "to express *xingqing*" and for the viewer "to cultivate *xingqing*."[109] Actually art was seen as a form of self-cultivation as well as expression for the artist. The ultimate Confucian aim of self-cultivation was to realize the ideal of *junzi* (a Confucian perfected gentleman), i.e., to achieve the *Dao* (the Confucian Way). Therefore the cultivation of *xingqing* through the arts had ethical as well as aesthetic implications. Zhou's frequent quotation of the time-honored sanctum, "Literature is an instrument to carry the *Dao*," could equally be applied to painting.[110]

This moralistic view of art, which was hardly unique to Zhou Lianggong, has been succinctly discussed by James Cahill and summarized by Arthur Wright:[111]

> Briefly, this theory held that the quality of a painting lay in the character of the artist . . . it should reflect the perfection of the character of the artist, and this perfection — perceived in the painting — in turn inspires the beholder to try to attain a comparable perfection. In a new context and with a new vocabulary the centrality of moral perfection was reiterated, and painting was raised above the status of avocation or artisanship; it became instead a means of expressing the attributes of the Confucian perfected man and of inspiring others to cultivate his qualities.

Zhou's embrace of this commonly held view is evident in such statements as, "If the literary works of a literatus can be passed down to later generations, it is because he possesses that [virtuous character] which enables his works to be passed down. . . ."[112]

Therefore, Zhou, like other critics of his day, looked for "the attributes of the Confucian perfected man" in a painting — attributes that would allow for the viewer's cultivation of his own Confucian qualities. One important attribute Zhou sought was a "scholarly spirit," whose antithesis was "vulgarity." Zhou had little tolerance for vulgarity, by which he usually meant a superficial elegance and a tendency to follow the common trend in order to please the taste of the ignorant public. Zhou preferred the art of learned men who were possessed of a lofty character and expressed a "scholarly spirit" in paintings. His contempt for vulgarity was often expressed in his praise of those who were devoid of it. For example, he commented on one of Xu You's (ca. 1620–1664, DHL 3/3) paintings: "Yujie's painting is like his poetry; hoary, clear, and distinct — totally devoid of vulgar habits." Zhou's appraisal of paintings thus basically repeated the age-old aphorisms of traditional Chinese criticism which divided the world into the two polar opposites: "vulgarity" and "scholarly spirit." This basic critical standard was applied to paintings either directly or indirectly throughout the *Du Hua Lu*.[113]

The following comment on Zou Dian's work exemplifies Zhou's use of this critical terminology:[114]

> In his painting, his brushwork possessed a lofty and refined character without sweetness and vulgarity. He was good enough to be able to look down upon mediocre painters.

Similar terms were also used in the criticism of poetry as is evident in Zhou's endorsement of the following statement by a Chen Houcun: "Complexity and gorgeousness are inferior to simplicity and tranquillity; straightforwardness is inferior to indirectness; heaviness and turbidity are inferior to lightness and limpidity; solidness and obscurity are inferior to the void and cleanliness."[115] These descriptive terms were not unique to Zhou but had been the focus of Confucian aesthetic values ever since the Northern Song, when scholars began to believe that art had to go beyond the imitation of nature and express the spiritual qualities of the artists themselves. Similar terms were frequently used by critics in painting and poetry from the Northern Song period onward.

It was only natural that Zhou's *xingqing* theory emphasized the relative importance of education in art, since this was the backbone of the literati tradition. Zhou often attributed an artist's success to his education. He made the following comment on Yun Xiang (1586–1655) in the *Du Hua Lu* (DHL 1/16) (fig. 30; cat. nos. 8, 22): "Since he stores many books in his bosom, his work has little of an eye-pleasing, vulgar air. The same is true of his poetry. . . ." To emphasize the importance of education in painting, he quoted Dong Qichang: "Yunjian [Dong Qichang] once said that those who did not read books were not worth talking with about painting. I agree with him completely."[116]

In his discussion of painters Zhou seldom fails to point out their accomplishments in literary composition and calligraphy. Throughout the *Du Hua Lu*, Zhou criticizes only one painter, He Faxiang (DHL 4/11), the professional painter of bird-and-flower subjects, of "shallow learning:"[117]

> He was skilled at painting birds and flowers. Although he is a grandson of Master Xuetai, since his father Yuzhi is vulgar and cunning, Zizhang's learning is shallow. Thus he finally ended up with vice and nothing else. My collection has only one work by him, which is a painting of mynah birds.

This shows that Zhou firmly accepted the traditional literati emphasis on the importance

Fig. 30. Yun Xiang (1568–1655). "Snow Landscape." Hanging scroll, ink on paper, 121 cm x 53.5 cm. Wang Chi-ch'ien collection, New York. (Cat. no. 8)

of education and that he shared the common belief that a good general education was a prerequisite for the artist.

Zhou's interest in paintings and his belief in their moral efficacy and their value in self-cultivation was therefore perfectly consistent with the so-called "literati theory of art." Art for Zhou was part of an "all-embracing system of cultivation" and an effort to achieve total balance.[118] It seems clear then that Zhou pursued the orthodox path to sagehood. Although the peculiar complexities of his time and milieu as well as his own personal idiosyncrasies and taste were inevitably reflected in his critical judgment, this orthodox view of art was to remain the backbone of his connoisseurship and criticism.

AGAINST THE MANCHUS

IN NOVEMBER 1642 and January 1643, while Zhou was still in Wei Xian, Manchu forces led by Abahai (Norhaci's seventh son) attacked and occupied much of northern Shandong and northern Jiangsu.[119] A large number of cities were sacked. We are told by Zhou that Wei Xian, under his leadership, was the only city to withstand the assault. Rallying local officials and conscripted townsfolk to defend the city against great odds, Zhou proved himself a capable strategist and an effective military leader, as he was well versed in military strategy and excelled in archery.[120] A number of poems he wrote at this time, which were later published under the title *Tongjin* (Poems of Rage), vividly portray his fear that the Ming dynasty was crumbling and express his sorrow over the sufferings of the people. One reads:[121]

> With horses lined up, the barbarian army crossed
>   the Wei river at night.
> Wounded and feeling sad, I am lying on a pillow alone.
>   (my left shoulder was wounded by two arrows)
> My hometown [i.e., Kaifeng] is immersed under water
>   and my home has become a [barren] plain.
> Nearby cities have been shaken;
> The lives of the people are in great danger.
>   (Chang Village, east of Wei Xian,
>   and Shouguang to its west have been sacked)
> I felt abandoned and insignificant with my arm wounded three times.
> Sharing the resentment and tears of my people, I ascend
>   the parapets [on the city wall].
> Do not be shocked by the desolate sight of the suburbs;
> This is the time when seventy-some cities have already been sacked . . .
>
>   *   *   *   *
>
> A great victory to end the war is hard to come by.
> Worried over the national crisis, his Majesty has given
>   his trust to military generals.
> But we do not have [the Han general] Hou Qubing . . .
>
>   *   *   *   *
>
> Even weak women have ascended the city wall [to fight],
> But their strength cannot withstand [the enemy attack].
> I cannot but wonder how those military commanders can bear
>   to face the emperor's self-blame in his edict.

Zhou was prepared to fight to the death. It is recorded that he placed a large sign on his chest reading "Body of Zhou Lianggong, the magistrate of Wei Xian" to display his willingness to fight until death and to enable the identification of his corpse after the battle. It is also said that his concubine née Wang assisted in battle by beating a drum. Under siege and waiting for relief, Zhou felt abandoned and enraged by the helpless state of the government, which proved unable to prevent recurring Manchu invasions and rebel uprisings.

Meanwhile, Zhou learned the fate of his hometown, Xiangfu, which he left two years earlier. The rebel army of Li Zicheng flooded Xiangfu, drowning most of its inhabitants. His patron Zhang Minbiao and his family were among them. Zhou sent his brother to Kaifeng to camp out on the bank of the Bian River with provisions to assist the survivors. Only one son from the Zhang family survived; he was taken into Zhou's family.[122]

Zhou's *Poems of Rage* are a powerful realistic documentation of his confrontation with the mighty, disciplined military power of the Manchus. The poems express his despair over the military weakness of the Ming — which had no great military leader comparable to the Han general Hou Qubing — and his compassion towards his hungry and cold soldiers and the desperate populace.

In late 1643, in recognition of his achievement in defending Wei Xian, Zhou was chosen as one of the ten best local officials in the empire and called to Beijing.[123] Upon his departure, the Wei Xian people wept and followed his retinue in a long incense-burning procession. Soon afterwards they built a shrine in honor of Zhou which contained his portrait and a tablet of his meritorious deeds.[124]

THE FALL OF THE MING DYNASTY: BEIJING

IN BEIJING, Zhou was promoted to the post of imperial censor in charge of the Zhejiang circuit. During this dismal period, just prior to the fall of the capital, a sense of doom and a mood of apathetic hopelessness began to prevail in the city.[125] Nevertheless, the emperor and bureaucrats alike did not seem to have foreseen the disaster that was about to occur. The court even celebrated a great festival with all the scholar-officials in attendance the day before the arrival of Li Zicheng's army.[126] Officials like Zhou, whose ranks were not high enough to be included in the policy-making process, simply waited, hoping conditions would improve.

Although the record on Zhou's life in Beijing during this period is scanty, we know that he offered lodging to the seal carver Liang Qianqu and commissioned several dozen (lit. tens of) seals from him just as Li Zicheng approached the city. Zhou records that as a result he did not get even one seal.[127]

On the 19th day of the 3rd month of 1644 when Li Zicheng's army captured Beijing, Zhou had been promoted to the post of imperial censor less than ten days. The Chongzhen emperor (r. 1628–1644) immediately ended his life by hanging himself. After six weeks, and several battles against Li's troops, the joint Manchu–Wu Sangui forces[128] advanced towards Beijing. On the 30th day of the 4th month, Li Zicheng fled the city. When on the 2nd day of the 5th month, the Manchu–Wu forces reached Beijing, the Ming officials went outside the city wall to welcome them. Soon the Manchus proclaimed their sovereignty over China and the Shunzhi emperor (r. 1644–1661) was enthroned. In the following year, Yangzhou and Nanjing fell.

When Li's army entered Beijing, many officials, including Ni Yuanlu (1594–1644) and Fan Jingwen (1587–1644), committed suicide.[129] Many others, including Zhou Lianggong and his mentor Sun Chengze, are recorded to have attempted suicide but were prevented by their family members.[130] Zhou's action thereafter is obscured by the existence of two contradictory accounts. His chronological biography, which was most likely composed by a friend with the help of the family, records that Zhou soon heard, as many other officials of Beijing in fact did at the time, a rumor of the Chongzhen emperor's safe flight to the south. According to the same source, Zhou gave up the idea of committing suicide in deference to his parents and hid in a temple together with Zhang Yi for one night before escaping with other officials mingled among refugees to the south.[131]

Another account by an anonymous author, however, lists Zhou as one of the court officials who remained in the capital during the Li Zicheng interregnum.[132] The Li regime cruelly abused captured gentry and bureaucrats, whose malfeasance and selfishness they blamed for the fall of the dynasty. Brutal punishment was meted out to many officials; about one thousand were executed or tortured to death. Many were forced to pay a political ransom ranging from 1,000 to 100,000 taels.[133] According to this second account, Zhou was one of the officials who registered with Li's government and was soon herded into four encampments where they were treated like prisoners of war. In addition to Zhou Lianggong, Fang Yizhi, and Fang's father, Fang Kongzhao, Sun Chengze, Prime Minister Chen Mingxia, the scholar-painter Dai Mingyue (*jinshi* of 1634), and the eminent collector Liang Qingbiao were listed among the prisoners. The account singles out Zhou and two others as the only individuals who survived the encampment unharmed. Rumors of Zhou's favored treatment, whether true or not, may have made Prince Fu's court in Nanjing suspicious of Zhou's collaboration with the Li regime and may account for his imprisonment immediately after his arrival in Nanjing. While a number of officials who eventually escaped to Nanjing were executed for collaboration with the Li regime, Zhou was acquitted of all accusations and shortly released.[134] Zhou's acquittal casts doubt on the authenticity of the second account, at least to the extent that it implies collaboration with Li.

Fig. 31. Woodblock print illustration for Kong Shangren's 1669 novel Tao Hua Shan (Peach Blossom Fan). From the translation by Chen Shih-hsien and Harold Acton, with the collaboration of Cyril Birch. Berkeley: University of California Press, 1976.

This illustration depicts a moment in the story when Yang Wencong and Ruan Dacheng appear before Prime Minister Ma Shiying, who protests that they are being too ceremonious. The three then sit down together and Ma proclaims, "Now the world belongs to us!"

By the time Zhou reached Nanjing, the Prince of Fu (Zhu Yusong) already had been enthroned with the support of Ma Shiying (DHL 4/19) and Ruan Dacheng (ca. 1587–1646) over the opposition of Shi Kefa (d. 1645), who instead favored the Prince of Lu (Zhu Yihai) (fig. 31).[135] Those serving the Nanjing court by the 8th month included Qian Qianyi, Huang Daozhou (1585–1646), Liu Zongzhou (1578–1645), Huang Zongxi, Qi Biaojia (1602–1645), Wang Duo, Wu Weiye, Chen Zilong, Cheng Zhengkui, Yang Wencong, and some other Fushe members and sympathizers. Zheng Zhilong (1604–1661), the former pirate leader, was made commander of the troops in defense of the capital; his son Zheng Chenggong (1624–1662), was put under the tutelage of Qian Qianyi in Nanjing in this year.[136]

Factional conflict, if anything, intensified after the fall of Beijing, perhaps due to the absence of any strong central leader. Ma sought to become the most powerful man of the Nanjing court over the opposition of Shi Kefa. The Fushe members openly maneuvered against Ruan Dacheng, the former Donglin member who was thoroughly despised by the Donglin and Fushe members for his betrayal when he became an adopted son of the Donglin's enemy, the eunuch Wei Chongxian. Ruan in turn sought revenge against the Fushe.[137] Upon his arrival, Zhou evidently reported to the Nanjing court and sought to receive a position. He retained his official rank and title, but before he received actual duty, he was slandered by a former imperial guard named Feng Kezong for surrendering to the Li regime. He was imprisoned for a short while and then released when he was found innocent.[138]

Meanwhile the Ma-Ruan faction sought to eliminate all opposition, including all Donglin/Fushe elements from the court. They offered Zhou an official post under the one condition that he memorialize the throne impeaching Liu Zongzhou, the former Donglin member and acting president of the Censorate at the Nanjing court. Liu, who was respected by a great number of scholars, had been attacking the corrupt practices (such as bribery and sale of offices, etc.) of Ma and Ruan. Dismayed at the proposal, Zhou finally decided against any involvement with the Nanjing court and retired to Mount Niushou, south of Nanjing, with his parents sometime before the end of 1644.[139] It was during this time that Zhou seems to have befriended Qian Qianyi and Wang Duo, as well as such *Du Hua Lu* painters as the monk-painter Kuncan who lived on the same mountain, Yang Wencong, Cheng Zhengkui, Zou Zhilin (DHL 1/18), Gong Xian, Gao Cen, Zhang Feng (d. 1662), and Fang Hengxian (a cousin of Fang Yizhi). Fang Yizhi and Wan Shouqi were also briefly in Nanjing towards the end of 1644.

THE FALL OF THE MING: YANGZHOU AND NANJING

ON THE 25th of the 4th month of 1645, Yangzhou fell to the Manchus. The news reached Nanjing before the 3rd of the 5th month, when the Prince of Fu, Ma, and Ruan fled.[140] By the 15th day of the 5th month, when the victorious army of the Manchu prince Dodo arrived outside the Nanjing city gate, everyone in Nanjing knew of the ten days of plunder and massacre which the residents of Yangzhou had suffered at the hands of the same Manchu army for their spirited resistance led by Shi Kefa. They obviously feared suffering the same fate for what must have seemed a hopeless cause. The populace probably was indifferent to the Ming cause and the few soldiers that remained did not want to fight. In fact, the chief commander for the city's defense had already secretly conveyed his surrender to the Manchus before they arrived.[141] Two Ming generals, Gao Jie and Liu Liangze, and fourteen others along with 23,830 soldiers had already surrendered and the two Ming forces charged with the defense of the Southern capital under the command of Zheng Hongkui (the uncle of Zheng Chenggong) and general Cao had failed to prevent the Manchu army from crossing the Yangzi river and were already in retreat to Fujian.[142] Nanjing was thus virtually abandoned. It was clear that the Southern Ming officials who remained had to choose between martyrdom and surrender. The former course not only guaranteed their own deaths, but the destruction of the city. It can be imagined that they were faced with tremendous public pressure to spare the city. In fact, they probably could not have organized a loyal resistance force even if they had wanted to.

When Dodo's army arrived, the city gate was still tightly closed. But before the Manchu army took any action, the remaining officials were assembled and led out the gate by the commander-in-chief Zhao Zhilong to welcome Dodo and his army, just as their Beijing counterparts had done one year earlier. Dodo's memorial to the Shunzhi emperor reporting his takeover of Nanjing gives a complete list of the thirty civil officials who welcomed him on this day outside the city gate. Included on the list were the President of the Board of Ceremonies Qian Qianyi, the Grand Secretaries Wang Duo and Cheng Zhengkui, as well as seventy-two military officials.[143]

Zhou Lianggong's name was not mentioned. This strongly suggests that Zhou was still in hiding, probably on Mount Niushou. After Dodo entered Nanjing, all former officials were ordered to surrender. Wang Duo was in charge of their presentation to Dodo.[144] At least two officials were recorded to have been executed for failing to surrender and a number of others committed suicide.[145] While the exact date and circumstances are not clear, Zhou went to Dodo's headquarters and surrendered.[146]

Following the fall of Nanjing much of the south remained outside Manchu control, and many of Zhou's Fushe comrades — including Jin Bao, Fang Yizhi, Wan Shouqi, Huang Zongxi, and Qi Xiongjia — were directly involved in the loyalist resistance. To some loyalists at this time, Zhou's surrender probably was considered abandonment and betrayal. Zhou never discussed the issue openly — at least not in the surviving records — and we must therefore examine the decision in light of Zhou's background and personality, and in the context of events surrounding his surrender during the chaotic transition period.

Certainly the fall of Nanjing was crucial to both Ming officials and the Manchu court. To the latter, it was tantamount to the conquest of the entire area south of the Yangzi river. Thus when the fall of Nanjing was confirmed, the Manchu court in Beijing announced in an imperial declaration, on the 29th of the 5th month, the "Great Victory News of the Pacification of Jiangnan." Except for the most ardent loyalist Ming officials, the prospects for a Ming revival must have appeared hopeless. For many military officials and the general populace, loyalty for the Ming cause appears to have no longer been a great matter of concern. The calamitous events of the years leading up to the Manchu's occupation of Beijing had undoubtedly eroded support for the Ming cause. Military men who lacked proper leadership or remuneration lost all incentive to fight. Commoners, who for two decades had suffered from the ravages of wars and rebellions, probably sought a return to stability. For many, further resistance must have represented only further suffering and pointless sacrifice. Moreover, the legitimacy of the corrupt Southern Ming court under the dominance of Ruan and Ma must have been increasingly questioned. By 1645, the Manchus had pacified most of north China and had begun to set up a working administration in Beijing with the assistance of many prominent Ming officials. The Manchus boosted their claim to legitimacy by not attempting to alter existing Chinese political and social systems. Officials who chose to collaborate could with justification assert that the new rulers were worthy of the mandate of heaven.

The fall of the dynasty, however, was a traumatic calamity that raised very serious immediate moral problems for Confucian scholar-officials, both active and retired, as well as for degree holders and intellectuals. They had to decide, often at great personal costs, whether to uphold the strict Confucian doctrine of *zhong*, or "loyalty" to the ruler.[147] One choice was to become a collaborator by serving the Manchus, the other was to become a loyalist by committing suicide, joining a resistance army, or forsaking the world as a monk or hermit. The choice was often based on the varied circumstances of each individual — socioeconomic status, native place, age, personality, philosophy, religion, academic status, talent, and ambition all were relevant. Each chose according to his own conditions and needs.

ZHOU LIANGGONG'S SURRENDER

THE COMPLEX QUESTION of why Zhou Lianggong chose to serve the Manchus while many of his close friends remained loyalists can never be fully answered. It has been suggested that Zhou Lianggong might have surrendered in order to protect his Fushe comrades from the alien regime. The strong sense of trust and dependency displayed towards Zhou by his loyalist friends, many of whom were Fushe members, adds credence to this explanation. Moreover, certain evidence exists which hints that there might have been a kind of loose coalition among collaborators who shared loyalist sympathies despite their surrender. Some contemporaries seem to have believed in Zhou's loyalty and good intentions despite his collaboration. The noted scholar and bibliophile Huang Yuji went as far as to say that it "was for the sake of the people that Master Zhou came forward and answered the call [of the new government]."[148] It remains unclear, however, what Zhou's main motivation was at the time.

Having fought a desperate battle against the Manchu army as magistrate of Wei Xian, Shandong, Zhou knew from first-hand experience the mighty strength of the Manchu military force and the helplessness of the Ming armies. He probably had a clearer appreciation of the futility of further resistance than others who had no military training or experience. Zhou's economic and social background also had an important bearing on his decision to collaborate. Coming from a struggling lower gentry background, his drive to succeed and his sense of responsibility for his family were very powerful. Unlike literati from wealthy elite families, Zhou endured considerable hardship and sacrifice in his advance into the ranks of the scholar-official class and was obviously loath to give it all up at the very beginning of his career. Moreover, his personal character was not that of a martyr or recluse. He was a man of action, outgoing and gregarious. Influenced by his father and by the activist goals of the Fushe, he had a strong commitment to public service.

In fact, this was not the first time the question of "withdrawal" became a serious issue in Zhou's life. In about 1641, around the time he received his first appointment, still under the Ming, Zhou exchanged letters with his friend and mentor Zhang Minbiao, and expressed his commitment to public service despite all the potential dangers. Zhang's response reveals the depth of Zhou's commitment and highlights the dilemma faced by individuals like Zhou who felt compelled to serve:[149]

> You think you can fulfill your noble intention [in government service]. I always have this thought in my mind: that it is easy to be an official in order to benefit only oneself but it is difficult to be an official to serve the court and the people.

If one plans only for himself, then what he has to do is to try to establish connections. How does one make connections? I do not have to mention it here. Do you think there have been only one or two who have become rich and prominent since the ancient times? Do you think there have been only one or two who have been loyal to the emperor and the people, put into practice what they believe they must do to serve people, and incur jealousy and accusations and eventually lose their lives? The "wise man" who keeps silent and the "virtuous gentleman" who hides from the actual world would not be any good to the world. I know. [On the other hand] why should one drink bitter tea as if it is sweet? [However] I do understand your volition.

A great amount of surviving biographical information testifies that Zhou held a firm conviction that a man's actions should be governed by their social utility. Even after suffering for years in a dangerous post in Fujian and then being slandered, sentenced to death and jailed for six years, he refused to consider retirement. It was only when he fell seriously ill that the idea of retirement was temporarily considered. At this time, in 1664, he wrote a letter to his son-in-law which reveals his activist temperament:[150]

> I have been requesting retirement from my post. . . . Officials usually like to talk about retirement. But I am not such a type [as you know]. I think you are the only one who probably understands me.

The desire to assist loyalist scholars and artists and to safeguard Chinese culture offers another possible explanation for Zhou's decision to collaborate. It also points to a new meaning and dimension given to Zhou's patronage after the fall of the Ming. Zhou clearly respected the loyalists and felt a deep sense of responsibility to help them. He was keenly aware of their hardships and sufferings. Forsaking an official career, many became poor artists. Zhou lamented their fate in his *Yinren zhuan*:[151]

> Alas! All these bright and outstanding people, who are regarded as useful men by the people, did not meet the right time. Therefore only with their art can they fulfill themselves. What a pity!

Indeed, loyalists who abandoned their scholar status and became *buyi* (plain-clothed) were given special attention throughout the *Du Hua Lu* and *Yinren zhuan*.

Zhou also took it as his responsibility to safeguard Chinese culture under the alien rule. Du Jun (1611–1687), the famous one-time Ming loyalist, pointed this out in a letter written to Zhou in which he requested that Zhou write the biography of their deceased mutual friend, the painter-seal carver Huang Jing (b. ca.1595–d. 1663, DHL 3/1), and sponsor the posthumous publication of a book Huang wrote:[152]

> You have always considered literati culture as your responsibility. So I assume that even if this were someone else, you would still diligently help him. Then how much more so when it [my request] concerns Huang! So I hope you will keep this in mind all day. Then his friendship with you while he lived will not have been in vain.

While initially many loyalists may have felt abandoned and resentful towards collaborators, in general the relationship between the collaborators and loyalists seems to have been cordial and without bitterness. The position of both sides was evidently widely accepted at the time. There are some isolated cases in which collaborators such as Qian Qianyi were scorned by some contemporaries for having acted immorally or for being more than just unwilling "collaborators." Some "loyalists" took a longer time to accept collaborators, though the vast majority eventually did. Loyalists and collaborators in fact frequently continued to be close friends. Qian Qianyi maintained close ties with many staunch loyalists such as Huang Zongxi.

Zhou seems to have been confident that his contemporaries would understand his collaboration, or at least recognize the redeeming beneficial aspects of it. In writings throughout the rest of his life, Zhou gives no hint of his having suffered from shame or guilt as a collaborator as our sentimentalism might lead us to believe; instead he seems to have taken a fatalistic approach to dynastic change and to have preserved his dignity by pursuing the "right way" in his official duties and by safeguarding Chinese culture under the alien rule. Although confident about the judgment of contemporaries and about the propriety of his actions, Zhou does seem to have feared the judgment of history. This uncertainty, which became particularly acute towards the end of his life, will be discussed below.

CHAPTER 3

Collaboration and Patronage

RECOVERY IN YANGZHOU
AND THE BIOGRAPHIES

AFTER JOINING the new regime, Zhou was reappointed to his original rank of censor and sent by Dodo on a peacemaking mission to Yangzhou, where he assisted in restoring order. His friends arranged a farewell party for him at the waterside pavilion of the old Fushe member Ding Jizhi at Qinhuai.[153] Qian Qianyi was present and composed a farewell poem for Zhou which betrays a mixture of emotion and a veiled hope for the Ming revival:[154]

> Under a dim light, the wine at this farewell party
>   fails to add to our amusement.
> Rosy clouds pregnant with snow darken Qinhuai.
> During turmoil, it is difficult to communicate with each other.
> At [this] critical moment, we can only talk by means of
>   our eyebrows.
> At midnight, villagers cry and, with battle unfinished,
>   [we hope] to raise Lu Yang's halberd.
> Let us enjoy *lizhi* [fruit] while it is ripe and *luyu* [fish]
>   while it is fresh.
> Let us get drunk, play the silver *zheng*, and sing out loud.[155]

Yangzhou, which was probably devastated more than any other city during the entire Manchu conquest, was in ruins when Zhou arrived, probably in the autumn of 1645. Upon his arrival, Zhou persuaded merchants and salt makers to return to their abandoned businesses. In the same year, he was appointed salt controller of the Lianghuai region. Zhou's contribution to the restoration of Yangzhou is detailed by Huang Yuji:[156]

> [Thanks to him] the Lianghuai region returned to peace. First he established the [Lianghuai] *yenfadao*. When Master Zhou took up his duty there, Guangling had experienced the Ten-day Massacre and it was still in ruins. [Salt] merchants had not yet regained their breath. The salt which had accumulated formed a *tanyan* [salt wall]. Merchants had fled and all the salt had been confiscated by the

government. Master Zhou devised various plans to get these merchants back. He asked the government to return the *tanyan* to the merchants. He arranged it so that all the unemployed got back their old jobs. He also asked the court to abolish the old system of levies on salt merchants and carried out his new system. As a result, a large number of merchants returned and the government revenue increased.

During his two years in Yangzhou, he played a key role in helping revive the ruined Yangzhou city as the salt capital of the nation. He reformed the old regulations and revised and updated the tax quotas.[157] Based on his experience, he authored a book on salt administration.[158] The following year, he was transferred to the post of intendent of the Huaiyang circuit, where he served until 1647.

When free from official duties, Zhou was actively involved in cultural activities. He frequently gathered at Huaiyang with Wan Shouqi, Wang Shilu, and Chen Taisun. The monk-painter Wan Shouqi had become friends with Zhou in 1630 while both were Fushe members in Nanjing. Chen obtained his *jinshi* in the same year as Zhou. Wang Shilu, who was a scholar-official and poet and the elder brother of the celebrated poet Wang Shizhen (1634–1711), was serving in the area during this time (cat. no. 1, leaf AA). Zhou wrote of their time together at Huaiyang as follows:[159]

> In the years of 1645 and 1646 when I was posted in Weiyang [Yangzhou], Wang Xueqiao [Wang Shilu] was serving in Sizhou [in northern Jiangsu]. Several times when we both went to Huai [Huaiyang] on official business, my *tongnian* Chen Jiliu [Chen Taisun] invited us to drink. He would always invite Ro [Wan Shouqi's *zi*]. Xueqiao could not drink, but he liked to compose poems. Whenever we drank, we assigned a rhyme to each of us. Ro's poems were good and his calligraphy was beautiful. Whenever I got his works on fans, I always kept them. . . .

Since 1645, Wan Shouqi had taken up residence in Huaiyang. According to his official biography, Wan never abandoned his ambition to raise a loyal resistance army.[160] Together with many Ming loyalists, including his close friend Yan Ermei (1603–1679), Wan pledged resistance to the Qing. Evidence suggests that Wan's home was a gathering place for Ming loyalists. Chen Taisun had become a lifelong friend of Zhou and presented him with a boat at this time as a gift. Zhou turned the vessel into a floating art gallery which he named "Jiuyuan."[161]

Zhou and his friends spent many leisurely hours aboard the Jiuyuan viewing his collection, and subsequently he was often called by this name himself. Gao Fu wrote of Zhou's boat: "He kept the mist and clouds (calligraphy and paintings) in his boat wherever he went. Cases of paintings were tied to the upper rudder. When the boat was moored, he invited his friends to join his imaginary journeys enjoying his collection of art works."[162] Since Nanjing was to be reached only a short distance down the canal from Yangzhou, then up river, Zhou probably frequently used his new boat to visit Nanjing, where his parents and family still lived. Zhou also remained in close contact with the artists of Nanjing, as evidenced by an album in the collection of the British Museum (cat. no. 1) executed for Zhou around this time by such Nanjing painters as Hu Yukun, Zou Zhe, Zhu Ruiwu, Gao Cen, and Shi Lin (DHL 4/17).[163] Nanjing artists also visited Zhou in Yangzhou. Hu Yukun was a frequent house guest, Zhu Ruiwu came from Nanjing and painted an album for Zhou, and Shi Lin contributed two paintings to an album now in the National Palace Museum (cat. no. 6).

Scattered references indicate that Zhou actively sought out talented artists, poets, and scholars. For example, he met with Cheng Sui (1602 – after 1690, DHL 3/5) (fig. 32), a painter from Anhui, and Zong Hao (DHL 3/10), a painter from Zhejiang, who were both living in Yangzhou.[164] Zhou probably renewed his friendship with Gong Xian, who had moved from Nanjing to Wucheng in the Yangzhou prefecture at approximately the same time that Zhou was in Yangzhou.[165] Fang Qiyi (1619–1649), the brother of his friend Fang Yizhi, came to see him and stayed on his Jiuyuan boat. During his stay, Fang carved one seal and wrote calligraphy on several fans for Zhou.[166]

As indicated in Zhang Yi's preface to the *Du Hua Lu*, it was during this Yangzhou period that Zhou first began to collect notes on the lives of painters (fig. 33):

> Posted in Huaiyang [Yangzhou], he spent much of his leisure time on a boat where he would take up albums at random. As his thought wandered, he would write a biography [of a painter whose work was included in the album]; write about the circumstances under which the work was painted, narrate the entire history of the work, or inscribe a poem or a colophon — sometimes elaborate and sometimes simple.

Zhou also began to seriously study and collect antique and contemporary seals. Wherever he went he looked for old seals and seal carvers. By this time Zhou had already become quite well known for his interest in seals and attracted seal carvers from various regions who sought his attention and approval of their works. Zhang Yi's description of Zhou's method of compiling the biographies of painters in the *Du Hua Lu* is echoed in the preface of Zhou's *Yinren zhuan*, which Zhou probably also started writing during this period:

> Since he [Zhou] was well versed in the Six Scripts [i.e., philology], seal carvers came from all four directions to meet him. Master Zhou from time to time made evaluations of some of these seal carvers, who thereafter became very well

Fig. 32. Cheng Sui (1602 – after 1690). "Wintry Landscape." Fan, ink on gold paper, 22.86 cm x 48.26 cm. H. Christopher Luce collection. (Cat. no. 25)

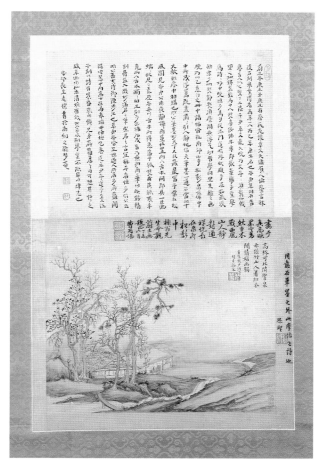

Fig. 33. Gao Cen (fl. 1650–1679). "Landscape." Accompanied by the artist's biography composed and inscribed by Zhou Lianggong in 1651. Two album leaves mounted as a hanging scroll, ink and color on paper, painting size 24.7 cm x 32.0 cm. Freer Gallery of Art, Smithsonian Institution, F80.116. Transferred from the Department of the Treasury, U.S. Customs. (Cat. no. 9)

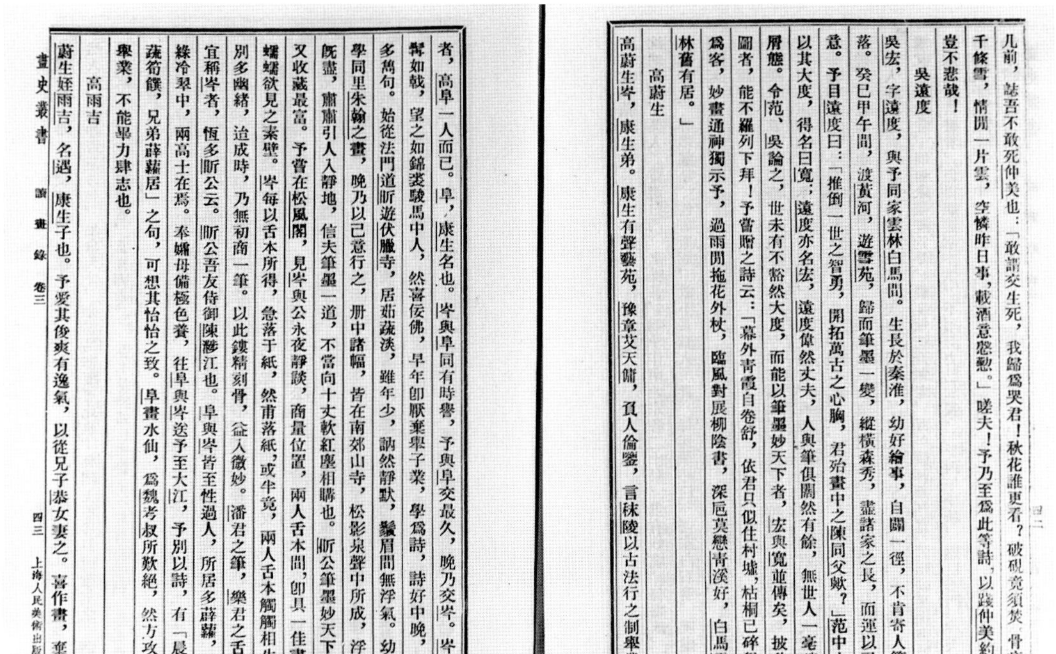

高蔚生岑，康生弟。康生有聲藝苑，豫章艾天晡，頁人倫鑒，言林陵以古法行之制樂業。

高遠度

爲客，妙畫通神獨示予，過雨聞拖花外杖，臨風對展柳陰書，深巵莫戀青溪好，白馬雲林舊有居。」

圖者，名不罹石至村墟，枯桐已碎猶

屑態。今范、吳論之，世未有不怒大度，而能以筆墨妙天下者，宏與寬亜傳矣，披此

以其大度，予詣遠度曰：遠度亦名宏，遠度偉然丈夫，人與筆俱闊然有餘，無世人一毫

意。予目遠度曰：「推倒一世之智勇，開拓萬古之心胸，君殆畫中之陳同父歟！」范中立

落。癸巳甲午間，遊黃河，遊雲苑，歸而筆墨一變，縱橫森秀，靈諸家之長，而運以己

吳宏，字遠度，與予同家雲林白馬間。生長於秦淮，幼好繪事，自闢一徑，不肯寄人籬

吳宏

豈不悲哉！

千絛雪，情聞一片雲，李檎昨日事，裁酒忌慈憨。」嗟夫！予乃至爲此等詩，以踐仲美約，

几前，甚苦不敢死仲美也！「敢謂交生死，我歸爲哭君！秋花誰更看？破硯竟須莢，骨痩

蔚生姪雨吉，名遇，康生子也。予愛其俊爽有逸氣，以從兄子恭女妻之。著作書，壘栗

高雨吉

業，不能畢阜志也。

蔬筍饌，兄弟蘖藟居」之句，可想其怡怡之致。早畫水仙，爲魏考叔所歎絕，然方攻制樂

綠冷翠中，奉嫣毌備極色養，往阜與岑途至大江，予別以詩，有「晨昏

宜稱岑者，恆多昕公云。昕公善友侍御陳鬣江也。

別多幽緒，造成時，或半宵。潘君之筆，樂君之舌，兩人舌本觸觸相生，

蠟螺欲見之素壁，岑每以舌本所得，然甫落紙，急落時，乃無初商一筆。以此鏤精刻骨，

又收藏最富。予嘗在松風閣，見岑與公永夜靜談，兩人舌本間，卽具一佳畫。

危盡，蕭廎引人入靜地，信夫筆墨一道，不常向十丈軟紅塵相購也。昕公筆墨妙天下，

學同里朱翰之畫，晚乃以己意行之，冊中諸幅，皆在南郊山寺，松影泉聲中所成，浮巒

多萬句。始從法門道昕遊臙寺，居茹蔬淡，雖年少，訥然靜默，鬢眉間無浮氣。幼時

帮如戟，望之如錦襄駿馬中人，然喜伏佛，早年卽厭葷摹子業，學爲師詩，詩好中晚，恆

者，高阜一人而已。阜，康生子也。岑與阜同有時譽，予與阜交最久，晚乃知岑。岑鬢

畫史叢書　諸畫錄　卷三　四三　上海人民美術出版社

Fig. 33a. Gao Cen's biography in the Du Hua Lu, *identical with the colophon in Fig. 33. Omitted in the biography is Zhou's inscription in the last column dated 1651 in the colophon.*

Collaboration and Patronage 67

known. He carried the seals in his collection wherever he went. With the seals arranged on his left side, he wrote short biographies of these seal carvers.

Zhou hosted seal carvers, such as Liang Danian, at his official residence for several months at a time to carve seals for him.[167] He even collected seals by a woman seal carver, Han Yuesu (*hao* Xige Nuzi), who was famous in her time for tiny seals.[168] Her biography in the *Yinren zhuan* contains several interesting remarks by Zhou about contemporary women artists:[169]

> I have compiled a *yinpu* [collection of seal imprints] which represents less than 10 of her seals. . . . Alas! Those contemporary women [who were famous in the same period] as Xige, such as Wang Xiuwei, Yang Wanxu, and Liu Rushi [Liu Shi, 1618–1664, Qian Qianyi's concubine], all are known by their poems. However, in truth, they achieved their fame by relying on their famous and eminent husbands. [But] Xige is a weak woman. She is only skilled at seal carving. Since she is married to an old and poor scholar, she has not been recognized. But those who have her tiny seals always treasure them as if they were gold and jade. Therefore, Xige also will be remembered by later generations for her seals. Alas! An insignificant craft though it is, it is still enough to enable one to be known to posterity like this.

The *Yinren zhuan* preface also records the preface author Qian Lucan's conversations with Zhou. The conversations are very important in that they reveal Zhou's motives and objectives in compiling the *Yinren zhuan* and, by extension, cast light on his intentions to write the *Du Hua Lu*:

> In the past, I heard Master Zhou saying that "literature originated in characters. Characters are made of horizontal and vertical strokes. In each character, there are *zi*, *mu*, *yin*, and *yi*." This is why every three years he made a list [of ancient characters]. There was certainly an important reason why he did this every three years. He also said, "From the Qin and Han periods up to now, forms of characters have been distorted and their pronunciation has changed. We don't even know how much has been changed. Therefore it is the scholar's duty to research the ancient forms through the characters on seals."

This shows his interest in seals was not only artistic, but also philological. Zhou began to advocate emulation of the style of Qin and Han seals because this represented the earliest form of seal script; he began to judge seal carvers accordingly. But he felt frustrated over the rarity of quality seals: "I have always been crazy about seals. I always look around the country doing a great deal of research. But it is very seldom I find someone who meets my standard. . . ."[170] Throughout his life, Zhou was to continue this search. He wrote a good deal about the art of seal carving and its evolution during the late Ming and early Qing. This enduring effort finally resulted in his book *Yinren zhuan* (Lives of Seal Carvers), a book which greatly contributes to our understanding of this disappearing art.

GOOD GOVERNMENT AND
LITERATI PURSUITS IN FUJIAN

AFTER SPENDING about two years in Yangzhou, Zhou was posted in Fujian. From 1647 to 1649 he served as a provincial judge and then from 1649 to 1653 as a junior financial commissioner. Finally in 1653 he was promoted to senior financial commissioner and held that post until 1654. Fujian was the last stronghold of Zheng Chenggong's army on the mainland and a large part of the province was still under Zheng's control when Zhou arrived. Constant warfare raged between the Qing government forces and Zheng Chenggong's army, and order was regularly disturbed by large numbers of roving bandits. During these years Zhou successfully defended several cities from Zheng's army as well as from local bandits and once again proved his leadership qualities and military abilities.[171]

At this time, Fujian cities repeatedly changed hands among Zheng's army, the Qing army, and the bandits. The Ming restoration army and the Qing army were equally threatening to the local populace. In addition to sporadic pillaging, both armies frequently punished the local populace, when territory changed hands, for its collaboration with the former occupant.[172] Cities previously occupied by Zheng's army were punished by the Qing army. Cities taken over by Zheng's army were sacked and pillaged unless they peacefully surrendered. Even if they surrendered in peace, the cities often had to meet unreasonable demands for provisions and other military levies. One suspects that the local populace, battered from all sides, was at best indifferent to the imperial claims of the conflicting armies.

Under the circumstances, it is not surprising that the pressing need to ease the suffering of the people and restore order, rather than any self-righteous commitment to Ming loyalty or "emotional devotion to the principle of loyalty itself," commanded Zhou's attention. Zhou had already chosen to cast his lot with the triumphant Qing; the Ming cause by this time certainly appeared even more hopeless than it was immediately following the fall of Nanjing. Moreover, the validity of Zheng's claim to represent the fallen dynasty must have seemed tenuous even to the loyalists.

The surviving records indicate how Zhou intervened on the citizens' behalf. First, he was able to save a thousand people from massacre by the Qing army. The Fujian coastal people at this time were sandwiched between Zheng's army, which demanded that they supply provisions, and the Qing army, which was enraged by their collaboration. When a Manchu general ordered the execution of all the inhabitants of more than ten coastal towns and the destruction of their homes, Zhou intervened at the critical moment.[173]

On another occasion a military commander was about to demolish fourteen counties in Quanzhou prefecture in order to eliminate the possibility that the inhabitants would form allegiances with the Zheng Chenggong army. Zhou once again intervened. By swearing the local populace's loyalty to the general over the bodies of one hundred members of his own family, he convinced the general to spare the fourteen counties.[174]

Zhou also cracked down on local bullies. In one case he severely punished a group of strongmen who troubled the people by criminal practices. This was later to become one of the direct causes of his impeachment in 1655, which nearly cost him his life (see below). A passage in Zhou Zaijun's *Xingshu* describes this incident and his father's role as a model official:[175]

In the year of *guisi* [1653], my late father was promoted as senior financial commissioner. He was the first Chinese since this dynasty was established to serve in this position, and served in the Fujian frontiers in many places. He understood the difficulties of the people and acting as a model official he tried to relieve them from their difficulties. He eliminated bad customs and wrote signs at the entrance of his hall. One said, "When I receive the silver money, I don't take the melting fee. I send the silver out in its original sealed condition."[176] Another one was, "When the document arrives, I begin to gather the tax. As soon as I finish, I send it out immediately." For a while, the Fujian people almost forgot about the hardships of tax-payment. There were many cunning people in the provincial capital who formed a clique named Wu Toushe. They troubled the villages and good people were harmed by them. But the officials did not dare to accuse them. He [my father] arrested them and had them punished by law.

Time and again throughout his life, Zhou Lianggong demonstrated an extraordinary ability to make the best of the most difficult circumstances. Even in the midst of war, whenever he found free time, Zhou continued to pursue his cultural interests. He continued to seek out local scholars and artistic talents — many of whom were Ming loyalists — and remained an active collector and patron even in war-torn Fujian.

During the Ming period, Fujian was famous for book publishing, and even though its quality was not comparable to that of the Jiangnan area, it produced such eminent bibliophiles as the families of Xie Zhaozhe (1567–1624) and Huang Zhuzhong (*juren* of 1585). Zhou befriended both families and from this time on seriously began to collect books himself.[177]

During the early Qing, Fujian suffered incessant warfare, which began before Zhou's arrival and did not really end until the death of Zheng Chenggong in 1662. The fact that many scholars and artists fled the province is noted in a passage in Zhou's *Yinren zhuan*:[178]

> Fujian was disturbed [by attacks] from the sea. Many of the scholars and artists fled and could not return. People like [the two scholar-seal carvers] Wu Chin and Lin Xiong [who left the province] therefore cannot be enumerated. It is lamentable.

Compared with Beijing and Yangzhou, not to mention Nanjing, which was the art capital of the country during the early Qing period, Fujian had little to offer the connoisseur. Zhou's direct contact with works of art consequently must have become restricted. But art was nevertheless constantly on his mind. Even when in 1647 he was stranded for eight months in Shaowu, Fujian, near the border of Zhejiang (see map 1) and forced to lead the local defense against bandits, Zhou built a pavilion to which he gave the name of Shihualou and enshrined the Song poet Yan Yu's tablet.[179] He also renovated an old hall in the *yamen* (office), which was surrounded by plantains (*jiao*) and named it "Jiaotang."[180] The Shihualou and the Jiaotang became gathering places for Zhou and local literati friends known for poetic talent.[181] Zhou published the poems of local literati under the title *Wanshan zhongshi*. Twenty years later Zhou recalled his eight-month stay at Shaowu:[182]

> Every day I was engaged in fighting. Qiaoquan [Shaowu] is surrounded by

many mountains. As a result, things for amusement cannot reach Qiaoquan or be known to scholars there. Therefore these scholars have no other hobbies [besides poetry] for their amusement. Occasionally some of them presented poems to me. I always ground ink to write poems in response. I have compiled the *Wanshan zhongshi* for them. More than twenty some years have passed. Even now their names are still clear in my mind.

On New Year's Eve, at Shaowu, Zhou organized a gathering to sacrifice to ink ("Jimo") with wine and to compose "Jimo" poems. He was joined by the painter-seal carver Cheng Sui, Hu Yukun, and other friends. This became a custom which Zhou seems to have followed each New Year's Eve thereafter.[183] While in Shaowu, Zhou also finished three books: *Tongshu* (miscellaneous notes and anecdotes), *Ziqu* (divination by the use of ideographs), and *Jiaotangshi* (a collection of poems from Jiaotang). He also began to write two other books called *Yiyang* and *Minxiaoji* (notes on the customs, products, and people of Fujian).[184]

The following year, when Zhou finally reached his destination, Fuzhou, he turned his official residence and the Shewu Pavilion in Fuzhou into gathering places for local scholars, poets, painters, and seal carvers. Zhou was especially delighted to meet Xu You, a Ming loyalist and poet-painter-calligrapher who was a close friend of Chen Hong-shou.[185] Zhou records that he went directly to visit Xu You, whom he had never met, upon his arrival at Fuzhou in 1648. Xu was a *shengyuan* degree holder and studied under Ni Yuanlu in his youth.[186] His father, Xu Zhi, was a famous scholar and a Fushe member, who lived as a recluse in Fujian after the fall of the Ming. Zhou esteemed Xu You as the best calligrapher among the Fujian artists in running and cursive scripts and indicated that he took Xu Wei (1521–1593) and Chen Hongshou as his models (figs. 48, 49).[187]

Another close friend Zhou met in Fujian was Song Zijian (d. 1660), the nephew of Song Jue (1576–1632), who inherited his uncle's fame as a calligrapher. Because of the close relationship that Song Zijian, Xu You, and several other friends maintained with Zhou, they were all later implicated in a legal case brought against Zhou and sent with him to Beijing (see below). Song died while imprisoned in Beijing, while Xu You died in 1664, no more than three years after his release.[188] Zhou also met Guo Dingjing (DHL 4/13), who excelled in poetry, painting, and calligraphy (fig. 34; cat. no. 10),[189] the portrait painter Guo Gong (DHL 4/14), who was a student of Zeng Jing, and the poet-painter-calligrapher-seal carver Li Gen (DHL 4/3). The three artists, who have long been forgotten, all painted and wrote calligraphy for Zhou. Zhou felt that Li's Buddhist paintings were indistinguishable from those of the late Ming painter Wu Bin.

Scholars and artists from Nanjing and Yangzhou also came to Fujian to visit Zhou. For example, the famous seal-carver and painter from Yangzhou, Cheng Sui, and the doctor and seal carver Zhou met in Kaifeng, Cheng Lin, both made visits.[190] Hu Yukun and Le Yao (Zhou's classmate from his youth) from Nanjing accompanied Zhou to Fujian and stayed at Zhou's *yamen*. Zhou brought his collection of paintings with him and built a studio called "Bai Tao fang" (Gallery of a Hundred Poems by Tao [Qian]) at his *yamen* to house the hundred paintings the Nanjing artist Ye Xin (act. 1661, DHL 3/19) painted as illustrations for selected Tao Qian poems.

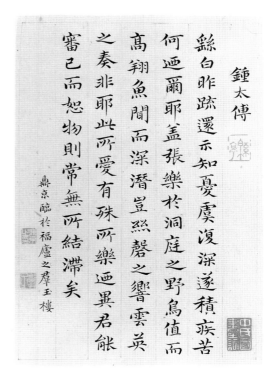

Fig. 34. Guo Dingjing. "Landscape." Dated 1647. Artist's calligraphy at right in imitation (?) of Zhong Yao. From an album of twenty leaves, ink on paper, 22.2 cm x 15.3 cm. Guan Lu Yuan collection. (Cat. no. 10)

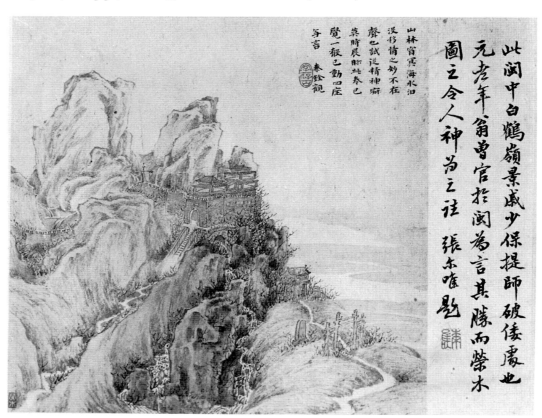

Fig. 35. Ye Xin (active 1661). "Baihe [White Crane] Ridge." Album leaf, ink and color on paper, 24.8 cm x 33 cm. The Metropolitan Museum of Art, New York. Seymour Fund, 1964, 64.268.2. All rights reserved. (Cat. no. 11)

A PASSION FOR SEALS AND EPIGRAPHY

During this Fujian period, Zhou continued to pursue his interest in seals. Zhou rediscovered the book *Jinshi yunfu*, a collection of ancient metal and stone inscriptions compiled by a Ming scholar, Zhu Shiwang. With the help of two local scholars, Zhou began to annotate and expand upon the work. He later completed the work and published it in Nanjing.[191] Zhou also actively sought out scholars and professionals who excelled in seal carving. Those who heard of Zhou's craze for seals also came to see him. Among many seal carvers Zhou met during this time was the Anhui seal carver living in Fujian, Jiang Haochen, who was the country's best-known carver of jade seals.[192]

In about 1648 while in Fujian, Zhou reflected on the art of seal carving and on his addiction to seals:[193]

> The study of the Six Scripts [i.e., philology] has died out. It is only in seal carving that some of the scripts [i.e., seal script] have survived. Among my hobbies, I have been most crazy for this [seals]. Of all that I have collected over the last twenty years, the seal collection is the richest. . . .[194]

Seal carvers frequently remained as Zhou's house guests for extended periods of time. Lin Jin (YRZ 3/15), for example, stayed at his Bai Tao fang and carved quartz seals for him. Zhou often commissioned a large number of seals at a time. Huang Qiyou (*jinshi* 1628), who stayed at his Fuzhou office, carved one hundred and ten seals. Zhou also commissioned seal carvers active in other cities. He also collected old seals by the famous Ming seal carvers, Qiu Min and Gu Yuanfang (YRZ 3/14) from Suzhou.[195] Once when Zhou was unable to buy a Song seal at a local scholar's home, he bought some pages of imprints instead. Thereafter he began to collect the imprints of seals, past and present, which he could not acquire. He began to compile the imprints in album format (i.e., *yinpu*) and to study them (fig. 36).

While Zhou supported virtuous men of mediocre talent, he was especially concerned about discovering hidden or unrecognized talents. Zhou's support for the Fujian seal carver Xue Juxuan (ca. 1580s–1650s, YRZ 3/16) offers an example of Zhou's sympathy for suffering artists and his concern for hidden talents. Xue, who lived in Fuzhou, was an educated man and a competent carver, but failed to gain any recognition.[196] When Zhou summoned Xue, the carver was so moved by the attention and appreciation he received from Zhou, he cried and said:[197]

> "I am an old man. I have been in this craft for the last forty years [but] nobody knows me. My family was poor and had nothing to depend on for their livelihood, so I took this up to feed my wife and children. Every day I sit in my shop by the Kaiyuan temple and [carve seals] for people I don't even know. I charge those who come for my seals by the character; they fetch from ten some [copper] taels, down to three some taels. But even if one character does not fully meet their satisfaction, the customers demand that I carve a new seal. I have lived like this for several decades. I never expected that I would meet you now." When he finished talking, he cried again. His tears wet the seals he had engraved.

Upon hearing Xue, Zhou reflected on the fate of seal carvers — a fate shared by most artists — during periods of disorder:

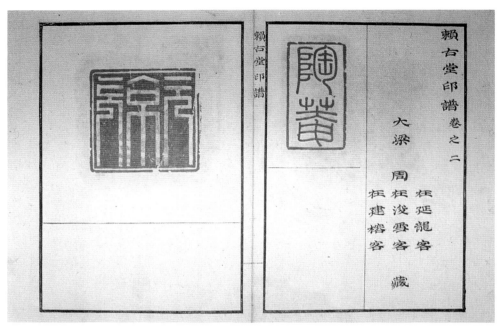

Fig. 36. Imprint of two of Zhou Lianggong's seals. Both seals are in homage to Tao Qian. The seal at left reads "Yuanliang" and refers to Tao Qian's pen name. Imprint at right reads "Tao-an," a reference to Tao Qian's hut. From Laigutang yinpu *(Book of imprints of Zhou Lianggong's personal seals), completed ca. 1672. Library of the Tokyo National Museum.*

I only lamented that in peacetime, such seal carvers as He Zhuchen [He Chen], Wu Wushu, and Zhu Xiuneng, all busied themselves at this craft, while scholar-officials around the whole country all treated them with respect. Sometimes they would kneel in front of them to offer money and when they got a single seal, their happiness rose to their eyebrows, and they were even more proud of themselves. In my opinion, Hongbi's [Xue Juxuan] seal carving entered the chamber of the Qin and Han masters and he could have sneered at all others. Yet his name did not even reach out beyond his village. He sat in his shop every day and faced the ridicule of people whom he did not know. What a sad fate! Fujian people considered Hongbi's meeting with me was like Jiang Yaozhi from Huicheng being known to me and [then] becoming prominent. Alas! How could I place enough esteem on Hongbi?

Although Zhou was clearly influenced by his sympathy for struggling artists, he did not lack critical standards and an ability to distinguish the good from the bad. His search for talented artists was also driven by the instincts of a true collector and the desire to acquire quality works. He was no mean collector, but a connoisseur who knew how to discover and assess the various qualities contained in works of art. Zhou once proudly wrote:[198]

Although contemporary seal carvers present their seals to me with my name carved, if the seal does not satisfy me even a bit, I go back to the carver and ask for a replacement. The carver also agrees with me and appreciates that I understand the art of seal carving.

With his wide exposure to the flourishing art world of Jiangnan, the cultural center of his day, Zhou was strongly influenced by Jiangnan tastes and critical standards. It is thus not surprising that Zhou found Fujian art to be provincial and rather limited. As mentioned above, Fujian had no major artists during the early Qing period and Zhou's rather low opinion of Fujian art can be inferred from the following passage in the biography of the native Fujian artist Weng Ling (DHL 2/11):[199]

> His [Weng Ling's] early paintings were characteristic of Min [Fujian painting style]. But when he went to Moling [Nanjing] and became friends with Vice-president of the Board of Works Cheng Duanbo [Cheng Zhengkui], his painting changed. He moved his family to the Gonglubu [of Huaiyang, Jiangsu]. At this time *xiaolian* [*juren*] Wan Nianshao [Wan Shouqi] also moved to that district. They were together day and night. As a result, his painting changed again. In this way, Shouru's painting changed several times. Therefore his work reached the highest perfection and the people in Jiangnan [lower Yangzi valley] regarded him highly.

Zhou's comments on the transformation and "perfection" of Weng Ling's art under the influence of successive Jiangnan artists suggest that he judged the Fujian artist by the standards of Jiangnan art.

One painter Zhou reserved the highest esteem for throughout this period, yet was unable to entice into accepting his patronage, was his old friend Chen Hongshou. Zhou's repeated requests for paintings from Chen, who retired to his native Hangzhou in 1643, were ignored. While Zhou probably had not seen Chen since they parted in Beijing in 1641, the two men were destined to meet again on Zhou's first trip out of Fujian.

ZHOU LIANGGONG AND CHEN HONGSHOU

IN THE 10th month of 1649, Zhou left Fujian on an official mission to Beijing to report on the Fujian situation. He was accompanied by the two famous Fujian scholar-poets Chen Kaizhong and Xu Yanshou.[200] When the party reached Hangzhou, Zhou ran into Chen Hongshou at West Lake. Chen was by this time the best-known figure painter in the country. This meeting was as poignant as their second meeting in Beijing (see above) when Zhou, the new *jinshi*, renewed his boyhood acquaintance with Chen, the scholar-official aspirant turned court painter. This time Zhou, of course, was an official in the Qing court, while Chen had become an estranged loyalist scholar-professional painter.

Chen had returned to Hangzhou from Beijing in 1643 during the turmoil which attended the collapse of the Ming. Greatly affected by the fall of the Ming and the tragic deaths by suicide or execution of his teachers, Liu Zongzhou and Huang Daozhou, and friends, such as Qi Biaojia, he initially entered the priesthood. Whether this was an act of political protest or an attempt to escape life's misery is unclear. Probably, to some degree, it was both. But soon after entering the priesthood, Chen realized that he was not fit to be a monk. Prior to Zhou's visit, he had returned to layman's status and was living as a professional painter. Taking wine and women as an escape, his painting was both an emotional outlet and a means of livelihood.

His outlook at this time was wryly expressed in a poem entitled "No Virtue," which he wrote under the guise of the poet Tao Qian on a handscroll he painted for Zhou in 1650 (fig. 37; cat. no. 12): "Buddhism is distant, [but] the rice wine is near; I cannot reach the distant, therefore I embrace the near." The handscroll illustrates episodes of Tao Qian's life, the scenes of which are accompanied by short poems Chen composed to serve as explanatory notes. In actuality, the notes were largely drawn from his own life. For example, the poem quoted above mentions Buddhism, a religion which never really influenced Tao Qian, but which had an important impact on Chen's life.

Since their separation in 1641, Zhou seems to have tried in vain to get Chen's paintings, probably through requests relayed by mutual friends or letters. In a colophon on another Tao Qian handscroll that Chen eventually painted for him (figs. 38a–c, 39), Zhou described the frustration he felt in attempting to get Chen to paint for him:[201]

> Zhanghou [Chen Hongshou] and I have been friends for twenty years. It was only when we were in the capital [Beijing] that he painted a scroll of "Gui qu lai tu" [Painting of "Returning Home"] for me. I requested more paintings again

Fig. 37. Chen Hongshou (1599–1652). "Scenes from the Life of Tao Qian." Dated 1650. Handscroll, ink on paper, 30.48 cm x 308.9 cm. Honolulu Academy of Arts. Purchase, 1954 (1912.1). (Cat. no. 12)

until my mouth was dried out and my brushes worn. But he was not responsive at all . . . .

It is quite possible that Chen consciously or unconsciously avoided friends who were serving the new regime for some time after the fall of the Ming, until the intensity of his emotions lessened. Zhou also pointed out in his biography that Chen carried all the familiar prejudices of the literati painters: he could not stand the patronizing tone of any requests and generally refused to paint for dignitaries or vulgar people. On the other hand, according to Zhou, "he especially liked to paint for poor scholars with unfulfilled ambitions in order to help them financially. . . ."[202] Since Chen had, in fact, painted for other scholar-officials who served the new regime before Zhou's visit in 1649,[203] Ming loyalty alone can not have been the cause for his refusal to meet Zhou's requests. It is possible that there was some personal reason for his refusal rather than any political one. He may have reacted self-consciously to the idea of having the younger man, whom he had first met under vastly different circumstances, as a patron.

Whatever the reason for his refusal, something important must have happened that

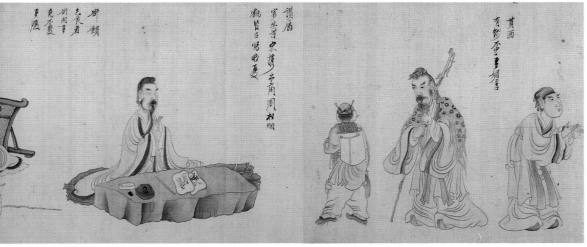

Fig. 38a. Chen Hongshou (1599–1652). "Illustration to Tao Qian's Ode 'Returning Home'." Zhou Liang-gong's colophon appears on the painting proper. Handscroll, ink on paper. Present collection unknown.

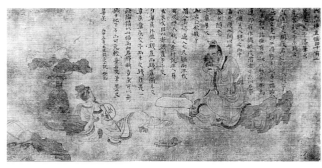

Fig. 38b

Fig. 38c

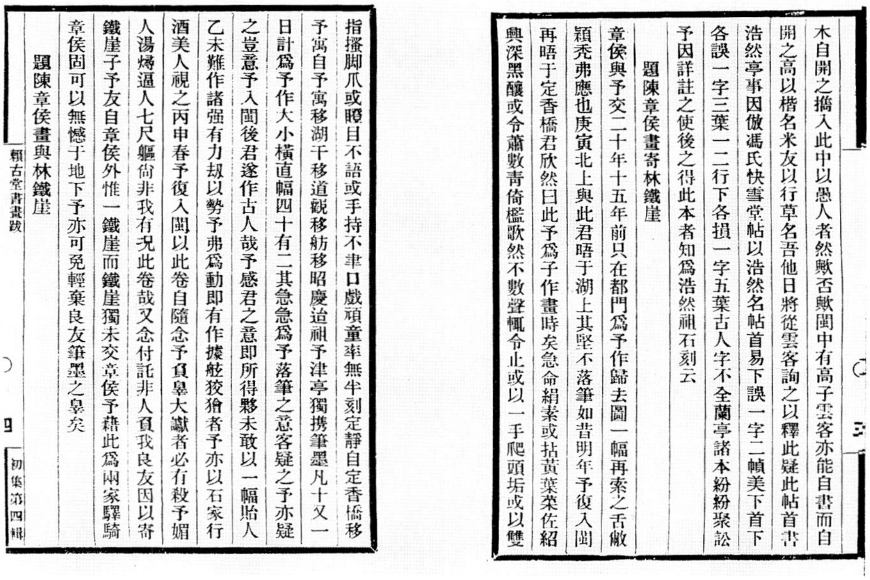

Fig. 39. A transcription of Zhou Liang-gong's colophon in Fig. 38. From Laigutang shuhuaba.

題陳章侯畫與林鐵崖

鐵崖子予友自章侯外惟一鐵崖而鐵崖獨未交章侯予藉此為兩家驛騎
人湯煑逼人七尺軀倘非我有兄此卷哉又念付託非人負我良友因以寄
乙未雖作諸強有力劫以勢予弗為動即有作擾舷猶者予亦以石家行
之豈意予入閩後君遂作古人哉予感君之意即所得弊未敢以一幅貽人
日計為予作大小橫直幅四十有二其急急為予落筆之意客疑之予亦疑
予為自予寓移湖干移道覘移舫昭慶道祖予津亭獨携筆墨凡十又一
指搖腳爪或瞪目不語或手持不聿口戲頑童率無半刻定靜自定香橋移
章侯固可以無憾于地下予亦可免輕棄良友筆墨之皋炎
酒美人視之丙申春予復入閩以此卷自隨念予負皇大讎者必有殺予媚
鐵崖子予友自章侯外惟一鐵崖而鐵崖獨未交章侯予藉此為兩家驛騎

題陳章侯寄林鐵崖

章侯與予交二十五年前只在都門為予作歸去圖一幅再索之舌儆
穎禿弗應也庚寅北上與此君晤于湖上其堅不落筆如昔明年予復入閩
再晤于定香橋君欣然曰此予為子作畫時矣急命絹素或拮黃葉榮佐紹
興深黑釀或令蕭敷青儉歌然不數登楓令止或以一手爬頭垢或以雙
予因詳註之使後之得此本者知為浩然祖石刻云
各誤一字三葉一二行下各損一字不全蘭亭諸本紛紛聚訟
浩然亭事因倣磗氏快雪堂帖以浩然名帖首易下誤一字二幀美下首下
開之高以楷名米友以行草名吾他日將從雲客詢之以釋此疑此帖首書
木自開之摑入此中以愚人者然歟否歟閩中有高子雲客亦能自書而自

forced Chen to change his mind about Zhou Lianggong. This change was evident when they met again after several months when Zhou returned from Beijing. In the summer of the following year, 1650, Chen anxiously waited for Zhou's return to the lake and even sent a poem to welcome him.[204] Upon Zhou's arrival, he happily announced to Zhou, "Now is the time I will paint for you." And paint he did. Chen produced altogether forty-two paintings for Zhou in eleven days — an enormous outburst of creativity for such a short period of time.

Perplexed though he was at Chen's sudden, unexpected generosity, Zhou somehow understood his friend's intention: he was chosen by Chen to safeguard and transmit his art to posterity. Thus Zhou wrote on the same handscroll:

> Within approximately eleven days [when we were together], he painted large and small handscrolls and hanging scrolls, altogether forty-two pieces. Others present and I myself could not understand why he had to paint for me in such a hurry. Was it because he at that time had a premonition of his death after I returned to Min [Fujian]? I was deeply moved by his intention and although I had so many of his paintings, I dared not give away even a single work . . . .

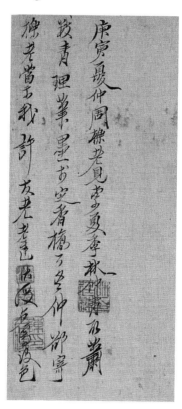

Included among these forty-two paintings Chen did for Zhou is one of Chen's masterpieces, a handscroll cited above and now in the collection of the Honolulu Academy of Arts illustrating episodes of Tao Qian's life. In the case of the Honolulu scroll, Chen himself knew what he had accomplished and felt proud. Therefore, he even asked Zhou to show the painting to his close friend, Xu You, who, as mentioned above, had become intimate friends with Zhou and lived in Fuzhou, Fujian. Chen wrote the following inscription on the painting (fig. 40):

> In the *gengyin* year [1650], in the mid-summer, my old friend, Zhou Lilao [Zhou Lianggong] saw me and asked for paintings. Therefore, during the summer season Lin Zhongqing [Lin Tinglian] had [the singer] Xiao Suqing attend me with ink and brushes at the Dingxiang Bridge [at West Lake, Hangzhou]. In mid-winter I post this painting to Lilao. Please do show this painting to our old friend, Xu You. Laozhi, Hongshou, painted this scroll and [my fourth son] Mingru [Chen Zi] applied the colors.

Fig. 40. Chen Hongshou (1599–1652). Detail, inscription from Fig. 37.

ZHUGE IN SERVICE, TAO IN RETIREMENT: PERSONIFICATIONS

OF THE forty-two paintings done by Chen for Zhou, one painting which is of special interest is a handscroll depicting two scholar-gentlemen engaged in debate (fig. 41 a–c, cat. no. 13). The two figures are seated facing each other against the background of a landscape. The figure on the viewer's left is talking with his one hand raised, while the other figure is listening attentively, leaning against a table with a deep frown on his forehead. The work is executed with Chen's unmistakable brushlines and his sense of composi-

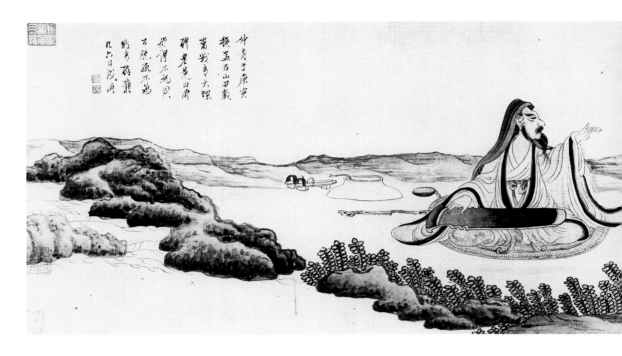

Fig. 41. Chen Hongshou (1599–1652).
"Zhuge Liang versus Tao Qian."
Dated 1650. Frontispiece by Lin Chong:
"In service, he is Gongming [Zhuge
Liang]; in retirement he is Yuanliang
[Tao Qian]." Handscroll, ink on paper.
Present collection unknown.
(Cat. no. 13)

林寵書　元則爲　則爲廬　隃爲孔　出則

tion.[205] Above the shoulder of the figure on the viewer's left, we find the artist's inscription, which, though cryptic, identifies Zhou Lianggong as the recipient. The left figure wears a long cloth headdress of Daoist origin, has a jar of wine at his side and a *qin* on his lap — all attributes which are associated with Tao Qian. The frontispiece and colophons written by two of Zhou's Fujian friends, Lin Chong and Guo Dingjing, confirm the Tao Qian identification and explain that the figure opposite to him with a deep frown is Zhuge Liang (181–234 A.D.).[206] The frontispiece written by Lin Chong in running-standard script reads:

> In service he is Gongming [Zhuge Liang];
> In retirement he is Yuanliang [Tao Qian].

The two figures in the painting represent two contrasting historical personalities — Tao Qian, the eremite poet, and Zhuge Liang, the man of action. Tao Qian was an extremely popular classic model of the disillusioned official who turned his back on government service and sought solace in wine and poetry. When he resigned from public office, he composed his famous ode, "Returning Home," which expresses his longing for a quiet life in retirement. Tao Qian became a symbol of eremitism in Chinese culture; his

life episodes, his famous odes, "Returning Home," and "Peach Blossom Spring," the chrysanthemum (his favorite flower), and the "three paths" of his humble garden became popular eremite symbols in Chinese art and literature.[207]

Zhuge Liang was a scholar, Daoist magician, and military strategist who had lived in retirement during the period of political and social disorder of the Three Kingdoms until he was persuaded by Liu Bei, one of the three contenders for the empire, to forsake his retired life and join his cause. During his campaign against the other two contenders, Zhuge wrote two famous memorials, called "Memorials on Sending Forth the Army," (transcribed by Lin on this scroll), which have been admired for their heroic spirit and expression of loyalty.[208] In later history Zhuge Liang became a respected symbol of a man of action.

Zhuge Liang's commitment to political participation stood in sharp contrast to the eremitic spirit of Tao Qian. For later generations, Tao Qian and Zhuge Liang became "romantic" role models representing the classic moral and political choice between service and retirement. Most Confucians had to face this choice at some point in their careers and either model was sanctioned in Confucian tradition. In practice, the timing of the decision, the legitimacy of the government, and conflicting filial obligations all affected the appropriateness of the model. The role of Zhuge Liang was more difficult and dangerous during a period of political crisis. In a period of dynastic change the question of dynastic legitimacy was by no means clear cut and the decision to serve an unsuccessful contender would result in eternal condemnation of the would-be Zhuge Liang as immoral and disloyal. Thus the role of Tao Qian often emerged as the most viable model in periods of political disorder.

Chen Hongshou initially chose to pursue a government career, but after becoming increasingly disenchanted with the Beijing political environment and with his failure to succeed in an official career, finally decided on permanent withdrawal. As early as 1641, the life episodes of Tao Qian and his eremitic ode "Returning Home" became favorite subjects for his paintings.[209] On a boat on the way home to Hangzhou from Beijing in 1643, he took Qu Yuan (ca. 340–278 B.C.), a late Zhou statesman who committed suicide in exile, as the subject for a painting.[210] Later when he was offered a position at the Southern Ming court at Nanjing, he declined to accept it. It is clear that Chen romantically identified his fate with that of Qu Yuan and Tao Qian. He also, however, struggled throughout his life with the Zhuge/Tao debate, for despite his decision to withdraw, he never seems to have overcome his sense of failure in attaining the status of a scholar-official.

Zhou Lianggong also confronted the same debate, albeit from the perspective of a successful Ming scholar official. Zhou was aware that the time was not right to go into government service even before he assumed his first government post in 1641. In his debate with his teacher Zhang Minbiao, a retired scholar who tried to persuade Zhou against pursuing an official career, he argued that a man of volition should try to achieve his goal of public service regardless of the perils.[211] Notwithstanding this commitment to service, there were conditions under which he would not serve. For example, when Ma Shiying and Ruan Dacheng, the two powerful men of the Nanjing court, offered him a post in exchange for his denouncement of Liu Zongzhou, Zhou refused and retired to Mount Niushou in Nanjing. But Zhou's strong predilection for service and action are clearly evident in his decision to become a Qing official after the fall of Nanjing.

Zhou was deeply committed to the basic Confucian principle that man's true virtue must be made manifest in actions benefiting the people, a principle often identified with Zhuge Liang. But, at the same time, he understood the value of the life of detachment and contemplation symbolized by Tao Qian and admired Tao's lofty character. The deeper he became engaged in war and politics, the more he had to struggle to achieve some balance between his active and contemplative life. Zhou thus cultivated the Tao Qian ideal — like poetry and painting — as a practical means of spiritual cultivation. Evidence of this is abundant. For example, wherever Zhou was posted, he put aside one room which he named "Tao-an" (literally "hermitage," in honor of Tao Qian) and used a seal with these two characters (fig. 36). He hung a portrait of Tao on which he transcribed the "Returning Home" ode in this room, and offered sacrifices to the portrait.[212] Zhou commissioned the Nanjing painter Ye Xin to illustrate as many as a hundred of Tao Qian's poems and built a special studio called the Bai Tao fang to house them.[213] He adopted Tao's *hao* Yuanliang and had seals made with the legends reading "Yuanliang" and "Xue Tao" (to emulate Tao Qian) (fig. 36).[214] Finally, he repeatedly requested Chen Hongshou to paint Tao Qian and was delighted when the artist painted his (Zhou's) portrait in the *persona* of Tao Qian.[215]

Zhou's attraction to Tao Qian seems to have been similar to that of Zhao Mengfu (1254–1322), the famous scholar-official calligrapher-painter, who, like Zhou, served a foreign court despite his links with the former native dynasty and his friendship with avid loyalists. Zhao also shared Zhou's practical mindedness and his commitment to the preservation of Chinese culture. Zhao painted Tao Qian[216] and composed a poem in which he expressed his admiration for the man. Zhao's confession in this poem that for him Tao Qian represented an unreachable ideal, no doubt would have been seconded by Zhou:[217]

Each person lives his life in this world according to his own time;

Whether to come forth and serve, or to retire in withdrawal,
is not a fortuitous decision.
Consider Tao Yuanming's [Tao Qian] poem "Returning Home";
The excellence of his course is not easily explained.
Subsequent ages have much admired him,
Closely imitating him, sometimes well and sometimes crudely.
And in the end, themselves unable to withdraw,
They remain, irresolute, in this dusty world.
But this man Tao truly possessed *Dao*.
His name hangs aloft like the sun and moon.
He followed his lofty way, noble as the green pines.
He was like a chrysanthemum, touched by the frost and still bright.
How readily he gave up his official position,
And bore poverty, dozing contentedly by his north window.
Rolling up this painting, I sigh repeatedly;
How long since the world has known the likes of this Worthy!

An example of another contemporary painter, besides Chen Hongshou, who was fond of painting Tao Qian and Zhuge Liang was Zhang Feng. Zhang's case further illuminates the psychology behind such a portrayal. Zhang Feng was from a prominent military family from Nanjing and had won the *shengyuan* degree under the Ming. According to Zhou, he was a man of martial, heroic character and seems to have joined a certain Ming resistance movement right after the fall of Nanjing in 1645.[218] But despite this heroic spirit, Zhang was forced to earn a meager living through painting and calligraphy, and by teaching children. Frustrated, widowed, poverty-stricken, and suffering from a stomach illness which eventually proved fatal, painting seems to have become not only a means of survival but also his only means of spiritual comfort.

Zhang's attachment to Zhuge and Tao, and his communication with them through their portraits, are recounted in the record of a dream his brother Zhang Yi had after Zhang Feng's death in 1662. The artist appeared before his brother in the dream and said:[219]

> It is so comfortable to live as a leisurely immortal in heaven. I have a newly built small house and have painted portraits of Zhuge [Zhuge Liang] and Chaisang [Tao Qian]. I have set up in the house these two portraits. So I still communicate with all immortals by means of painting.

Zhang's simultaneous attachment to Zhuge and Tao once again suggests the universality of this theme, but at the same time suggests the special relevancy of the two ideals and the heightened tension between the choices they represented during periods of disorder.[220]

Given the importance of the Zhuge Liang/Tao Qian debate for both Chen Hongshou and for Zhou Lianggong, as well as for Zhao Mengfu, Zhang Feng, and many others, Chen's paintings can be interpreted from two different perspectives. On the one hand, the painting can be seen as a symbol of the conflicting claims of two important values in Confucian life, which of course had a special relevance to both Chen and Zhou. On the other hand, it can be interpreted as an expression of the actual debate between

Chen Hongshou, who retired, and Zhou Lianggong, who continued to serve. If read from the latter perspective, Tao Qian in this painting should be seen as Chen Hongshou's self-portrait and Zhuge Liang as the portrait of Zhou Lianggong. If read from the former perspective, the picture represents one man, either Zhou Lianggong or Chen Hongshou, who experiences both sides of the Zhuge/Tao debate throughout his life.

An interesting account narrated by Zhou's eldest son, Zhou Zaijun, suggests this painting might have been Chen's portrait of Zhou Lianggong:[221]

> Chen Hongshou from Kaiji [near Hangzhou] thought that in service he [my father] was Zhuge Wuhou [Zhuge Liang] and in retirement he was Tao Pengze [Tao Qian]. He frequently painted them together in one painting. But my late father humbly refused such honor.

Zhou Zaijun's phrase, "in service he was Zhuge Liang and in retirement he was Tao Qian," is almost identical with Lin Chong's frontispiece for Chen's Zhuge/Tao scroll, which suggests that he might be specifically referring to the painting under discussion. It is very possible that Chen indeed painted the picture as a portrait of Zhou Lianggong — in admiration and with a certain sense of flattery for a man who entertained both ideals. But the complexity of the Zhuge Liang versus Tao Qian debate in Confucian life suggests that the painting can be interpreted on a variety of different levels both personal and universal.

The tragedy of Chen and Zhou was that neither felt comfortable in their respective roles. Zhou lived in fear of historical judgment of his decision to serve in the foreign regime. Chen, on the other hand, never overcame his resentful feelings over his fate. A man of worldly ambition rather than eremitic disposition, he never really achieved the contentment of the idealistic world of Tao Qian.[222] This conflict between an idealistic illusion and bitter reality was reflected in Chen's paintings. The Tao Qian he created in his poems and paintings was a wry, embittered man who was frustrated over the necessity to paint for his livelihood. Thus Chen Hongshou's portrayal is a romanticized, idealized vision of the debate between Zhou and himself as well as the internal struggle that each of these men carried on within themselves.

What made Chen Hongshou a great artist was his ability to translate the irony, contradiction, and poignancy of his period and his life into a powerfully persuasive pictorial language all his own, which is at once imaginative, mischievous, and eccentric. Chen's figures are often portrayed in exaggerated and distorted forms with elongated faces, square jaws, long eyes and eyebrows, and flamboyant gestures. Drapery folds are schematically drawn with superb control and "a calligraphic rhythm of irrepressible iron-wire lines," which endow his "archaic and weird" figures with a life and emotion of their own.[223] The ease and control he achieved in his paintings is a tribute not only to his natural talent, but also to his ardent studies of the ancient models. For example, Chen studied Gu Kaizhi (ca. 344–406) for his brush method, Guanxiu (832–912) for eccentric figure types, and Tang landscape painting for rocks. The Zhuge Liang vs. Tao Qian painting is not as shocking or eccentric as some of his other works. But we can still trace much of Chen's characteristic artistic personality in its tension-charged brushwork and its vivid facial expressions.

Chen's rare artistic talent lay in his ability to comprehend stylistic and iconographic traditions of the past and to recreate them in his own special style of "schematic archaism." This archaism, as Wen Fong has pointed out, was not meant to evoke nostalgia for the past but was to repudiate the present — to shock and amuse — as a form of personal retreat or protest.[224]

In addition to the emotional and political content of his art, Zhou appreciated Chen's inborn talent as a painter and the eccentricity of his artistic personality:

> He was naturally talented in painting, something which can not be obtained through strenuous study alone. . . . People only know of him as a painter of figures and do not know his landscape painting is exquisite. People only express astonishment at the weirdness of his art. But they do not know his every brush-stroke is based on precedent. . . . When I was just about to leave for Wei Xian [following his appointment as magistrate], Zhanghou [Chen] presented the painting, "Returning Home." I could understand his far-reaching thought [from this work].

This brief statement about Chen reveals Zhou's critical frame of mind and two important critical concepts of Chinese art and literature — personal expression and archaism. We observe that in addition to Chen's expressive quality, Zhou appreciated Chen's adherence to tradition expressed in the disguise of individuality. He warns those who found Chen's art too alienating due to its excessive departure from the past that Chen's art, though weird, was based on a knowledge of the ancient masters. Thus, even in his appreciation of this major individualist of his era, Zhou inserts a notion on the importance of the past. This "classicist" appreciation prevails throughout the *Du Hua Lu* in Zhou's discussion of other artists. This was not due to some peculiar fixation of Zhou's, but rather is evidence of the fact that neither Zhou nor contemporary artists including Chen Hongshou and Gong Xian, the foremost individualists of their time, could completely free themselves from the past. While Zhou's criticism reflected his own aesthetic experience at different stages of his life, it was clearly bounded by the degree of development of aesthetics and historical thought of his time.

It is uncertain exactly when Zhou wrote Chen's biography. But considering the fact that he had already begun to accumulate biographical notes for the *Du Hua Lu* from the mid-1640s (with the earliest datable entry being Gao Cen's, written in 1651), and considering the intensity of his feeling towards Chen, it is reasonable to assume that it was written not long after Chen's death in the early 1650s. The time when Chen was dominant in the art world as a "major style-setter" and had captured Zhou's admiration was a period when strong *yimin* (left-over subjects of a fallen dynasty) sentiment prevailed among intellectuals and when the arts joined the critical moral and political struggles of the day.[225]

During the last two decades of his life, Chen Hongshou produced highly individualistic and expressionistic paintings. Borrowing Zhou's terms, he can be viewed as the foremost *xingqing* artist and as one who exemplified the role of the artist as social critic. It is thus understandable that Zhou, who had been an active participant in the reactionary literary movement of his friend Qian Qianyi against late Ming formalism and the imitative mode, was particularly attracted to Chen's work. By the time of their meeting in 1650, Chen must have understood Zhou's keen appreciation and so decided to make Zhou Lianggong the guardian of and the spokesman for his art. Chen's reliance on Zhou and his gift of so many paintings to him makes it clear that Zhou, with his sincerity and genuine appreciation of art, was able to convince even the most stubborn of literati artists that he was no mean, ordinary collector.

Zhou evidently also convinced Chen of his political stance — if in fact this had been an issue in the past — by sharing with the artist his criticism of the alien rule. One of Chen's forty-two works, entitled "Modoujian" (Just Touch your Helmet), seems to have been painted to caution Zhou against speaking his mind.[226]

History proved that Chen's faith in Zhou was not misplaced. Zhou's biography of Chen is one of the fullest and best researched biographies in the *Du Hua Lu*.[227] Written in Zhou's best prose and containing some of his keenest critical insights, it portrays Chen with an unusual sense of intimacy as a unique man and a great artist.[228]

ZHOU LIANGGONG AS ART CRITIC

ZHOU'S ABILITY to appreciate different qualities in different artists is evident in a brief review of some of his favorites. Chen Hongshou, whom Zhou regarded in the 1650s as the greatest of his day, was praised for his inborn talent and eccentricity. Gong Xian was understood and appreciated for his unique individual achievements:[229]

> In his paintings, he stays clear of the commonly traveled paths and goes forth alone into the unknown and unusual. Of himself he has said: "There has been nobody before me and there will be nobody after me." I believe this is not an erroneous remark.

In the case of Yun Xiang and Fang Hengxian, he recognized the value of their direct contact with nature in their artistic development. Zhou was attracted to the "impressionistic" atmosphere in Hu Yukun's works, despite the fact that this mode was not popular during this period due to its association with academy paintings and the contemporary preference for calligraphic brush lines over ink.

As these various comments on different artists suggest, Zhou demonstrated an uncommon ability to appreciate individual qualities in each artist. Zhou created an impression among his contemporaries, as well as later generations, that he was a man of universal tastes, respected for his impartiality and his openness to diverse ideas and modes of artistic expression. Zhou's strong moral commitment to support worthy scholars and artists may have influenced his taste and broadened the focus of his patronage activities. Zhou zealously sought out talented artists without regard to schools, social classes, or geography. Therefore we can view his appreciation of Wang Hui, a young artist with unquestionable talent, as in keeping with his broad taste and past patronage activities.

In terms of Zhou's development as an art critic, the 1650s was a time when Zhou was under the heavy influence of two of the major art critics of his time: Ai Nanying, who was the successor of the Tang-Song literary movement, and Qian Qianyi, who was the foremost advocate of the direct expression of individual emotion and the harshest critic of the former and latter Seven Masters for their formalism and parochialism. The strong feelings and needs of this particular political period and the influential aesthetic and theoretical thinking of Ai and Qian were reflected in Zhou's critical judgment of the arts in the late '40s and '50s, and account for his emphasis on the expression of emotion —

in Zhou's terminology, *xingqing* (personal disposition and emotion, i.e., personal expression).[230]

A renowned poet and literary critic of his time, Zhou's views of painting were very much in accord with his theory of literature. Although Zhou's extant writings do not contain any sustained theoretical writings on painting, his biographies of painters and seal carvers reveal an aesthetic and critical consistency with his theory of literature. This is not surprising, since the convergence of theories of painting and poetry was a common phenomenon in the late Ming and early Qing. Zhou's literary theory therefore provides an important key to our understanding of his theory of painting and art criticism.

The following passage is representative of the critical concepts employed in Zhou's poetic criticism:[231]

> When the ancients composed poems, they did not concentrate on *gediao* [form and sound, i.e., formal style], nor did they disregard *xingqing* [personal disposition and emotion]. Contemporaries emphasize *gediao* but neglect *xingqing*. This is why their poems are no longer archaic. Poetry is to express *xingqing* . . . [people have] different emotions. Nowadays, [poets] have nothing to say, they just compose; they have nothing to lament yet they shed tears and snivel. To compose poems specializing in [the expression of] sadness or happiness without [real] emotion is the so-called beating of drums and bells with no harmony in rhythm. Yet [contemporary poets] carry their anthologies under their armpits and boast: "I, [after] the Prince Tang," or "I, [after] the Six Dynasties." I do not approve of them, but mundane opinions seldom agree with mine.

Xingqing refers to the content of a work, that is, the personal expression of deeply-felt emotion, while *gediao* means the style, as well as, in its extended meaning, the stylistic tradition.[232] During the late Ming, the conflicting claims of *xingqing* and *gediao* were an important element in the split between individualism and orthodoxy in the art world.[233]

As a serious art and literary critic and friend of all the major critics of his day, Zhou was right in the middle of the major controversies that divided the art and literary world. In the above-quoted passage, Zhou emphasizes the importance of *xingqing* in the arts and expresses his opposition to those who placed an inordinate emphasis on the formal dimension of poetry, that is *gediao*. In this regard Zhou closely follows the main emphasis of Qian Qianyi. Zhou also followed Qian's opposition to the late Ming orthodox masters, the former and latter Seven Masters, and in the above statement actually intended to criticize the late Ming orthodox masters, especially Li Panlong (1514–1570), Wang Shizhen (1526–1590), and their followers. Zhou severely criticized the orthodox masters' excessive emphasis on the *gediao*, i.e., formalism, their imitative tendency, and their display of false emotion all his life.[234]

It is important to note, however, that Zhou's *xingqing* was classicist in origin, while Qian's *xingqing* was unconventional and iconoclastic in attitude. Zhou's concept of *xingqing*, as we have discussed in connection with Hu Yukun in chapter two, presupposed the Neo-Confucian didactic view of art as a means of spiritual cultivation, whereas Qian tended to either dismiss the familiar Neo-Confucian didacticism or to shift his emphasis towards the expressive element of art. Furthermore, as an active participant in the *fugu* ("return to the past") literary movement led by Ai Nanying, Zhou admired the

Eight Great Masters of the Tang and Song, especially Ouyang Xiu, and adhered to their theory that art should express emotion as a form of social and political censure. He accepted their belief that the single most important element of classic literature, such as the Book of Poetry, Qu Yuan's poems, and the histories written by the two Han historians Ban Gu and Sima Qian (ca. 145–86 B.C.), was the expression of their authors' "sincere innermost emotion" as a form of social and political censure.[235] Therefore art which failed to express such *xingqing* was no longer considered "archaic," the quality which Zhou obviously viewed as the standard quality of a good art.

It is not surprising that such a view was popular among artists and critics during this period of strong *yimin* emotion. The "far-reaching thought" Chen conveyed to Zhou through his painting of Tao Qian and Zhuge Liang was undoubtedly viewed as an expression of the artist's "sincere innermost feeling" and his political and moral criticism, which we may call "political eremitism." It is important to recognize that Zhou's appreciation of the expression of political eremitism and protest found in Chen's works and in many other *Du Hua Lu* artists' works is indicative of his own complex political feelings and psychological needs during the early Qing transition period. Viewed in this light, it would not be an overstatement to conclude that the *Du Hua Lu* was a means by which Zhou joined the political protest of his time.[236]

TO BEIJING

AFTER SPENDING eight years in Fujian, Zhou Lianggong was finally called to Beijing in 1654 to receive a new appointment as a court official in the Censorate. His family and friends considered it unusual that he was forced to serve for such an extended period of time in such a remote and dangerous province. They even believed that there was a conspiracy against his transfer to the court by those who wished to keep him far away from the throne.[237] Whether it was conspirators that blocked Zhou's promotion and arranged for his extended appointment in Fujian can not be determined. While Zhou made the best of this predicament, he hinted at the hardship and loneliness he felt during this prolonged "exile" in farewell poems composed for Hu Yukun, who left Fuzhou for Nanjing in 1650 after staying with Zhou:[238]

> When I just crossed the mountain pass,
> I said that it was too late to turn back.
> Now I lament how long I ended up staying at this place,
> As my thoughts of home deepen.
> A weary traveler has been disillusioned by a "blunt sword"
> [i.e., unfulfilled ambition].
> Even reading requires the aid of wine.
> I ask you to relieve my friends of their worry [about me]:
> The heavy air and humidity are gradually getting bearable.

Zhou was not without high-official supporters at the court to intercede on his behalf. But the times demanded extreme caution; in many ways court politics had become much more complicated under alien rule. The hostility between the Donglin/Fushe faction and their enemies continued. But added to this was the enmity between the bannermen and Chinese officials, and the factional conflict within the Manchu ruling house involving regents, princes, and military leaders. Chinese officials inevitably became embroiled in these conflicts even if they sought to avoid them. One wrong move could not only ruin a career but also place one's life in jeopardy. Given this situation at court, Zhou's friends might not have felt strong enough to arrange for his transfer.[239]

The Manchu prince Dodo to whom Zhou offered his surrender in 1645 in Nanjing evidently liked Zhou and was responsible for his initial appointment. It is therefore possible that Zhou was opposed by enemies of Dodo. Although Dodo died of an illness in 1647, he was posthumously condemned for treason in 1652, one year after his brother Dorgon met the same fate. Perhaps Zhou's affiliation with Dodo tainted his record and weakened his position at court.[240]

At last, at the end of 1653 or early 1654, Zhou's mentor, the President of the Censorate Sun Chengze, who concurrently held the honorary title of Grand Guardian of the Heir Apparent, recommended Zhou for the post of senior vice-president of the Censorate with the help of the Grand Secretary Cheng Kegong (1608–1691).[241] Sun probably acted with the help of another of Zhou's close friends, Senior President of the Censorate Gong Dingzi. Sun and Gong in turn depended on the protection of Grand Secretary Chen Mingxia, who was not only the highest ranking official among the Han Chinese, but also was a former Fushe member.[242] Sun was a Donglin sympathizer, while Gong was a Fushe member. Because of the cohesiveness of Fushe members and their political strength, the Fushe group must have been particularly feared by the bannermen, the court, and their traditional political opponents. Therefore, Sun's recommendation of Zhou Lianggong was no doubt closely watched by court officials and may have been interpreted by opponents as an attempt to increase the power of the Fushe clique.[243]

Fig. 42. Xiang Shengmo (1597–1658). "Autumn Landscape." Dated 1654. Album leaf, ink and color on paper, 24.8 cm x 31.1 cm. The Metropolitan Museum of Art, New York. Seymour Fund, 1964 (64.268.1). All rights reserved. (Cat. no. 14)

Zhou Lianggong's survival at court was largely dependent on these allies, especially Chen Mingxia and Sun Chengze. Unfortunately for Zhou, both men would fall from power before he arrived in Beijing.

Zhou left Fujian in the late autumn of 1654 right after he served as an examiner for the Fujian provincial examinations.[244] According to Zhou Zaijun's account, the locals bid him an emotional farewell which included a thirty *li* long incense procession.[245]

On his northward trip, Zhou passed through Suzhou and went to call on Qian Qianyi at nearby Yushan. He asked Qian to write a preface for his anthology of essays written by contemporary scholars, *Laigutang wenxuan*.[246] In Suzhou, Zhou probably saw Zhang Xueceng (fl. 1634–1657, DHL 3/2), one of the so-called "Nine Friends in Painting" who had just been appointed the new prefect of Suzhou.[247] It is also possible that he saw Xiang Shengmo (1597–1658, DHL/SL), who painted for him in this year (fig. 42).

In Hangzhou, Zhou was joined by Qi Zhijia (still active 1682, DHL 1/19), who accompanied him to Nanjing. Zhou stayed in Nanjing with his parents for a month, during which time Qi was his house guest.[248] Zhou undoubtedly renewed his friendship with artists active in Nanjing at this time, including the two monk-painters Fang Yizhi and Kuncan.[249] After a month, Zhou proceeded to Yangzhou by boat, again accompanied by Qi, who painted for him along the way. Zhou and Qi were welcomed by Cheng Sui and Chang Xun (DHL 3/6). The four got together at the Pingshan tang in Yangzhou.[250]

Finally arriving in Beijing in the first month of 1655, his spirits must have been dampened by the ominous political developments that occurred while he was en route. Just before Zhou arrived in Beijing, Chen Mingxia was executed after being accused of treason by another grand secretary, Ning Wanwo (d. 1665), who was a Chinese bannerman of the Plain Red Banner and a meritorious retainer at the founding of the Qing dynasty. Zhou's old friend and supporter Sun Chengze was accused of being a follower of Chen and was permanently relieved of office. In the following year, another of Zhou's powerful friends, Gong Dingzi, whom Zhou worked under briefly in Beijing in the Censorate, was indicted and deprived of his office and titles. With his most important supporters eliminated from office — or on the way out in the case of Gong — Zhou must have

Fig. 43. Cheng Zhengkui (1604–1676). "Dream Journey Among Rivers and Mountains." Detail. Handscroll, ink on paper. Present collection unknown.

Fig. 44. Cheng Zhengkui (1604–1676). "Dream Journey Among Rivers and Mountains." Dated 1655. Handscroll, ink and light color on paper, 19.7 cm x 282 cm. The Art Institute of Chicago. W. L. Mead Fund, 1953.161. Photography by Greg Williams. Photograph © 1996, The Art Institute of Chicago. All rights reserved. (Cat. no. 15)

approached the prospects of his new appointment with considerable apprehension and misgivings. Although it is uncertain whether the conflict between Chen Mingxia and his followers and their opponents had any direct impact on Zhou's fate in Beijing, certainly it left him much more vulnerable.

Nevertheless, once in Beijing, Zhou again refused to retire. Moreover, he continued to pursue an active cultural life — often in the company of his fallen friends, Sun and Gong. Sun Chengze, who was living in retirement in the vicinity of Beijing, often invited Zhou and other friends such as the former Fushe member Fu Mengzhen to his house to drink and to view his collection of paintings as well as Zhou's.[251] Sun had amassed a few hundred famous paintings which originally belonged to the Ming palace collection right after the fall of Beijing. He was now devoting most of his time to connoisseurship.[252] It was probably during this time that Sun presented Zhou an album of paintings by Li Liufang (1575–1629, DHL 1/6) as a gift.[253] In the spring of 1665, Zhou was in the constant company of Gong Dingzi.[254]

Zhou Lianggong also renewed his acquaintance with the painter Cheng Zhengkui, a former Fushe member, who came out of retirement to serve the Manchus in 1649. At the time they met, Cheng was serving as president of the Board of Rites. In 1649, the first year of his government career under the Qing, Cheng made a resolution to paint a series of one hundred landscapes under the title, *Dream Journey Among Mountains and Streams*" (figs. 43, 44). An introverted man, Cheng devoted himself to this task with the utmost seriousness and a near religious fervor. The act was not unlike that of a Buddhist devotee copying sutras for spiritual repose and salvation or a Neo-Confucian practicing quiet-sitting to achieve tranquillity of mind. Painting was clearly part of Cheng's spiritual life and was viewed as an important means to cultivate his own mind and spirit as well as that of others. He explained his rationale for undertaking such a project as follows:[255]

> There are three difficulties to living in Changan [Beijing]: there are no mountains and rivers to enjoy, no calligraphy and painting to study, no collectors from whom I can borrow. Therefore I decided to produce a hundred scrolls of *Dream Journey Among Rivers and Mountains* to be circulated [in substitute for the real thing] in order to save those friends who are in service. I have completed so far about thirty scrolls, all of which have been taken away by art-lovers, except this scroll which I now inscribe and present to Wugong . . . .

Zhou became one of the art-lovers cited by Cheng who managed to secure one of Cheng's paintings. The work, like all other extant paintings from Cheng's *Dream Journey* series, aims to achieve the quality of *pingdan* (placidity and plainness) through the use of

subdued brushwork, the sparse application of ink, and a stylistic reference to Huang Gongwang of the late Yuan, who was one of the most admired *pingdan* artists in the history of Chinese painting. Cheng, who had studied painting under Dong Qichang, had absorbed from Dong the orthodox theory of art and an affection towards Huang Gongwang, who was the major source of inspiration for the entire *Dream Journey* series. Zhou found Cheng to be an ideal practitioner of the orthodox Neo-Confucian theory of art. He regarded Cheng as one of the three foremost scholar-official (*shidafu*) painters of his day together with Fang Hengxian and Gu Dashen (DHL/SL, *jinshi* of 1652) (fig. 45).[256]

Fig. 45. Gu Dashen (jinshi 1652). "Aged Pine and Swirling Waterfall." Hanging scroll, ink on paper. Osaka Museum of Art collection.

By the mid-17th century it was rather difficult to find artists who were amateur scholar-official painters in the true sense. Zhou notes, "Among the scholar-officials in the world who are famous for their painting, Cheng Zhengkui [fig. 44], Gu Dashen, and Fang Hengxian can be considered the legs of a tripod."

CHAPTER 4

The Six-Year Trial, 1655–1661: Causes and Effects

IMPEACHMENT

DURING his first year in Beijing, Zhou was rapidly transferred from the Censorate to the Board of Finance, and finally to the Board of Civil Office. It is possible that these frequent transfers, which probably undermined Zhou's influence, were due to opponents of the former Fushe leader Chen Mingxia and Zhou's mentor-protector Sun Chengze.[257]

In the autumn of 1655, about one year after his arrival in Beijing, Zhou was granted an audience with the Shunzhi emperor. The audience was given in recognition of Zhou's successful defense of Fujian cities and for the purpose of discussing his recent memorial containing proposals for Fujian defense and military strategy.[258] During his audience, as Zhou was reporting on the affairs of Fujian, an impeachment memorial charging Zhou with corruption and brutality was handed to the Emperor. The memorial was written by Tong Dai, a Chinese Plain Blue Bannerman and the new governor-general of Zhejiang and Fujian. As a result, in the 11th month Zhou was deprived of his title and office and put on trial. For the next six years he was imprisoned while waiting the final outcome of a very complicated series of trials. Whether or not his case was directly related to the Chen Mingxia case and the downfall of Sun Chengze, their demise certainly left him vulnerable to attacks from the likes of Tong Dai. His case was closely intertwined with the byzantine politics of the day, both at court and in Fujian, and it is impossible to fully explain all the various contradictory charges and countercharges exchanged. However, since the case marked such a crucial turning point in Zhou's life, it is important to examine it more closely.

A section of Zhou's official biography quite matter of factly describes some of the background details of the case:[259]

> In the 12th year [1655], Zhou Lianggong sent in his memorial in which he provided a military strategy for dealing with the coastal areas of Fujian. He said that Quzhou in Zhejiang, Jianning in Fujian, and Guangxin in Jiangxi were areas where bandits frequently collaborate with the enemy from the sea [i.e., Zheng Chenggong]. [He then proposed that] since Guangxin is located only 100 *li* from Quzhou, the court should order the governor-generals of both Zhejiang and Fujian provinces to take charge of the city together to avoid any mistake in the strategy. [He further proposed that] since the sea-based enemy had Xiamen [Amoy] as its base, the court should send a secret order to the governor-general

of Guangdong to order the troops stationed at Chaozhou to jointly attack the enemy's rear. He recommended the court strengthen the naval force in order to guard the coast.

His memorial, in turn, was sent down to the [provincial] officials to check on its credibility. Zhou also requested that the court execute Zheng Zhilong and stop asking Zheng Chenggong to surrender. Instead, he recommended that the court send a force to destroy him immediately. His memorial received [imperial] recognition. . . .[260] Consequently Zhou Lianggong was promoted to the post of junior vice-president of the Board of Finance.

When Zhou Lianggong was serving as provincial judge of Fujian, the *wuju* (military *juren*) Wang Guobi, the *gongsheng* Ma Zhichang, Cai Qiupu, Cai Kainan, Shi Donglai, and some other locals founded political societies such as the Nanshe, Xishe, and Lanshe. Their numbers increased rapidly and they violated the law. Zhou Lianggong reported their crime to the governor and indicted them. He had the names of Qizhang and other members carved on stone. The four men died in jail.

In the 5th month of the same year [1655], when Tong Dai took up his post as governor-general [of Fujian], the relatives of Qizhang and others [prosecuted by Zhou] sent in a petition charging [Zhou] with injustice. Tong Dai listed Zhou Lianggong's misdeeds in several categories such as greediness [i.e., corruption], cruelty, and the like. The court, upon hearing the accusation, asked Zhou Lianggong to report. He was dismissed from his post and sent to Fujian [i.e., Fuzhou] for trial. . . .

Even before Zhou reached Fujian, Tian Chilong, the provincial judge of Fujian, and others, based on the evidence, made up a verdict in which they accused Zhou of accepting bribes worth more than 40,000 *liang* [silver taels]. Tian sentenced him to death by decapitation and ordered the confiscation of his property. When Zhou arrived to face the witnesses, all these accusations were found false. Governor Liu Hanzou suspected that such officials as Tian Chilong might actually have been bribed to fabricate the case. So he arrested both [Tian and Zhou] and sent them to the Board of Punishments.

In the 16th year [1659], because the [alleged] bribery involved amounted to the considerable sum of several ten thousand taels and because [he was found guilty by] the earlier verdict made by Tian Chilong and others, the Board of Punishments considered the crime to be very grave and decided Zhou should be executed right away and have his property confiscated. The emperor reviewed the case and found the discrepancy between the former and latter verdicts. He orderd the Three High Courts again to conduct a more thorough investigation. In the 17th year [1660], the verdict of the Three High Courts came out the same as [the earlier one] before. But by special grace of the emperor, [Zhou's] sentence was reduced by one degree, to banishment to Ningguta [in the winter of 1660, see map 1]. [However], before it was carried out, there was an amnesty [upon the Shunzhi emperor's death] and Zhou was released.

This account indicates that the charges against Zhou were vague and certainly not very well substantiated. The overall impression gained is that Zhou's trouble ultimately stemmed from his involvement within the complex, unstable local Fujian political environment. The case also illustrates the enmity between Chinese bannermen and Chinese scholar-officials, and that the absence of high-level protectors left Zhou vulnerable to the enemies he made in the course of his official career in Fujian.

In his own memorial about Fujian Zhou touched upon two of the most sensitive issues of the time: the problem of the southeast coastal defenses and Zheng Chenggong. This memorial in fact led to the arrest and eventual execution of Zheng Chenggong's father, Zheng Zhilong. It was reported in other sources that Zheng greatly resented Zhou's role and sent money to Fujian to promote a plot against him.[261]

Zhou's proposal for the coastal defense may help to explain the new governor-general Tong Dai's opposition. Tong Dai disagreed with Zhou's proposal and in fact submitted his own memorial on the subject in the same year.[262] Tong Dai argued that instead of strengthening coastal defenses, as urged by Zhou, the coastal inhabitants be prohibited from sailing in coastal waters in order to cut off Zheng Chenggong's source of supplies. Zhou's proposal reveals his concern over the livelihood of the inhabitants of the 88 some *xian* situated along the Fujian coast, who had depended on fishery, salt-manufacturing, and other sea-based businesses for generations. Zhou's policy was to strengthen the coastal defense force in order to prevent Zheng's army from approaching the coast. Zhou also felt that ultimately the government must seek to dispose of Zheng completely in order to relieve the prolonged misery of the Fujian people. The fact that Tong Dai's proposal had considerable support is suggested by the fact that even after Tong's dismissal, the court in 1662 ordered the massive removal of the coastal people of Shandong, Zhejiang, Fujian, and Guangdong for a distance of 30 to 50 *li* inland. History proved this policy to be more disastrous to the people of the coast, especially those of Fujian, than to Zheng Chenggong.[263]

Another explanation offered by Zhou himself of his impeachment could be a personal grudge Tong developed against him as the result of an incident that occurred in late 1654.[264] According to Zhou's account, in the same year he went to Beijing to receive his new appointment, Tong Dai, the newly appointed Zhejiang-Fujian governor-general, thought his boat passed Zhou's on the way to Fujian. Tong was told by a boatman that a northward bound boat full of music and laughter belonged to a certain Master Zhou. Having previously heard about Zhou and knowing that he was being transferred from his Fujian post, he mistook this man as Zhou Lianggong, though the latter had already arrived at Beijing by then. Assuming that Zhou would certainly pay a visit, Tong waited for him with an elaborate banquet. When the boat sailed away, Tong Dai was so humiliated he vowed that he would get even with him. Huang Yuji repeated the same story and noted that "when he received reports about the province [upon his arrival], he came upon Zhou's name so often that he hated him the more."[265]

Tong Dai, whose alternate name was Duntai,[266] was from the famous Tong clan of Fushun, Liaodong, from which the Kangxi emperor's (r. 1662–1722) mother and one of Kangxi's own consorts came.[267] Some members of the Tong clan were officials under the Ming. Most of the clan members joined the Manchus some years before the fall of Ming and entered the Chinese Plain Blue Banner where they fought successfully against the Ming army. After the Manchu takeover of China they were given high official ranks and exercised considerable political power. Tong Dai was the younger brother of the famous Tong Yangliang and a cousin of Tong Yangxing (d. 1632) who was instrumental in establishing the Eight Chinese Banners.[268] The biography of Tong Dai in the Qing official history represents him as quite an audacious figure with a quick temper. Interestingly, Tong was also related to Tong Guoqi, who was the former governor of Fujian (until 1655) and a strong supporter of Zhou.[269] If Tong Dai had been on good terms with his clansmen, it is unlikely that he would have been so vengeful towards Zhou, who clearly had established a close relationship with Tong Guoqi. It is even possible that some form of ill will or hostility between the Tong Dai and the Tong Guoqi branches of the Tong clan also influenced Zhou's case.

Another factor cited in Zhou's *Xingzhuang*, written by Huang Yuji, which may have contributed to Zhou's legal trouble was the fact that Zhou created enemies among certain military generals stationed in Zhejiang and Fujian. For example, while he was in Fujian, Zhou reportedly infuriated one general who had proposed the marriage of one of his children to Zhou's daughter. Zhou, who apparently did not regard the family as respectable, flatly refused. He then offended another general when he rescued a man whom the general had falsely accused of being a bandit. The two men reportedly plotted against Zhou and also sent accusations to the court.[270]

Still other possible sources of the accusations against Zhou were his fame and his art collection. While some no doubt resented his fame, others probably coveted his collection. By this time Zhou had become famous as a scholar and art patron. He was not an obscure man who could avoid trouble by keeping a low profile. Zhou's Fujian friend Xu Yanshou warned him about the dangers of his growing fame:[271]

> A magnet has no intention to pull, but all the metals are attracted to it. You are like a magnet. Without your intention, they surround you. You will be finished just like that. What a pity that a white lamb would not even make a cry when people try to kill it.

By this time Zhou's collection in fact had become enormous. It represented many painters and seal carvers, and might include several dozen to a hundred works by the same artist. He collected paintings, calligraphy, bronzes, seals, and ink-sticks, both antique and contemporary. According to his son and his friends, Zhou carried them with him wherever he went, be it by cart or boat.[272] He was also a bibliophile and had amassed a library of considerable scale. Song Wan, a former Fushe member and Zhou's close friend from Shandong, described Zhou's collection and suggested the possible link with his prosecution as follows:[273]

> When I looked through them [Zhou's collection of contemporary paintings], they were done by painters who were from as far [away] as Yunnan, Guizhou, Shanxi, and Sichuan, and [from] as near as Hebei, Yangzhou, Jiangsu, and Zhejiang — regardless of what they were, prominent officials or hermits, Buddhist or Daoist monks, he collected their works. . . . What the Master [Zhou Lianggong] owned was a houseful of books and paintings. Thus when he moved, he had to have wagons to load them. It is highly possible that those who slandered the Master used his collection as an excuse. . . .
>
> Nevertheless [Zhou] was not even slightly discouraged. On the contrary, he has persisted [in collecting] as if he were pressed for time. Isn't this one of the habits of the literati who dedicate their minds to such activity?

All the examples cited above by Song Wan point to the fact that the jealousy or suspicion aroused by his collection may have been at least in part responsible for Zhou's downfall. It is interesting that Gong Dingzi, another of Zhou's close friends, made the same comparison of Zhou to Ma Yuan in his colophon to a painting Zhou owned.[274]

THE TRIAL IN FUJIAN
AND THE JOURNEY NORTH

IN THE 11th month of 1655, Zhou was ordered to leave Beijing to face his accusers and witnesses at the Fujian provincial court over which he once presided as chief judge. Accompanied by the painter Hu Yukun, Zhou stopped briefly in Nanjing to see his parents.[275] In the 1st month of 1656, Zhou left Nanjing, and Qian Qianyi, Gu Mengyu (1599–1660), and other friends composed farewell poems for him. Qian, who had experienced imprisonment himself, saw Zhou off at Shicheng and comforted him. He also gave him a painting by Bian Wenyu (act. 1620–1670), one of the Nine Friends in Painting, as a farewell gift.[276] Besides Hu Yukun, four other friends followed Zhou to Fujian. [277] By the time they reached Fujian, Tong Dai had already left, having been recalled by the court.

At the trial, which occurred in Fujian in 1657, the original accusations against Zhou were proven false. The new provincial judge Cheng Zhongyu, after looking into the case, concluded that Zhou had been set up. Five judges handed down a verdict of innocent.[278] The Fujian governor Liu Handuo (served 1656–1659), however, was afraid to take a stand on the case and thus shifted the responsibility for a final decision to the central government by sending up both the earlier verdict of guilty and the later verdict of innocence. Liu also promptly resigned his post. Besides the seriousness of the corruption charge, the fact that the impeachment was brought by a bannerman against a Chinese scholar-official, and both were high ranking officials, made the case extremely delicate. One can assume that there was a great deal of behind-the-scenes maneuvering by both Zhou's supporters and those who opposed him. The discrepancy between the two verdicts was so drastic that the court sent officials down in the 5th month of 1658 to arrest Zhou and 108 other people including the five judges who acquitted him, witnesses, and those accused of being Zhou's accomplices. Together with Zhou they were all transported to Beijing.[279]

Among the 108 people sent to Beijing were several of Zhou's friends, such as Xu You and Song Zijian, who were arrested for "guilt by association." On a mid-summer day when the officials sent from the court left Fujian escorting the defendants, the Fujian people strongly protested: merchants closed their shops, commoners wailed, and local scholars and elders sent representatives to the capital with a memorial of appeal. Among the scholars who protested was Gao Zhao, a student of Zhou's in Fujian. He wrote the "Minren siqi ji" (Account on the Fujian people shedding tears at the four different places [for Zhou Lianggong]), which vividly chronicles Zhou's last days in Fuzhou. Gao's account indicates the unusual outpouring of support which Zhou received from the local populace at the time and is a testament to his eight years of service to the Fujian people.[280] Their outpouring of anger and protest may explain why the Fujian governor Yi Yonggui risked memorializing the throne in 1656 while Zhou's trial was underway to explain that

Zhou not only saved the city from the enemy's attack, but was also loved very much as a local hero.[281]

The flotilla of boats carrying the 108 defendants, envoys, and guards, followed by the friends and students of the prisoners,[282] must have caused quite a stir as it traversed the grand canal on its northward journey to Beijing. When they reached Hangzhou, Zhou was received by his son-in-law Wang Rongji and friends who had been waiting to accompany him. Among them were the painter Zhu Zhichao and Zhou's childhood friend Gao Fu (the brother of the painter Gao Cen).[283] At Yangzhou, Cheng Sui, Zong Yuanding (1620–1696), and many others were waiting for his boat.[284] At Wucheng, Gong Xian came to Zhou's boat to comfort him.

Arriving in Beijing in the 11th month of 1658, Zhou and others were confined to the South Prisons, which occupied the southwest corner of the compound of the Board of Punishments.[285] There they were to spend the next three years while the case was under investigation. Zhou, who had formerly served as a provincial judge and as a member of the Board, must have been fully aware of the grim prospects for justice under the traditional legal system, which "focused on the need to assign suitable punishments to acts already known to be criminal."[286] In Zhou's case, it is indeed doubtful that the Board of Punishments and the Three High Courts were concerned with determining whether the accused were guilty or innocent. They showed an extreme reluctance to acquit Zhou despite the considerable evidence in his support. Luckily cases involving capital punishment had to be endorsed by the emperor. After several trials, the Board and the Three High Courts repeatedly memorialized the throne for approval of Zhou's execution. Many of Zhou's biographers believe that the Emperor certainly knew of Zhou's innocence and was reluctant to approve the death penalty.[287] In fact, the Emperor repeatedly ordered a closer investigation of the case. The only hope for Zhou seemed to be a special imperial amnesty.

With no close allies at court to defend him, Zhou's chances were slim. At the time he was impeached, he was virtually the last high-ranking official among the surviving Fushe members. The scholar-painter Cheng Zhengkui was President of the Board of Rites, a position of high rank but of no real power, and he adhered to a policy of nonaction and non-involvement befitting his introspective personality. Cheng resigned his office and retired in 1657.[288] In the same year another high ranking official of the Fushe background, Wu Weiye, resigned.[289]

LIFE, ART, AND FRIENDS IN JAIL

Zhou was detained for almost three years in Fuzhou, Fujian, and for about three years in the Board of Punishments compound in Beijing before being released in the spring of 1661. During this six-year period Zhou nearly became a pauper. While it was common for officials to accumulate great wealth during their years of government service, Zhou's financial status prior to his arrest is unclear. In the opinion of his family and friends, Zhou was a frugal family man and acted as an upright official.[290] It is thus unlikely that he amassed a great fortune. On the other hand, even upright officials who remained within the customary boundaries of official practice had the opportunity to live rather well. Zhou supported a large family of more than one hundred, including his brother's family. He also actively patronized poor scholars as well as painters and seal carvers beginning in 1641, the year he entered government service.[291] His patronage activities, including his comprehensive collection of paintings and seals, suggest that he enjoyed the wealth expected of a man of his high position, but these activities must not have left him with much extra money for this kind of emergency.

While his trial was underway, Zhou had to sell many of his possessions in order to support his family and meet expenses associated with the trial. Although the surviving record makes no explicit mention of expenses, we may assume they were extremely severe given the seriousness of the accusations and length of time the case dragged on. As Derk Bodde and Clarence Morris conclude in their study of Chinese law, "Any entanglement with the Chinese imperial penal system was a personal disaster. The long periods of imprisonment awaiting appeals, the venal cruelty of jailers and wardens, the interferences with normal family life and the involvement of the accused person's relatives added up to a terrifying experience — even when the final punishment was lenient."[292] In addition, traditional Chinese jails provided no provisions to prisoners. Thus, besides needing to support himself, Zhou probably had to provide for his jailed friends who were suffering on his account.

Except for a handful of Chinese scholar-officials who strictly avoided involvement and who were extremely lucky, all of the famous scholar-officials of Zhou's time seem to have experienced either dismissal from office or imprisonment at some point in their career. The aforementioned Song Wan was imprisoned in 1661. Song suffered even more than Zhou, evidently because he lacked the means to pay off the jailers and wardens and to provide for his own comforts:[293]

> His [Zhou Lianggong] case was a relatively minor case compared to mine. When I was slandered, I was thrown into a prison cart to be transferred to the Board of Punishments and then was imprisoned for two years in a dark local prison. My suffering was much harsher than his. [Unlike him] I did not own such collectors' items as bronzes and seals to sell for the money and congee which I needed. . . .

To avoid the corporeal suffering of Song, Zhou was forced to sell a large portion of his collection. The personal anguish which this drastic step caused is vividly expressed in his poems entitled "Poems on the sale of my four collections."[294] A portion of Zhou's collection of contemporary paintings were spared, in part because they commanded so little value on the open market. Song Wan records the following conversation with Zhou Lianggong right after Zhou's release in 1661:[295]

> Master Liyuan [Zhou Lianggong] was slandered for his uprightness and honesty; people throughout the country knew of his innocence. Thanks to the imperial benevolence and forgiveness, he could finally take off his prison clothing and return to office. In the year of *xinzhou* [1661], when Master came to the [West] Lake, he looked at me and said with a sigh: "In my whole life, I have had no other habits except collecting famous calligraphy and paintings, and bronzes and seals by the ancients, which I appreciated day and night and treasured all my life. Most of these collections have been sold. All that is left are the several hundred pieces by contemporary scholars and painters in these albums, for which I was often offered a low price. . . . Therefore they were not sold and still remain in my chests."

Zhou also sought to keep his favorite paintings from certain "powerful people" who sought to take advantage of his difficulty to force him to liquidate his collection. By mid-summer of 1656, he lost all hope of being released and began to fear his execution. Zhou also began to worry about the fate of his collection after his death. He was especially concerned about the works by his deceased friend Chen Hongshou, as he confesses in the colophon he wrote in this year on one of Chen's Tao Qian scrolls that he entrusted with friends (figs. 38, 39):[296]

> In the *yiwei* year [1655], when I fell into adversity, powerful people used their authority to force me [to give up my paintings]. But I did not give in. Although there were some people who used trickery to get my works, I took it very calm-ly as if watching a beautiful lady serving wine at a rich man's home. In the spring of the *bingshen* year [1656], when I returned to Min [for trial], I carried this handscroll with me. I was thinking at that time that someone like me who was involved in a serious legal case would surely be condemned to death; certainly there would be someone who would kill me to please others or pour boiling water over [me] to force me [to give up my paintings?]. If I could not even pro-tect my own body, what would become of this handscroll? I was also thinking that if I give it to the wrong person, I would be ungrateful to my good friend. This is the reason why I chose to give it to Tieyai [Lin Sihuan]. Tieyai was my only true friend besides Zhanghou. But Tieyai never met Zhanghou, therefore I wrote this in order to introduce these two men to each other. Zhanghou would certainly not be sorry [for my decision] from his grave and, at the same time, it would also save me from the blame for being too rash in giving away a painting by my good friend.

It was not until late in 1660 when the death penalty recommended by the Court was finally approved by the Emperor — who ordered a postponement of the execution and a decrease in the form of execution by one degree — that Zhou was actually locked up as a prisoner.[297] Prior to the Emperor's approval of his sentencing, Zhou apparently was accorded the more flexible terms given to high-ranking officials. Thus in early 1659, he was allowed to build a hut in the detention compound of the Board of Punishments which he named *Yinshuwu* (Because-of-Trees Hut). The name was derived from one of his poems which reads: "My hut, because of tall trees, does not get light even when it is autumn. . . ." He also planted two elm trees on the eastern side of the hut and chry-santhemum and cedar trees on the western side.[298]

During these six years in jail, Zhou wrote a large number of poems, which were lat-er published under the title *Laigutang shiji*. Another collection of his jail poems from Bei-jing, *Beixueji*, was also circulated.[299] Many friends exchanged poems with Zhou in which they shared Zhou's pain and sorrow. Throughout Zhou's confinement, Gong Dingzi wrote poems for Zhou, many of which followed the rhyme pattern of Zhou's poems. Gong repeatedly reaffirmed his friendship and sought to keep his friend's spirits up.[300]

In addition to composing poetry, Zhou also began to reflect on his life and his own place in history. He was acutely aware that he would be known by posterity largely through the writings he left behind. Zhou was a great admirer of the Han historian and biographer Sima Qian and sought to emulate Sima Qian's *Shiji* in his biographical writ-ing including the *Du Hua Lu*.[301] Now that Zhou was imprisoned, his identification with the Han historian, who wrote his monumental work while suffering imprisonment and punishment by the Han court, no doubt strengthened.

Zhou further sought to emulate Sima by leaving posterity with important scholarly works.[302] He promoted the publication of a collection of his own poems[303] and also worked incessantly on a collection of miscellaneous writings on such varied subjects as literary criticism, painting, drama, calligraphy, tea, wine, history, phonology, and biography.[304] Much of the work was random jottings drawn from memory. Therefore when it was completed towards the end of 1659 or early spring of 1660 — about one year after it was started — the work was given the title *Yinshuwu shuying* (Shadows of Books [Written] at the Yinshu Hut) and is better known in short as *Shuying*.[305]

Zhou's seemingly calm resignation to his fate, his absorption in writing *Shuying*, and his composition of numerous poems, won the great admiration and respect of his friends. They all compared him with Sima Qian and later judged that he was even better than the Han historian because his *Shuying*, unlike Sima's work, did not express anger.

Whatever the outward appearances, Zhou did suffer severely during his long confinement.[306] Nonetheless, Zhou must also have felt hurt and disillusioned by the cooling attitude of some of his friends who no doubt feared being associated with him: "After I was involved in the legal case, those who used to socialize with me seldom visited. . . ."[307] However, Zhou did not lack loyal friends who kept in touch with him and visited him in jail. When he went back to Fujian for trial in 1656, he was accompanied by the faithful Nanjing painter Hu Yukun and four other friends. The loyalty of these five friends moved the Fujian painter Gao Gong (whose biography is found in the *Du Hua Lu*) to make a pictorial record of the event under the title "Entering Fujian in the *bingshen* year [1656]" to present to Zhou.[308]

While the trials dragged on in Fujian, Zhou was comforted by his close friends — including Xu You and Hu Jie. Xu would later in 1658 be arrested with Zhou and sent to Beijing. Zhou frequently gathered with local scholars often at Xu You's studio or his own studios, Jianzhai and Ganyuan.[309] Zhou was greatly moved when Wu Di, one of his friends, who received the *jinshi* degree with him in 1641 but who had gone into hiding after the fall of the Ming, suddenly visited him when he was detained in Fujian. Unable to afford a carriage, this old friend traveled 500 *li* on foot to make the visit.[310] The Qinhuai painter Fan Qi (1616–after 1694, DHL 3/16) sent a landscape painting in 1657 to comfort Zhou (fig. 46). He received olives sent by Gao Zhao from Fujian; others sent medicines; some sent plum blossoms. Seal carver friends presented Zhou with seals to comfort him.[311]

Of the four artist-companions who accompanied him while imprisoned in Beijing, Hu Yukun had been Zhou's live-in guest off and on ever since they first met in Wei Xian, Shandong, in 1641.[312] In 1660, Hu finally had to return to Nanjing, leaving Zhou behind in prison. Upon his departure Zhou composed a farewell poem:[313]

> I lived with you by the old Qingqi [in Nanjing]
> And we rode horses together passing Mount Yan [in Hebei] five times.
> In my old age I have been imprisoned.
> If I can return alive, it will be thanks to you.
> Over the wine in the goblet,
> The spring clouds cast shadows in disorder.

Fig. 46. Fan Qi (1616 – d. after 1694). "Sail Boats by a River Shore," detail. Dated 1657. Handscroll, ink and colors on paper, 29 cm x 318 cm. Liaoning Provincial Museum collection. (Cat. no. 16)

Over the jagged outline of green trees
The setting sun shines obliquely.
As I think of the last twenty turbulent years of my life,
It is only with tears that I can remember my friends.

Knowing how much Nanjing meant to Zhou Lianggong, after returning Hu sent Zhou an album of paintings called "Historic Spots in Nanjing" which included the Qinhuai canal area where Zhou was born and grew up (fig. 47, cat. no. 17). Many poems Zhou composed while away from Nanjing express his longing for this city and the Qin-huai. Hu Yukun's "True View landscape" painting was an approach also followed by many late Ming and contemporary Nanjing painters, and allowed the artist to devise his own composition and to depart from the stereotyped compositions of the old masters. In addition to his impressionistic handling of colors and ink and empty space, the "His-toric Spots of Nanjing" also exhibits his skillful handling of mountain forms: they swirl and twist upward, executed with dry texture strokes harmonious with the forms and movement of the hovering clouds. With this album Hu successfully integrates the Yuan tradition through the Suzhou heritage to arrive at a very atmospheric personal style.

The fourth friend was Xu You, a *shengyuan* under the Ming, a student of Ni Yuanlu and the son of a Fushe member, who lived as a recluse in Fujian after the fall of the Ming. He first met Zhou through Chen Hongshou's introduction in 1648 when Zhou was transferred to Fuzhou, Fujian. Zhou esteemed Xu You primarily as a good poet and as the best calligrapher among the Fujian artists in running and cursive scripts (fig. 48).[314] In painting, bamboo was Xu's chief subject (fig. 49).[315] But after his detainment, he switched to painting old trees. To Zhou's great lament, Xu You survived less than three years after their release.[316]

Together Zhou and his four artist companions drank, composed poems, discussed the arts, painted, and wrote calligraphy. As might be expected under the circumstances, they expressed their sadness and despair as well as their anger and political censure through their art. Though coming from all different backgrounds, they shared, "loyalist" and "collaborator" alike, a common sadness over the loss of their country and a common suffering of injustice under foreign rule.

Fig. 47. Hu Yukun.
"Shicheng." Dated 1660. From
an album of twelve leaves,
"Historic Spots in Nanjing."
Album leaf, ink and color on
paper, 25.5 cm x 18.4 cm.
Guan Lu Yuan collection.
(Cat. no. 17, leaf L)

Hu Yukun was a close,
lifelong friend of Zhou Liang-
gong. To comfort Zhou at a
time when he was imprisoned
for several years, Hu Yukun
painted this album of scenes
from Zhou's hometown. Its
receipt must have been partic-
ularly meaningful for Zhou,
who had by this time lost all
hope for his release and was
waiting for execution.

Fig. 48. Xu You (ca. 1620–1664). "Calligraphy." Fan, ink on paper. Taitsu Hashimoto collection.

Fig. 49. Xu You (ca. 1620–1664). "Rock, Bamboo, and Trees," detail. From a collaborative work with six other painters. Handscroll, ink and light color on paper. Hou-chen-shang-chai collection.

"SONG OF COLD CROWS"

ONE COLD winter night in 1659, Xu You painted the "Qunya hanhua tu" (Crows' Conversation in Cold). The work was created out of the depth of despair and dramatically symbolized both their personal tragedy as innocent prisoners awaiting probable execution and the tragedy of the entire country under alien rule. The work inspired Zhou to compose a poem called "Song of Cold Crows" and Sun Ziqian to respond with his own poem in rhyme with Zhou's.[317] The scroll also received colophons by other scholars, including their mutual friend Gong Dingzi.[318] The painting is no longer extant, but it is described by Zhou with such intimacy that its general appearance can be imagined. Vividly expressing the artist's political protest and personal rage, Xu used cold crows in winter to symbolize himself and other Ming subjects under alien rule.

Zhou's long poem captures and intensifies the artist's mood, and is also his autobiographical statement. The characteristic reticence and caution Zhou employed throughout his career in order to avoid prosecution and literary inquisition were here discarded, and, inspired by Xu's bold artistic statement and embittered by their helpless predicament, Zhou threw caution to the wind. In the poem Zhou first introduces the painter and portrays his character. Then Zhou turns to a description of their prison cell. Because of its length, we will skip the first section, and move directly into an analysis of the poem, section by section, below:[319]

> In the South Prison, at night the northern wind is severe;
> He [Xu You] called for wine, but no one was there to give it to him!
> With the ink-stone frozen and wine cup empty,
>   he was unable to sleep.
> His worn brush was leisurely lain beside the cold brick bed.
> He breathed on [the frozen tip of] the brush and,
>   shaking, he painted on a discarded paper.
> Devoid of leaves and branches, the tree [he painted] was
>   twisted beyond its normal form.
> Yet under the lamplight one could still vaguely discern
>   the appearance of a dragon and a tiger.
> Unconsciously the tree wanted to die, but it could not.
> How starved the dragon was, beaten and whipped
>   by the rain and wind!
> It grasped to the left, but was unable to reach anything;
> It reached to the right, but again found nothing to grasp.
> With pity he tried to add some colors [to give it some life].
> But beautiful colors had no place [in this somber painting].
> By applying light ink, he made the branches look as if
>   they were covered with frost.
> By applying deep ink he made the branches look as if
>   they were covered with snow.
> The white area looked like a skeleton of this dilapidated dragon,
>   while the dark area looked like hard iron.
> And it could not be mistaken as firewood.

Although this master [i.e., the withered old tree] was bitter,
    he cherished a novel mind.

Despite the fact that Zhou's prison accommodations were superior to those of common criminals, his short description of the room where Xu painted indicates the hardships he and his friends were forced to endure. The description of the withered old tree, destitute and twisted, makes a clear allusion to the predicament of the country during the dynastic change. The dilapidated dragon seems to allude to the Ming court, so "beaten" and "starved," that it unconsciously seeks death.

Zhou then goes on to discuss the crows Xu painted perched on this wintry old tree:

At midnight, he suddenly heard the clamorous noise of crows.
Ya-ya ja-ja, [they cawed] while the bright moon was setting.
Luxuriant trees never attract cold wings [crows].
The crows [therefore] didn't know to whose house
    they could fly to find shelter.
Watching the crows, Xu Sheng [Xu You] heaved a long sigh.
Suddenly, thousands of nests appeared in his mind.
[So he spoke to them]:
    You crows, come here; you crows, come here!
    I am going to build a nest for you with my wondrous ink.
    My tree, though withered, has survived a good many years.
    The southern branch is not fragile, the northern branch
        still sturdy.
The mountains and rivers are cold under the snow.
Why don't you think of finding a place to rest?
Then you can freely fly and dance and even move
    to another place.

The cold crows symbolize the Ming subjects, both collaborators and loyalists, who have survived the turmoil. The reference to luxuriant trees seems to refer to Li Zicheng's short-lived regime and to the Manchu regime, which Zhou evidently regarded as a temporary interregnum before the revival of the seemingly withered tree, and the reappearance of a native dynasty.

In the next section, Zhou incarnates himself as one of these crows and sings an autobiographical *aria*, in which he briefly describes his experience at the Qing court and suggests that his heart remains nevertheless with his own people and the fallen court:

When the night was deep, the crows started talking to each other.
They perched above and beneath [the tree] in all four directions.
Cao-cao, jie-jie, they chattered [noisily]
    without reservation.
[One crow said to the others]: "I will sing, and you harmonize.
    Please don't refuse."
[Then he began to sing]:

    In the morning I returned from the Jaoyang palace.
    All the palace doors suddenly opened wide.

There was a loud sound of beating drums, and the dancing
      was at its climax.
I saw with my own eyes Zou Yan playing the lute.
The turtledoves were happy to have such a spacious room;
      the magpies roared with laughter;
They came with wine to congratulate me.
But how could we [crows] forget the sound of
      the blowing cold wind,
When we had to perch together on an old withered tree?
We could not forget the time when we had to hide ourselves
      among weeping willows in Paimen [Nanjing].
We remembered the time when we wished to fly away to no avail,
      as the sun was setting.
Our hearts longed for a running stream somewhere beyond
      a solitary village.
We could not say whether this place was good or permanent.

The reference to Zou Yan of the Warring States period (475–221 B.C.), who was slandered and imprisoned during the reign of King Hui, seems to allude to Ming scholar-officials, like Zhou, who would be similarly slandered and imprisoned at the Manchu court. Turtle doves here refer to the Manchus, magpies the collaborators, and the setting sun to the predicament of the fallen Ming. Zhou wistfully recalls his longing for refuge from the political turmoil while hiding on Mount Niushou in Nanjing in 1645.

In the last section, Zhou returns to reality, to the painting and the painter. His expression appears to become even more seditious:

The wind blew so severely at the thatched hut that he could not
      finish his painting.
Hence he put aside his brush and talked with the crows
      about the bitterness of life.
He even forgot whether they were within his painting
      or on the tree [outside].
As the moon waned, the crows bade him farewell.

Xu Sheng [Xu You], when you paint bamboos, they possess feeling.
Xu Sheng, when you paint crows, they seem to cackle.
But with one or two dots of ink,
Why do you have to constantly struggle with the crows?
Xu Sheng, do not grieve over the coldness of the rising sun.
When you, instead, wield your ink with great splendor,
It will be possessed of a miraculous breath.
Then you may hear the phoenix singing loudly
      in the sky.
And every day you will paint myriad Wutong trees.

While expressing his sympathy for the painter and his own sadness, Zhou nevertheless makes his poem a message of encouragement and hope rather than an unrelieved lament of despair. He thus concludes with a call to action. He says that they should not grieve over the present situation, but rather work more positively towards the revival of the country. The "rising sun" seems to be a disguise of the character "ming" which is the dynastic name for the Ming, whose classic meaning is the "rising sun." The phoenix, a symbol of the imperial court, according to tradition, perches only on Wutong trees.

The "Song of Cold Crows" helps place Zhou's role as collaborator in perspective and offers an explanation of his close friendship with many Ming loyalists. The poem suggests that Zhou's loyalties and intentions, despite his collaboration, were not very different from those of his loyalist friends. This perhaps explains why even when Wan Shouqi and his friends were secretly planning to raise a force against the Manchus after 1645, they trusted and kept close ties with Zhou Lianggong, who was already openly serving the Manchus. All this suggests the possibility that there was a certain loose informal coalition between the so-called collaborators and some of the Ming loyalists which worked towards one common goal — the restoration of native rule.

One illuminating example which supports this thesis is Zhou's relationship with the Nanjing painter and Ming loyalist Zhang Feng. According to Zhou, while imprisoned in Beijing, he received from Zhang a painting accompanied by the artist's poem:[320]

> After I was slandered, Dafeng [Zhang Feng] painted [for me] a man with a sword: his hand was caressing the sword and his two eyes were fixed on it; he also had a gourd. His brushwork was very extraordinary and archaic. He inscribed on the painting: "Although the sword is not sharp, it is not dull either; He secretly fondles his sword, showing his great hatred." I was moved by his intention. I have treasured this painting until now.

The fact that Zhang would send such a painting and seditious poem to Zhou clearly demonstrates that Zhou was Zhang's trusted confidant.

Most of the time, Zhou was very skillful in avoiding direct criticism of the Manchus and cautious of every move he made. In fact many of his writings contain statements which easily could have provided grounds for his enemies to accuse him of sedition.[321] Some of the poems he wrote for Hu Yukun and Huang Jing, which are included in both the *Du Hua Lu* and the *Laigutang ji*, for example, seem particularly dangerous.[322] Chen Hongshou's warning to Zhou in 1651 which urged him to watch his criticism was not just idle talk.

In a colophon to Xu You's painting, Gong Dingzi sympathized with both Xu You and Zhou Lianggong:[323]

> The old man Li's [Zhou Lianggong] new poem follows
>   the tradition of *yuefu* [of the Han dynasty].
> The worn-out brush of Xu You paints blue frost
>   [i.e., lofty wintry forest].
> On a tall branch are numerous birds in silence.
> It is only you who unceasingly chirp about the setting sun
>   [i.e., conquering the dynasty].

In this colophon, Gong appears to confirm that Zhou's "Song of Cold Crows" is not simply a description of Xu's painting but contains political allusions. Moreover, Gong identifies Zhou Lianggong as a cold crow — one of the few that, after a decade and a half of the Manchu rule, still "unceasingly chirp" (i.e., lament) about the fate of the Ming dynasty.

Gong also wrote another poem — this time in response to a collection of Zhou's prison poems, "Beixue ji" (Poems of Northern Snow) — in which once again he referred to the cold crow as a political symbol:[324]

> Where do the Poems of Northern Snow come from,
>   drifting about alone.
> The sad wind blows lonely and my heart is broken into pieces.
> I bitterly remember the time the crows perched in the dark night;
> They cried until they vomited blood at midnight.
> With a failing lamplight and no wine left, I cast aside and
>   shatter my wine cup.

Gong states he wrote this poem in rhyme with "Bitter and Cold Journey," a poem by the Tang dynasty poet Du Fu (712–770). This association further intensifies the feeling of bitterness and homelessness.

Taken together, Xu You's painting "Crows' Conversation in Cold," Zhou Lianggong's poem "Song of Cold Crows," and Gong Dingzi's colophon and his version of "Bitter and Cold Journey," all confirm that cold crows had become a form of private symbolism to represent the fate of the Ming subjects, both loyalist and collaborator, under the alien occupation.

FREEDOM AND RESOLUTION

IN 1660, as his trial was nearing its conclusion and the death sentence appeared almost certain, Zhou began to express a sense of urgency in his writings and other activities. He counted the days before his execution and reported breaking out in cold sweat at the sound of footsteps. He wrote to Huang Jing: "Today I will receive an imperial order [for my execution]. Therefore I am dressed up waiting for it. This is really like what people mean by saying 'When the time comes, I shall go.'" Or, "Today I still have not received the imperial order. I can live one more day." Thereupon he asked Huang Jing to carve a seal which read, "One more day."[325] All the surviving records indicate Zhou had completely given up hope by 1660. Until then, he seems to have had some hope that his life would be spared, based on the emperor's obvious reluctance to have his sentence carried out and based on the assumption, or rather the hope, that the Shunzhi emperor knew of his innocence.[326] Shunzhi was known to be a conscientious and lenient ruler who "had only reluctantly approved any death sentences" and was also blamed by his own people, including his mother, for his preference for Chinese officials over Manchus.[327] Furthermore Shunzhi had personally met Zhou and expressed his gratitude for his achievement in Fujian.[328] All this, together with the contradictory evidence and an understanding of the complex political pressures involved, helps explain the reluctance of the emperor to approve the death sentences repeatedly handed down by the court. In 1660, much as Zhou seems to have feared, the emperor finally approved the death sentence, but ordered its commutation by one degree and a stay of Zhou's execution.[329]

In the same year, celebrating the Dowager Empress's birthday, the court declared an amnesty for prisoners by commuting punishments by one degree. Zhou was thus saved from death and ordered banished to Ningguta in the winter of 1660. In the 1st month of the following year, before Zhou's departure, the Shunzhi emperor died.[330] The official history records that right before he died he issued an edict of amnesty for prisoners which included a special order for the release of Zhou Lianggong. In the 3rd month of 1661, Zhou's six-year ordeal ended and he was officially released.[331]

On his way home, Zhou could not help but feel sorrow for his friends who were involved in his case, some of whom lost their lives during the ordeal. At a gathering of friends in Yangzhou he said:[332]

> I frequently think of the one thousand odd people who have been involved in my legal case. One hundred odd people were almost beaten to death because of me. Among those officials who tried to prove my innocence, one died on the road [while being deported to the capital from Fujian], two died of sickness [in jail], and the rest were on the edge of death many times. Nevertheless, none of them changed their mind and made a false confession against me. How can I count all those who changed their names and hid away to assist me in secret. Alas! Why did they treat me so kindly? I have thought of this day and night [and reached the conclusion that] it is because I have never done anything that I would regret since I [first] took office when I was young.

By the time Zhou was released and returned, he had become truly a national figure: the *Laigutang shiji* and the *Laigutang wenxuan* had been widely circulated in the literati world. Moreover, through poems and other types of writings exchanged with his close literary friends from all over China, his jail life had been closely monitored by the literati. Many came to admire his courage and sagacity in coping with adversity. His reputation as a scholar-official loyal to the people became widely recognized as a result of his admirers from the provinces where he had served. His passionate commitment to the arts and his protection and support for worthy scholars also had become common knowledge.[333]

In the summer of 1661, Zhou buried his parents on the foot of Mount Banzi, south of Nanjing, and began to observe the mourning period at the Gaozuo temple. In the meantime, the court proclaimed that the original accusations against Zhou were all unfounded. Citing Zhou's meritorious deeds in the defense of Fuzhou while detained in 1656, the Boards of Civil Office and Punishment were ordered to reinstate him.[334]

In the autumn of 1661, he went to Yushan to pay a visit to his old friend Qian Qianyi, who was then eighty years old. Zhou asked him to write an epitaph for his father, Zhou Wenwei.[335] This grand old man of politics and poetry, who twice suffered imprisonment, had been living in retirement since 1648. Zhou had maintained close relations with Qian over the past seventeen years. He was seen off by Qian when he took up his first post in Yangzhou under the Manchus.[336] When he was slandered and sent back to Fujian, Qian saw him off in Nanjing. Qian also wrote two prefaces for Zhou's books and sent him numerous correspondence. Zhou edited his biographies of poets.[337] But the true nature of their relationship is as elusive as Qian Qianyi himself. Their lasting friendship however suggests that they had a deep mutual understanding and it is quite possible that their positions towards the Manchu regime were similar.

By the end of the Ming, Qian had become a celebrity; a prominent politician, a nominee for a prime minister position, the foremost poet and critic, a respected Donglin associate (once jailed for his affiliation), and a flamboyant man with elegant taste. Perhaps because of his stature, his "open" allegiance to the Manchus provoked more controversy and attention than other collaborators. In the early years of the new regime, he was denounced in writings as a traitor, and a riot was staged in which his house was set on fire.[338]

Nevertheless, Qian had many supporters and friends among both loyalists and collaborators. In fact certain circumstantial evidence suggests that Qian played the role of loyalist and collaborator at the same time. Qian was in communication with a number of arch Ming loyalists, and was even imprisoned in 1647 under suspicion of communicating with the Ming loyalist army. Although he was able to defend himself successfully from the charges and was shortly released, the episode points out that his Manchu loyalties were suspect.[339] Qian, if the evidence of the chronicler of Qian's *nian pu* can be trusted, secretly communicated with his former student Zheng Chenggong and raised funds for Zheng's all-out, yet ill-fated, attempt to take over Nanjing in 1659.[340]

A letter written by the noted scholar Ji Dong (1625–1676) to Zhou Lianggong sheds some light on the divided opinion among contemporaries towards Qian Qianyi:[341]

> Last spring, I was in Beijing. There was a certain person from Loudong [Taicang] who wrote an essay entitled "Zhengqianlu" [An Attack on Qian Qianyi]. He was trying to find all small faults to attack him. When I heard this, I slowly said to a friend: "I have just come from Shandong where I climbed Mount Tai. When I reached the Erguan peak, in great awe, I suddenly wanted to relieve myself. So I hurriedly went down about 40 *li*. But I could no longer hold it, and therefore did my business on the side of the peak. I was afraid of being punished. However, many people do it and Mount Tai is so big that it does not care about such things." Yesterday, Wu Meicun [Wu Weiye] said my analogy is correct. Therefore I write this to you to see what you think about it.

Through this analogy comparing Qian Qianyi to Mount Tai, Ji Dong conveys the message that a man of Qian's stature would not be moved by his petty attackers. In a passage from a letter Qian wrote to Zhou Lianggong within two or three years of his death, Qian Qianyi himself alludes to his cherished, unfulfilled goal of Ming restoration:[342]

> The Gao bridge and Silver *zheng* are still wrapped in tears of blood. I will have to sail back and stay for a while to continue the story of Luyang [to bring back the sun] . . . .

Neither Qian nor Zhou lost the respect of their close friends and followers, many of whom were ardent Ming loyalists. This suggests that both men, albeit under different circumstances and perhaps for different reasons, were playing the role of loyal collaborator. If the above evidence of Qian's secret activities is correct, Qian assumed a more active loyalist role than Zhou, who limited himself to the more passive role of preserving the well-being of his fellow countrymen under the foreign rule.

By the time of their 1661 meeting, all of Qian Qianyi's hopes and ambitions had been shattered. Not only had he suffered public misunderstanding and condemnation for his collaboration, but his family fortune had been dispersed and much of his famous collection of books and antiques destroyed.[343] Finally, his last hope for the Ming restoration had been shattered when Zheng Chenggong's final effort in 1659 failed and Zheng committed suicide in Taiwan in 1662.[344] At this stage in his life, Qian deeply immersed himself in Buddhism, hoping for ultimate salvation from his worldly suffering.[345]

Zhou, who was an unknown young official at the time of his surrender to the Manchus in 1645, never seems to have suffered public condemnation of his collaboration like the celebrated Qian. Nor did he suffer from feelings of guilt like Wu Weiye. Nevertheless Zhou did suffer as a result of his involvement in the early Qing government. Zhou's six-year imprisonment and the strain of living under the shadow of a death sentence for many years inevitably affected him both physically and mentally. Before his legal entanglement, Zhou always had good health and was admired for his tall, imposing stature.[346] When he was released from prison at age fifty, however, he showed signs of sudden aging — loss of teeth, impaired eyesight, white hair — and suffered lung and stomach ailments.[347] The poems and letters written after his release are rarely without some reference to his imprisonment and are infused with a sad awareness of aging and thoughts of his approaching death.

Unlike Qian Qianyi, however, Zhou was never attracted to Buddhism,[348] but tirelessly sought solace within Confucianism. Fundamentally, he viewed himself as a *junzi* (a Confucian perfected man) locked in a struggle against *xiaoren* (petty men).[349] Further, Zhou maintained an activist Confucian commitment to this world which contrasts sharply with Buddhism's renunciation of secular preoccupations. While he did practice "quiet sitting" and cherished the ideal of Daoist eremitism, he did so only in the Confucian sense as a rather practical measure aimed at achieving the proper balance or equilibrium. Even after his dangerous political entanglements and his six years of imprisonment, Zhou remained stubbornly Confucian and sought to achieve an integration of objective (Confucian) principles, his own subjective motivations, and his actual conduct in order to fulfill the ideal of a *junzi*.[350]

During the final decade of his life, to which we turn now, Zhou not only returned to active political life but also continued his devotion to the arts and scholarship. As a respected official, scholar, connoisseur, and patron, Zhou was by now not only viewed as a model official, but also recognized as an arbiter of taste in the cultural world.

CHAPTER 5

The Final Decade

THE 1660S ART WORLD, NANJING AND BEYOND

ZHOU SPENT the first two years after his release in Nanjing. From the 1st month of 1663, Zhou served in Shandong as Intendent of Coastal Defense of the Qingzhou circuit. In the winter of 1664, he made an official trip to Beijing and returned to Qingzhou in the 4th month of 1665. In the fall of 1666, Zhou was promoted to the Nanjing-based post, Intendent of Grain Transportation for Jiangnan. Zhou returned to Nanjing in the 8th month of 1666 and took up what was to be his last government position in 1667. In the following year, Zhou again went to Beijing on official business. In all these capacities, he appears to have been the same upright official he was in his earlier career. A number of anecdotes in his various biographies indicate that he displayed the same concern for the public welfare and the same tenacity in rooting out wrongdoings. As a consequence, in 1669, he was once again slandered and put on trial. In 1670, when he was found innocent, he finally retired. He died two years later in 1672. All in all, Zhou spent seven and a half of the eleven years in Nanjing after his release from prison until his death.

The art world of Nanjing in the 1660s was still dominated by Zhou's old friends. All of these artists experienced the fall of the Southern Ming court, the rise and fall of Ma Shiying and Ruan Dacheng, the humiliation of Nanjing's surrender to the Manchu prince Dodo in 1645, and the public execution of Ming loyalists, including the eminent scholar-official, philosopher, and calligrapher-painter Huang Daozhou in 1646.[351] The tragic ends which many of their talented friends and acquaintances met, many of whom had been Fushe associates, weighed heavily on their minds. During the first decade or so under the Manchu rule, the atmosphere of Nanjing was grave and austere.

But by the early 1660s, active resistance in the Jiangnan area had subsided and the intense *yimin* emotions among the populace had begun to ease. The death of Zheng Chenggong in 1662 inaugurated a new era of peace in the south. The Manchus had retained most Ming institutions and pursued a policy of employing Chinese officials in government service. While Chinese commanders Wu Sangui (1612–1678), Shang Kexi (d. 1673), and Geng Jimao (d. 1671) continued to exercise considerable independence in their rule over the Three Feudatories (Yunnan, Guangdong, and Fujian respectively), order had largely been restored.[352] The Manchus became more and more confident in their rule, and the Chinese increasingly accepted their sovereignty over China. When

Kangxi assumed personal rule in 1667, it signified the passing of Manchu leadership to a new generation born and raised under Chinese influence and with deeper respect and understanding of Chinese institutions and culture. A generation change also took place among the Chinese literati who entered the ranks of officialdom and to whom the Ming was at best a distant memory of their youth. At the same time, many of the Ming loyalists of Zhou Lianggong's generation had already died. Many more would be gone by the end of the decade. Thus, for many the Qing dynasty became an accepted fact.

By the time Zhou gained his freedom, the whole art world knew of Zhou's passion for collecting, his discriminating taste as an art critic, his noble efforts as a generous patron of art and literature, his power as a writer, and his influence in the cultural world. Of course, many artists had been very active in Nanjing during the previous decade and a half. But during most of this period the Nanjing art world still lacked the major figures — artists and patrons — or the critical mass necessary to promote any significant new movement or trend.

By Zhou's return in 1661, Nanjing had substantially recovered from the disruption and disorder that attended the establishment of a new dynasty. Although it had not recovered the gaiety and frivolity of the city's heyday during the late Ming, the art world had already begun to recover its vitality as many of the artists who had left the city began returning.

Gong Xian, Fang Hengxian, and Cheng Zhengkui, returning to Nanjing prior to Zhou, must have given a significant boost to the art world. Gong and Cheng, though rather introspective and discriminating in their choice of friends, were strong artistic personalities and probably exerted considerable influence upon their returns. Fang, a former imperial censor, was more sociable and outspoken than the other two and perhaps played a more important role in revitalizing the Nanjing art world during the 1660s. Zhou regarded Fang as one of the three great *shidafu* painters of his time. After his exile to Ningguta, Fang had lost all interest in the pursuit of a government career and devoted himself entirely to artistic pursuits as a painter, connoisseur-critic, and art patron.

Fang came from the prominent Fang clan of Tongcheng, Anhui, which produced a number of *jinshi* and *juren* for successive generations. The Fang family — which included Fang Hengxian's father Fang Gongqian (*jinshi* of 1629), his two brothers Fang Xiaopiao (*jinshi* of 1649) and Fang Yusheng (*juren* of 1629), and his uncle the eminent scholar and former Fushe member Fang Wen (1612–1669) — was one of the most prominent in Jiangnan. The Fangs were important art patrons of major contemporary artists. Zhou Lianggong was close to all of the Fang family members and eventually became their relative through the marriage of his fourth son, Zaijian (b. 1655), to Fang Yusheng's daughter. Wang Gai (born ca. 1650), one of the young artists the Fang family patronized, eventually became a relative of Fang Hengxian by marrying Fang Wen's daughter.[353] Wang Gai's eventual success in the Jiangnan art world probably owes much to this marriage connection.[354]

Gong Xian, the poet-painter who had left Nanjing during the turmoil of the early 1640s, returned sometime around the turn of the 1660s. The old master remained in the city for more than twenty years until his death in 1689 and attracted many students and imitators (figs. 50, 51; cat. no. 26).[355] Zhou figured very prominently in Gong Xian's life during the 1660s as a sympathetic friend and patron.

Cheng Zhengkui had resigned from the post of President of the Board of Ceremo-

Fig. 50. Gong Xian (ca. 1620–1689). "Peach Blossom Studio." Dated 1671. Album leaf, ink and color on paper, 24.13 cm x 44.45 cm. The Nelson-Atkins Museum of Art, Kansas City, Missouri (Purchase: Nelson Trust), 60–36/1–11. (Cat. no. 26)

Gong Xian executed this painting in memory of his artist friend Zhang Feng, who died in 1662.

Fig. 51. Gong Xian (ca. 1620–1689). "Landscape." From an album of sixteen leaves, "Ink Landscapes with Poems." Album leaf, ink on paper, 27.5 cm x 40.8 cm. The Metropolitan Museum of Art, New York. Gift of Douglas Dillon, 1981 (1981.4.1). All rights reserved.

ny in 1657 while Zhou was in prison and had been living in retirement dividing his time between Nanjing and his hometown Xiaogan, Hunan. He had already painted more than three hundred paintings in the *Dream Journey* series by the early 1660s and religiously continued this endeavor until his death in 1676 (figs. 43, 44). Throughout his life Cheng stubbornly remained a single-style, single-theme painter, and regarded Huang Gongwang as his idol. He was aloof from the rest of the painters' world, but appreciated the works of Gong Xian and Kuncan. As noted above, Zhou had obtained at least one of Cheng's *Dream Journey* paintings before he was imprisoned. He also had some small works by him from this period, as well as colophons (cat. no. 6, leaf F).

Wu Hong had been back from Kaifeng since his patron Hou Fangyu died in 1654. He lived in the same neighborhood as Gao Cen in Shicheng. Zhou compared Wu's broad-minded personality with the Northern Song master Fan Kuan (d. after 1023) and recognized the influence of Wu's direct study of the northern collections (with a heavy emphasis on the Northern Song) on his subsequent development (fig. 52).

Kuncan and Chen Shu were active in the southern suburb of the city. Kuncan, the abbot of the Changgan Temple, seems to have studied ancient paintings (especially those from the Yuan) and developed his own style of landscape painting independent from contemporary fashions and trends in Nanjing, of which Kuncan painted a hanging scroll of a landscape for Zhou in 1661 (fig. 53). At least five more paintings Kuncan painted for Zhou can be documented, two of which are still extant (cat. no. 6). Chen Shu, a friend of Kuncan's, lived on the bottom of the Yuhuatai (fig. 54). Zhou wrote a long letter requesting paintings from him sometime during this period. Not much is known about

Fig. 52. Wu Hong (active 1670–1680). "Landscape." Hanging scroll, ink and light colors on silk, 85.5 cm x 46 cm. University of California at Berkeley; gift of Isabel Pollard, San Francisco (1968.1).

Chen. His extant works are of high quality and suggest that he was familiar with the Wen school paintings as well as Dong Qichang's.

Hu Yukun, who accompanied Zhou Lianggong to Beijing, returned home to Nanjing in 1660. Zhou at one point said that Hu contributed the largest number of paintings to his collection, since Hu had been his live-in guest for much of the preceding twenty years (figs. 4, 28, 29, 42; cat. nos. 1, 17). His brother Hu Shikun had been active in the city and enjoyed moderate esteem for landscapes and orchid paintings (fig. 55). Zhang Feng, who went to the North around 1645, had returned by 1660. While staying at the Gaozuo temple in 1662, Zhou invited Zhang to visit and the artist stayed with him for several days and painted (figs. 56, 57).[356]

Most of the Qinhuai masters who had been Zhou's childhood friends never left Qinhuai in Nanjing (see map 3). Zou Zhe continued to work at the painting studio, *Jiexia ge*, which he inherited from his father Zou Dian (fig. 8). Fan Qi and his brother Fan Yi (act. ca. 1658–1671) were leading a contented life quietly absorbed in painting at their studio by the Huiguang temple (fig. 46). Xie Cheng was still living in the neighborhood of Zhou Lianggong's family home. But Gao Cen,

Fig. 53. Kuncan (1612–after 1692). "Landscape." Dated 1661. Hanging scroll, ink and light colors on paper, 102.5 cm x 29 cm. Formerly in the collection of Huang Chün-pi, Taipei; present collection unknown.

Kuncan, the abbot of the Baoen Temple, freqently encountered Zhou, who was observing the three-year mourning period for his parents at the nearby Gaozuo Temple.

Fig. 54. Chen Shu (still active 1687). "Landscape," detail. A collaborative work with Zhu Ruiwu. Handscroll, ink and light colors on paper. The Shoto Museum collection, Tokyo. Chen Shu and Zhu Ruiwu were close friends who lived outside the southern gate of Nanjing.

Fig. 55. Hu Shikun. "Orchids and Rocks." Dated 1664. Handscroll, ink on paper. From Shina nanga taisei, Tokyo, 1935, vol. XV, pp. 38–39.

Fig. 56. Zhang Feng (d. 1662). "Landscape." Dated 1644. Album leaf, ink and color on paper, 15.4 cm x 22.9 cm. The Metropolitan Museum of Art, New York. Edward Elliott Family Collection, Gift of Douglas Dillon, 1987 (1987.408.2[A–L]). All rights reserved. (Cat. no. 24, Leaf B)

Though poverty-stricken, Zhang Feng remained loyal to the Ming dynasty after the Manchu conquest. The poem reads in part, "The red dust [of the mundane world] does not pollute my doorstep . . . ."

often called Gao the Whisker, seems to have moved to Shicheng near Mount Qingliang and was training his nephew Gao Yu as a painter at their *Bi le* studio (fig. 33; cat. nos. 1, 9). Other boyhood friends of Zhou's in Nanjing at the time included: the prolific artist Ye Xin (fig. 35; cat. nos. 6, 11, 23); the well-known flower painter Hu Cao (DHL 3/17);[357] the renowned lotus painter Zhang Xiu, who was living in seclusion next to the Qiufeng temple; the plum painter Yao Ruoyi, who was fond of using real petals of plum blossoms from Mt. Zhongshan in his paintings; and the amateur landscape painter Zhang Yi. Both Yao and Zhang became Zhou's house guests in Qingzhou, Shandong.

During the first two decades of the Qing the professional painters at Qinhuai, who for the most part remained in Nanjing throughout this period, developed a unique stylistic trend, which was based, no doubt, on their combined interpretation of the available

Fig. 57. Zhang Feng (d. 1662). "Listening to the Waterfall." About 1658–60. Hanging scroll, ink on paper, 94.3 cm x 40.9 cm. The Art Museum, Princeton University. Gift of Mrs. Edward L. Elliott (y1984-53).

In his biography of Zhang, Zhou Lianggong wrote, "He had a very dignified appearance with a beautiful beard. He looked like a Daoist alchemist who came from the depths of the mountains."

stylistic sources near at hand and the natural scenery around Nanjing. Among their most prominent stylistic sources was the Northern Song tradition as practiced by Wu Bin and his circle, in which the solid formal construction and the careful, detailed *gongbi* brush technique were employed.

Conversely, the Qinhuai artists toned down the dramatic and fantastic quality of the works of the late Ming followers of the Northern Song. The Qinhuai artists' use of calculated pictorial effects by formal abbreviations (often by the arbitrary use of mist) and the overall "scholarly" mood of their works was probably indebted to such late Ming masters as Wen Jia (1501–1583), Zhao Zou, and Shao Mi (ca. 1592–1642), as well as Dong Qichang. They also employed various Western techniques brought in by the Jesuit missionaries, as is evident in their use of unusual compositions and horizons.

Finally, the Qinhuai professional artists drew on the true-view landscape tradition inherited from the late Ming in their approach to nature. As a whole, they did not display much interest in the revival of a past tradition, and thus their large-format paintings often failed. Fan Qi was probably one of the most instrumental in the formation of this latter stylistic trend (fig. 46). To a greater extent than most Qinhuai artists, Fan preserved some of the fantastic expression of the late Ming professionals of Nanjing. Overall his influence is perhaps most clearly evident in Gong Xian's works as well as the younger Wang Gai's.

In addition to Wang Gai, some of the new artists Zhou found in Nanjing after his return were Liu Yu (DHL/SL) and Gao Yu. Zhou was distantly related to Wang Gai through the Fang family and recognized the artist's talent while he was still only in his late teens. Wang painted four Buddhist paintings for Zhou around 1670.[358]

The long and diverse list of painters cited above represents Zhou Lianggong's circle in Nanjing. With the exception of Liu Yu and Wang Gai, whose names are found in the supplementary list, they all have biographies in the *Du Hua Lu*, and probably represent the best of the Nanjing art world. Zhou singled out Gao Yu, Liu Yu, and Wang Gai by including Gao Yu's biography in the *Du Hua Lu* and Wang and Liu in the book's supplementary list. But he seems to have considered Wang Gai as the most promising young

Fig. 58. Fu Shan (1607–1684). "Wudong Tree Studio." Album leaf, ink on paper, 23.4 cm x 32.8 cm. The Art Museum, Princeton University. Gift of Wen C. Fong and Constance Tang Fong (y1962-109). (Cat. no. 19)

talent. Wang's biography was included in the *Yinren zhuan*, which probably makes him the youngest artist of whom Zhou wrote a biography.

Given the large number of artists in Jiangnan and Nanjing from which to choose, it is obvious that Zhou Lianggong was forced to be very selective in writing biographies for the *Du Hua Lu*. This must not have been an easy task given the inevitable social pressures; yet Zhou was considered by his contemporaries as a rare connoisseur. His expertise in the contemporary art field was such that the compilers of the new 1668 edition of the Nanjing Gazetteer entrusted the section on artists to him.[359] The traditional grouping, the "Eight Nanjing Masters," which includes some of the above-listed artists, has been attributed to Zhou, though there is no evidence in Zhou's own writings that he ever used such a grouping.[360]

Given Zhou's extensive travels and his insatiable search for talent, his contacts with contemporary artists stretched far beyond Nanjing even before his imprisonment. Zhou's friend Song Wan noted the wide geographical distribution represented in Zhou's collection right after his release.[361] The extent and geographical diversity of Zhou's artistic activity suggested by Song Wan is confirmed by a brief review of his acquaintances. In addition to the many artists from Nanjing, Kaifeng, and Fujian, by the early 1660s Zhou knew painters from Anhui (Hongren, Xiao Yuncong [1596–1673], Zha Shibiao [1615–1698], Cheng Sui), from Yangzhou (Zheng Yuanxun and Zhang Xun from Shanxi), from Wujin (Yun Xiang, Zhuang Qiongsheng [1626 – after 1647], Zou Zhilin), from Suzhou (Shao Mi, Shen Hao [act. 1630–1650], Zhang Hong [1577 – ca. 1652], Yang Bu [1598–1657], Xie Bin [act. 1650]), from Jiaxing (Xiang Shengmo), from Taicang (Wu Weiye), from Songjiang (Gu Dashen and Zhao Zou), from Hangzhou (Cheng Hongshou, Qi Zhijia, Zhang Xueceng, Lan Ying [1585–1664], Liu Du, Zhang Gu [act. ca.

1640–1660]), from Sichuan (Wang Sui), and from Guizhou, Jiangxi (Yang Wencong and Ma Shiying), as well as the northern artists from Henan (Wang Duo) and Hebei (Dai Mingye).

As his financial situation improved after his reinstatement as an official, he started to collect paintings and seals again with no less zeal than before his arrest. He also tried by all possible means to recover works, both contemporary and antique, from his original collection which he was forced to sell or give away during his imprisonment. For example, according to a passage in Ye Xin's biography, Zhou managed to get back Ye's one hundred paintings illustrating Tao Qian's poems:[362]

> I built Bai Tao fang [Gallery of the Hundred Paintings of Tao Qian] at my office in Fujian [in 1648] to store these works. During that period I carried them with me for self-enjoyment. But during my period of distress [1655–1661], Zhang Qiaoming took them away. Recently I got them back from his son Haixu. Now they are back where they originally belonged. [I am so happy that] both my eyebrows want to dance. . . .

Zhou was also apparently less tied down by official duties at this time than he was during his tenure in Fujian and therefore traveled and socialized extensively. Since he spent most of his remaining years based in Nanjing, he frequently used his Jiuyuan boat to visit other major art centers of the Jiangnan area — Wujin, Yushan, Suzhou, Taicang, Hangzhou, and so on. He kept in constant contact with old painter friends and seal-carvers, and naturally met many new artists.

Zhou probably met Le Mu (1622 – d. after 1706) from Jiangxi and Fu Shan (1602–1683) from Shanxi during this period, as evidenced by a poem Zhou composed for Le[363] and the two paintings Fu Shan painted for Zhou (fig. 58; cat. no. 19). He probably also befriended Mei Qing (1623–1697) from Anhui at this time.[364] Another artist Zhou probably met was Yu Zhiding (1647 – d. after 1709), who painted his portrait (fig. 1). It is interesting to note that Zhou makes no reference to Zhu Da (1625 – d. after 1705), active in Nanchang, Jiangxi, whom modern scholars consider as one of the major painters from this period. We also have no clear evidence that he met the monk-painter Daoji (1641 – ca. 1720) or Dai Benxiao (1611 – d. after 1691).[365]

THE THREE WANGS OF TAICANG

OTHER prominent artists Zhou first met in the 1660s were Wang Shimin and Wang Jian from Taicang, their student Wang Hui from Yushan, and Wang Hui's intimate friend Yun Shouping (1633–1690) from Wujin. The three Wangs have been considered the leading masters of the so-called Orthodox School. It is understandable that Zhou had never met Wang Hui and Yun before this time, since they were fairly young. But it is surprising that he had not previously met the two elder Wangs (figs. 59, 60). Zhou's writings contain no reference to them until 1662, when Zhou wrote a colophon on Wang Shimin's copy of Zhao Mengfu's "Autumn Colors on the Qiao and Hua Mountains."[366] About the same time Wang Shimin wrote a long colophon on an album Zhou showed to him.[367]

Of the four, Wang Hui impressed Zhou the most and received the highest praise of any artist in the *Du Hua Lu*. The remaining three are only included in the book's sup-

Fig. 59. Wang Shimin (1592–1680). "Land-
scape in the Style of Huang Gongwang."
Dated 1666. Hanging scroll, ink on paper,
134.5 cm x 56.5 cm. The Metropolitan
Museum of Art, New York. Gift of Douglas
Dillon, 1980 (1980.426.2). (Cat. no. 30)

Fig. 60. Wang Jian (1598–1677). "Landscape." Album leaf, ink and color
on paper. Guan Lu Yuan collection.

plementary list. Zhou seems to have met Wang Hui right after his return from Shandong
in 1666, though he knew of him before 1664. Thereafter Zhou made an all-out effort to
acquire Wang's works. Wang frequently visited Nanjing to see Zhou, both on his own
initiative and at Zhou's invitation. Wang is recorded to have painted at least two albums
(one with 16 leaves and the other with 24 leaves) and four other works for Zhou. Extant
are one album leaf and a handscroll, both of landscape, to be discussed below.

With the exception of the painter Wu Li (1632–1718),[368] to whom Zhou makes no
reference, Zhou thus met all the major artists of the Taicang group. Zhou's active
patronage of both the Nanjing and Taicang artists is significant in that it implies that
close links were maintained between these two important artistic centers of the seventeenth century. Zhou's multi-regional collection, which embraced works from both centers, was not only viewed by the artists of both, but his travels to Taicang and his hosting of Taicang artists in Nanjing suggest that artists from Taicang and Nanjing were
keenly aware of the trends and styles in both cities.[369] Indeed the comprehensiveness of
Zhou's contemporary art collection and the extent of his patronage during this period
were such that it would not be an exaggeration to conclude that he served as an important link between all the important art centers in contemporary China. The fact that

Zhou usually took his collection with him on his extensive travels increased the exposure it received and added to its art historical importance. Zhou's studios and his gallery boat, Jiuyuan, were virtually private museums of contemporary art where artists or connoisseurs could view a wide range of works and obtain encyclopedic information on contemporary painting, including the opinions of renowned connoisseurs and critics.

The important impact that his collection had on leading contemporary artists, critics, and patrons is evident in many of the colophons from his collection and in many contemporary letters and poems. Gao Cen, for example, sent the following letter to Zhou requesting to borrow his albums to study:[370]

> People say that albums of paintings by contemporary painters in your collection are marvelous and that through them one can see kaleidoscopic scenes. I sincerely hope you would lend several albums to me, so that I could see more clearly what I have [briefly] seen [before]. I do not mean that I want to take them simply as models.

Wang Shimin mentions viewing twenty of Zhou's albums, and gives the artist's own assessment of the important contribution that Zhou's collection made to the art world:[371]

> Vice-president Master Zhou Liyuan is an eminent man. He is a leading man of our time in his elegant manner and refined literary style. He has long been famous. In his leisure time, after his literary and administrative work, he also cultivates himself in the art of painting, and finds great pleasure in paintings. Whether [artists] be scholar-gentlemen, commoners, Daoist monks, or Buddhist monks, as long as they are engaged in painting, with great enthusiasm, he collects their works — even by mail — and purchases them at a high price. After years of collecting, he has mounted the works into twenty albums which have title labels in brocade on their embroidered covers. When one opens the case to browse, it feels as if you are searching through a garden of jades and a forest of pearls; constantly changing forms and visionary images spread before you. This [collection] is certainly a great achievement in the art world, which was only made possible by his lofty interest [in contemporary art]. . . . It is my great honor to see this sumptuous view at my old age. It makes me feel so insignificant. I inscribe this at the end of this album to record this memorable event and also to congratulate myself on this fortunate opportunity to see this album.

It is interesting to note that Wang, like Song Wan, points out that Zhou's collection represented a diverse group of artists from all different levels of society and with a varying degree of accomplishment and fame.

Aside from the important role his collection played in exposing artists to a wide selection of contemporary works, Zhou also served as an important social catalyst, stimulating contacts between Nanjing artists and connoisseurs and linking them with their counterparts from other regions. A glimpse of this social interaction can be seen in the detailed account in the *Du Hua Lu* of the famous party Zhou Lianggong threw in 1669 at his home. In the mid-winter of that year, right after Zhou was dismissed from his official post after being slandered, the painter Wu Qiyuan (DHL 4/18) from Dantu, Jiangsu, whom Zhou met while he was in Qingzhou, Shandong, came to Nanjing to comfort

Zhou and stayed at Zhou's home as a house guest for some time. On this occasion Zhou threw a big party at his Du Hua pavilion which Zhou himself described as the most exciting event in Nanjing for several decades. More than seventeen friends attended the party, including Wu Qiyuan, Huang Yuji, Hu Yukun, Fan Qi, Fan Yi, Wu Hong, Zhang Xiu, Zou Zhe, Xia Sen, Chen Zhe, Ye Xin, Wang Gai, and Ni Can (1627–1688), all of whom were from Nanjing. Wang Hui from Yushan also attended with his pupil named Hu Jie. Gao Cen and Gong Xian were also invited but were unable to attend.[372] Most guests were renowned painters of their time. Such gatherings, though their scale might widely vary, were one important channel through which ideas were exchanged and trends of art discussed.

Certainly Zhou was not the only patron-collector and art critic of his time, but he impressed his contemporaries more than anyone else as a man of catholic taste and broad-mindedness, and as one who appreciated each individual effort. Artists and critics felt compelled to present their works and their views to Zhou for his approval. This sometimes seems to have resulted in controversies and even arguments. Thus Huang Yuji, Zhou's student and a member of his inner circle, wrote:[373]

> The true connoisseur Sinong [Zhou Lianggong] has built
>   the Du Hua pavilion.
> It houses a complete collection of golden colophons
>   and beautifully ornamented scrolls [i.e., valuable paintings and calligraphy].
> I have climbed up to the pavilion and viewed them all.
> My only regret is that there is so much disagreement at fine gatherings.
> How could I expect that [we all] could shake hands tonight?
> At this corner of the city we have such an elegant gathering
>   with no loud accusations and reprovals.

Colophons written on Zhou's albums frequently discuss some of the most significant aesthetic and art historical issues of the time. In one colophon Gong Xian reasserted the supremacy of the *yipin* (untrammeled class) over the *shenpin* (divine class) and outlined a redefinition of literati painting and painters (fig. 2). Gong's view was then refuted by Fang Hengxian in a colophon to Zhou in which he insisted on the *shenpin* above *yipin* theory.[374] Fang Yizhi wrote a colophon on a work Zhang Xuezeng painted for Zhou in 1651 in which he asserted the importance of both *fa* (method) and *wufa* (no method) in painting.[375] A colophon by Wang Duo on an album of paintings in Zhou's collection outlines Wang's criticism on the works contained in the album.[376]

Letters that contemporaries exchanged on the arts also figure prominently among the correspondence included in Zhou's anthology of letters in three volumes.[377] These letters are not only important documents on mid-seventeenth-century Chinese painting, but also are an indication of the seriousness and the critical attitude with which the authors approached contemporary painting and art theory. The inclusion of so many letters with this type of discussion implies a conscious effort on Zhou's part to circulate and preserve these artistic ideas.

As indicated above, the most significant of all Zhou's activities during the period of the 1660s was Zhou's new interest in the Taicang group of artists, especially Wang Hui. Zhou's keen attraction to the Taicang group not only proved to be a critical step in his own aesthetic and critical development but also may have had an important impact on the contemporary art world, since his patronage activities helped to open a dialogue between Nanjing, where "individualists" were concentrated, and Taicang, the center of the "orthodox" masters.

ZHOU LIANGGONG AND WANG HUI

ONE OF the most exciting events of the last decade of Zhou's life was no doubt his "discovery" of Wang Hui from Yushan, Jiangsu. Zhou first met the young artist, who was a student of Wang Shimin and Wang Jian from Taicang, sometime between 1661, the year of his return, and 1664. Zhou's old friend Qian Qianyi, who was from Wang Hui's hometown, wrote a long letter of introduction to Zhou. Qian's letter, which was written at the artist's request, was accompanied by a painting Wang executed for Zhou as a gift. The letter reads in part:[378]

> Some two hundred years after Huang Zijiu [Huang Gongwang] died, the school of Shen [Zhou] and Wen [Zhengming] arose. Recently in Lujiang [at Yushan] the student Wang [Hui], *zi* Shigu, studied with the prefect of Yuanzhao [Wang Jian] and followed the [former] Fengchang [sub-director of the Court of the Sacrificial Worship] Yanke [Wang Shimin]. He thoroughly studied their collection of famous Song and Yuan paintings. He is skillful in description, and mist and clouds are exuberant on his paper. The artisans who paint inch by inch are incomparable to him. . . .
>
> Shigu feels comfortable with his poverty and adheres to it stubbornly. His disposition is elegant and peaceful. He is truly far from the vulgar and the mundane. [His personal disposition] has already achieved something of Zijiu's [Huang Gongwang] and the quality of his painting is also something similar. In the past, people said that Zijiu's paintings of mountain peaks always resembled that of Feisui [in Yushan] and Shuming's [Wang Meng] always resembled that of [Mount] Huanghe [near Wuxing, Zhejiang]. The two gentlemen truly had mountains and rivers in their bosom. They took the books in their bosom as *fenben* [a sketch]. Therefore, as soon as they laid their brush on paper, they captured the resemblance [of those mountains]. The same can be said of Shigu's paintings.
>
> My humble hometown has produced many artists such as Zijiu in painting . . . but there have been no successors up until now. Only Shigu has inherited the habit and bowl [tradition] of Zijiu. Since you are a connoisseur of calligraphy and painting, Shigu presents his work to you for your instructions. I have spoken above about Shigu in great detail, because I am certain that he is one who is capable of succeeding Huang Gongwang as I have described above. Since you are a fine connoisseur, you certainly will not consider my words groundless.

Qian's letter reveals that he was very proud of the cultural heritage of his hometown Yushan and was anxious to assist the talented native son, Wang Hui, secure the approval of his friend Zhou Lianggong.

Wang Hui, who was only in his early thirties when he met Zhou, was from a family which had produced professional painters for generations. Despite his professional background, he evidently received sufficient education and cultivated a refined manner which facilitated his social acceptance among the literati elite. Qian's description emphasizes that Wang adhered to the literati ideals — he was "comfortable with his poverty . . . elegant and peaceful . . . far from the vulgar and the mundane." The Nanjing scholar Huang Yuji, who met Wang at Zhou's home, said Wang's "elegant demeanor was like the slow flowing waves in the spring."[379] Unlike many contemporary painters with some literati leaning, Wang never seems to have attempted to take a government examination and showed no feeling of regret or ambivalence about being a professional artist.

In 1651, when he was twenty years old, Wang Hui contacted Wang Jian through a mutual friend from his hometown, in much the same manner that he later approached Zhou Lianggong. He subsequently became a live-in student of Wang Jian and Wang's older friend Wang Shimin and, as indicated in Qian's letter, studied their rich antique collection. The two elder Wangs were from old powerful gentry families of Taicang, whose forefathers had held high government positions.[380] Both had lived all their lives in Taicang, except for a short period of government service away from home at the end of the Ming. They both had received government appointments through the merits of their illustrious forefathers, rather than through the regular channel of civil examination. While young, they received instructions from Dong Qichang, the founder of the orthodox tradition of painting, and were actively engaged in painting from the 1620s. They do not seem to have achieved any real literary fame but were mainly known as painters, calligraphers, collectors, and connoisseurs.

Wang Shimin and Wang Jian led leisurely lives and maintained little contact outside Taicang and the immediate Lake Tai area. Their lack of contact with Nanjing, the cultural capital of the country since the end of the 1620s, is particularly noteworthy. While isolation was, in part, probably a function of the proud regional loyalties and conservatism of the Taicang/Lake Tai area, it also might have been related to their involvement in the factional conflict of the late Ming-early Qing period. Wang Shimin was a follower and close friend of the notorious prime minister Wen Tiren (d. 1638), who led the opposition against the Donglin/Fushe factions.[381] Wang's retirement in 1638 coincided with the fall and death of Wen and appears to have been a political act. Although Wang shunned active political involvement after retirement, he and his family opposed the Fushe in Taicang. In addition to a personal animosity that developed between Wang and the Fushe's local founders, the society's liberal teachings apparently were viewed as a threat to the family's established position.[382] Wang became the leader of a group of painters in Taicang that included his close friend Wang Jian. Wang Shimin's association with Wen Tiren, who became one of the six men listed under the biographical section *Jianchen* ("evil officials") of the Ming official history, along with Ma Shiying,[383] and his anti-Fushe affiliation might have been damaging to his reputation in the Jiangnan area, particularly in such Fushe strongholds as Nanjing.

The failure of the two Wangs to associate with the Nanjing individualist painters or connoisseurs like Zhou prior to the 1660s may be explained by Zhou's close association with the Donglin and Fushe. As explained above, many of the scholars, artists, and young students in Nanjing such as Gong Xian, Fan Qi, Fang Hengxian, Cheng Zhengkui, Fang Yizhi, to name only a few, either joined the Fushe or had close associations with Fushe members. Political divisions thus may have influenced the art trends of the period.[384]

One interesting figure who seems to have bridged this political gap was the scholar-painter from Taicang, Wu Weiye.[385] Wu became a leading Fushe member and was the favorite student of the local Fushe founder Zhang Pu, the arch-enemy of Wen Tiren and Wang Shimin. In fact, Zhang's reputation and popularity as a teacher reportedly increased sharply when Wu passed the metropolitan examination as the *zhuangyuan* (ranked number one) in 1631. Wu, however, seems to have been a cautious man and to have taken a moderate stance in this factional conflict. He kept a cordial relationship with Wang Shimin's circle and, as an artist himself, recognized Wang's artistic talent. Wu later became a spokesman for their art.[386] Until the end of the Ming, however, Wu was actively engaged in the Fushe movement in Nanjing and preoccupied with politics. He befriended Zhou Lianggong in 1630, and it was probably through his friendship with Wu that Zhou eventually met Wang Shimin and Wang Jian.

Wu's recognition of the two Wangs notwithstanding, prior to the 1660s little contact seems to have been made between the Taicang circle and the Nanjing art world. After Wu Weiye retired to Taicang in 1657 and devoted himself to poetry and painting, his relationship with Wang Shimin and Wang Jian deepened, and he became a great admirer of their art. He also no doubt helped to introduce the Taicang circle to the contemporary art of Nanjing and beyond based on his own extensive exposure during the previous twenty-five years. However, it was chiefly through Zhou Lianggong's contact with the two Wangs and their student Wang Hui, beginning in the early 1660s, that real two-way communication between the two important centers of seventeenth-century painting opened up.

DONG QICHANG AND THE ISSUES OF ORTHODOXY AND INDIVIDUALISM

IN ORDER to understand the art historical implications of Zhou's role in this two-way communication and of his ardent patronage of Wang Hui, we need to first briefly examine the basic differences between the Taicang circle and the leading individualist painters active in Nanjing. The Taicang group considered themselves the true inheritors of Dong Qichang's orthodox doctrine of painting, but made important adjustments to suit their own ultraconservative predisposition. According to Dong's original theory, the creative process of painting consisted of two basic stages of development. In the first stage the artist has to master the rules and conventions of the orthodox tradition, as represented by the literati "Southern School" masters whom he grouped together as the masters of *dunwu* (sudden enlightenment) — as opposed to the professional "Northern School" masters of *jianwu* (gradual enlightenment).[387] Dong believed that a thorough analysis and assimilation of "an assemblage of enlightened specimens" from the orthodox tradition would enable one to obtain intuitive control (i.e., internalization) over the formal medium (or method, i.e., "brush movement and spatial dynamics") of one's models, and ultimately achieve *shenhui* (spiritual correspondence). In the second and final stage, the artist achieves transcendence from tradition through *bian* (transformation) and moves towards self-realization (i.e., achievement of one's own formal and spiritual identity). In other words, in order to achieve the second *bian* stage, one had to go through a process of unlearning.[388] Wang Shimin and Wang Jian, both in theory and practice, altered Dong's concept of *bian*. They believed that "fidelity to the ancients meant fidelity to one's inner self" and "thus to be a good imitator, one can only create." In other words, they viewed artistic creativity as the total identification with one's model, internally and externally.[389] Imitation of the works of the enlightened ones — the repositories of the Principle of Nature (a process known as *fang*) — was thus the only way to become an enlightened master of painting. Imitation for the two Wangs was the key to creativity and an end in itself. It was in a way a shortcut to enlightenment by learning through a master who has already become enlightened.

The two Wangs came to believe that the purity of the ancient models should be kept unspoiled and that each individual's attempt to express his own ideas and to establish his own identity would only "scatter evil seeds," provide "false directions," and bring "disaster." This ultra-classicist attitude also removed the Taicang school from the natural world. Although nature was often overshadowed by Dong's emphasis on the study of antiquity, it was nonetheless viewed as important. By adopting this doctrinaire interpretation of the neo-classicist principles of Dong's theory they became conservative and formalistic.[390]

The so-called "individualist" artists active in Nanjing and elsewhere probably would have been considered by the two Wangs as leaders of the "false direction." But it is important to recognize that the individualist artists were also very much influenced by Dong Qichang's art theory. By the 1620s, Dong's theory of the Northern and Southern School and his belief in the supremacy of the latter school came to be accepted by the entire art world, "orthodox" and "individualist" alike. Dong's theory had become the point of departure for all art criticism. The importance of studying old masters to promote one's artistic development had become a norm. Moreover, most of the contemporary art world also followed Dong's assertion that the Four Great Masters of the late Yuan were the most appropriate models to emulate.[391] The professional Zhe School art was accordingly downgraded at the time. "Scholarly spirit" was the ultimate attribute that most artists tried to convey and which most connoisseur-critics sought to discover. Calligraphic brushstrokes were considered the most expressive means to convey this attribute.

Given this broad acceptance of the basic tenets of Dong Qichang's art theory, the main difference between the Taicang circle and the individualists lay in their attitude towards the use of the past. While the Taicang circle made their main goal the restoration of the Southern School masters in the purest possible form, the individualists sought a more creative use of the past. The individualists had a keener sense of subjectivity than the Taicang group and had a greater sensitivity towards the natural world. Although they also revered the past, instead of engaging in exhaustive studies of antiquity, they often concentrated on a narrow stylistic range and exhausted its potentials and possibilities in order to create their own pictorial vocabulary and means of personal expression. Such "intense exploitation of narrowly limited technical means along a singular line of stylistic development," as Marc Wilson aptly points out, "could hardly help but lead to individualistic expression."[392]

Far from rejecting Dong Qichang, the individualists in certain respects adhered more closely to his original theory than Dong's direct students in Taicang. Gong Xian, for example, probably appreciated and practiced Dong's *bian*, or transformation to a stage of self-expression and individual creativity, more than artists from the Taicang circle. Gong Xian echoes Dong's *bian* theory in the following passage:[393]

> In painting it is [first] necessary to make a systematic and ordered synthesis of Song and Yuan painting, but then, by dispersing [the synthesis into its constituent veins and principles], painting can be made to arrive at the "untrammeled" class. Although the strokes might be few, the Six Canons [of painting] will all be fully realized.

Gong Xian's major departure from Dong Qichang's orthodox tradition was that he did not exclusively follow the orthodox ideals of using "the brushwork of the Yuan to move the peaks of the Song" and of using a calligraphic modeling brush method. He instead often by-passed the Yuan to unravel on his own the secrets of pre-Yuan Southern School masters. This was especially true with respect to the ancient master he admired the most — Dong Yuan (act. 937–975).[394] Gong Xian's new discovery from his study of Dong Yuan's art was the true possibility of the chromatic use of ink and dots and their expressiveness as an artistic form. Gong certainly did not discredit the old master for his invention of the calligraphic modeling stroke known as "hemp-fiber texture stroke," which had been practiced as the appropriate literati brush mode from the Yuan onwards. But while he himself sometimes used this stroke,[395] he was not completely committed to the orthodox idea that lines are superior to any other elements in painting. This conviction was in fact the primary distinguishing characteristic of his work and became a major cause of contemporary ambivalence towards his art.

As exemplified by Gong Xian, the artistic concern of the leading individualists was to create a unique style in the form of a renewal or an expansion of a chosen tradition. This was seen as both a means of self-expression and a means by which they sought to establish their own independent place in the tradition of Chinese painting.

By the time Wang Hui contacted the two Wangs in the early 1650s, Wang Shimin and Wang Jian had been fully occupied with unraveling the mystery of the ancients through making endless copies of their works. They believed that the *qiyun* (spiritual breath and resonance) of the ancients could be captured or visualized through imitation of their "brush movement and spatial dynamics." When they discovered the promising young painter Wang Hui, they hoped he would succeed where they themselves had failed. Wang Hui turned out to be a willing and accomplished student. He adopted their views with fervor, and the two teachers soon came to view his works as the ultimate expression of their ideals. An example of Wang Shimin's praise can be seen in the following (fig. 61):[396]

> When Wang Shigu [Wang Hui] arose he again introduced the great masters of the Tang, Song, and Yuan dynasties by imitating and copying them very closely. As soon as one opens a scroll of his, one is impressed by the strong and rich coloring, and whatever the design or the "short cuts" may be, they are quite in keeping with those of the old masters, and in his brushwork and spirit-resonance he is superior to them. Furthermore, when he imitates a master of old, he is entirely like this particular model and does not do it by introducing elements from various masters. If the picture is not signed, it cannot be distinguished

from the original. No artist before him could do that; even Wen Zhengming and Shen Zhou did not reach as far.

As Wang matured and became more independent of his teachers, he must have felt a need to reach out beyond the rather confined world of Taicang and Yushan. The importance which Wang Hui placed on winning Zhou Lianggong's recognition is evident in his receiving strong recommendations from both Qian Qianyi and later Wang Shimin.[397] Wang Hui sought Zhou's patronage undoubtedly because he was clearly in a better position to assist him in gaining national recognition. Zhou's *Du Hua Lu* project was well known by this time and there is ample evidence that Wang Hui was also very much aware of it.

Although a meeting with Wang Hui was not arranged immediately after Qian Qianyi's letter, Zhou Lianggong certainly appreciated Wang Hui's painting and took Qian's words seriously. The delay of their meeting was probably due to Zhou's three-and-a-half year stay (1663–1666) in Qingzhou, Shandong. Although the exact year of their first meeting is unknown, Zhou invited Wang Hui to come to Nanjing probably soon after the 8th month of 1666, when he returned from Shandong to Nanjing. For this first meeting, Wang Hui prepared a handscroll painting for Zhou and asked Wang Shimin to write a colophon (fig. 61). Wang Shimin and Zhou had been in contact since 1662. In his colophon, Wang Shimin emphasized the significance of the meeting of Zhou in Wang's career:[398]

This autumn, [Wang Hui] will go to visit Liyuan Xiaosinong [Zhou Lianggong] at his invitation and he will bring this painting as a present. Therefore, he has shown this to me and asked me to inscribe it for him. Liweng [Zhou] is a man of elegance and broad learning. He is the leader of scholar-officials and the patriarch of connoisseurs. He and Shigu [Wang Hui] have a great admiration for each other, therefore it is certain that they will strike a great accord when they meet. Furthermore, Shigu is moved by his friendship and thus will completely exhaust his inspired heart and marvelous fingers to create precious objects at their elegant and secluded gatherings. It is [an example of] the quote "He who becomes a disciple of Confucius will make his name more renowned." Although

Fig. 61. Wang Hui (1632–1717). "Summer Mountains and Misty Rain." Colophon by Wang Shimin. Handscroll, ink on paper, 43.81 cm x 246.38 cm. Asian Art Museum of San Francisco, The Avery Brundage Collection. Gift of the Tang Foundation. Presented by Leslie Tang, Martin Tang, and Nadine Tang to the Asian Art Museum of San Francisco in celebration of Jack C. C. Tang's sixtieth birthday (87D8).

he could not meet Wenmin [Dong Qichang], he can now meet Sinong [Zhou Lianggong], which is enough to celebrate all his life. Why should he lament that he was not born when he [Dong Qichang] was still alive?

By all accounts Zhou was immediately captivated by Wang Hui and his art. A number of letters and a poem Wang Hui received from Zhou, as well as Wang's biography in the *Du Hua Lu*, are a testimony to their intimate relationship and to Zhou's extraordinary esteem for the artist. Wang Hui frequently visited Nanjing after their first meeting. Zhou wrote in a letter to Wang Hui sometime towards the end of the 1660s: ". . . whenever you pass by here, you never fail to visit me to celebrate the New Year. I hope you can visit me with your disciples. . . ." As noted above, Wang Hui and his disciple Hu Jie were guests at Zhou's 1669 party.

Zhou's estimation of Wang Hui had reached an extreme by the time he wrote the following letter to Wang after receiving a painting from him:[399]

> In the "Clear Sky after Snow" by Right Prime-minister [Wang Wei] which you copied [for me], you have reached the zenith; you have emulated and even surpassed the ancients. As for the rest of the painters, it is not worth talking about. Thank you. Thank you.

It is possible that Zhou might have used similar expressions of praise in private correspondence to his other favorite artists and that the above compliment was unique only in the sense that it has survived thanks to Wang Hui's rather conspicuous publication of the letters he received praising his works. But Zhou's proclamation of Wang Hui's supremacy over other painters in the *Du Hua Lu*, a book which he surely intended to publish and leave for posterity, carries a special significance and probably accurately reflects his true estimate of the artist. A passage from Wang's biography, which was written around late 1670, just two years before Zhou's death, reads:[400]

> Shigu's copies after Song and Yuan masters are absolutely faithful to the originals. The people in Wu used to ask him to paint, and then they mounted his paintings in the fashion of old masters' works, so as to fool connoisseurs. Even those who were good at connoisseurship could not tell that these paintings were

done by a contemporary artist. Among all the painters who copied the old masters, there are really only two: Zhao Cheng and Shigu. The former is very closely bound by the established rules, and does not have spontaneous expression, whereas Shigu is a great genius by nature, youthful and strong. What he paints may indeed be placed on a level with the old masters' works. He is the greatest painter who has appeared for a hundred years.

This glowing assessment of Wang Hui at first blush would appear surprising and perhaps even inconsistent, given his earlier praise of individualist artists such as Chen Hongshou. However, it appears Zhou's appreciation of the Taicang school late in life was both a reflection of his catholic tastes and the result of a natural transition in his development as an art critic.

What is important to notice, however, is the intensity and seriousness with which he speaks of Wang Hui and the striking similarity between his appraisal and that given by Wang Shimin and Wang Jian. Zhou's exaltation of the young "transcriber" Wang Hui as the greatest painter who had appeared for a century (here Zhou clearly means the greatest painter since Dong Qichang) indicates that he, like Wang Shimin and Wang Jian, considered Wang Hui's art as the ultimate expression of the orthodox ideals. Zhou's comparison of Wang Hui and Zhao Cheng in the above excerpt demonstrates his appreciation of the distinction between a spontaneous copy as a true work of art equal to the ancient model and a labored imitation. In so doing, he also seems to be accepting the emphasis on *gediao* adopted by Wang's literary counterparts, such as Li Dongyang and Li Mengyang, two of the former Seven Masters. On the face of it this would appear to be a reversal in his thinking, since he had previously followed Ai Nanying and Qian Qianyi and been harshly critical of the orthodox former and latter Seven Masters.

But again the inconsistency of his new appreciation of Wang Hui and his apparent acceptance of orthodox theory with his former views is more apparent than real. Despite Zhou's past emphasis on *xingqing* (personal disposition and emotion) in his art criticism under the great influence of Qian Qianyi, as discussed in connection with Chen Hongshou in chapter three, Zhou never ignored *gediao*, or formal style and stylistic tradition. In fact, he viewed both elements — *xingqing* and *gediao* — as indispensable. His advocacy of *xingqing* was largely a result of his critical reaction towards the late Ming orthodox poets for their inability to recapture or evoke the true spirit [i.e., *xingqing*] of the ancients. He believed that this was the result of their superficial focus only on the formal level (i.e., *gediao*), which meant that they failed to achieve a spiritual correspondence (*shenhui*) with their models. Even Qian Qianyi, the rebel of his generation, never ignored the ancient tradition or denied its importance for students of poetry. Qian's real goal was to warn students against the dogmatism and formalism inherent in the orthodox theory as expressed by its founder Yan Yu (1180–1235) and his later followers.[401]

As Zhou entered the decade of the 1660s, he seems to have shifted his interest and emphasis from *xingqing* to *gediao*. This shift may reflect a general change in the ideological environment of the day, but undoubtedly it was influenced by the broadening of Zhou's contacts with the major orthodox masters of literature and painting. Prior to the 1660s Zhou's mentors and friends consisted largely of men who were considered unorthodox such as Ai Nanying, the arch enemy of Chen Zilong; Qian Qianyi, the rebel of his century; and individualist artists such as Chen Hongshou and Gong Xian. But during the final decade of his life, Zhou's circle expanded to include all the major orthodox masters of literature and painting such as Wang Shimin, Wang Jian, Wang Hui, and Wang Shizhen. Zhou's admiration for Wang Hui, the authentic *gediao* artist, is an important indication of this expansion and shift.

Another significant indication can be found in Zhou's great enthusiasm for the young scholar-official poet Wang Shizhen, who became Zhou's intimate friend from 1661. The considerable number of colophons and poems that Wang Shizhen wrote for Zhou testify to their congenial relationship and frequent communication.[402] Wang, who was at this time just emerging as the principal literary critic of his age, stood up against Qian Qianyi in defense of the former and latter Seven Masters. Wang's principal thesis was based on poetic *samadhi* (enlightenment or intuitive understanding) and *buji buli* (nonconformity and detachment) — goals which he believed were only attainable through the artist's perfect identification with the formal medium of the orthodox patriarchs. To Wang Shizhen, "innovation can only have meaning in the context of tradition."[403] Wang Shizhen's literary theory is, in the final analysis, the reassertion of the fundamental concepts of the orthodox tradition. According to Wang, poets could attain their own poetic enlightenment by thoroughly assimilating the formal style of "enlightened" orthodox masters. Wang Shizhen's success in translating this theory into practice in his own poetry, which demonstrated a new vigor and sophistication, may have been critical in winning Zhou's acceptance of his theoretical ideas. The same may have been true of Wang Hui and the orthodox theory expressed by Wang Shimin and the Taicang circle. Wang's brilliance as an artist may have been critical to Zhou's new interest in *gediao*. Clearly the works of Wang Hui provided Zhou with another pivotal aesthetic experience, as important as his earlier experiences with works of Hu Yukun and Chen Hongshou.

While the shift in emphasis that occurred in Zhou's thinking during the final decade is important, it would be a mistake to view this as a repudiation or reversal of his earlier thinking. For in many ways, despite his early affiliation with the individualists, Zhou had been orthodox in his own right all along. His belief in the function of poetry and painting as a means for self-cultivation and fulfillment of sagehood, for example, was firmly within the orthodox tradition. Even his understanding of the importance of *gediao*, and his criticism of its misuse in the hands of the late Ming orthodox school, was within the orthodox tradition. The ancient models for poetry and prose he advocated were also from the orthodox tradition. While Qian Qianyi discarded Yan Yu (who was in fact the true mentor for Dong Qichang's orthodox theory), Zhou revered him and even built a pavilion in his honor while he was in Fujian. Zhou had been deeply engaged in the revival of ancient literature and the seal-script of the Qin and Han from his youth onwards. In his own prose writing, including the *Du Hua Lu* and *Yinren zhuan*, he tried to emulate the true spirit of the literature of Sima Qian and Ouyang Xiu.[404]

The shift which occurred in the final decade of Zhou's life is evident in the biographies of the men he associated with in the period. In general, more attention is devoted to art itself and less to political issues and social concerns. Wang Hui's biography, which was written around 1670, contains none of the political sentiment so commonly found in the chapters on such individualist painters as Chen Hongshou, Gong Xian, Xu You, and Zhang Feng. Nor do we find political sentiment expressed in Wang's own writings and correspondences. Art clearly was Wang Hui's major concern. It should not be surprising that Zhou not only had to change his literary tools but also his critical mind in dealing with Wang Hui, a post-generation painter and an orthodox master.

In the final analysis, Zhou was a profound antiquarian all his life. He described himself as "antiquarian in disposition,"[405] with the implication that he, too, looked for perfection in the art of the past with a romantic belief in the premise that the past is better. Even in his appraisal of Chen Hongshou, one of the foremost individualists of his time, he did not fail to insert a statement on the importance of tradition in Chen's development. In spite of the fact that many of his painter friends were individualistic in their artistic personalities, it was only Zhang Feng who Zhou felt was truly independent of tradition (figs. 56, 57):[406]

> In his painting Dafeng followed no special teacher and casually painted according to his own ideas; yet he achieved a transcendent quality. His paintings were elegantly placid and far reaching. In his brushwork he did not follow any set rules. Among the Nanjing painters, he was the only one who truly followed an independent style.

Wang Hui and his counterpart in the literary realm, Wang Shizhen, were the last major new figures of the art and literary world that Zhou met. Wang Shizhen contributed comments to Zhou's collected paintings as exemplified by his inscription on a Ye Xin leaf in the Taipei album (cat. no. 6). The two represented a new post-war generation of painters and literary critics, for both were in their childhood at the fall of Ming in 1644: Wang Hui was thirteen and Wang Shizhen was only eleven. Wang Hui and Wang Shizhen were both immersed in the orthodox tradition. While Wang Hui worked to achieve a great new synthesis of the ancient tradition of painting, Wang Shizhen emerged as an equally great synthesizer and practitioner of various literary theories of earlier orthodox masters. It is remarkable that the two faced such a similar struggle with their respective orthodox traditions and emerged with similar solutions. It is not surprising that Wang Shizhen became a friend and patron of Wang Hui.[407]

Zhou's contact with the three Wangs from the orthodox camp and his passionate patronage of Wang Hui at the height of his influence in the cultural world probably played a key role in opening up artistic communication between Nanjing and the relatively isolated, conservative world of Taicang. For Wang Hui, this contact with Zhou Lianggong's circle of painters centering around Nanjing seems to have marked a turning point in his early career and artistic development, for this was his first real contact with the art world beyond the Lake Tai area and the tutelage and patronage of his two teachers, Wang Shimin and Wang Jian.

The frequent visits Wang Hui made to Nanjing upon Zhou's enthusiastic invitation enabled Wang Hui to meet the major figures in the Nanjing art world. The many references to gatherings of Zhou's artistic friends, Wang Hui, and Wang's students suggest that this exposure was intense. Zhou's close friend, the scholar-calligrapher and amateur painter Ni Can wrote in a letter to Wang Hui long after Zhou's death:[408]

> I have been a friend of Master Shigu's [Wang Hui] for thirty years. When Master Zhou Liyuan [Zhou Lianggong] was in Nanzhong [Nanjing], Shigu stayed with him day and night whenever he visited Master Zhou. I have deeply admired his sincerity and solitary disposition. His attitude is so easy. If people see him through his painting, then they know him only skin-deep.

WANG HUI AND GONG XIAN

OF ALL Zhou's Nanjing painter friends, the one who most impressed Wang Hui was no doubt Gong Xian, who in turn recognized Wang Hui's talent. From Gong Xian's letters written to Wang Hui, we learn that the two admired each other and exchanged poems, letters, and paintings. In one letter to Wang, Gong Xian wrote:[409]

> When Zilao [unidentified] came, I received your most valuable treasure [painting]; my wish was granted. But how could I dare to send my work to you? It makes me feel ashamed of myself. I hope you can discard it with a smile. My own clumsy poems and other gentlemen's have also been sent to you. Lu Qian and his brother have left in advance. They asked me to send their regards to you. I have transcribed a poem, which I had composed previously, on a piece of paper the size of a small album leaf. I will write another one if someone comes to the south of the city.

Wang Hui's interest in Gong Xian was such that Gong Xian's younger friend and student, Liu Yu, who had known Wang Hui for some time, wrote to Wang Hui protesting his neglect of others (including Liu Yu himself) when he came to Nanjing.

It is clear that Wang Hui not only directly exchanged paintings with such Nanjing painters as Gong Xian, but also that he had an ample opportunity to closely view the contemporary paintings in Zhou's extensive collection. In fact, all the painters, connoisseur-collectors, and critics in Zhou's wide circle of friends studied and communicated through Zhou's collection. They wrote inscriptions directly on the works as well as letters and poems about the collection and held intense discussions during their many gatherings.

Wang Shimin, for example, who had not had much exposure to Nanjing art prior to meeting Zhou, was one of the many who studied Zhou's collection carefully. Although a detailed assessment of the impact of Zhou's collection and Wang Hui's exposure to Nanjing artists is beyond the scope of the present study, it seems reasonable to speculate that this new stimuli had an important impact. The fact that Wang Hui "produced the finest works of his entire career," during the 1660s and 1670s may be more than just a coincidence. An examination of some of his works in this period suggests the possible influence of the Nanjing artists. For example, the "Colors of Mount Taihang," which was

Fig. 62. Wang Hui (1632–1717). "The Colors of Mt. Taihang," detail. Dated 1669. Handscroll, ink and color on silk, 29.84 cm x 304.80 cm. The Metropolitan Museum of Art, New York. Gift of Douglas Dillon, 1978 (1978.423). All rights reserved.

painted in 1669, shows an increasing interest in surface quality, pictorial effects of formal omission, the overall sense of design, and the use of illumination (fig. 62).[410] The whole approach is very modern in keeping with the Nanjing mode represented by Gong Xian and Fan Qi rather than the orthodox Taicang mode. Although the Northern Song master Guan Dong has been identified as the source of the work, the link seems rather tenuous and obscured.[411] The work is similar to Fan Qi's works[412] and prominently displays characteristics commonly associated with the Nanjing mode.

It is more difficult to assess how Gong Xian reacted to the works produced by artists from Taicang. This influence may have had some bearing on the intensification of Gong Xian's intellectual (i.e., art historical and theoretical) interests at the time. But it is also possible, despite the polite compliments offered in correspondences with Wang Hui, that Gong viewed Wang's works as simply unusually good imitations of the ancient masters which in the final analysis lacked self-expression. While the influence of the Taicang circle on Gong Xian and others of his generation seems to have been limited and difficult to access, their influence on such post-war generation artists of Nanjing as Liu Yu and Wang Gai appears to have been stronger.[413]

By the late 1660s, Wang Hui had become widely sought after by friends, collectors, and affluent citizens as well as forgers in Jiangnan. Thus it became increasingly difficult even for Zhou Lianggong, Wu Weiye, and Wang's mentors Wang Shimin and Wang Jian to secure his works. Many of their letters from this time reveal their frustration.[414] Zhou's letters to Wang reveal how anxious and obsessive he had grown over Wang Hui's paintings. At the time he utilized whatever influence he had to induce Wang Hui to paint for him. He even tried to use the influence of Wang Shimin and Wu Weiye, as seen in a letter Wang Shimin wrote to Wang Hui on behalf of Zhou.[415]

In the winter of 1669 or the early spring of the following year, right after Wang left, Zhou had to write a letter of apology to the artist for not paying him enough. He explained that this was a result of his recent dismissal from the government service because of an accusation brought against him:

> You came all the way. I do not know how I can repay your kindness. Now since I have just been dismissed from my office, I am in a very precarious position. Therefore I could only present you a little bit of money for your travel expense, which made me feel so uneasy that I felt almost like dying. However, am I a person who would forget to repay you? I hope you will be understanding. After I have been able to slightly recover from this shock [lit., gasp], I will someday repay you.

Just before his death, Zhou wrote a preface for Wang Hui's collection of poems in response to the artist's request. Zhou's desire for Wang Hui's work was such that in one letter he even seems to have made subtle use of the *Du Hua Lu* (which he called by the generic title, *Huaren zhuan*, Lives of Painters), to try to persuade the artist to be more cooperative:[416]

> I had been waiting for your great work for one year until recently when I saw it while visiting Wumen [Suzhou] by boat. Dong Wenmin [Dong Qichang] said: "An excellent painting is much more enjoyable after dreaming about it several times." Yours is the one I have dreamed of several hundred times. Wasn't I surprised and pleased when I got hold of it! Meicun's [Wu Weiye] preface [attached

to it?] is a great literary work. . . . The *Huaren zhuan* [i.e., *Du Hua Lu*] can be finished by next spring. When it is done I shall send you a copy for you to browse through.

Wang Hui was decidedly the most admired painter of the period. Already from the late 1660s, his success was truly phenomenal. Wang's popularity among the powerful scholar-official patrons as well as the wider public, and even at the court of the Kangxi Emperor, marked him as "the leading painter of the empire."[417] Wang Hui was first recognized by Wang Shimin and Wang Jian, followed by Qian Qianyi, Wu Weiye, and Zhou Lianggong. He then was recognized by the country's foremost collectors and connoisseurs Liang Qingbiao, Zhu Yizun (1629–1709), Song Lao, Gao Shiqi (1645–1703), An Qi (b. 1683?), as well as the Kangxi Emperor. Each of these men contributed in varying degrees to Wang Hui's success. Zhou's contribution to Wang's reputation was certainly a considerable one, through his early patronage and more importantly the *Du Hua Lu*, which praised the youthful artist as the greatest of the century. Unlike many of the artists included in the *Du Hua Lu*, Wang lived on for almost a half century after the work's publication and enjoyed the fame his biography brought during his life.

The Wang Hui "phenomenon" was deeply rooted in the spiritual temper of the century and the very tradition of antiquarianism, which dominated Chinese traditional culture. Wang Hui was uniquely able to satisfy the demands of the time and to synthesize the works of the ancients by means of his brush and ink. His art was the eloquent conclusion of his time and civilization. It also represented the conclusion of Zhou Lianggong's own artistic quest. While Zhou appreciated such individualist painters as Chen Hongshou and Gong Xian, he was not one to raise the banner for a truly individualistic movement of art. His tastes and his whole intellectual framework for understanding art were too orthodox and too antiquarian.

Wang Hui's success had another important implication from a broader historical point of view. The fact that Wang, as a professional painter coming from a long line of professional painters, emerged as the undisputed heir of the orthodox literati tradition in succession to Dong Qichang, signified a notable turning point in the history of Chinese painting. Intellectual professional painters not only established themselves as the "scholar painter" equals of literati painters, but began to assume a dominant role in the development of Chinese painting.

THE BURNING OF BOOKS: DOUBTS AND FEARS

As Zhou's fame grew and as he became increasingly aware of his impending death, fears and doubts began to grow about his place in history. He became increasingly fearful of how later generations would judge him when all of his friends, witnesses, and sympathizers were gone. He himself never doubted that his integrity and service to the people compensated for his collaboration with the Manchu regime. He had served the alien regime for the good of his country and his people and was understood and appreciated by his fellow men during his own life. On the other hand, he felt very vulnerable at the hands of later historians. Since the object of history was to teach statecraft by precedents and to promote Confucian morality by praising the good and condemning the bad, Zhou clearly sensed that he was open to condemnation for his failure to adhere to the rigid Neo-Confucian notion of dynastic loyalty.[418]

At times, this fear of history, which was intensified by his own personal vanity, seems to have made Zhou restless, emotional, and even cynical. No better description of his mental state during this period can be made than the one Zhou himself gave in the following letter written in 1664 from Shandong to his son-in-law, the *juren* Wang Rongji:

> It has been a long time since I have seen my son-in-law, the first on the list of *juren* candidates. As I get older, this longing for him gets deeper. Now I am fifty-three years old. I see those who passed the [metropolitan] examination with me in the same year [1640], some even older than I, are still in government service. The new prefect of Dongzhun is one example. His is now eighty-three. Compared to him, I am still young in age. I did not expect that I would suddenly get older this year. My beard and hair have all turned white and I have lost all my teeth. My right hand and foot are gradually becoming numb. All of a sudden I feel like I am seventy or eighty years old. People are startled when they see me. Luckily, my mind is still clear.
>
> All my life I have not been very good at poetry and other literary composition. But I do like to write. It has been more than one year since I came here [Shandong]. But I have written only some ten poems. When Wu Jiezi left, I composed these two lines: "I pour the dew-like wine in front of the wind, and appreciate Yunmen after snow." They are yet to be finished. I have written very few prose poems. To hold a brush is like stretching a heavy bow. When I just think about what to write, I immediately begin to have a headache. . . .
>
> As soon as someone starts to play music [on New Year's day, and I see] the decorations set up, my tears start to fall. [Recently] on a moonlit night, I sat with my son Jun (Zhou Zaijun) in [my] Zhenyi [True Intention] Pavilion. After a couple of drinks, I suddenly remembered [old friends] who were my seniors. Their passing has already made me feel sad enough. Now Zunying [Xu Zunying] and Yujie [Xu Yu] have also died suddenly. Human life is not *aksobhya* [i.e., immovable, changeless]. This old man just cries and cannot stop. Yes, I know old people easily get emotional. But they do not become emotional with little things. I know this is not a good sign. . . .
>
> Now you mentioned the old shrines [built in honor of me]...in my opinion [the fame they represent] is nothing but an illusion. All throughout my life wherever I have been posted as an official, I have never left one couplet, not even one name plate for a hall. This is because I am afraid that if I leave my name behind for later generations, they will sneer at me. . . . I pleaded with people not to build [the shrines] in the first place. . . . Recently when I passed through Beihai [Wei Xian, Shandong], I saw my portrait and tablet still enshrined there. So I destroyed the portrait and burnt the tablet. I told the local elders, "They have been here enjoying honors for more than twenty years. That is enough. Please save this lot for your own banquets and parties. Wouldn't that be better?"
>
> Recently Wang Zhouce [Wang Ji] came to see me and asked for the poems and prose pieces written while I was in Yangzhou. Although he repeatedly asked for them, I refused. To me, they are nothing but a dream. Several years [from

now] when this old man enters his grave, he will no longer be able to enjoy beautiful pines and cypress trees. How much more so with fame in this world! That is why I did not respond to him. . . .

Ever since the civil official system was established, numerous shrines and tombstones have been erected in this world. Of all the shrines of living officials which have been recorded in local gazetteers, how many of them are still extant? I frequently visit big cities and see a great many tombstones. I try to remember the names, but as soon as I walk away, I already have forgotten them. I try hard to remember the names of many gentlemen recorded in local gazetteers, but I forget the names even before I close the books. Those names I keep in my mind and cannot forget are never learned from monuments and stone tablets, nor from the record of local gazetteers. Judging from this, it [worldly fame] is only a dream. It serves no good at all. When I saw Zhouce, I told him about this. The ten some poems I wrote at Yunmen have been printed. But one night I asked my son Jun to destroy all the blocks.

In my life, all my troubles have been caused by my poking into others' business. Recently I began to repent and try intentionally to keep myself from [unnecessary involvement], hoping that there will be no involvement at the time of my death. When you, my dear son-in-law, read this letter, you will say these are ominous words. Yet [don't we know] "auspiciousness" also has its inherent ominousness? Lu Wei is an old man of seventy, but he plans to live to one hundred. Whenever someone mentions the word "death," he becomes unhappy. One day when he passes away, what he leaves behind will be a host of unrelated people in his house. Although I am stupid, I shall not be so stupid as he. . . .

Zhou began to think seriously of retirement when he took up his Shandong post in 1663. When he was promoted in 1666 to the Nanjing-based post, Intendent of Grain Transportation of Jiangnan, Zhou was determined to retire. He asked to be relieved from this appointment on the grounds that, although he was officially registered in Xiangfu, Henan, his family and his ancestral tombs were in Nanjing. Although civil officials were prohibited from serving in their native province,[419] the regulations did not take into account actual family residence or "second" hometowns. His request was therefore rejected and in 1666, he had to take up his appointment in Nanjing. Zhou certainly must have known of the troublesome nature of his new duties. The administration of grain transportation was the source of considerable contention and often was associated with corruption. Having experienced slander and imprisonment earlier and having committed himself to avoiding future entanglements, he naturally sought retirement.

As implied in the letter, destroying his own shrines and the printing blocks of his poetry collection were deliberate attempts to reduce his fame and eliminate relics which he imagined might become objects of desecration by later generations. Zhou knew that in the cold balance of historical judgment, all of the other virtues he could rightly claim before his contemporaries would be useless in the face of the charge of disloyalty. Since the degree of condemnation only increased in proportion to one's fame and status, Zhou sought to reduce his own fame and the traces of his life before his death. Zhou was familiar with the fate of many great men in the past who suffered posthumous condemnation and sought to avoid a similar fate. If Zhao Mengfu, who served the Yuan, for example, had only been a mediocre man during his life, leaving nothing noteworthy behind, his disloyalty would not have been such a highly charged issue for later generations. Zhou had already witnessed the impact that popular condemnation had on the life and art of his friend Qian Qianyi, who had just died in 1664. He also had witnessed the fate which Ma Shiying suffered, though the latter's case was not linked to the question of loyalty.

Zhou's leniency towards Ma Shiying and his willingness to include him in the *Du Hua Lu* certainly owes much to the peculiar political situation of his time and his own life experience. Contemporary opinion held Ma in contempt for his unscrupulous dealings at the Nanjing court and blamed him for the failure of the restoration of the Ming. He was active as a painter in Nanjing before his involvement in the Southern Ming politics and his reputation as an artist suffered along with his political reputation. As a result, his works have been completely effaced from Chinese art history.[420] Ma's case illustrates the fact that in Confucian society, art and politics not only mix, but often become inextricably fused.[421]

Zhou's biography of Ma Shiying recognized his artistic achievement and noted how his artistic reputation was completely ruined by his political involvement:[422]

Ma Shiying, [*zi*] Yaocao, is a native of Guiyang [in Guizhou]. After he retired from his office of *fengdu* [governor-general], he moved to Baimen [Nanjing]. He devoted himself to painting. He studied [the art of] Dong Beiyuan [Dong Yuan] and was able to transform it and establish his own ideas. His works were quite remarkable. . . . If Yaocao had ended his life while he was still a governor-general, although he could not have matched the ancients, his reputation might not have fallen so precipitously into the "so and so" [i.e., "bad last minister"] category.

Noting the relativity of human affairs and the brutality of history, Zhou then proceeded to take issue with this popular condemnation of Ma and his art:

Sometimes it is fortunate to have achievement, fame, riches, and honor, but sometimes it is not. What a pity! Wang Yishang [Wang Shizhen] said: "Cai Jing's calligraphy was comparable to that of Su [Su Shi] and Huang [Huang Tingjian]. Yaocao also had in his bosom hills and valleys." . . .Yaocao became the ridicule of later generations like this, but I would say he might have been a good man, who unfortunately fell under the evil influence of Huaining [Ruan Dacheng]. Some scholars are lucky to leave their literary works, calligraphy, and paintings to posterity. But if you do not act properly in the slightest way, later generations will launch a merciless attack whenever they get hold of a piece of your work. [Therefore those who enjoy fame] are not so lucky as those who know nothing of poetry, literature, calligraphy, and painting, and whose names later generations rarely see [on works of art], hence sparing them from severe accusations. Isn't this a great pity! When Yaocao became famous [as a painter], so many people vied with each other to buy his paintings that he could hardly meet the demand. Therefore he had Shi Lin paint for him in substitution.

The tone of this passage is strongly autobiographical and reflects back on his own life and feelings of vulnerability as an *erchen* (an official who served two ruling houses).

From the experiences of Ma and others who suffered at the hands of history, Zhou apparently concluded, in his typically practical way, that, although it was too late to effectively change his reputation, he still could save himself a certain degree of posthumous humiliation by reducing the exposure of his name to future generations. Zhou also began to reflect on the fundamental cause of his predicament. He became more and more conscious and cynical of the psychological motive behind fame: ambition. He concluded that part of the solution to the problem of fame, which in his case was sure to beget historical condemnation, was to rid himself of ambition. He also noted, as indicated in the above letter to his son-in-law, that fame was only transitory and ultimately futile anyway.

One early spring night in 1670, while the investigation into charges against Zhou was still going on, Zhou gathered his books and printing blocks and set them on fire.[423] Although he immediately regretted this impulsive act, it demonstrates the depth of his fears and frustrations. Zhou wrote about the incident to Zhang Yi:[424]

> On the fifth day of the second month, I burnt all those [writings] that had been carved into blocks and those which had not yet been carved, as well as random writings. . . . Nevertheless I regretted what I did soon afterward, and then I realized that it is difficult to be rid of the desire for fame. This proves that I can not learn the *Dao*, because I am still concerned and involved [with mundane fame].

This incident occurred while Zhou was under investigation, after he was slandered by the governor-general of Jiangsu Yan Bo, a Chinese bannerman, in the 8th month of 1669 for mishandling government funds. Zhou had been dismissed from his post after the accusations were made. The investigation lasted a year and he was finally found innocent. During his earlier legal trouble Zhou always seems to have managed, despite his despair, to contain his frustration and resentment. He also maintained his faith in the ultimate triumph of the *junzi*. He was even able to offer a touch of hope to his fellow inmate Xu You in his otherwise bitingly critical "Song of Cold Crows." This time, however, physically ill and mentally weakened, Zhou could not contain his feelings of bitterness and resentment. Hope seems to have given way to despair. After the incident, sometime in the autumn of 1670, Zhou expressed his bitterness in a letter to Zhang Yi:[425]

> I have been in a hot boiler for the last ten months. Since I have been detained [that long], I had hoped my case would be resolved soon. But it is still dragging on. My mind is in turmoil and I am filled with all kinds of bitterness. Added to this situation is [the fact] that my younger brother died on the 25th day of the 7th month. He was my only brother. He also left me behind. I wept near to death over his coffin. Do you think I can stand all this at my old age?

Zhou despaired that his seemingly endless social commitments only seemed to bring him personal disaster. His mood after his dismissal was expressed in the name he chose for a hall at his homestead: "Hall of an Angry Old Man" (*Nu lao tang*) after his dismissal. Behind these comments and gestures, including burning his books, was a complicated mental state of personal rage, self-reprimand, doubt, and fear.

When Zhou Zaijun re-collected his father's writings from his friends after Zhou's death and named them "Writings Remaining after the Burning," which would later become known as *Laigutang ji*, he asked the outspoken Ming loyalist Lu Liuliang to write a preface. In his preface, Lu first lists several famous precedents of book burning in history and gives the motives behind these acts. He then points out the uniqueness of Zhou Lianggong's burning of his own writings and outlines his motives. Lu concludes with his own interpretation of Zhou, which is colored by a certain sarcasm and lack of sympathy towards collaborators:[426]

> Liyuan burnt all his writings. It was not because he thought anything was wrong with his works [as we see from the fact that] he continued to write even after the burning. . . . It was certainly due to something very unbearable in his bosom. Therefore I would rather lament his ambition than mourn his books. . . . [While young], he looked down upon those narrow-minded scholars and stupid men who lived and died in a small village without getting any official rank or academic degree. However, when he became old and experienced many adversities, he became exhausted and turned to reality. When he thought of his young ambition which resulted in nothing, he felt that even those worthless scholars and stupid men, with their easiness under the sky and above the earth, were better off than he. When he wanted to speak out about his feelings, he could not make even a sound; when he thought of it, he felt ashamed. Such feeling and his inability to make a sound ultimately left him no desire to live on. . . . He just thought of burning himself right away, as well as his poems and other writings. . . . [But] that which should have been burnt was his ambition, not his books. The only one who really knows the reason why [Zhou] burnt his writings is [his eldest son] Xuege [Zhou Zaijun]. [He knows] that [Zhou] knew his act of burning was wrong, but this act saved him from burning himself.

Lu, who criticized "the defeatist spirit of his fellow Chinese," thought that Zhou late in life finally came to realize the wrongness of his ambitions which drove him to collaborate with the Manchus. He saw Zhou's veiled act of burning his books as the desperate attempt of a collaborator to try to undo his shameful act. But Zhou was not at all ashamed of his collaboration, nor would he have agreed with Lu that his collaboration "resulted in nothing." Rather, he feared that later generations would draw precisely the same simple-minded, self-righteous conclusion on the issue of the collaboration as Lu Liuliang.

The psychological damage suffered by collaborators, symbolized by Zhou's book-burning, is perhaps most vividly portrayed in a poem entitled "In Time of Sickness," written by Wu Weiye, one of the most prominent poets of the day and a collaborator:[427]

> The world presses, and white hairs multiply.
> Gong Sheng refused to serve, "died young" at eighty,
> And left a name imperishable.
> Medicine knows no cure for this sickness of mine,
> This bright flame of blood in my breast.
> Can I sprinkle it here in offering
>   to the west wind and waning moon,
> Take out my heart and lay it on the ground,
> Ask the magician Huate to loosen the knot in my entrails.
> I think on past follies and sob aloud.

So many stalwart friends, men of high constancy;
And I, because I wavered at the crucial moment,
I hide in the reeds on borrowed time.
Burn *moxa* between the brows,
    clear the nose with gourd stalks,
Nothing brings relief
    as old disasters come again a thousandfold.
Too hard to sacrifice wife and children, cast them off
    like an old shoe,
And still I can boast not a penny to my name.
Why are some lives so flawed when others find wholeness?

Wu Weiye could not find medicine for his sickness. He laments that no matter how upright and honest an official he was, history would judge him as a flawed man in contrast to those who refused to serve.

No doubt all men of intellect and consciousness who lived through the Manchu conquest, loyalists and collaborators alike, experienced suffering and had misgivings about their chosen response. Collaborators and loyalists had an acute appreciation of each other's role and the peculiar dilemma each had to face. In fact, loyalists frequently depended on collaborators for support and protection, while collaborators depended on loyalists to express their heartfelt ideals.[428] The responsibility for the maintenance of Chinese culture under the alien rule and the protection of the populace from the whim of unruly Manchu and Chinese bannermen fell heavily upon the shoulders of such collaborators as Zhou Lianggong. Loyalists, on the other hand, those men without "flaw" living "under the sky and above the earth" (in Lu's description), lamented their fate and sought their own salvation in art, philosophy, and religion. Ironically, later in life the tables seem to have been turned. In their twilight years, collaborators like Zhou began to fear that they would be the outcasts when future generations passed judgment on their lives, while loyalists on the contrary felt a certain smug satisfaction at having endured a life of poverty and having retained their purity.

Zhou Lianggong and Wu Weiye's deepening doubts and fears as they approached the end of their lives contrast sharply with the sentiment of men who lived "unflawed" lives. In 1671, the loyalist poet painter Gong Xian concluded with a contented smile that his life was not so bad after all, compared with "those who move attentively in the circle of ceremony and regulations":[429]

On New Year's Day of the *xinhai* year [1671], sprinkling some tea about that I had specially set aside, I made sacrifice in the mountains to the Vast Heavens. I sealed my door and sat quietly, communicating with neither relatives nor friends. Having washed my ink-stone and tried out my brush, I brought out this plain album. I painted away like this for some ten days, but then, my "flower-activities" became somewhat burdensome, and it was already the end of Spring before I finished it. I dare not say that I have enjoyed in full measure the unalloyed happiness of [this world of] man, and yet, compared with those who move attentively in the circle of ceremony and regulations, is not what I have attained much more? And so, I record this here with a smile. Resident of Half-Acre (*Banmoujuren*), Gong Xian.

But as Gong himself recognized elsewhere, he was quite dependent on those men of ceremony and regulations:[430]

> The time passed, both the flourish of summer and the depths of winter. What was there to disturb me in my lofty seclusion? The years and seasons changed. Now it is the *renxin* year [1682], 11th month, and I have just completed it [this album]. I have titled it "Streams and Mountains Without End."
>
> I recall that at the age of thirteen I was able to paint. Fifty years later, I am exerting myself in the "inkstone field" [i.e., painting for a living]; what I plow in the morning is my evening harvest. But there is barely enough to support myself. You might call me crude, but gentlemen and officials do not consider me crude. In their tall carriages, drawn by four steeds, they come personally to my rustic door. Can it be [only] because my dry brush and left-over ink are highly valued among men? I took this album with me on my journey to Guangling [Yangzhou]. When my boat arrived at Yingluanzhen, they sat me highest among their friends. Directly, I met the sub-prefect, Xu Hueian [unidentified], who invited me to his aged residence, then put me up and gave me food. . . .

Zhou Lianggong, of course, was one of the officials on whom Gong Xian depended.

Even at the height of their careers, Qing collaborators looked upon the loyalists with a certain respect and envy. Gong Dingzi contrasted his life as a Qing official with that of Gong Xian and the loyalist painter from the Yuan dynasty, Gong Kai (1222–1307):[431]

> My clansman the Recluse Banqian [Gong Xian] is very aloof and solitary in his spiritual resonance. His paintings are lofty, hoary, luxuriant, and elegant; not even a single dot in his painting has a vulgar spirit. A court official in the mundane world, I shiver with chill facing this quiet forest and [these] withered trees. I feel so ashamed before the two Gongs.

From the perspective of the Buddhist monk painter Kuncan, both loyalists and collaborators were mere puppets on Nature's stage. Kuncan, who watched the fall of the Ming from a mountain in the south of Nanjing, reflected on his life and the world surrounding him in a letter addressed to another Ming loyalist, Zhang Yi, sometime after 1670:[432]

> After we departed from each other, there passed summer, fall, and winter. All the events that happened in the past are like an old dream in the last life. Now, I just drag on day after day. As for the rest [of my life], though there will be renewals of coldness and heat, it is only a fit of pain or a fit of itch. I just look at myself, that is all. Since Nature built this theater, it can hold but only a puppet show. These puppets are really without feeling, since if they had [any], they should have beaten their chests with their hands and fled from the stage. I, Shitouren, now do not have the patience to watch this show. I only doze off all day long, as you, Songfeng Daoren, create your world while drinking. Now, when you are compared with a dozer [like me], are we alike or not alike?

To Kuncan, loyalists and collaborators alike were men of human desires, selfishness, and egotism. One was embroiled in the self-righteousness of loyalism and its consequences, and the other in political ambition and its consequences.

What adds a sense of irony and human tragedy to Zhou's life was his struggle to square his inescapable ambition and absorption in the present world with his understanding that all of his accomplishments and fame would only bring further disgrace to his name in history. At times, this fear of history seemed to take the upper hand, compelling him to urgently cut himself off from social and political entanglements and to attempt to efface any trace of his accomplishments. But at other times he focused primarily on present concerns and continued his very active life filled with many social and artistic engagements as well as political commitments.

THE FINAL DAYS

DESPITE HIS FEARS, he could not help but continue writing, even after he burned all his books. He was a literary man to the core and only death could quiet his brush. He therefore resumed work on his anthologies of letters, the *Du Hua Lu*, and the *Yinren zhuan*. In his letter to Zhang Yi quoted above, which he wrote right after the book burning, he asked Zhang to find noteworthy prose writings for him to edit:[433]

> [Before my trouble started], at my leisure I had been devoting myself to selecting and editing letters sent by friends. . . . Now that my mind is in such turmoil I can not review these letters. I would like to ask you to browse through this volume of twelve chapters. . . . One letter by Shigong [probably Kuncan] is marvelous. I have it already printed. But I detest recent letters written by Wugong [probably Fang Yizhi] because he likes to talk in the Chan manner, which makes me feel nauseous. But the one you have transcribed is quite elegant and vivid, which is unusual for him. Therefore I have included it. . . . Do you know if there are any collected works by contemporary literati I can edit? If you do not have them in your possession, please give me the titles so that I can ask someone to try to locate them. . . .[434]

Not only did Zhou keep on writing, but he continued his activities as a patron with undiminished zeal. The fervor with which he pursued Wang Hui's paintings is evident in the following letter written to the artist around 1672:[435]

> . . . We have been separated for quite a while. How can I not lament the separation! Suddenly, I received your letter, in which you still express your abundant longing for a commoner [Zhou was now without an official post] like me. . . . My humble birthday is unworthy of mentioning. But when I hear that you intend to present a painting to me [as a birthday gift], I begin to think of my birthday on each of the 360 days. However, my birthday is on the 7th day of the 4th month, which is not too far from now. I am afraid that the able affair [artistic creation] can not be rushed, yet days go fast. Therefore I only hope you can keep this in mind. If you can kindly give it to me one day earlier, I would live one more year. Please send it to me as soon as you finish it. Do not have it mounted. If your poetry collection is published, I hope you can mail it to me soon. . . .

In the spring of 1672 Zhou went to Yangzhou and gathered together with Cheng Sui, Wang Qi, Wu Jiaji, Sun Zhiwei, and other friends. They all knew Wu Weiye had just died. They also knew that their old friend Fang Yizhi had killed himself in the previous year after he learned of an order for his arrest under suspicion of treason.[436] Zhou Lianggong and others tried to help Fang but were too late.[437]

As Zhou sailed home from the gathering, he wrote the biography of a Taicang seal carver, in which he complained of severe pain in his eyes.[438] Zhou continued to work on his biographies of artists right up until his death. His persistence despite ill health was no doubt due to the sense of obligation he felt to the many artists he had still not written about. Perhaps the one artist to whom he felt the most indebted was Xu You, who suffered with him in prison and died two years after being released with Zhou in 1661. On one early spring day, Zhou took out several of Xu You's seals, made imprints, and proceeded to write his biography for the *Yinren zhuan*, despite the fact that he had already written Xu's biography for the *Du Hua Lu*.[439] Right after his sixtieth birthday, while working on the *Yinren zhuan*, he seems to have feared that he would not be able to complete the work before his death:[440]

> On the right I have put together all the imprints of Jin Guang's seals which his students collected for me. [Now] Jin Guang's *yinpu* is done. This is the *renzi* year [1672]. I just had my birthday. Now I have become sixty years old. How can I hope to see the completion of this work [the *Yinren zhuan*]?

In the 5th month, Zhou showed further signs of illness. His student Huang Yuji kept him company. Before his death, in his last conversation with Huang, Zhou said one of his greatest regrets was that he had not been able to publish a collection of Xu You's poetry.[441] Zhou finally died on the 23rd day of the 6th month in the *renzi* year (1672) at his home in Qinhuai, Nanjing.

Chronology of Zhou Lianggong's Life (1612–1672)

Zhou Lianggong was born in Nanjing. His father, Zhou Wenwei, was a *shengyuan* and a fellow at the Imperial Academy in Nanjing.	Dong Qichang (age 55) was in retirement in Huating. Ding Yunpeng (age 66) was residing at a temple on Tiger Hill in Suzhou. Cheng Hongshou (age 15) probably began to paint, studying under Lan Ying in Hangzhou. In Nanjing, painters such as Wu Bin, Gao Yang, Gao Yu, Wei Zhihuang, Wei Zhike, Hu Zongren, Hu Zongxin, Zeng Jing, Zheng Zhong, and Xue Daoling were active.	1612
(age 13) Zhou visited his father, who had been posted at Zhuji, Zhejiang, as district registrar, and met Chen Hongshou, who traveled with him to Mount Wuxi.	Zheng Chenggong (Koxinga) was born.	1624
(age 17) Zhou participated in a revival movement of the ancient style of literature with Gao Fu and other friends. His talent was recognized by Ai Nanying, a prominent literary figure of his time. In autumn, Wei Zhihuang and Wei Zhike painted for Zhou.	Fushe was organized. The pirate Zheng Zhilong surrendered to the Ming. Uprisings were staged by Li Zicheng and Zhang Xianchong.	1628
(age 23) In Xiangfu. Zhou met Sun Chengze, the magistrate of Xiangfu. Sun recognized Zhou's talent and selected him as first in the list of successful *shengyuan* candidates. Sun also bought farm land for Zhou so that he might support himself.	Uprising in Tongcheng, Anhui. Fang Yizhi moved his family to Nanjing. Song Lao and Wang Shizhen were born.	1634
(age 24) Scoring first in a qualifying examination, Zhou was able to enter the Xiangfu Academy. In the winter, he married the daughter of Feng Yumin, a student at the Imperial Academy.	Li Rihua died at 71 and his book, *Liuyan zhai biji*, was published.	1635
(age 25) In Xiangfu, Zhou failed the provincial examination. He met the painter Feng Yujiang at Zhang Minbiao's home. He met Cheng Lin, a seal carver from Huizhou living in Wulin, who was visiting Kaifeng.	The Manchus proclaimed the Qing dynasty. Fang Yizhi probably met Hou Fangyu, who was then living in the city. Mao Xiang had a riverside villa in Nanjing, where they all often gathered. Dong Qichang died at 82. Zou Zhe was born.	1636
(age 28) In Xiangfu, Zhou obtained the *juren* degree. Zhou went to Shangqiu to visit the Xueyuan of Hou Fangyu, where he met Song Quan, the father of Song Lao.	Manifesto against Ruan Dacheng was published by some Fushe members. Manchus attacked Zhili. Fang Yizhi passed the provincial examination in Nanjing; Hou Fangyu began his stay in Nanjing from this year to 1640. Hou Fangyu failed the same exam. Chen Jiru died at 83.	1639

1640 (age 29)

In the spring, Zhou left Xiangfu and went to Beijing with Zhang Minbiao to take the metropolitan examination. He passed the metropolitan and palace examinations and received the *jinshi* degree. Zhou renewed his friendship with Chen Hongshou, who had just arrived in Beijing that year. He became friends with Fang Yizhi, who passed the same examinations, and Zhang Yi, a brother of Zhang Feng. In Beijing Zhou also met Liang Zhi, a Yangzhou seal carver (living in Nanjing), who carved seals for him. Zhou's first son, Zaijun, was born.

Fang Yizhi, Chen Taisun, Qi Xiongjia, Jin Bao, Xiong Huaguo, Zhang Fengyi, and Wu Di received *jinshi* degrees. Chen Hongshou purchased a fellowship to enter the Imperial Academy of Beijing and arrived at Beijing in the spring; he was able to see the imperial collection of old paintings.

1641 (age 30)

In Beijing, Zhou was appointed district magistrate of Wei Xian, Laizhou fu, Shandong province. Upon his departure, Chen Hongshou painted for Zhou, as a farewell gift, the "Guizhu tu" (an illustration of Tao Qian's ode "Returning Home"). Fang Yizhi, then appointed as a Hanlin scholar, and Zhang Yi visited Zhou together to bid him farewell.

In Wei Xian, Zhou founded the Wei Society to promote local talents. One of its members was the future scholar-painter Fa Rechen. Fang Yizhi visited Zhou in Wei Xian accompanied by Hu Yukun; Hu remained with Zhou after Fang left and painted for him. Prompted by Hu's paintings, Zhou began full-fledged collecting this year, particularly paintings in the album format.

Cheng Sui stayed at a temple in Nanjing.

1643 (age 32)

Selected as one of the ten best administrators of the country, Zhou was summoned to the court. It was probably in this year that a shrine in honor of Zhou was erected by the residents of Wei Xian.

Chen Hongshou returned to Hangzhou from Beijing. Ma Shiying was in Nanjing and painted "Mount Niushou." The printing of Qian Qianyi's *Quxueji* was undertaken by Qian's student Qu Shisi. Cheng Jiasui died at 79 in Huizhou. Zhang Zhou died at 67.

1644 (age 33)

In Beijing. Early in the 3rd month, Zhou was made a censor in charge of the Zhejiang circuit. Within ten days after this new appointment, on the 19th day of the 3rd month, Beijing fell under Li Zicheng's army and the Chongzhen emperor hung himself. Zhou was jailed by Li's army along with many Ming officials including Fang Yizhi and his uncle Fang Gonggan (Fang Hengxian's father), but was released without torture. He soon left Beijing and fled to Nanjing with other officials in disguise among refugees. Zhou was imprisoned in Nanjing when a former imperial guard, Feng Gezong, accused him of surrendering to Li Zicheng's army while in Beijing. He was deprived of his official title but it was soon restored after his innocence was proved. Zhou went into seclusion with his family on Mount Niushou south of Nanjing.

On the 19th of the 3rd month, Beijing fell under Li Zicheng's army. In the 5th month, the Manchus entered Beijing and Li Zicheng fled with the Crown Prince as hostage. In the same month, Prince Fu (Zhu Yusong) was enthroned in Nanjing. In the 6th month, Qian Qianyi was appointed president of the Board of Ceremonies in Nanjing. In the 10th month, the Manchus moved their capital from Shenyang to Beijing.

Before the fall of Beijing, Yang Wencong, who had been serving as magistrate of Jiangning, was charged with corruption and dismissed. Zhu Da and Daoji became Buddhist monks after the fall of Beijing.

1645 (age 34)

In Nanjing. Zhou was among such scholar-officials as Qian Qianyi and Wang Duo who surrendered to the Manchus, presumably after consultations among themselves. Based on his original censorial rank, the Manchu court conferred on Zhou the post of Intendent for Salt Transportation of the Lianghuai circuit with his office in Yangzhou. Gu Jianshan (DHL/SL) and Hu Yukun

On the 15th of the 5th month, the Manchu army led by Prince Dodo captured Nanjing. In the 6th month, Prince Tang (Zhu Yushan), endorsed by Huang Daozhou, was proclaimed emperor at Fuzhou, Fujian. Li Zicheng committed suicide. In the 8th month, Prince Lu was proclaimed emperor at Shaoxing, Zhejiang; Ming loyalist armies were raised throughout the country by Ming officials as well as by commoners.

were his guests in Yangzhou. Chen Taisun gave Zhou a boat which Zhou named "Jiuyuan."

Fang Yizhi, Ni Jiajing, Sun Zixiu, and Jin Bao were at the Shiji temple in Zhejiang. Ming loyalists Liu Zongzhou and Qi Biaojia committed suicide. Gao Shiqi was born.

(age 36)
In Yangzhou. Shen Hao contributed a leaf of calligraphy to the Taipei album. Shi Lin painted two album leaves of landscape (cat. nos. 1 [leaves G, H], 21). Zong Hao painted for Zhou on a boat in Gaoyu, Yangzhou. Promoted as provincial judge of Fujian, Zhou went to his new post via Nanjing. He was halted on his way to Fuzhou by bandits and rebels and had to stay in Shaowu, Fujian, for eight months. In Shaowu, Zhou built the Jiaotang, where he finished three books: *Tongshu* (8 *zhuan*), *Zichu* (6 *zhuan*), and *Jiaotang shi* (1 *zhuan*). Zhou attracted many local scholars, who often gathered at the Shihualou with him. When he came to Fuzhou, Zhou was accompanied by Hu Yukun from Nanjing. Hu stayed with Zhou at Shaowu and was later joined by Cheng Sui. They held a "Rite to Ink" (*Jimo zhihui*) at Zhou's place.

Wen Zongjian (DHL/SL) died at 75. In the 3rd month, Qian Qianyi was imprisoned and charged with giving aid to Ming loyalist armies.
1647

(age 37)
In Fujian. While in Shaowu, Zhou built the Bai Tao Fang, where he kept the hundred paintings Ye Xin had painted for him illustrating the poems of Tao Qian which Ye asked Zhou to select. In early summer, he arrived at Minhou Xian, Fuzhou. Upon his arrival at the city, he proceeded directly to the home of Xu You, whose studios, Miyu tang and Taoping, were to become gathering places of local literati clustered around Zhou. He met a local painter, Guo Gong, in Minhou Xian, whom, he requested to paint for him the *Jiaotang se zhu tu*, a portrait of him in the Jiaotang in Shaowu. This work was based on Zhou's own description. The same subject was painted by Chen Hongshou, Hu Yukun, and Xu You for Zhou within a few years. Zhou wrote *Bamin jishou shao shimo*, and printed collected poems of all the scholars he met at Shaowu with the title *Wanshan zhongshi*. Probably from this year he had a garden named Kanyan in Fujian. Zhou frequented the Shiwulou with his circle in Fuzhou.

Zheng Chenggong initiated a campaign along the seacoast of Fujian, taking Tongan and other cities. In the spring, Qian Qianyi was released. Kong Shangren was born.
1648

(age 38)
In Fujian. Zhou became the Junior Financial Commissioner of Fujian province and was ordered to go to Beijing for official business. He left Fujian in the 10th month, accompanied by Chen Jun and Xu Yanshou. Passing Hangzhou, Zhou saw Chen Hongshou at West Lake, and asked him for some paintings.

Zhangpu and Yuanxiao, Fujian, were taken by Zheng Chenggong's army. Cheng Zhengkui began to paint the *Jiangshan woyu tu* (Dream Journey Among Rivers and Mountains) series. Qian Qianyi was back in Nanjing by the 1st month.
1649

(age 39)
On the way to Beijing, Zhou met Wang Duo who viewed an album of paintings by Fan Qi which Zhou carried with him. In the 6th month, he began his return trip to Fujian, going via Yangzhou, Nanjing, Yunjian, and Hangzhou, accompanied by Hu Yukun and Luo Yao. In Nanjing he saw many friends. Gao Cen and Gao Fu saw him off at Shicheng. Chen Taisun prepared several tens of leaves of paintings by his literary society

In the 11th month, Guilin was captured by Qing troops and Chu Shisi was executed. Zeng Jing died at 83. Jiang Zhaoshu's book, *Wusheng shishi*, was probably circulated.
1650

members to give to Zhou. He composed poems with Wan Shouqi and Wang Shilu at Chen Taisun's Gongshu studio. In Hangzhou he saw Chen Hongshou again, who on this occasion painted forty-two works for Zhou, some of which must have been finished later in the year. By the 6th month, he was back in Fujian. In the 7th month, Huang Shu, the governor of Fujian, wrote an inscription on a landscape album leaf by Chen in Zhou's possession as well as on a portrait of Zhang Minbiao that Zhao Cheng painted in Beijing upon Zhou's request. In mid-winter, Zhou received the "Returning Home" scroll from Chen Hongshou; Chen, in his inscription, asked Zhou to show it to Xu You.

	(age 40)	
1651	In Fujian. In the autumn, Zhou took up his office at Yanping and went to Shaowu to subdue the Rebellion of Genghu. Probably in the spring, he received the painting "Modoujian" from Chen Hongshou and sent a poem in return. Zhang Xuezeng painted for Zhou.	Qing troops led by Ma Degong and Huang Shu seized Amoy during Zheng Chenggong's absence. Zheng began a campaign of retaliation along the Fujian coast. Fang Yizhi was ordained as a Chan Buddhist monk. Qian Qianyi was in Nanjing.

1651 — In Fujian. In the autumn, Zhou took up his office at Yanping and went to Shaowu to subdue the Rebellion of Genghu. Probably in the spring, he received the painting "Modoujian" from Chen Hongshou and sent a poem in return. Zhang Xuezeng painted for Zhou.

Qing troops led by Ma Degong and Huang Shu seized Amoy during Zheng Chenggong's absence. Zheng began a campaign of retaliation along the Fujian coast. Fang Yizhi was ordained as a Chan Buddhist monk. Qian Qianyi was in Nanjing.

(age 44)

1655 — In Beijing. In the 4th month, Cheng Zhengkui painted a handscroll for Zhou in Beijing (cat. no. 15). In the 6th month, Zhou was promoted to the rank of Junior Vice President of the Board of Finance and soon thereafter was again promoted to Senior Vice President of the Board of Civil Office. In the 6th month, Duntai, a Chinese Blue Bannerman and governor-general of Zhejiang and Fujian, accused Zhou of various crimes. He put together charges from different people who had held a grudge towards Zhou and sent to the court a memorial in which he charged Zhou Lianggong with cruelty and bribery during his Fujian service. In the 9th month, Wang Yuanqu painted the 16th leaf of the Taipei album for Zhou in Beijing. In the 11th month, Zhou was discharged from his position and ordered to go to Fujian for the investigation and trial. On his way to Fujian, accompanied by Hu Yukun from Beijing, Zhou stopped in Nanjing to see his parents. Zhou's fourth and fifth sons, Zaijian and Zaidu, were born.

The army of the Manchu prince Jidu forced Zheng's troops to withdraw from Hui-an, Nan-an, Tong-an, and Zhangzhou and to concentrate in Amoy. In the 10th month, Gong Dingzi was also indicted and deprived of his office and titles. Yun Xiang died.

(age 45)

1656 — In the 1st month, Zhou left Nanjing for Fujian; he arrived accompanied by Hu Yukun and other friends. In mid-summer, worried about the future of his collection, he gave some paintings to his friends. He gave Lin Sihuan, the Intendent of Coastal Defense in Fujian and one of the editors for Zhou's *Chidu xinchao*, the Tao Qian handscroll Chen Hongshou painted for him in 1650. He also gave him Bian Wenyu's painting that was originally given to him by Qian Qianyi in 1655. In the fall, Guo Gong (DHL 4/14) painted the *Bingshen rumin tu* ("Entering Fujian in the *bingshen* year [1656]") for Zhou which depicted Zhou and five friends, including Hu Yukun, who accompanied him when he returned to Fujian for his trial. In the 9th month, Zhou's mother and his son Zaiyang died in Nanjing.

Prince Gui (Zhu Yulang) fled to Yunnan.

(age 46)

In Fujian. At the trial the original accusations against Zhou that were made before his arrival were proven false. The five judges in charge handed down a verdict of innocent, which was celebrated by the local people. Fan Qi painted a landscape handscroll for Zhou that is now in the Liaoning Provincial Museum (see fig. 46, cat. no. 16).

(age 47)

In Fujian. Fearing involvement and responsibility in Zhou's case, the governor-general of Fujian sent the court both the earlier verdict of guilty and the later verdict of innocent. Vexed by the contradictory contents of the reports and the seriousness of the offense, the court ordered the Board of Punishments to arrest Zhou along with the five judges who declared his innocence and those who initially spoke out against him and later changed their minds. The Board was also ordered to reopen the judicial investigation of the case after the above-mentioned people had been transported to Beijing. In the 11th month, Zhou arrived at Beijing. Soon after his arrival, Lin Sihuan, to whom he had given the paintings of Cheng Hongshou and Bian Wenyu, was also arrested on an unrelated charge and sent to Beijing. In the 12th month, Zhou's father died in Nanjing.

(age 48)

In Beijing. Zhou built a hut at the Baiyun temple and called it "Yinshu Hut." Here he worked on his books *Shuying* and *Beixueshi* while waiting for his verdict. Xu You, detained with others at the Baiyun temple together with Zhou, painted "Night Conversation of Cold Crows," on which Zhou wrote a long poem. Zhou sold part of his collection of paintings, seals, ink-sticks and other antiques, as well as his poems written in his own calligraphy for money to provide for himself. Despite the confirmation of Zhou's innocence by all the accused, the Board of Punishments pronounced the death sentence for Zhou and the confiscation of all his property. The emperor, intrigued by the drastic difference between the original and second verdicts, ordered the judges to make a closer reexamination of the case. Zhou's second son, Zaiyang, died.

(age 49)

In Beijing. During the investigation of the case several people died under torture, including Lu Tolong, one of the five judges who defended Zhou's innocence. The Three High Courts of Judicature recommended capital punishment, which was met with the Shunzhi emperor's rebuke. He ordered postponement of the execution and a decrease of the punishment by one degree. Zhou was then locked up in jail. The trial began in the autumn, but before it was complete, a general amnesty was announced in celebration of the birthday of the empress dowager. Zhou's sentence was commuted from a death sentence to banishment to Ningguta, Liaoning. On the 5th day of the 12th month, Zhou learned the news of his exile to Ningguta and wrote letters to his friends in Nanjing, including Hu Yukun, as

Dong Qichang's book, *Huachanshi suibi*, edited by Yang Bu, has been published. Cheng Zhengkui resigned from office and returned to Nanjing, where he took the name Qingqi daoren. Wu Weiye resigned and returned to the south. Fang Hengxian and his family were exiled to Ningguta, Jinlin. Yang Bu died at 60.

1657

Zheng raised his largest army and captured a number of cities along the sea-coast of Zhejiang. Gong Xian probably returned from Yangzhou to Nanjing this year. Xiang Shengmo died at 62.

1658

In the 7th month, Zheng Chenggong took Jinjiang and Huizhou. In the 8th month, Qian Qianyi met Zheng's envoy at Songjiang. Zheng lost a battle on his way to Nanjing and was forced back to Amoy.

1659

Sun Chengze's book, *Gengzi xiaoxia ji*, was published. Lin Tieyai was released and returned to Fujian. Tai Mingye resigned from his office. Gu Mengyu died.

1660

well as his friends in Fujian. In the spring he asked his son Zaijun to print a collection of his poems entitled *Laigutang shi* or *Laigutang shiji* in Nanjing. These poems were collected and edited by Wu Daiguan while he was with Zhou during his imprisonment. Zhou finished writing *Shuying*. Hu Yukun painted an album of landscapes for Zhou entitled "Historic Spots in Nanjing" (cat. no. 17).

(age 50)

1661 The Shunzhi emperor died in the 1st month. On his death bed he sent down an edict of amnesty for prisoners which cited a special order for the release of Zhou Lianggong. The court proclaimed that the original accusations against Zhou were all unfounded and ordered the boards of Civil Office and of Punishments to reinstate Zhou in consideration of his meritorious deeds in the defense of Fuzhou while detained in 1656. Huang Jing came to Nanjing to see Zhou and stayed with him at his Qinghua Studio for more than a month, during which time he produced several paintings for Zhou. Kuncan painted a hanging scroll of landscape for Zhou on which Wu Yusheng wrote an inscription.

In the spring Zheng Chenggong captured Taiwan. The Suzhou Incident occurred during public mourning for the Sunzhi emperor. Wu Weiye was implicated in the incident and imprisoned in Beijing. In the 10th month, Zheng Zhilong was executed at Lingguta.

(age 51)

1662 In Nanjing. Zhou invited Zhang Feng to the Gaozuo temple; Zhang stayed with him several days and painted several album leaves; he also presented Zhou with a small album. Zhang Feng died of an illness shortly afterward. The boards of Civil Office and Punishments recommended to the court the reinstatement of Zhou with the rank of *qianfu* (signitary official) to the post of intendent of the Qingzhou circuit, Shandong province, and in the 10th month he received his appointment. While on his boat, Jiuyuan, Zhou wrote an inscription on Wang Shimin's landscape painting, dated 1606, painted after Zhao Mengfu. Zhou saw Wang Shizhen in Zhenzhou and Wang contributed another inscription to the Taipei album.

In the 4th month, Wu Sangui executed Prince Gui in Yunnan. On the 8th day of the 5th month, Zheng Chenggong died at 39. Probably in this year, Gong Xian moved to the south of Qingliang temple, where he named his garden Half-acre Garden.

(age 52)

1663 In the spring Zhou took up his duty at Qingzhou, Shandong. His sixth son, Zaiqing, was born. Zhou purchased Xu Yi's paintings through his friend Du Yanfen. He also produced a hanging scroll of calligraphy, transcribing one of his own poems in *qiyanliu* style.

Huang Jing died in the early winter. Hongren died at 54. Hu Jie died at 49.

(age 53)

1664 In Qingzhou, Shandong. Fang Yusan visited Zhou to congratulate him on his birthday and gave him three seals he had carved. Zhou wrote a long letter to Chen Shu in which he requested Chen's paintings. Hu Shikun, the brother of Hu Yukun, painted a handscroll of ink orchids for Zhou (fig. no. 55). Zhou wrote poems to mourn Xu You's death. In a letter to his son-in-law Wang Rongji, Zhou asked Wang to destroy the shrines built in his honor in Yangzhou, Fujian, and Shandong.

Fang Yizhi became abbot of the Qingyuan temple, Jiangxi. In the 5th month, Qian Qianyi died at 83. Xu You apparently died also in this year.

(age 54)

1665 In the summer, Wu Qiyuan visited Zhou in Qingzhou and painted for him two landscapes after Huang Gongwang. Wang Shizhen wrote another inscription on the Taipei album for Zhou at the Zhenyi pavilion.

(age 55)
Zhou was promoted to the post of Grain Intendent of Jiangnan.

Xie Cheng died.

1666

(age 56)
Fu Shan painted for Zhou a landscape handscroll that has a colophon by Zhang Yi and is now in the National Palace Museum, Taipei. In the winter Zhou published the *Yinshu wu shuying* (with prefaces by Jiang Chenglie, Gao Fu, etc.) and the *Zizhi xinshu* in Nanjing (*Shuying*, with preface by Zhou Zaijun).

The Kangxi emperor, at 14, assumed full administrative responsibilities.

1667

(age 57)
Wu Qiyuan sent Zhou an album of his paintings from Beijing. Wang Hui painted for Zhou the landscape handscroll *Xiashan yanyu tu* ("Summer Mountains and Misty Rain") which was presented with a long colophon by Wang Shimin.

Weng Ling probably died.

1668

(age 58)
In the 10th month Zhou was criticized by Yan Bao, the commander-in-chief of Transportation, for his handling of the government money outside of Zhou's jurisdiction. Zhou was dismissed from his office and deprived of his title pending trial.

Fa Rozhen was made lieutenant-governor of Anhui. Xu Yi and Fang Wen died.

1669

(age 59)
In Nanjing. Zhou was sentenced to death by strangulation. In the 2nd month, Zhou burnt his life's work including the *Du Hua Lu* as well as printing blocks including those of the *Shuying*. In the 7th month, Zhou's brother, Zhou Liangjie, died. In the 10th month, Zhou was acquitted of Yan Bao's accusation.

Fa Rozhen was dismissed from office for allegedly concealing a shortage in Zhou's accounts.

1670

(age 60)
Zhou saw Wang Hui in Nanjing and soon afterwards composed a congratulatory poem for Wang Hui's 40th birthday. Xie Bin painted Zhou's portrait when Zhou met him at West Lake. Yao Youbu wrote an inscription on the 6th leaf of the Taipei album at the Shengen temple in Nanjing, and He Cai wrote the frontispiece. In the autumn, Fang Hengxian was with Zhou looking at seals.

Wu Weiye died at 63.

1671

(age 61)
Wu Jin wrote his inscription for Zhou in the Taipei album at the end of spring in Zhou's Shulao tang. In the 1st month, Zhou went to Yangzhou and gathered with Wang Qi, Cheng Sui, Wang Jun, Sun Zhiwei, Wu Jiaji, and others, and returned in the 2nd month. In the 5th month, Zhou suddenly fell ill, and died the following month.

1672

Frontispiece by He Cai (fl. late 17th c., jinshi 1649) for cat. no. 6 (see p. 163). Reads: "Enchanted to my heart's content!" From Album of Landscapes by Famous Masters Collected by Zhou Lianggong. *Ink on paper; each leaf 29.2 cm x 34 cm. National Palace Museum, Taipei, collection.*

Catalogue

1. ALBUM OF LANDSCAPES BY FAMOUS
MASTERS COLLECTED BY ZHOU LIANGGONG
(ZHOU LIYUAN SHOUJI MINGREN HUACE)

Hu Yukun (fl. ca. 1630s–1670s DHL 2/5)
Chen Hongshou (1599–1652 DHL 1/15)
Zou Zhe (1636–d. ca. 1708 DHL 1/12)
Zhu Ruiwu (fl. mid-17th c. DHL 1/13)
Gao Cen (fl. ca. 1645–1689 DHL 3/14)
Shi Lin (d. ca. 1672 DHL 4/22)

Album of 16 leaves
Paintings: 8 leaves (A–H), specifications and
    measurements (see below)
Colophons: 8 facing leaves (AA–HH), measurements
    approximately same as paintings
Collection: The British Museum, London

Leaf A
    Hu Yukun
    "Mount Qi"
    Before 1652
    Colors on paper, H 24.8 cm; W 32.3 cm
    Artist's seal: "Yukun" (square relief, lower right)

    Colophons (painting)
    1. Wang Duo (1592–1652): one column of running
        script (upper right)
        Signature: Wang Duo
        Seal: "Wang Duo" (double seal, both square
            intaglio)
    2. Shen Hao (1586–after 1661 DHL 3/11): six
        columns of free-style standard script (upper
        middle)
        Inscription: "This painting looks like Zhao
            Daonian's [Zhao Liangrang, fl. 1070–1100]
            work. But its ultimate source is Sengyu's
            [Zhang Sengyu, fl. 500–550] boneless paint-
            ing. Shen Hao."
        Seal: "Langqing" (rectangle intaglio)

    3. Yu Dong (1618–1704): seven columns of running
        script (upper left)
        Signature: Huan Dong. Seal: "Huian" (square
            intaglio)
    4. Zhao Dao (fl. mid-17th c.): three columns of
        standard script (middle left)
        Signature: Dao
        Seal: "Dao" (oval relief)

    Colophons (silk mounting)
    5. Yang Sisheng (1621–1644, *jinshi* 1646): one
        column of running script (right top)
    6. Ji Zhi (*jinshi* 1658): two characters reading "Wu-
        mo" ("No ink") in running script (right
        bottom)
        Seal: Ji Zhi zhi yin (square relief)
    7. Shen Yifang (fl. mid-17th c.): ten columns of
        running script (top right)
        Signature: "Shen Yifang inscribed this."
        Seal: Zi Weisi (square intaglio)
    8. Ni Can (born 1627): eight columns of running
        script (top left)
        Signature: "Yanyuan, Ni Can inscribed this."
        Seal: Chen Zan (square, half relief, half intaglio)
        Collector's seals: Deng Shi (modern): Deng Shi
            (square intaglio, lower left corner)

Leaf AA
    Colophons
    1. Ji Yingzhong (1609–1689): ten columns of
        archaic standard script (leaf proper)
        Signature: "On a summer day, I happened to
            read a history of paintings where I found the
            above-quoted writing . . . by Xuanzhai [Dong
            Qichang, 1555–1636]. It is as if he anticipated
            what Hu Yuanrun would accomplish in his
            painting. I wrote this to make Liweng [Zhou
            Lianggong] smile. Yingzhong, *hao* Bomian-
            gong."
        Seals: Ji Yingzhong yin (square intaglio); Bozi

(square relief); Meian (square relief, upper right)

2. Wang Shizhen (1634–1711): twenty-one columns of running script (silk mounting, top)
   Signature: "Wang Shizhen from Langye."
   Collector's seal: Deng Shi: Qiumei baoai (square relief, lower right corner)

Leaf B

Chen Hongshou

"Landscape after Mi Fu"

ca. 1650

Ink and colors on paper, H 24.7 cm; W 32.1 cm

Artist's signature: one column of running script: "Hongshou painted this upon the request of my Buddhist sworn-brother Yuanlao [Zhou Lianggong]"

Artist's seal: Hongshou (double seal, both square intaglio)

Colophons (silk mounting)

1. Wang Jun (fl. mid-17th c.): two columns of running script (right top)
   Signature: Wang Jun. Seal: Qiurun (square relief)

2. Unidentified: one column of running script (right bottom)
   Signature: Lu? Li. Seal: Wu? Gong (rectangle relief)

3. Wu Shan (fl. late 17th c.): seven columns of running script (top)
   No signature
   Seal: Wu Shan (square, half intaglio and half relief)
   Collector's seal: Deng Shi: Qiumei (square relief, lower right corner)

Leaf BB

Colophon

1. Huang Shu (fl. mid-17th c. DHL fn. 173): ten columns of running script (quoted by Zhou Lianggong in DHL 1/E.15)
   Signature: "In the year of *kuiwei* [1643], I bade farewell to Zhanghou at the capital. The following year, I received in Jin Daoyin's [Jin Bao] mail-case a letter from him accompanied by a painted fan. They were intended to give me earnest advice. Only this old man did not utter hackneyed words at all. In the year of *jiqiu* [1649], I visited Hulin [Hangzhou]. At the office of Nan Shenglu [*jinshi* 1637], I saw dozens of nature-sketches that Zhanghou had painted for him. They were powerful and unusual and had a three-dimensional quality. I

said, "We should take good care of Laochi's wrist [i.e. his paintings]. We should not let him paint again, since [such talent] may incur the wrath [i.e. jealousy] of dragons, thunder, and demons who may snatch him away from us. Again the following year [1650] when Liyuan took out four albums of paintings to show me, I saw more of Zhanghou's paintings. I felt as if I had seen Zhanghou in person, bareheaded and shirtless with his right hand holding a wine cup and the left scratching his head and stroking his feet; while discussing old current affairs his mouth jutted out and his eyes opened wide. [With all these paintings and talents] he has not been snatched away by dragons, thunder, demons. He certainly must have a divine aura and a primordial destiny which safeguards him. Ill-fortuned man that I am, every dot and line by Hongshou in my collection was burnt during the war. Not even a single painting remains. Some other day I will have to beg Shenglu for some paintings or Liyuan for some albums. On the 18th day of the 7th month in the *gengyin* year [1650], after the night watch struck three times, I wrote several words, while trying to keep the lamp wick straight. Lamentations over ink [painting] causes the meeting and separating of friends, and [grief and joy in] human affairs of life and death are not so much different from each other. How much more so do I feel since I have just finished inscribing a posthumous portrait of Master Zhang Linzong [Zhong Minbiao, 1570–1642]! How can it not deepen my sense of loss? Guduo daoren, Huang Shu wrote this at Diyi Pavilion at Sanshan." (This colophon, except the last paragraph, is recorded in Zhou Lianggong's biography of Chen Hongshou in DHL 1/15. See my annotated translation.)
   Seals: Shu (square relief); Qiwen tang (tall rectangle relief)
   Collector's seal: Deng Shi: Fengyu lou (square relief, lower right)

Leaf C

Zou Zhe

"Landscape"

before 1665

Ink on paper. H 25.5 cm; W 32.8 cm

Artist's seals: Zou Zhe zhi yin (square intaglio, lower left, top); Zi Fanglu (square intaglio, lower left, bottom)

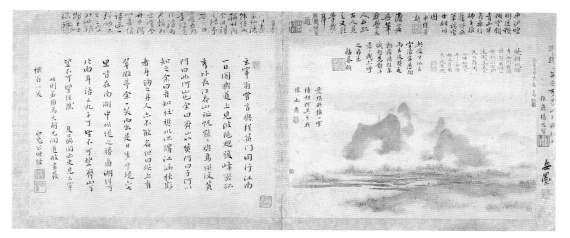

Leaf AA   1   *Leaf A*

Leaf BB   1   *Leaf B*

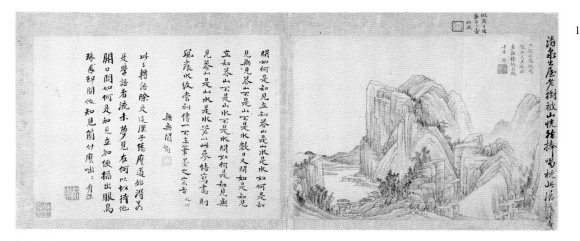

Leaf CC   1   *Leaf C*

Colophons

1. Shao Qian (1581–1665): four columns of standard script (painting, upper right)

   Signature: Qian

   Seal: Qiantian si yin (square intaglio)

2. Cao Erkan (1617–1690): one column of running script (silk mounting, right)

   Signature: Gu an.

   Seal: damaged (square intaglio)

3. Unidentified: two columns of running script (silk mounting, top)

   Signature: Shijun

   Seal: damaged (square relief)

   Collector's seals: Deng Shi: Qiumei (square intaglio)

Leaf CC

Colophons

1. Fang Yizhi (1611–1671 DHL 2/7): five columns of standard script

   Signature: Wuwu guan Zhixing

   Seal: Zhi (square relief)

2. Cheng Zhengkui (1604–1676 DHL 2/6): four columns of standard script

   Signature: Qingqi

   Seal: Cheng Zhengkui (square intaglio)

   Collector's Seal: Deng Shi: Shun-de Deng Shi Fengyu lou zhenzang guwu ji (square relief, lower left)

Leaf D

Zhu Ruiwu

"Landscape"

Undated

Ink and colors on paper. H 25.5 cm; W 32.8 cm

Artist's signature: Seng Wu

Artist's seals: Qishi (rectangle relief); Seng rui zhi yin (square intaglio, left)

Colophons

1. Zhao Jizheng (fl. 17th c.): one column of running script (silk mounting, right)

2. Zhao Dao, dated 1669: ten columns of running script (silk mounting, top)

   Signature: "On the sixth day of the fifth month in the *jiyu* year [1669], after the full moon, Gong Banqian [Gong Xian] and I viewed this album together and admired Liyuan's [Zhou Lianggong] profound appreciation of art and connoisseurship. Zhao Dao inscribed this."

   Seal: Zhao Dao zhi yin (square intaglio)

3. Unidentified: ten characters of running script (silk mounting, bottom): "The scene in this painting resembles the autumn and winter scenery at the Zhanggan temple [in Nanjing]."

No signature

Seal: [ ]-ding (damaged, rectangle relief)

Collector's seal: Deng Shi: Deng Shi (square intaglio)

Leaf DD

Colophons

1. Chen Ke (fl. mid-17th c.)

   (a) three columns of running script.

   Signature: "Jingmei, Chen Ke inscribed this."

   Seals: Chen Ke zhi yin (square, half intaglio and half relief)

   (b) eleven columns of running script: "Earlier people said that unless one reads ten thousand books and rids himself of the mundane dust from his heart he can not paint, nor can he understand the art of painting. I remember it was only in the *bingshu* [1646] year when I spent a year at the home of my old friend Zhang Buzin from Zhongahou [Kaifeng], the magistrate of Shanghai, that I at last had an opportunity to see Master Liyuan's [Zhou Lianggong] writing on a small piece of paper, in which he said, 'My only pleasure is to buy books.' Later I had an opportunity to read a fine edition of the collected works of Ruan Tachong [Ruan Hanwen, fl. early 17th c.] and Zhang Linzong [Zhang Minbiao, 1570–1642] which Master Zhou published. The two books contained a number of poems [written over twenty years expressing a] longing to meet Master Zhou for almost twenty years. Suddenly I am able to see an album from Master Zhou's eyes and looked at it so many times. What the album contains is so extraordinary and unprecedented. I have regretted that I could not meet the "sage" [Zhou Lianggong]. Now I feel I can simply put myself amidst Master Zhou's ten thousand books [reflected in his collection and paintings]."

   Signature: "In the 1st month of autumn in the *xinchou* year [1661], Chen Ke from Wumen [Suzhou] inscribed this again."

   Seals: Jingmei xiaoyin (square relief); Xiaoguan (square intaglio)

   Collector's seal: Deng Shi: Deng Shi (rectangle relief, lower right)

Leaf E

Gao Cen

"Landscape"

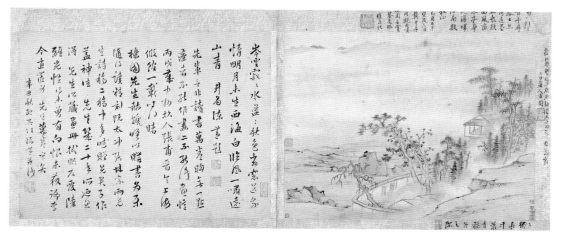

Leaf DD   Leaf D

Leaf EE   Leaf E

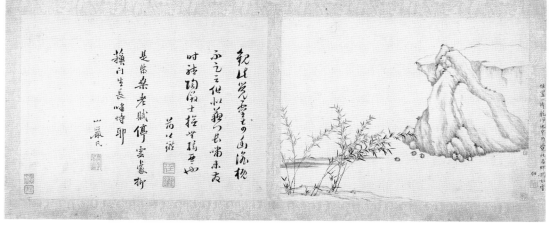

Leaf FF   Leaf F

Ca. late 1640s
Ink on paper. H 24.8 cm; W 32.3 cm
Artist's seal: Gao Cen (lower right corner)

Colophons
1. Dai Mingye (*jinshi* 1634), dated 1650: one
   column of standard script (silk mounting,
   right, top)
   Signature: "In the second month of the *gengyin*
   year [1650], Dai Mingye viewed this to receive
   his instruction."
   Seals: Dai Mingye (square intaglio); Daomo
   (square intaglio)
2. Yang Sisheng (fl. 17th c.): one column of standard script (silk mounting, right, bottom):
   undeciphered
   Signature: Yang Sisheng. Seal: Yulong (oval
   relief)
3. Jin Junming (1602–1675): ten columns of
   running script (silk mounting, top)
   Signature: Jin Chen
   Seal: Jin Junming yin (square intaglio)
   Collector's seal: Deng Shi: Deng Shi (square
   intaglio, lower left)
   One seal: damaged (square intaglio, lower right,
   above the artist's seal)

Leaf EE
Colophons
1. Chen Daisun (*jinshi* 1640): three columns of
   running script
   Signature: "The above-quoted poem . . . is from
   an inscription Dongpo [Su Shi] wrote on his
   painting. It perfectly illustrates this painting.
   Therefore, I copied it here to make Taoan
   [Zhou Lianggong] smile. A junior, Taisun."
   Seal: Yue An (rectangle relief, upper right)
2. Chen Hongshou: two columns of running script
   Signature: Lianlao.
   Seal: Hongshou (square intaglio)
   Collector's seal: Deng Shi: Fengyu lou (square
   relief, lower right)

Leaf F
Gao Cen
"Landscape"
Undated
Ink on paper. H 24.8 cm; W 32.4 cm
Artist's seal: Gao Cen (square relief, lower right)
Colophon by an unidentified writer: one column
   of standard script (silk mounting, right).
Signature: Hong.
Seal: Nengren (square relief)

Collector's seal: Deng Shi: Qimei (square intaglio,
   left, above the artist's)

Leaf FF
Colophons
1. Zhuang Tinglong (died ca. 1662): three columns
   of running script
   Signature: Zhuang Tinglong
   Seal: Tinglong (double seal, square relief)
2. Wu Shan: two columns of running script
   Signature: Shanyan shi
   Seal: Yanzi Wushan (rectangle relief)
   Collector's seals
      1. Deng Shi: Fengyu lou (square relief)
      2. Gao Yanru (modern): Yanru xinshang
         (square relief)

Leaf G
Shi Lin
"Landscape after Ni Zan"
Undated
Ink on paper. H 24.7 cm; W 32.2 cm
Artist's seals: Shilin si yin (square intaglio); Shi
   Yujian (square intaglio)
Colophon by Zhao Dao: two columns of running
   script (silk mounting, right)
Signature: Yiren, Zhao Dao
Seal: Zhao Dao zhi yin (square intaglio)
Collector's seals: Deng Shi: Qiumei (square
   intaglio, left)
Zhou Lianggong's seal: Xue Tao (rectangle
   intaglio, damaged, lower right)

Leaf GG
Colophon
1. Zhao Jizheng: four columns of running script.
   Signature: "To receive Master Liweng's [Zhou
   Lianggong] [instructions?], a younger stu-
   dent Jizheng from Xijin [Nanjing] [wrote
   this]."
   Seal: Zhao Jizheng yin (square intaglio); Zhuo
   zhai (rectangle intaglio)
   Collector's seals
      1. Deng Shi: Fengyu lou (square relief)
      2. Gao Yanru (modern): Yanru xinshang
         (square relief)

Leaf H
Shi Lin
"Landscape"
Dated 1647
Ink on paper. H 24.7 cm; W 32.2 cm
Artist's signature: "Two days before the 1st month

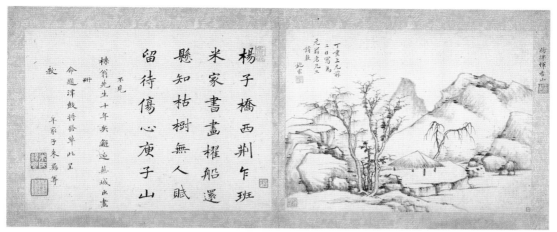

Leaf GG   *Leaf G*

1

Leaf HH   *Leaf H*

of the *dinghai* year [1647], I painted this in order to receive Yuanweng's [Zhou Lianggong] instruction. Shi Lin."

Artist's seals: Shi Lin yin (square intaglio); Shi Yujian (square intaglio, left)

Colophon by Wang Yun (fl. mid 17th c.): one column of standard script (silk mounting)

No signature

Seal: Wang Yun zhi yin (square intaglio)

Collector's seal: Deng Shi: Qiumei (square intaglio, lower right)

Leaf HH

Colophon

1. Zhu Yizun (1629–1709): four columns of free-style standard script

   Signature: "I had not seen Master Liweng for ten years until I happened to see him at Wucheng [Yangzhou]. He took out this album and asked for my inscription. Since my

boat was about to leave, I hurriedly wrote this for his instruction. Zhu Yizun, a son of your colleague."

Seals: Xiushui (rectangle relief, upper right); Zhu xichang shi (square intaglio); Wosheng zhi qu sui zai shu wei dahuang loyue zai ji zhiang wangzhi guiyu shi (square relief)

Collector's seal: Deng Shi: Fengyu lou (square relief)

Published

Zhou Liyuan [Zhou Lianggong] shouji mingren huace. Shanghai: Shenzhou guoguangshe, 1966

Roderick Whitefield. "The Aesthetics of Ch'ing Paintings," in *Apollo*, vol. CVI, no. 188 (October 1977) (paintings only)

Yu Yi, ed. Ming Chen Hongshou huaji, Taipei: Zhonghua shuhua chubanshe, 1974, p. 52 (Leaf B only)

2. PLAYING THE QIN (*Fuqin tu*) (Portrait of Zhou Lianggong)

Yu Zhiding (1647–1701? 05?)

Two album leaves (A, AA) mounted as a hanging
    scroll
Painting Leaf (A): ink and colors on paper, H 31.8 cm;
    W 34.3 cm
Colophon Leaf (AA): H 31.8 cm; W 34.3 cm
Collection: Wang Chi-ch'ien (modern), New York

Leaf A
    Undated
    Artist's inscription: "I painted this *Fuqin tu* ("play-
        ing the qin") for the eminent literatus Lilao
        [Zhou Lianggong]."
    Signed: Yu Zhiding from Guangling [Yangzhou]
    Artist's seal: "Shangji" (square, half relief and half
        intaglio)
    Collector's seal: "Zhichen sicang" (square relief),
        Zhu Zhichen (modern)

Leaf AA
    Colophon by Zhou Ming (fl. 17th c.; DHL, fn. 541):
        11 columns of archaic standard script. Inscrip-
        tion: "I respectfully inscribed the painting of
        my respectful uncle Liweng [Zhou Lianggong]
        'Playing the Qin,' your nephew Ming."
    Seals: "Lufeng" (round relief); "Chen Ming seyin"
        (square intaglio)

2

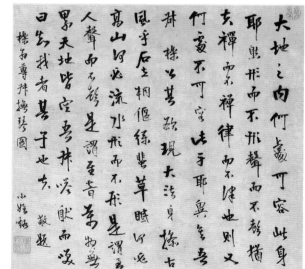

3. TEN BAMBOO STUDIO PAINTING MANUAL

Late 17th – early 18th century edition (first published
    in Nanjing in early 17th century)
16 vols., with a total of 106 double pages
Woodblock print
Each page: H 25 cm; W 15.3 cm
Guan Lu Yuan Collection

One leaf: "How the raised hand should hold the
    brush."
Compiler: Hu Zhengyen
Proof-reader: Gao Yang
Co-proof-readers: Ling Yunhan, Wu Shenguan, Wei
    Zhihuang, Wei Zhike, Hu Rongshi, Gao Yu
Yang Wencong's colophon
Xie Cheng's flowers
Gao Yang's banana and rock
Two anonymous paintings of fruits and vegetables

4. CALLIGRAPHY [a couplet composed and written by Zhou Lianggong]

Zhou Lianggong (1612–1672)

Two hanging scrolls
Ink on paper
Each: H 114.6 cm; W 25.2 cm
Guan Lu Yuan Collection
5 characters on the right scroll read: "I use my own
    method"
5 characters on the left scroll read: "I also love my hut"
Artist's signature: Zhou Lianggong
Artist's seals: Zhou Lianggong *zi* Yuanliang (square
    intaglio); Liyuan (square relief)

5. CALLIGRAPHY [POEMS DEDICATED TO SOME OF THE *Du Hua Lu* PAINTERS AND FOUND IN THE *Du Hua Lu*]

Zhou Lianggong

Album of 28 leaves
Ink on paper
Calligraphy proper, each: H 26.5 cm; W 16 cm
Guan Lu Yuan Collection
Title (4 characters written by Zhou Lianggong):
    "Zhenyi ding shi" (Poems from the Zhenyi pavilion)
Poems are dedicated to: Wang Shilu, Zou Dian, Fan

Qi, Wu Hong, Hu Yukun, Hu Shikun, Gao Cen, and others.

Artist's inscription: "I wrote [these poems] for my senior Youlao for his instruction. [Written by] Junyi Zhou Lianggong respectfully"

Artist's seals: Zhou Lianggong yin (square intaglio); Zhoushi Lianggong (square relief)

6. Album of Landscapes by Famous Masters Collected by Zhou Lianggong (Zhou Lianggong ji mingjia shanshui ce) [not in exhibition]

Xie Cheng (1612–1666 DHL 3/12)
Yan Shengsun (1623–1702)
Wang Hui (1632–1717 DHL 2/11)
Zhu Ruiwu (fl. mid-17th c. DHL 1/13)
Gu Fu (fl. ca. 1658–1679 DHL/SL)
Kuncan (ca. 1612–1693 DHL 2/8)
Sheng Dan (fl. mid-17th c. DHL 4/15)
Xiang Shengmo (1597–1658 DHL/SL)
Ye Xin (fl. ca. 1640–1673 DHL 3/19)
Zhou Quan (fl. mid-17th c. DHL/SL)
Cheng Zhengkui (1604–1676 DHL 2/6)
Wang Yuanqu (fl. mid-17th c. DHL/SL)
Gong Xian (1619–1689 DHL 2/15)
Yun Xiang (1586–1655 DHL 1/16)

Album of forty leaves
    Frontispiece (a–d): ink on paper, each leaf,
        H 29.2 cm; W 34 cm.
    Painting: eighteen leaves (A–R), specification and
        measurements (see below)
    Colophons: eighteen facing leaves (AA–RR), mea-
        surement approximately same as the paintings,
        except Leaf OO (H 27.1 cm; W 17.6 cm)
    Collection: National Palace Museum, Taipei
    Frontispiece (a–d) by He Cai (fl. late 17th c., *jinshi*
        1649): Four character title in running script
        (one character on each leaf): "Enchanted to my
        heart's content!" (*xin huai*). Seals: Qunji ting
        (tall rectangle relief); Xinhai [corresponding to
        1671]; Wenduan gong sun (square relief); He
        Cai (square relief) (see p. 154)

Leaf A
    Xie Cheng
    Undated
    Ink and colors on paper. H 24.8 cm; W 32.3 cm.
    Artist's seals: Xie Cheng zhi yin (square intaglio);
        one seal undeciphered
    Colophon by Cao Erkan (1617–1690): nine

columns of running script.
    Signature: "I have composed a poem in the tune of
        the "Jianzi mulanhua" [a type of *ci* invented by
        Wei Zhuang in the Five Dynasties] using the
        characters in the inscription by Langqing [Shen
        Hao] [on the facing leaf], to present it to Mas-
        ter Liweng [Zhou Lianggong] for his instruc-
        tion. Cao Erkan from Wutang [Suzhou] wrote
        this."
    Seals: Lufang (rectangle intaglio); Erkan (square
        relief); Gu-an (square intaglio)
    Collector's seals: Qing imperial seals
        1. Gaozong (Qianlong, r. 1736–95): Shiqu
            baozhi (square relief); Baozhi san bian
            (square relief)
        2. Renzong (Jiaqing, r. 1796–1820): Jiaqing
            yulan zhi bao (oval relief)

Leaf AA
    Colophons
    1. Shen Hao (1586 – after 1661 DHL 3/11): four
        columns of standard script
        Signature: "Landao zhe inscribed this."
        Seal: Langqing (square relief)
    2. Wang Shizhen (1634–1711): seven columns of
        running script
        Signature: Chanti [Sanskrit, *kasanti* (tolerance)],
            Wang Shizhen inscribed this."
        Seals: Jiazai boshan jinshui zhi jian (tall rectangle
            relief); Wang Shizhen yin (square intaglio);
            Chanti (square relief)

Leaf B
    Wang Hui
    ca. late 1660s
    Ink and colors on silk. H 25.1 cm; W 21.8 cm
    Artist's inscription: "[After] Li Cheng's 'Mountains
        after Snowfall.'"
    Collector's seal: Sundi (Emperor Xuantong, r.
        1909–1911): Xuantong yulan zhi bao (oval
        relief)

Leaf BB
    Colophon by Wang Shizhen (dated 1670): fifteen
        columns of running script: "In the summer of
        the *yisi* year [1655] (corrected to 1666 [by Wang
        Shizhen]), I, Zhen, stayed at [Zhou Liang-
        gong's] Zhenyi Pavilion in Qingzhou [Shan-
        dong] and inscribed albums of paintings for
        him. I also remember I inscribed poems on
        paintings for him when I was in Yangzhou in
        the *xinchou* year [1661] as well as in Zhenzhou
        in the *renyin* year [1662]; they are all together
        no less than thirty to forty pieces. I have done

this time and again, because I never knew where I would again see him. Feeling sad, I am [again] writing a few words at the end.

"In the summer of the *gengshu* year [1670], he [Zhou] had just got into trouble while working in Nanjing. I, Zhen, was then a sojourner in Yuanfu [Songjiang, Jiangsu]. He asked the eighty-year-old Ding Jizhi to visit me with a letter he had written and four albums which he asked me to inscribe. I understood his intention. Lately living like a good-for-nothing in a difficult situation, I have long abandoned my brush. Appreciating his sincerity I wrote a little more than twenty colophons for him. It has been already four or five years since the last time I wrote [on his paintings]. Whenever I think of current affairs, I become tearful. He lives aloof and unworldly. Although he has been trapped in the "gan" [a Yijing hexagram for "danger"], he keeps himself calm. I am certain he will be saved from the danger. I do not know when Master Ding will be back at his gate and when he will be able to read what I have written down. If he remembers what we said to each other in Qingzhou, Zhou would also certainly break into laughter as I do. On the 1st day of the 5th month under lamplight, junior Wang Shizhen from Yuanfu village respectfully wrote this."

Seals: Zhishi ju (tall rectangle intaglio, upper left corner); Wang Shizhen yin (square intaglio, lower right corner)

Leaf C
Gu Fu
Dated 1668
Ink on paper. H 27.2 cm; W 26.3 cm.
Artist's inscription: six columns of running script: "Earlier people said that it is almost impossible to learn to paint like Ni Zan [1301–1374]. Even the divine and marvelous master Shen Zhou [1427–1509] regretted that he could not achieve the essence of Ni Zan. In fact this is because Yunlin's [Ni Zan] achievement was through [spiritual] resonance. Therefore all efforts to learn to paint like Ni are fruitless. In the winter of the *wushen* year [1668], I playfully imitate [Ni Zan's] painting, "Anchu Studio," in my family collection. Although my idea is somewhat similar to his, the result is a pitiful imitation. What can I do?"
Artist's signature: Gu Fu
Artist's seals: Dongzhai (rectangle intaglio); Gu Fu

(double seal, square, half relief, half intaglio); Laihou (square relief, lower right)

Leaf CC
Colophon by Fang Hengxian (*jinshi* 1647 DHL 2/12): five columns of running script
Signature: "Asking for the instructions of Vice-minister Liweng [Zhou Lianggong]. Fang Hengxian."
Seals: Shifu zhai (round relief, upper left corner); Fang Hengxian yin (square intaglio); Shao-cun (square relief)

Leaf D
Sheng Dan
Undated
Ink and colors on paper. H 23.9 cm; W 31.1 cm
Artist's seal: Sheng Dan (square intaglio)

Leaf DD
Colophon dated 1670 by Yun Shouping (1633–1690 DHL/SL): nine columns of running script.
Signature: "In the 9th month of the *gengshu* year [1670], I wrote this to receive Master Liweng's instruction. Nantian caoyi, Yun Shouping."
Seals: Mojing (tall oval relief, upper right corner); Zhengsu (square relief); Shouping (square intaglio)

Leaf E
Ye Xin
Undated
Ink and colors on silk. H 19.1 cm; W 25.8 cm
Artist's seal: Rongmu (rectangle intaglio)

Leaf EE
Colophons
1. Wang Shizhen: three columns of running script
   Signature: "I inscribed Ye Rongmu's painting for Master Liweng [Zhou Lianggong] in order to receive his instruction. Wang Shizhen." (This colophon is recorded in Wang Shihzhuan, *Yuyang shizhuan*, 12/2, but curiously there it appears under a work by Cheng Zhengkui for Zhou Lianggong.)
   Seal: Wang Shizhen yin (square intaglio)
2. Li Liangnian (1635–1694), dated 1670: two columns of standard script
   Signature: "My boat was moored at Yangzi River. When I was about to leave for the capital, I visited Master Liweng to bid farewell. He took out several albums to show me, on which I respectfully wrote a poem in order to

Leaf AA   *Leaf A*

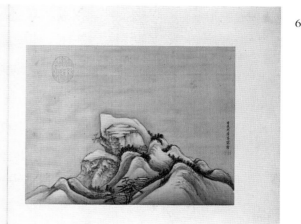

Leaf BB   *Leaf B*

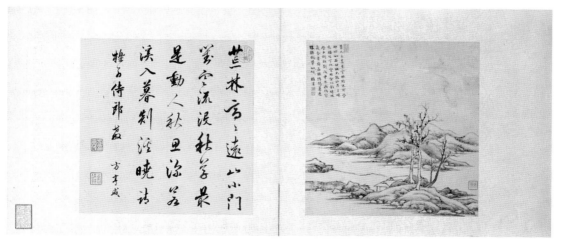

Leaf CC   *Leaf C*

6

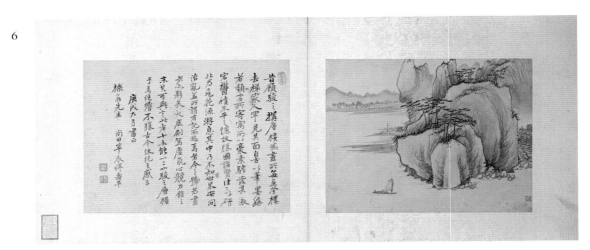

Leaf DD   *Leaf D*

6

Leaf EE   *Leaf E*

6

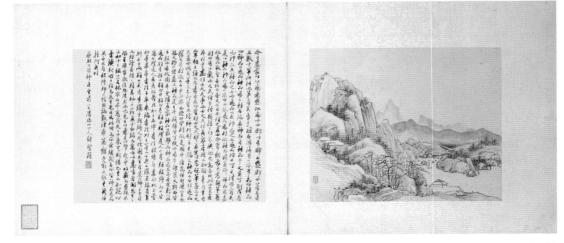

Leaf FF   *Leaf F*

receive his instruction. On the seventh day of the sixth month, in the summer of the *geng-shu* year [1670]. Li Liangnian from Jiaxing."

Seals: Li Shijiu (square relief); Wuzengfu (square relief)

Leaf F

Cheng Zhengkui

Undated

Ink on paper. H 23.6 cm; w 28.9 cm

Artist's seal: Zhengkui (rectangle intaglio)

Leaf FF

Colophon by Gong Xian (dated 1669): 23 columns of running script: "Nowadays, Jiangnan is the most important center of painting. Among its fourteen counties, however, the capital city of Nanjing is the most prominent. It has several tens of eminent painters. But if we count all those who can paint, the number exceeds one thousand. Now those men of fame fall into two schools and three classes. The classes are called *nengpin* (able class), the *shenpin* (divine class), and the *yipin* (untrammeled class). The able class is accomplished, but there is little more to be said for it. As for the divine class, there is nothing in the able class that can measure up to it. The divine class stands above the able class, while the untrammeled class stands even higher than the divine class. It is really quite impossible for words to describe the untrammeled class.

"The able and divine classes may be regarded as one school, namely, the orthodox school. The untrammeled class constitutes the heterodox school. Those in the able class are painting masters, while those in the divine class are patriarchs of painting. But those in the untrammeled class are rare sages, there is no category that can contain them; on the contrary, it is impossible not to speak of them simply as scholar-painters. Connoisseurs of today, when they see lofty and far-reaching paintings, say that these paintings have "scholar's spirit." And even men of no refinement, in words of praise that have the intent to ridicule, speak of a painting, "This is only a painting of a scholar-official." But isn't it clear that painting is not a matter of becoming a scholar-official, and that the scholar-officials do not constitute a particular category of painters? They do not know that Yan Liben was Li Tang's [Gaozi of the Tang dynasty] prime minister, and that Wang Wei also was deputy minister in the Shangshu Secre-

tariat? Were they not then scholar-officials? But if they decide to equate lofty and far-reaching paintings with the paintings of the scholar-officials, then what of Ni [Ni Zan], Huang [Huang Gongwang], Dong [Dong Yuan], and Ju [Juran], for what had they to do with the category of court-officials?

"In my opinion, the able class cannot disregard the untrammeled class; furthermore, the heterodox class can not disregard the orthodox class, then there would be no one in the world but noble Buddhist monks and Daoist priests and there would be no capped and robed scholar-officials. If in painting there were only an able class then Wang Dou and Yan Shou [of the Warring States Period, both subjects of King Xuan of Qi] and their like could all serve as court runner while Chao Fu and Xu You could be banished and made into grooms.

"Among the Jinling painters, the "able class" painters are most numerous. But the divine and the untrammeled class also have several artists each. At the head of the untrammeled class are the two "Qi," Shiqi and Qingqi. Shiqi is Can dao ren [Kuncan]. Qingqi is Vice-president Cheng [Cheng Zhengkui]. Both gentlemen live in Nanjing. Can dao ren's painting looks like a man with coarse clothing and disheveled hair; so it is like the calligraphy of Master Wang from Mengjin [Wang Duo]. Vice-president Cheng's painting looks like a man of icy flesh [cool appearance] and jade bones [lofty character]; thus, it is like the calligraphy of Master Dong from Huating [Dong Qichang]. In the discussion of the art of calligraphy for the last hundred years, both masters, Wang and Dong, should hold formidable positions. In the discussion of the art of painting, the same will be true of the two "Qi" from our days, for how could they relinquish their positions?

"The poet Master Zhou Liyuan [Zhou Lianggong] has a propensity for painting. He is a government official in this place [Nanjing]. He built the Du Hua Lou (Viewing Paintings Pavilion) where he stored his cases of [album] paintings, not to mention his collection of antiques. All painters of renown in this country, upon learning of his reputation, come fast [to visit him] like shooting stars or lightning, only being afraid to arrive late. How much more so when he summons them in writing and welcomes them with money. Therefore [their paintings] fill his desk and bed. His collection [of books] is not limited to the Thirteen Classics. It includes the twenty-one histories, the 5,000 chapters of Linzong [compiled by Guo Tai of the Eastern Han], and thirty cartloads of Maoxian [by Zhong Hua of the Zhen]. When I climb up to the pavilion, I am at a loss what to read first [among these books]. One day, I visited him by chance. He took out this album for me to see. I have carefully viewed it four times. They [the leaves in the album] are all in the class of divine and untrammeled. Among them, I especially liked the one leaf by Vice-president Cheng [Cheng Zhengkui]. Therefore I noted down several words. Luckily this album already has many writings by others [in which they expressed their admiration for him], otherwise my writing would have been criticized as mere flattery."

Signature: "In the reign of Kangxi, in the mid-winter of *jiyu* year [1669], one day before the 11th month, Gong Xian, a man from the foot of Mount Qingliang [in Nanjing], inscribed this."

Seal: Xian (rectangle intaglio)

(Translation is based on Lippe, "Kung Hsien," pp. 159–160, and Silbergeld, "Kung Hsien," pp. 208–210, with slight modification; see Fang Hengxian's critical comment on this colophon in DHL 2/12)

Leaf G
Gong Xian
Undated
Ink on paper. H 23.5 cm; W 33 cm
Artist's seal: Banqian (rectangle relief)

Leaf GG
Colophons dated 1671 by Rao Yupu (fl. mid. 17th c.)
1. Three columns of running script
   Signature: "In the 6th month of the *xinhai* year [1671] when I happened to stay at the Cheng-an Buddhist monastery [in Nanjing], Master Liweng [Zhou Lianggong] asked me to inscribe [this album]. Therefore I wrote this in order to receive his instruction. A younger student from Nanzhou [Sichuan], Rao Yupu."
   Seals: Wulu (rectangle intaglio, upper right corner); Rao Yupu yin (square intaglio); Jiangwen (square relief)
2. Three columns of running script
   Signature: "Yupu inscribed it again."
   Seal: damaged (square intaglio)

Leaf H
Yan Shengsun
Undated
Ink on paper. H 25.1 cm; W 31.7 cm
Artist's signature: Yan Shengsun
Artist's seals: Shengsun (square relief); Qiushui (square intaglio)

Leaf HH
Colophon dated 1670 by Wu Jin (fl. late 17th c.): thirteen columns of standard script, transcribing three poems by Wei Yingwu (b. 737).
Signature: "Eight days before the onset of the summer season in the *gengshu* year [1670], Wu Jin from Moling [Nanjing] wrote this at Shulao tang [a hall of Zhou Lianggong's in Nanjing]."
Seals: Moling (rectangle intaglio, upper right corner); Wu Jin (squat rectangle intaglio); Jieci (squat rectangle intaglio)

Leaf I
Zhu Ruiwu
Undated
Ink and colors on paper. H 24.9 cm; W 32.3 cm
Artist's seal: Ruiwu (square intaglio)
Colophon by Cao Erkan (1617–1690): six characters of running script (silk mounting): "[He] strives to achieve the likeness of the Yuan masters' [painting]."
Signature: Gu-an.
Seal: Erkan (square relief)

Leaf II
Colophons
1. Wu Taiguan (1624–after 1710, *jinshi* 1639. DHL/SL): two columns of running script.
   Signature: Shandao
   Seal: Taiguan (rectangle intaglio)
2. Mei Lei (fl. late 17th c.): three columns of running script
   Signature: Mei Lei
   Seal: Junzi (square relief)

Leaf J
Kuncan (Shiqi)
"Mount Niushou"
Undated
Ink on paper. H 24.3 cm; W 31.5 cm
Artist's inscription: five columns of running script: "When I turned around to look at the scenery after passing several peaks of Mount Niushou [in Nanjing], I think that they look like those in Old Mi [Mi Fu]'s paintings."
Artist's signature: Shitou

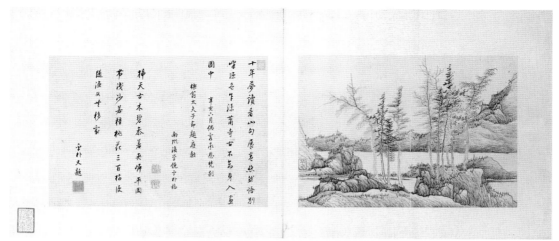

Leaf GG 　　　　　　　　　　　*Leaf G*

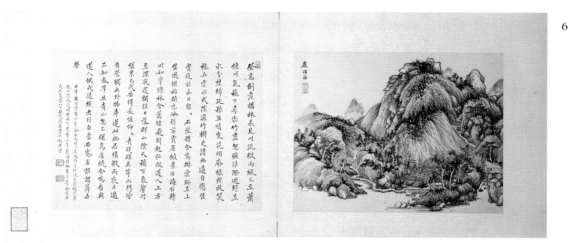

Leaf HH 　　　　　　　　　　　*Leaf H*

Leaf II 　　　　　　　　　　　*Leaf I*

6

Leaf JJ

Leaf J

6

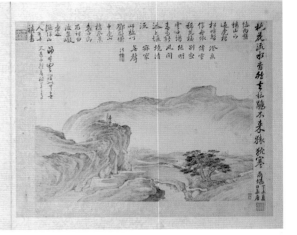

Leaf KK

Leaf K

6

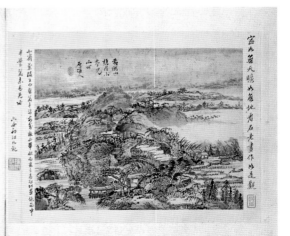

Leaf LL

Leaf L

Artist's seal: Jieqiu (double seal, broken oval, relief)

Colophon by Wang Shizhen: two columns of running script (silk mounting, right; this colophon is recorded in Wang Shizhen, Yuyang shizhuan, 19/3)
Signature: Di
Seal: Langye (tall rectangle relief)

Leaf JJ
Colophons
1. Zhu Yishi (*jinshi* 1642 DHL 4/9): five columns of running script
    Signature: Zhu Yishi
    Seal: Yishi (double seal, both square relief)
2. Zhou Ming (fl. late 17th c.): four columns of running script
    Signature: "Lufeng zi casually wrote this."
    Seal: Lufeng (round relief)

Leaf K
Ye Xin
ca. 1641
Ink and colors on paper. H 24.8 cm.; W 32.9 cm
Artist's seal: Rongmu (rectangle intaglio, lower right)

Colophons
1. Zhang Minbiao (1570–1642 *jinshi* 1592): eight columns of running script (painting proper)
    Signature: Fachuang
    Seal: Fachuang (double seal, both square relief)
2. Wang Shizhen
    (a) Two columns of running script (painting proper).
       No signature or seals.
    (b) Eighteen columns of running script (silk mounting, top).
    Signature: "Yuyang shanren, Wang Shizhen wrote this."
    Seal: Wang Shizhen yin (square intaglio)
3. Cao Erkan (1617–1690), dated 1667: one column of running script (silk mounting, right)
    Signature: "Erkan. On a summer day in the *dingwei* year [1667], I composed this with words collected from Tang [poems]."
    Seal: Gu-an (square intaglio)

Leaf KK
Colophon (ca. 1647) by Liu Xiangxian (fl. mid–17th c.): eight columns of draft cursive (*zhang cao*) script

Signature: "To the right is Zhenfu's [Ge Yilong, 1567–1640 DHL 4/4] colophon written for [Wang Wei's] 'Wang chuan painting' [which I transcribe here]. The respected [literary] society member Yuanweng [Zhou Lianggong] received his new appointment [in 1647] while in Weiyang [Yangzhou] and is about to leave for Bamin [Fujian]. Thereupon he asked me to inscribe this album he had put together. I therefore transcribed here Ge's poem [i.e., Ge's colophon mentioned above] to express my thought. For a thousand years [since Wang Wei's time], the works of the artists who were able to study Yucheng [Wang Wei] have also been handed down along with the 'Wang chuan.' All of that tradition is kept alive in this album. This proves that Master's [Zhou Lianggong] appreciation and connoisseurship reached the top. Liu Xiangxian."
Seals: Xiangxian (square intaglio); Fangchao (square intaglio)

Leaf L
Kuncan (Shiqi)
Undated
Ink on paper. H 24.8 cm; W 31.5 cm
Artist's inscription: four columns of running script: "Although I would never dream about becoming like Huanghe sanqiao [Wang Meng], this work can just pass [as of his style]!"
Artist's signature: Shidao ren
Artist's seal: indecipherable (oval relief)

Colophons
1. Unidentified: one column of running script (silk mounting, right)
    Seal: Yueshi (rectangle relief)
2. Sun Jianru (fl. late 17th c.): two columns of running script.
    Signature: "Sun Jianru from Liuhe [Zhejiang] viewed this."
    Seal: Sun Jianru (square intaglio)

Leaf LL
Colophon by Fang Hengxian: four columns of running script
    Signature: "Hengxian wrote this at [my studio] Shifu zhai."
    Seals: Fang Hengxian (square intaglio); Ziyue jiyu (square intaglio)

Leaf M
Xiang Shengmo
Ink on paper. H 25.3 cm; 33.5 cm

Artist's inscription: seven columns of running
    script: "'Hundred rapids carry the water;
    myriad valleys echo the pine wind.' These two
    lines are from Zhao Mengfu's inscription on a
    painting I have seen. Suddenly remembering
    this verse, I painted and inscribed this work for
    amusement."
Artist's signature: Xiang Kongzhang
Artist's seals: Zongwen sixiu shangxin leshi (square
    relief); Xiang Shengmo (square relief, low
    right)
Colophon by Fanglu (Zhou Lianggong's
    nephew?): one column of standard script
    (silk mounting)
Signature: Nephew, Fanglu.
Seal: Rinan (rectangle intaglio)

Leaf MM
    Colophons
    1. Zhuang Qiongsheng (b. 1627, *jinshi* 1647.
        DHL/SL): three columns of running script
        Signature: "Zhuang Qiongsheng inscribed this
            at the request of Master Liyuan [Zhou Liang-
            gong]."
        Seal: Zhuang Qiongsheng yin (square, half
            intaglio, half relief)
    2. Zhou Ming (fl. late 17th. c.): five columns of
        running script
        Signature: "I respectfully wrote for Liweng a
            poem, on the right, in the tune of the 'Ruan-
            lang gui' [a type of *ci* invented during the
            Song dynasty]."
        Signature: Your nephew, Ming
        Seals: Zhou Ming siyin (square, first and third
            characters in relief, second and fourth charac-
            ters in intaglio)

Leaf N
    Zhu Ruiwu
    Dated 1646
    Ink on paper. H 23.1; W 29.5 cm
    Artist's signature: two columns standard script:
        "On an autumn day in the *bingshu* year [1646]
        for Master Dao-an [Zhou Lianggong] [Signed]
        Ruiwu."
    Artist's seal: Hanzhi (rectangle intaglio)

Leaf NN
    Colophons
    1. Tang Yunji (fl. mid-17th c.): five columns of run-
        ning script: "Qi dashi [Zhu Ruiwu] is a man
        of noble and pure disposition. He looks
        down on government officials. His paintings
        are lofty. His art will last far beyond our gen-

eration. Those who study Ni Qingbi [Ni
    Zan] should take this painting as a guide. A
    poetic inscription Qingbi wrote on a painting
    has the following lines . . . That poem seems
    to have been written for this painting. Qishi's
    son [Zhu Zhichao, DHL 1/14], a *gongsheng*
    degree holder under the Ming dynasty, also
    excels in painting."
    Signature: Yunjia
    Seal: Tang Yunjia yin (square intaglio)
2. Wang Zehong (1626–1708, *jinshi* 1655), dated
    1670: four columns of running script
    Signature: "On a solstice day in the *gengshu* year
        [1670], Zehong from Jiangan wrote this."
    Seals: Zehong (squat oval relief); Mengyi ting
        (square, half intaglio, half relief)

Leaf O
    Zhou Quan
    Undated
    Ink on paper. H 25.4 cm; W 36.1 cm
    Artist's seals: Zhou Quan yin (square relief);
        Jingxiang (square intaglio)

Leaf OO
    Colophons
    1. Zha Shibiao (1615–1698 DHL/SL): three columns
        of standard script
        Signature: Meihe yuren Shibiao
        Seal: Zha Erzhan (square relief)
    2. Wang Jun (fl. mid-17th c. DHL/SL): two columns
        of running script
        Signature: Wang Jun from Hanjiang [Yangzhou]
        Seal: Qiurun (square relief)

Leaf P
    Wang Yuanqu
    Dated 1655
    Ink on paper. H 24.2 cm; W 31.7 cm.
    Artist's signature: one column of standard script:
        "On the 9th day in the *yiwei* year [1655].
        [signed] Wang Yuanqu."
    Artist's seal: Yuanqu (double gourd relief)

Leaf PP
    Colophon by Du Shouchang (b. ca. 1610s):
        fourteen columns of running script
    Signature: Du Shouchang
    Seals: Du Shouchang yin (square intaglio); Xiang
        cao (square relief)

Leaf Q
    Yun Xiang
    Undated

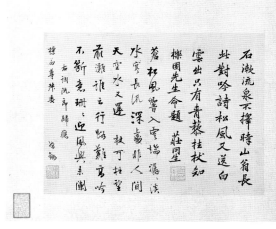

6

Leaf MM   *Leaf M*

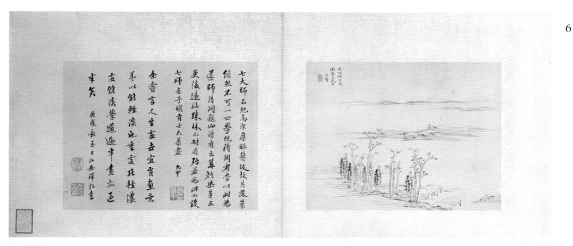

6

Leaf NN   *Leaf N*

6

Leaf OO   *Leaf O*

6

者倚書幾不修面彼袖淋漓
把捲捲卻来不滅三人頭小
稻子到安至隨而中乾色
勝夫坡大气芋者省十三力
向極風除云此将志兄丞舟
新活主福至至雲至雲至
子法龙深生子莊一江系
飄天漫手蒼亥学枝系
梅坐草隆上人酉本香梅
高倚偶余情睡寿語雲
莊煉祇林本子淡定
失籠橋淡气系有漁定
上石明云段
林巻署

Leaf PP   *Leaf P*

6

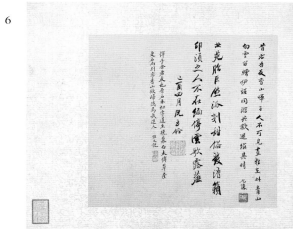
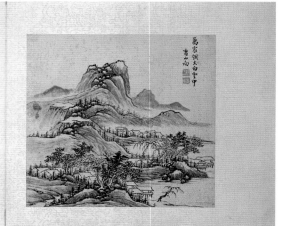

昔君秀友青山坪云人不可見畫稚至此青山
勾雲百瞻伊誰同游共歡適維其時兄陳
此苑脂色瀲添到甜倍發清籟
印須云人不在緔傳靈歌露難
之間四月尻立俗
評于茶老友此原牛牛程道主境森白大偉方度
史高列乎李山敬暗陰烏武廷人

Leaf QQ   *Leaf Q*

6

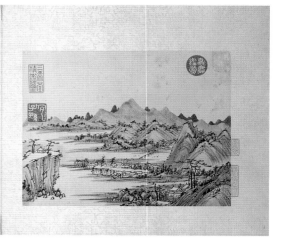

人家喬木杪漁艇
落英邊便欲尋源
入求耕不稅田
竹樹森森暗満塍
脉脉斜敲勤野鳥
嘆似喚我移家呈
樑翁老祖臺先生教
後學周家

Leaf RR   *Leaf R*

Ink on paper. H 27 cm; W 28.5 cm

Artist's inscription: one column of running script: "Myriad houses are enveloped by mist, smoke, and white clouds."

Artist's signature: Xiangshan Xiang

Artist's seals: Yun Benqu (square intaglio); Daosheng (square intaglio)

Leaf QQ

Colophons

1. Tan Yunjian (fl. mid-17th c.): two columns of running script: "My deceased friend Yun Xiangshan, though he is no longer around, has left his painting in this album. Why did he leave his green mountains and white clouds for? We used to roam around together reciting poems. Remembering that time, Yunjian wrote this."

   Seal: Yunjian

2. Ruan Yuxuan (fl. late 17th c.): two columns of colophons, one dated 1669:
   (1) Two columns of running script. Signature: "In the 4th month of the *jiyu* year [1669], Ruan Yuxuan wrote this."
   Seal: Ruan Yuxuan seyin (square intaglio)
   (2) Two columns of standard script. "Master Yun was an old friend of mine. His original name was Benqu, *zi* Daosheng. Late in his life, he admired Bai Juyi so much that he adopted Xiang as his given name and Xiangshang for his *zi*. He wished to retire and become a recluse. He was a native of Wujin [Jiangsu]. Xuan again inscribed [this]."
   Seal: Ruan Ding (rectangle intaglio)

Leaf R

Sheng Dan

Ink on paper. H 24 cm; W 31.5 cm

Artist's seal: Bohan (square relief, lower left corner)

Collector's seals: Qing imperial seals

1. Gaozong: Sanxi tang jingjian xi (tall rectangle relief); Yizesun (square intaglio)
2. Renzong: Jiaqing jianshang (round intaglio)
3. Sundi: Xuantong jianshang (square relief, right margin); Wuyi zhai jingjian xi (tall rectangle relief, right margin)

Leaf RR

Colophon by Zhou Huan (fl. mid-17th c.): six columns of standard script

Signature: "To present this to Master Liweng

[Zhou Lianggong] for his instruction. A junior Zhou Huan wrote this."

Seals: Shuxia (rectangle relief, upper right corner); Zhou Huan zhi yin (square intaglio); Dahu jushi (square relief)

Recorded: Gugong shuhua lu. Taipei, National Palace Museum, 1965, vol. IV, pp. 273–281.

Published

Zhou Liyuan Du Hua Lou shuhua jicui (Paintings in the Du Hua Lou collection of Zhou Liyuan). Beijing: Gugong Bowuyuan, 1931

Jin-Tang Wudai Song-Yuan-Ming-Qing minghua shuhua ji, Nanjing exhibition catalogue. Shanghai: Shangwu yinshuguan, 1943, pl. 269 (Leaf FF only)

Yu Yi, ed. Shiqi huaji, Taipei: Zhonghua shuhua chubanshe, 1976, pp. 34–35 (leaves J, L only)

Wang Hui huapu. Taipei: National Palace Museum, 1970, pl. 60 (leaf B only)

Wu, William D.Y. "Kung Hsien." Ph.D. Dissertation, Princeton University, 1979, fig. 22

Silbergeld, Jerome L. "Political Symbolism in the Landscape Painting and Poetry of Kung Hsien (ca. 1620–1689)." Ph.D. Dissertation, Stanford University, 1974

7. AUTUMN LANDSCAPE IN MIST

Hu Yukun (fl. 1640–1672; DHL 2/5); colophon by Tang Yunjia (fl. mid-17th c.)

ca. 1645

Album leaf

H 30 cm; W 32 cm

Artist's signature (far right): "While I was at Yuanweng gongzi's [Zhou Lianggong] official residence at Han River [Yangzhou], I painted this. Hu Yukun."

Artist's seals: Yukun (both, square relief)

The Art Museum, Princeton University (Y1962–110)

Colophons (on painting leaf)

1. Huang Shu (fl. mid 17th c. DHL fn. 173): one column of running script
   Signature: "Shu inscribed this."
   Seal: Shu (square relief)
2. Chen Zhi (fl. late 17th c.): one column of running script (far left)
   Seal: Shannong (tall rectangle relief)

Colophon (on facing leaf): calligraphy by Tang Yunjia (fl. mid-17th c.)

17 columns of standard script, transcribing Su Shi's essay on painting

Signature: "In the *dinghai* year [1647], Liangshui

yuren, Tang Yunjia examined the painting and inscribed it."

Seal: Yunjia (rectangle intaglio)

Collector's seal: unidentified (lower right corner)

8. SNOW LANDSCAPE

Yun Xiang (1568–1655; DHL 1/16)

Hanging scroll: ink on paper. H 121 cm; W 53.5 cm

Collection: Ming-te T'ang (Wang Chi-ch'ien), New York

Artist's inscription: five columns of running script: "Old tree branches put out new buds after snow. With a frozen brush I completed this painting at the Jiangtian Pavilion in Guabu to present it to my literary friend Yuanlao [Zhou Lianggong]."

Artist's signature: Xiangshan Yun Hsiang

Artist's seal: Yun Benqu yin (square intaglio)

Collector's seal: Wang Chi-ch'ien (present owner), one seal

Published

Suzuki Kei. comp. Chugoku kaiga sogo zuroku: daiikan, Amerika-Kanada hen (comprehensive Illustrated Catalogue of Chinese Paintings: vol. 1, American and Canadian Collections), Tokyo: University of Tokyo Press, 1982, pls. A 14-013.

9. LANDSCAPE [accompanied by Zhou Lianggong's calligraphy, "Biography of Gao Cen"]

Gao Cen (fl. ca. 1645–1689; DHL, 3/E.14)

Two album leaves (A, AA) mounted as a hanging scroll

Painting Leaf (A): Ink and colors on paper

H 24.7 cm; W 32.0 cm

Collection: The Freer Gallery of Art, Washington D. C.

Leaf A

  Gao Cen

  "Landscape"

  ca. 1645–1651

  Artist's seal: "Gao Cen" (double seal, both square relief, lower right)

  Colophons

  1. Wu Guodui (1616–1680; *jinshi* 1658): three columns of regular script (painting). Signature: "Mingyue qi ke." Seal: "Dui" (square intaglio)

2. Yang Sisheng (1621–1664; *jinshi* 1646; DHL, fn. 170) one column of running script (silk mounting, right)

  Signature: Sisheng

  Seal: "Yang Sisheng yin" (square relief)

3. Cao Erkan (1617–1690; DHL, fn. 193), dated 1667 eleven columns of running script (silk mounting, top)

  Inscription: "Upon the request of Master Liweng [Zhou Lianggong], I viewed this painting by Weisheng [Gao Cen] and inscribed it. In the sixth month of the *dingwei* year [1667], Cao Erkan."

  Seals: "Erkan" (squat rectangle relief); "Guan" (squat rectangle intaglio). No collector's seal

Leaf AA (mounted above the painting)

  Zhou Lianggong

  Calligraphy: "Biography of Gao Cen"

  Dated 1651

  Biography: seventeen columns of archaic regular script: "Gao Cen, *zi* Weisheng, is the younger brother of Kangsheng [Gao Fu], who is well known in the art world. Ai Tienyong [Ai Nanying] from Yuzhang [Dongxiang, Jiangsi] who is a good judge of personal character, said that the only person in Moling [Nanjing] who employs ancient methods in studying for government examinations is Gao Fu. Fu is the given name of Kangsheng. Both Cen and Fu are famous in our time. Fu and I have been friends for a very long time, but it was not until later that I became friends with Cen. He has a beard like a halberd and looks like a man dressed in an embroidered robe on a noble steed. However he takes pleasure from his belief in Buddhism. When young, he abandoned the task of passing the official examinations and studied poetry. In poetry he favored the mid and late [Tang] periods. He constantly produced fine verses.

  "He began to study under the monk Daoxin [Chen Danzhong] and went [to live in] the Fula Temple. He ate only vegetables. Despite his youth, he was serene and reticent. His face showed no sign of frivolity. As a youth, he also studied painting under Zhu Hanzhi [Zhu Rui-wu], who is his fellow townsman [from Hangzhou]. In his later years, however, he followed his own ideas. His paintings in this album were all done at a temple on a mountain in the southern suburbs [of Nanjing], amid the shade of pines and the gurgling of streams. Excluding all things frivolous and noisy, they quietly draw the viewer into a state of tranquillity. Truly [his paintings] attained the essence of brush and ink. It is certainly impossible to buy such paintings in the red dust [accumulated] as high as a hundred feet [i.e., city markets].

"The paintings by Master Xin [the monk Daoxin] are marvelous [creations] under heaven. He also has a very rich collection. I once stayed at the Songfeng Pavilion, where I watched Master Xin and Cen engaged in a quiet discourse late at night. They discussed composition [in painting]. During their discussion, they sketched a beautiful painting, so vivid that one could almost see it on a white wall. Whenever Cen grasped something from their discussion, he hastened to put it on paper. But as soon as he set the paper down or when he had only partly finished painting, the two would renew their discussion, bringing up many other subtle ideas. When [the painting] was finally finished, not a single brush-stroke of the original plan remained. He [Gao Cen] benefited profoundly from his discussion [with Daoxin], [and his paintings] became more and more subtle and refined: [Gao Cen's painting resembles the brush of Master Pan [Panyue], [while Daoxin's words resemble] the discourse of Master Yue [Yue Yi]. Those who acclaim Cen certainly praise Master Xin. Master Xin is my friend, the imperial censor of Chen Shejiang. Both Fu and Cen are of unusually fine character. The place where the two sages live is green and cool, full of vegetation and creepers. They supported their widowed mother well, attending to her meals and caring for her overall well-being. Fu Cen once accompanied me to the Great River [i.e., the Yangzi River], to see me off. I wrote a farewell poem for them which includes the following phrase: 'Eating vegetables morning and evening, the two brothers live among grass and creepers.' One can imagine the harmony they attained. The narcissus painted by Fu made Wei Gaoxu [Wei Zhihuang] sigh with admiration. However, he is committed to the task of passing the government examinations, thus he cannot completely devote himself to painting."

(This biography is contained in Zhou Lianggong's biography of Gao Cen in the DHL, 3/14. See my annotated translation, forthcoming.)

Inscription: "On a solstice day of the *xinmao* year [1651], the old Li wrote this at the Yanmeng Temple in Nanjian [Nanping, Fujian]."

Seals: "Zhou Lianggong" (square relief); "Yuan-liang" (square relief); "Yuequ" (oval relief, upper right)

Recorded: Zhou Lianggong, *Du Hua Lu*, in *Yishu congbian* (hereafter YSCB), vol. XIV, DHL 3/14 (Gao Cen's biography only)

Published
Nakata, Yujiro and Fu, Shen C. Y., eds. *Obei shuzo Chugoku hosho meisekishu* (Masterpieces of Chinese Calligraphy in American and European Collections), 5 vols., Tokyo: Chuokoron-sha, 1983, vol. IV, fig. 21 (p. 21)

10. LANDSCAPES AND OTHER SUBJECTS, AND CALLIGRAPHY

Guo Dingjing; 1647
Album of 20 leaves
Each, painting proper: H 22.2 cm; W 15.3 cm
(mounted H 25.7 cm; W 35.9 cm)
Guan Lu Yuan Collection

11. BAIHE (WHITE CRANE) RIDGE

Ye Xin (fl. ca. 1640–1673; DHL 3/19)
Undated
Ink and colors on paper.
H 25 cm; W 33.3 cm
Metropolitan Museum of Art, New York
Seymour Fund, 1964.268.1
Artist's seal: Rongmu (rectangle intaglio, lower left)

Colophons
    1. Qin Chuan (fl. 17th c.): six columns of standard script
    Signature: "Qin Chuan recorded this."
    Seal: Zi Cungu (oval relief)
    2. Zhang Xuezeng (fl. ca. 1633–1656; DHL 3/2): three columns of running script (silk mounting, right): "This is the view of Baihe Ridge in Min [Fujian], where the [Ming dynasty] general Qi Shaobao defeated dwarfs [Japanese pirates]. Yuanlao nianweng [Zhou Lianggong] was a government official. He spoke of the beauty of this ridge and Rongmu [Ye Xin] painted it. The painting allows one to travel there in imagination. Zhang Erwei inscribed this."
    Seal: Erwei (square relief)

Originally part of an album in the collection of Wang Chi-ch'ien (modern), New York. The pieces in cat. nos. 10 and 11 also originally were part of Wang Chi-ch'ien's album set. According to Mr. Wang, the original set also contained one leaf (landscape) by Fan Qi and one leaf (painting of plum blossom) by Chen Hongshou. He gave Chen's leaf to Osvald Sirèn and sold the rest to the Mi-chou Gallery.

12. "ILLUSTRATION TO TAO QIAN'S ODE, 'RETURNING HOME'" (GUIQU LAI TU)

Chen Hongshou (1599–1652)
Dated 1650
Handscroll, ink and slight color on silk
Painting proper: H 30.8 cm; L 310.3 cm
Collection: The Honolulu Academy of Art,
    Purchase, 1954

Frontispiece: calligraphy by Deng Erya (1884–1954): four characters in seal script: "Yuanming yixing" (The untrammeled spirit of Tao Qian)
Signature: Deng Erya. Three seals
Artist's inscription: each of eleven scenes (A–K) is preceded by an inscription with a two-character title and a prose poem. Poems are composed by the artist: three columns of running script (A, C, H), two columns of running script (B, D–G, J, K), and four columns of running script

A. Picking Chrysanthemums
   "Yellow flowers are just in bloom,
   A man-in-white brought [me] wine.
   What do I further desire?"

B. Sending A Laborer
   "A son of another serves my son [you],
   You serve another's son.
   [You] must not treat this worker as though [he were] someone else's son.
   [I] anxiously wrote this on this paper."

C. Planting Glutinous-Rice
   "Men are fighting for food from rice-barrels to gain raw strength.
   [I am] a man of stimulants, and need not feed on rice."

D. Returning Home
   "The pines are longing for me. Shall I not return?"

E. No Virtue
   "Buddhism is far, [but] the rice-wine is close.
   I cannot reach the far, therefore I embrace the close."

F. Renouncing The Official Seal
   "To make a living [I] come [to accept this post].
   [Forced to] kowtow I leave. This is one way out of the chaos."

G. Wine Credit
   "Money is not made to be guarded, but to please my mouth."

H. Comment on Fans
   "Living in the time of Jin and Song [i.e., the age of Tao Qian] and selling [ideas of the sages of] Shang and Zhou. The pine ink-stick and the crane brush should suffice to write my sorrow."

I. Refusing A Meal
   "The man was not ashamed to beg food [from friends], but refused a gift of meat. I, after all, do not love my stomach."

J. Begging
   "Dancing and submitting to fortune is as good as begging."

K. Filling Wine
   "Cap and gown are my burden. Yeast and distiller's rice serve my intoxication."

(Translation based on Tseng Yu-ho Ecke in "A Report on Ch'en Hongshou," p. 85, with minor modification)

Artist's signature: three columns of running script (towards the end of the painting): "In the *gengyin* year [1650], in the mid-summer, my old friend, Zhou Lilao [Zhou Lianggong] saw me and asked for paintings. Therefore, during the summer season Lin Zhongqing [Lin Tinglian] had [the singer] Xiao Suqing attend me [bringing] ink and brushes to the Dingxiang Bridge [at West Lake, Hangchou]. In mid-winter I post this painting to Lilao. Please do show this painting to our old friend, Xu Yu [DHL 3/3]. Laochi, Hongshou, painted this scroll and [my fourth son] Mingru [Chen Zi] applied the colors."
Artist's seals: Hongshou (double seal, both square intaglio); Woyong wofa (square intaglio, upper

right, painting). Both seals are located under
the last column of the artist's inscription.

Assistant's seal: Chen Zi; Chen Mingru yin (square
relief, under the artist's inscription)

Viewer's seal: Lin Tinglian (fl. mid 17th c.): Lin
Tinglian yin (square relief, under the first column of the artist's inscription)

Colophons: all dedicated to the collector Jiao
Meijing (modern)
Wang Guofeng: dated 1881. two seals
Zhang Yinhuan: dated 1881. one seal
Chen Rongguang: dated 1882. two seals
Chen Yi: dated 1882. two seals
Liu Shunian: dated 1885. one seal
Lu Jiguang: dated 1887. one seal
Li Wang: dated 1896. one seal

Collector's seals
Jiao Meijing (fl. 19th c.): two seals
Gu Yanru (modern): Yanru jinzang (square
relief, lower left corner, painting)
Unidentified: damaged (painting, lower left
corner); indecipherable (square intaglio,
frontispiece, lower left corner)

Published

Goepper, Roger H. ed. *Tausend Jahre Chinesische
Malerei* (Munich exhibition catalog), München:
Haus der Kunst, 1959, cat. no. 83

Sirèn, Osvald. *Chinese Painting: Leading Masters and
Principles*. 7 vols. New York: Ronald Press,
1956–1958, vol. VI, pl. 319

Huang Yongchuan. "Chen Hongshou," in *Zhongguo
minghuajia congshu*. Shanghai, 1958, fig. 12

Tseng Yu-ho. "A Report on Ch'en Hung-shou,"
Archives of Chinese Art, no. VIII (1959)

Ecke, Gustav. *Chinese Paintings in Hawaii*. Honolulu:
Honolulu Academy of Arts, 1965, pls. XXXIX, LXII

Kohara, Hironobu. "Chin Koju shiron" (On Chen
Hongshou), *Bijutsu-shi*, no. 62, 1966, fig. 19

Yu I, ed. *Ming Chen Hongshou hua-chi*. Taipei: Chung-
hua shu-hua ch'u-pan she, 1974, p. 51 (Scene, C, D,
J, K)

Cahill, James. *The Distant Mountains: Chinese Painting
of the Late Ming Dynasty, 1570–1644*. New York and
Tokyo: John Weatherhill, 1982, pl. 136 (Scene
H–K)

Suzuki Kei. comp. *Chugoku kaiga sogo zuroku: daikan,
Amerika-Kanada hen* (comprehensive Illustrated
Catalogue of Chinese Paintings: Volume 1, American and Canadian Collections). Tokyo: University
of Tokyo Press. 1982, pls. A 38-001 (pp. 386–388)

13. ZHUGE LIANG (181–234 A.D.) vs. TAO QIAN
(365–427 A.D.) [not in exhibition]

Chen Hongshou (1599–1652; DHL 1/15)
Dated 1650
Handscroll
Specifications and measurements unavailable
Collection: Present collection unknown (formerly in
the collection of Zhang Daqian)

Frontispiece: calligraphy by Lin Chong (fl. mid-
17th c.): ten characters in five columns of running
script: "In service he is Gongming [Zhou Liang-
gong]; in retirement he is Yuanliang [Tao Qian]."

Signature: "written by Lin Chong."

Artist's inscription: seven columns of running script:
"In the early autumn of the *gengyin* year [1650],
Zhongqing [Lin Tinglian, Chen Hongshou's
friend] carved with a small knife Xiao Shuqing's [a
famous singer and Chen's friend] Da-le bei. Laolian [I] said . . . It took me six days altogether to
complete this [painting]."

(In the passage left out of the above translation, Chen
makes a reference to Zhou Lianggong. But it is so
cryptic that it defies translation. Note the names of
Chen's friends, Lin Tinglian and Xiao Shuqing,
also appear in his inscription for the Honolulu
scroll, cat. no. 12)

Artist's seals: Hongshou (double seal, both square
intaglio)

Colophons
1. Lin Chong (fl. mid-17th c.): seventy-three
columns of standard script: a transcription of
Zhuge Liang's former Chushi piao
Signature: "In the early summer of the *renchen*
year [1652] on the Buddha-Bathing Festival
day [the 8th day of the 4th month] [i.e.,
Buddha's Birthday], when I visited Jianbu
[Fukien], I wrote this upon the request of
Master Liyuan [Zhou Lianggong]. Monong,
Lin Chong from Sanshan." Two seals.

2. Guo Dingjing (fl. mid-17th c.; DHL 4/13): thirty-
three columns of standard script: transcrip-
tion of Tao Qian's ode, "Gui qu lai ci," with
Tao Qian's preface to the ode.
Signature: "In the early summer of the *renchen*
year [1652], I wrote this for my teacher
Zhouweng [Zhou Lianggong]. His pupil
Guo Dingjing from Jin-an [Fujian]."
Seals: Dingjing zhi yin (square intaglio); Guo
Qujian (square intaglio)

3. Zhang Yuan (Zhang Daqian, 1899–1983):
(1) Three columns of running script between

前出師表

臣亮言：先帝創業未半而中道崩殂，今天下三分，益州疲弊，此誠危急存亡之秋也。然侍衛之臣不懈於內，忠志之士忘身於外者，蓋追先帝之殊遇，欲報之於陛下也。誠宜開張聖聽，以光先帝遺德，恢弘志士之氣，不宜妄自菲薄，引喻失義，以塞忠諫之路也。宮中府中，俱為一體，陟罰臧否，不宜異同。若有作奸犯科及為忠善者，宜付有司論其刑賞，以昭陛下平明之治，不宜偏私，使內外異法也。侍中、侍郎郭攸之、費禕、董允等，此皆良實，志慮忠純，是以先帝簡拔以遺陛下。愚以為宮中之事，事無大小，悉以咨之，然後施行，必能裨補闕漏，有所廣益。將軍向寵，性行淑均，曉暢軍事，試用於昔日，先帝稱之曰能，是以眾議舉寵為督。愚以為營中之事，悉以咨之，必能使行陣和睦，優劣得所。親賢臣，遠小人，此先漢所以興隆也；親小人，遠賢臣，此後漢所以傾頹也。先帝在時，每與臣論此事，未嘗不歎息痛恨於桓、靈也。侍中、尚書、長史、參軍，此悉貞良死節之臣，願陛下親之信之，則漢室之隆，可計日而待也。臣本布衣，躬耕於南陽，苟全性命於亂世，不求聞達於諸侯。先帝不以臣卑鄙，猥自枉屈，三顧臣於草廬之中，諮臣以當世之事，由是感激，遂許先帝以驅馳。後值傾覆，受任於敗軍之際，奉命於危難之間，爾來二十有一年矣。先帝知臣謹慎，故臨崩寄臣以大事也。受命以來，夙夜憂歎，恐託付不效，以傷先帝之明，故五月渡瀘，深入不毛。今南方已定，兵甲已足，當獎率三軍，北定中原，庶竭駑鈍，攘除奸凶，興復漢室，還於舊都。此臣所以報先帝而忠陛下之職分也。至於斟酌損益，進盡忠言，則攸之、禕、允之任也。願陛下託臣以討賊興復之效，不效則治臣之罪，以告先帝之靈。若無興德之言，則責攸之、禕、允等之慢，以彰其咎。陛下亦宜自謀，以諮諏善道，察納雅言，深追先帝遺詔。臣不勝受恩感激。今當遠離，臨表涕泣，不知所云。

嫩園先生命書
壬辰初夏嶺南日遇過浦
三山雲壑林寵

13　*Colophon by Lin Chong*

後出師表

先帝慮漢賊不兩立，王業不偏安，故託臣以討賊也。以先帝之明，量臣之才，故知臣伐賊，才弱敵強也。然不伐賊，王業亦亡，惟坐而待亡，孰與伐之？是故託臣而弗疑也。臣受命之日，寢不安席，食不甘味。思惟北征，宜先入南。故五月渡瀘，深入不毛，并日而食。臣非不自惜也，顧王業不可得偏全於蜀都，故冒危難以奉先帝之遺意也，而議者謂為非計。今賊適疲於西，又務於東，兵法乘勞，此進趨之時也。謹陳其事如左：高帝明並日月，謀臣淵深，然涉險被創，危然後安。今陛下未及高帝，謀臣不如良、平，而欲以長計取勝，坐定天下，此臣之未解一也。劉繇、王朗，各據州郡，論安言計，動引聖人，群疑滿腹，眾難塞胸，今歲不戰，明年不征，使孫策坐大，遂并江東，此臣之未解二也。曹操智計，殊絕於人，其用兵也，彷彿孫、吳，然困於南陽，險於烏巢，危於祁連，偪於黎陽，幾敗北山，殆死潼關，然後偽定一時耳，況臣才弱，而欲以不危而定之，此臣之未解三也。曹操五攻昌霸不下，四越巢湖不成，任用李服而李服圖之，委任夏侯而夏侯敗亡，先帝每稱操為能，猶有此失，況臣駑下，何能必勝？此臣之未解四也。自臣到漢中，中間期年耳，然喪趙雲、陽群、馬玉、閻芝、丁立、白壽、劉郃、鄧銅等及曲長、屯將七十餘人，突將、無前，賨叟、青羌，散騎、武騎一千餘人，此皆數十年之內，所糾合四方之精銳，非一州之所有；若復數年，則損三分之二也，當何以圖敵？此臣之未解五也。今民窮兵疲，而事不可息；事不可息，則住與行勞費正等；而不及今圖之，欲以一州之地，與賊持久，此臣之未解六也。夫難平者，事也。昔先帝敗軍於楚，當此時，曹操拊手，謂天下已定。然後先帝東連吳、越，西取巴、蜀，舉兵北征，夏侯授首，此操之失計，而漢事將成也。然後吳更違盟，關羽毀敗，秭歸蹉跌，曹丕稱帝。凡事如是，難可逆見。臣鞠躬盡瘁，死而後已。至於成敗利鈍，非臣之明所能逆睹也。

嫩園先生命書
壬辰初夏嶺南日遇過浦
三山雲壑林寵

13　*Colophon by Lin Chong*

歸去來辭 并序

余家貧，耕植不足以自給。幼稚盈室，缾無儲粟，生生所資，未見其術。親故多勸余為長吏，脫然有懷，求之靡途。會有四方之事，諸侯以惠愛為德，家叔以余貧苦，遂見用于小邑。於時風波未靜，心憚遠役，彭澤去家百里，公田之利，足以為酒，故便求之。及少日，眷然有歸歟之情。何則？質性自然，非矯厲所得。飢凍雖切，違己交病。嘗從人事，皆口腹自役。於是悵然慷慨，深愧平生之志。猶望一稔，當斂裳宵逝。尋程氏妹喪于武昌，情在駿奔，自免去職。仲秋至冬，在官八十餘日。因事順心，命篇曰《歸去來兮》。乙巳歲十一月也。

歸去來兮，田園將蕪胡不歸？既自以心為形役，奚惆悵而獨悲？悟已往之不諫，知來者之可追。實迷途其未遠，覺今是而昨非。舟遙遙以輕颺，風飄飄而吹衣。問征夫以前路，恨晨光之熹微。乃瞻衡宇，載欣載奔。僮僕歡迎，稚子候門。三徑就荒，松菊猶存。攜幼入室，有酒盈樽。引壺觴以自酌，眄庭柯以怡顏。倚南窗以寄傲，審容膝之易安。園日涉以成趣，門雖設而常關。策扶老以流憩，時矯首而遐觀。雲無心以出岫，鳥倦飛而知還。景翳翳以將入，撫孤松而盤桓。

歸去來兮，請息交以絕遊。世與我而相違，復駕言兮焉求？悅親戚之情話，樂琴書以消憂。農人告余以春及，將有事於西疇。或命巾車，或棹孤舟。既窈窕以尋壑，亦崎嶇而經丘。木欣欣以向榮，泉涓涓而始流。善萬物之得時，感吾生之行休。

已矣乎！寓形宇內復幾時，曷不委心任去留？胡為乎遑遑欲何之？富貴非吾願，帝鄉不可期。懷良辰以孤往，或植杖而耘耔。登東皋以舒嘯，臨清流而賦詩。聊乘化以歸盡，樂夫天命復奚疑！

楷則劇夫子書
壬辰初夏為
吾宗弟子郭鼎京

13　*Colophon by Guo Dingjing*

the frontispiece and the painting: "Laolian's [Chen Hongshou] painting method, brushwork, and composition, originate in the stone engravings of the Six Dynasties. His method in the use of color and ink is derived from Song masters. Not even a single dot [in his paintings] shows the bad habit of Qiu [Qiu Ying] and Tang [Tang Yin]. This handscroll was a work he painted for Zhou Lianggong one year before he died. It is a great accomplishment."
Signature: Daqian, Yuan. One seal.
(2) Four columns of running script (at the beginning of the colophon section immediately following the painting). Signature: Yuan. One seal. Collector's seals: Zhang Yuan. Nine seals.
   Viewer's seal: Lin Tinglian (fl. mid-17th c. Chen Hongshou's friend mentioned in Chen's inscription): Zhongqing (painting, lower right corner)

Reproduced: Princeton University, The Far Eastern Seminar, Photograph Archives

14. AUTUMN LANDSCAPE

Xiang Shengmo (1597–1658; DHL/SL)
Dated 1654
Album leaf from a collective album, dated 1654
Ink and color on paper. H 24.5 cm; W 31.1 cm
Metropolitan Museum of Art, New York
Seymour Fund, 1964.268.1

Artist's signature: "In the ninth month of the chia-wu year [1654], I painted this. Xiang Shengmo."
Artist's seal: Xiuzhou Xiang shi gongzhang so zuo (squat rectangle relief)
Colophons (on painting leaf)
   1. Wu Guodui (1616–1680; CS. 1658): five columns of standard script
      Seal: Yusui (rectangle, half relief, half intaglio)
   2. Wu Yun (1811–1883): two columns of running script (silk mounting, left)
      Seal: Wu Yun siyin (square intaglio). According to Wu Yun's colophon Leaf A was once in Gu Wenbin's (1811–1889) Guoyun Lou Collection.
      Collector's seals: Wang Chi-ch'ien: two seals

Colophon (on facing leaf) by Hong Ding (unidentified, fl. 17th c.): nine columns of cursive script.

Signature: "Yelu Yiya [I] viewed this and unexpectedly inscribed it."
Seals: Xuebu (oval relief); Hong Ding (square intaglio)
Collector's seal: unidentified (rectangle relief in blue)

Originally part of an album in the collection of Wang Chi-ch'ien (modern), New York. The pieces in cat. nos. 22 and 23 were also originally part of Wang Chi-ch'ien's album set. According to Mr. Wang, the original set also contained one leaf (landscape) by Fan Qi and one leaf (painting of plum blossom) by Chen Hongshou. He gave Chen's leaf to Osvald Sirèn and sold the rest to the Mi-chou Gallery.

15. "DREAM JOURNEY AMONG RIVERS AND MOUNTAINS" (CHIANG-SHAN WO-YU T'U)

Cheng Zhengkui (1604–1676)
Dated 1655
Handscroll
Ink and light colors on paper. H 7 3/4 in (19.9 cm); L 111 in (284.6 cm)
Collection: The Art Institute of Chicago, Purchase, W. L. Mead Fund, 1953
Artist's signature: four columns of running script: "In the 10th month of the yiwei year [1655], in Changan, I inscribed this painting again in order to receive my respectful colleague Yuanliang's [Zhou Lianggong] instruction. Zhengkui."
Artist's seals: Duanbo (square intaglio); Cheng (round relief, paper joint)

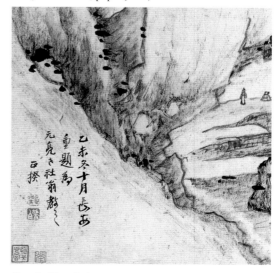

15

Detail of inscription

Colophon by Wang Chen (1720–1797): dated 1792. Seven columns of running script. Signature: "In the 10th month of the *renzi* year [1792], Wang Chen at seventy-three inscribed this." Two seals

Collector's seals: Song Lao (1634–1713)?: Lao (square relief, lower left). Three unidentified seals: Xiejun zhai shuhuaji (unidentified, rectangle relief, lower right corner); Jiale [ ]-cang (square relief, lower right); Zhenxian xinshang (square relief, lower left corner)

Published

Sirèn, Osvald. Chinese Painting: Leading Masters and Principles. 7 vols. New York: Ronald Press, 1956–1958, vol. VI, pl. 349 B.

Suzuki Kei. comp. Chugoku kaiga sogo zuroku: dai-ikan, Amerika-Kanada hen (comprehensive Illustrated Catalogue of Chinese Paintings: Volume I, American and Canadian Collections). Tokyo: University of Tokyo Press, 1982, pls. A3-014 (pp. 34–35)

16. SAIL BOATS BY A RIVER SHORE (JIANGPU FENGFAN TU) [not in exhibition]

Fan Qi (1616–after 1694; DHL 3/16)
Dated 1657
Handscroll
Ink and colors on paper. H 29 cm; L 318 cm
Collection: Liaoning Provincial Museum, Liaoning

Frontispiece by Zheng Yuan (modern calligrapher): photograph unavailable

Artist's signature: two columns of standard script: "In the *qinghe* [4th lunar month] of *dingyu* year [1657], in order to receive the instruction of the painter's companion and eminent literatus Liyuan [Zhou Lianggong].[I wrote this.] Fan Qi."

Artist's seal: Huigong (square relief)

Collector's seals: Zhou Lianggong: Yuanliang (square relief, lower left corner); Qingyuan cao tang (square relief, upper right corner). Five other seals: unidentified

Colophons: photographs unavailable

Published

Liaoning sheng bowuguan canghua ji. Beijing: *Wenwu*, 1962, pp. 91–92 (painting section only).

Chinese Paintings of the Ming and Qing Dynasties: XIV–XXth Centuries. A catalogue of an exhibition organized by the International Cultural Corporation of Australia Limited. Victoria: Wilke and Co. Ltd., 1981. Cat. no. 53

17. "HISTORIC SPOTS IN NANJING" (JINLING GUJI)

Hu Yukun (fl. ca. 1640–1672; DHL 2/E.5)
Dated 1660
Album of 12 leaves (A–L)
Ink or colors on paper (Ink: A, B, J, L. Ink and colors: C–I, K)
Average measurements, each leaf: H 25.5 cm; w 18.1 cm
Collection: Guan Lu Yuan
Artist's inscription (in seal script)
  Leaf A: Tianque
  Leaf B: Pingxu
  Leaf C: Sheshan [Qixia shan]
  Leaf D: Tianyin
  Leaf E: Meiwu
  Leaf F: Zhongshan
  Leaf G: Zitang [shan]
  Leaf H: Qinhuai
  Leaf I: Mochou [hu]
  Leaf J: Linggu [si]
  Leaf K: Pengtai
  Leaf L: Shicheng

Note: Some of these "historical spots" (Leaf C, F, H, I, J, L) of Nanjing can be located on my map.

  Artist's signature (Leaf L)
  "In the mid-summer of the *gengzi* year [1660], Hu Yukun painted this album of twelve leaves."
  Artist's seals (on each leaf): Yukun (square relief); Yuanrun (square intaglio)

Collector's seals
  1. Zhou Lianggong (1612–1672): Zhou Liang (oval relief, A, L); Lai gu tang (rectangle relief, D, F); Lianggong zhi yin (square intaglio, B, I); Li Li (rectangle relief, C, H); Liyuan (small square intaglio, G, J); Liyuan (large square intaglio, E); Lai gu tang dushu ji (tall rectangle relief, K)
  2. Huang Chün-pi (b. 1899): Nanhai Huang Chün-pi cang (square relief, K); Chün-pi? Zhencang (square intaglio, L, lower left)

Published

Ming-Ch'ing chih chi ming-hua t'e-chan, Taipei (National Palace Museum), pl. 9 (Leaf L only)

17A

17B

17C

17D

17 E

17 F

17 G

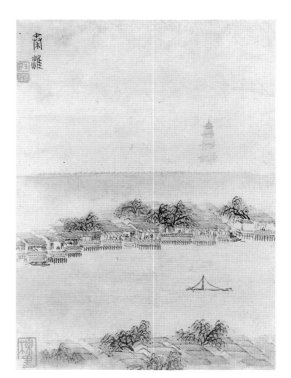

17 H

17 I

17 J

17 K

17 L

18. LANDSCAPE [not in exhibition]

Kuncan (Shiqi, ca. 1612–1693; DHL 2/8)
Dated 1661
Hanging scroll
Ink and light colors on paper. H 102.5 cm; W 29 cm
Collection: Huang Chün-pi, Taipei

Artist's inscription: twelve columns of running script:
    "Dongpo [Su Shi] said that the achievement in cal-
    ligraphy and painting should depend on the life
    breath and its reverberation, not on the mood of
    robustness; and that if one chose the latter, he
    would be trapped by vulgar conventions and [his
    painting] would not be worth being commented
    on. In our time Liyuan jushi [Zhou Lianggong] is
    not only an eminent man, but also a great connois-
    seur. He asked this monk Can to paint for him. I
    could not dare to present him my humble work.
    He asked me several times with such insistence that
    I had to wield brush and moisten it with ink to
    paint this. I feel my composition is rather nice, and
    the retired scholar [Zhou] also claps his hands, say-
    ing, 'Excellent! I am greatly honored!' What does
    this sound like?"
Signature: "Shidaoren. In the 8th month of the *xinqiu*
    year [1661] at Fuyun guan."
Artist's seals: Shiqi (square intaglio) Anju daoren
    (square intaglio)
Colophon by Wu Yusheng (modern): nineteen
    columns of standard script (silk mounting). Three
    seals.
Collector's seals: Tingyuan zhai (unidentified). five
    other seals (unidentified)

Published:
Ming-Qing zhi ji minghua tezhan. Taipei: National
    Palace Museum, 1970, pl. 29 (painting only)

19. WUDONG TREE STUDIO

Fu Shan (1607–1684)
Album leaf
Undated
Ink on paper. H 30 cm; W 32 cm
The Art Museum, Princeton University (y1962–109)

Artist's signature
"For Yuanliang sheweng [Zhou Lianggong], Painted
    by Fu Shan."
Artist's seal: Qingju (square intaglio)

Viewer's seal: Wang Shiyun (mid-17th c.): Guoqu seng
    (square relief, lower left)
No colophons
Collector's seals: unidentified (modern?): Meiqi shen-
    zang (square relief, lower left)

20. SUMMER MOUNTAINS AND MISTY RAIN

Wang Hui (1632–1717); colophon (dated 1669) by
    Wang Shimin (1592–1680)
Handscroll
Ink on paper
Asian Art Museum of San Francisco, 87D8

Title (4 characters written vertically by the artist):
    "Xiashan yinyu" (Summer Mountains and Misty
    Rain)
Artist's inscription: "In the 8th month of the year of
    wushen [1668], Wumushan zhongren, Wang Hui,
    painted this at a travel lodging in Suzhou."
Colophon dated 1669 by Wang Shimin: eighteen
    columns of standard script:
    "Calligraphy and painting have sometimes
    flourished, sometimes declined during past dynas-
    ties, but the wonderful works by Zhong [Zhong
    Yao] and Wang [Wang Shizhi] have seldom been
    reached. Students of painting in later times have
    tried to follow the superior path of Dong Yuan and
    Juran, but although the mountains and rivers
    inspired them with beauty, they were nevertheless
    dependent on the fashions of the time. After the
    Tang and Song periods the true current in painting
    was continued by the four great masters of the
    Yuan period, and by Zhao Mengfu. Later on in my
    country of Wu there were men like Shen Zhou,
    Wen Zhengming, Tang Yin, Qiu Ying, and finally
    Dong Qichang, who all used the brush differently,
    but nevertheless were all ardent students of the old
    masters and very close to them in every respect.
    But in recent times the Tao of art has been declin-
    ing; the old manners have been lost. Most men try
    to express their own ideas and scatter evil seeds
    about them. They wander in false directions and
    cannot be saved from disaster.
    "When Wang Shigu [Wang Hui] arose he again
    introduced the great masters of the Tang, Song,
    and Yuan dynasties by imitating and copying them
    very closely. As soon as one opens a scroll of his,
    one is impressed by the strong and rich coloring,
    and whatever the design or the 'short cuts' may be,
    they are quite in keeping with those of the old
    masters, and in his brushwork and spirit-resonance

he is superior to them. Furthermore, when he imitates a master of old, he is entirely like this particular model and does not do it by introducing elements from various masters. If the picture is not signed, it cannot be distinguished from the original. No artist before him could do that; even Wen Zhengming and Shen Zhou did not reach as far.

"This autumn [Wang Hui] will go to visit Liyuan Shaosinong [Zhou Lianggong] at his invitation and he will bring this painting as a present. Therefore, he has shown this to me and asked me to inscribe it for him. Liweng [Zhou] is a man of elegance and broad learning. He is the leader of scholar-officials and the patriarch of connoisseurs. He and Shigo [Wang Hui] have a great admiration for each other, therefore it is certain that they will strike a great accord when they meet. Furthermore, Shigu is moved by his friendship and thus will completely exhaust his inspired heart and marvelous fingers to create precious objects at their elegant and secluded gatherings. It is an example of the quote 'he who becomes a disciple of Confucius will make his name more renowned.' Although he could not meet Wenmin [Dong Qichang], he can now meet Sinong [Zhou Lianggong], which is enough to celebrate all his life. Why should he lament that he was not born when he [Dong Qichang] was still alive?

"On the 2nd day after Liqiu [the beginning day of autumn] in the year of *jizhou* [1669] during the Kangxi reign, the Xilu laoren Wang Shimin inscribed this at the age of seventy-eight."

Wang Shimin's seals: Wang Shimin yin (square intaglio); Xilu shanren (square relief)
Collectors' seals: Zhou Lianggong's 3 seals (Yuqing zhai juren; Laigutang; Liyuan), and others

21. MOUNTAIN RETREAT

Dai Benxiao (1621–1693) and Shi Lin (died ca. 1672; DHL 4/22)
Undated
Ink on paper. H 25 cm; W 31.4 cm
Metropolitan Museum of Art, New York
Seymour Fund, 1964.268.1

Artist's seals: Shi Lin si yin (square intaglio); Shi Yujian (square intaglio)
Colophon by Weng Ling (died ca. 1668; DHL 2/1): twenty-five columns of standard script.
Signature: "Weng Ling wrote this upon the request of

Master Liweng." Seals: [ ]-xing (rectangle intaglio); indecipherable seal (round relief, upper right)
Collector's seal: A–[ ] (rectangle relief, lower left corner)

Originally part of an album in the collection of Wang Chi-ch'ien (modern), New York. The pieces in cat. nos. 10 and 11 also originally were part of Wang Chi-ch'ien's album set. According to Mr. Wang, the original set also contained one leaf (landscape) by Fan Qi and one leaf (painting of plum blossom) by Chen Hongshou. He gave Chen's leaf to Osvald Sirèn and sold the rest to the Mi-chou Gallery.

22. MOUNTAIN UNDER SNOW [not in exhibition]

Yun Xiang (1586–1655; DHL 1/16)
Undated
Ink on paper. H 24.8 cm; W 32.4 cm

Artist's inscription: four columns of free-style standard script
Artist's signature: Xiangshan Xiang
Artist's seal: Yun Benqu (square intaglio); Daosheng (square intaglio)

Colophon (on painting leaf)
    Wu Guodui (1616–1680): four columns of standard script.
    Seal: Wu Guodui yin (square intaglio)
Collectors' seals: Wang Chi-ch'ien, two seals. Two unidentified seals.

Colophons (on facing leaf)
    1. Ji Zhi (*jinshi* 1658): four columns of running script.
        Signature: "Ji Zhi inscribed this."
        Seal: Ji Zhi (double seal, square relief)
    2. Cheng Zhengkui (1604–1676; DHL 2/6): three columns of free-style running script.
        Signature: "Qingqi." Seal: Zhengkui (square intaglio)
    3. Wang Shilu (1626–1673, *jinshi* 1652): four columns of running script
        Signature: "Lulian po dioa tu, Shilu inscribed this."
        Seal: Lulian po diao[?] (rectangle relief)

Collection: Unknown. Originally belonged to an album of 12 leaves, formerly in the collection of Wang Chi-ch'ien. The album leaves in cat. nos. 14 and 23 belonged to the same set.

21

22

23. SNOW LANDSCAPE [not in exhibition]

Ye Xin (fl. ca. 1640–1673; DHL 3/19)
Undated
Ink and colors on paper. H 24.8 cm; W 33 cm
No artist's signature or seals

Colophon (on painting leaf)
  Xu You[?] (ca. 1620–1664 DHL 3/3): seven columns
    of running script.
  Signature: "Xu You[?] inscribed Rongmu's [Ye
    Xin] painting."
  One seal.
Collectors' seals: Wang Chi-ch'ien; one seal.
  Two unidentified seals.

Colophons (on facing leaf)
  1. Lin Hongdao [Lin Chong?]: six columns of run-
    ning script
    Signature: "Lin Hongdao from Sanshan
      inscribed this."
    Seals: Lin Hongdao yin (square intaglio);
      Shouyi shi (square intaglio)
  2. Wu Guodui (1616–1680, jinshi 1658): two
    columns of running-cursive script.
    Signature: "Moyan."
    Two seals: Wu Guodui (square relief); Yusui shi
      (square relief)
Collection: Unknown. Originally belonged to an
  album of 12 leaves, formerly in the collection of
  Wang Chi-ch'ien. The album leaves in cat. nos. 14
  and 22 belonged to the same set.

23

24. LANDSCAPES

Zhang Feng (d. 1662)
Album of 12 Leaves
H 15.4 cm; W 22.9 cm
The Metropolitan Museum of Art, New York
Edward Eliott Family Collection
Gift of Douglas Dillon, 1987.408.2 (a–l)

25. FAN PAINTING

Cheng Sui (active 1650–1680)
Fan
H 16.5 cm; W 50.8 cm
H. Christopher Luce Collection, New York

26. LANDSCAPES

Gong Xian 1671
Album of 10 leaves
Ink or in color on paper
Each: H 24.1 cm; W 44.7 cm
Nelson-Atkins Museum of Art, Kansas City

27. ALBUM OF LANDSCAPES

Dong Qichang (1555–1636)
Dated 1630
Album of eight paintings and two facing pages of
     calligraphy

Ink on paper. H 24.5 cm; W 16 cm
The Metropolitan Museum of Art
Edward Elliott Family Collection
Gift of Douglas Dillon, 1986 (1986.266.5)

27

Catalogue 189

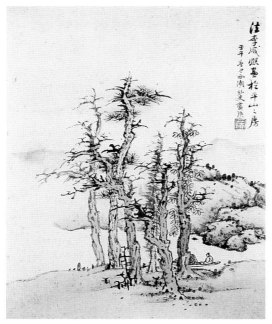

Leaf A

Leaf E

29

28. LANDSCAPES AFTER SONG AND YUAN MASTERS

Lan Ying (1585 – ca. 1664)
Dated 1642
Album of twelve painting leaves
Ink and color on paper. H 31.5 cm; W 24.7 cm
The Metropolitan Museum of Art
The Sackler Fund, 1970 (1970.2.2)

29. VIEWS OF NANJING: THE FOUR SEASONS

Wei Zhike (active ca. 1600 – after 1635)
Dated 1635
Handscroll
Ink and light color on paper. H 31.2 cm; W 11.8 m
The Metropolitan Museum of Art
Gift of J. T. Tai, 1968 (68.195)

30. LANDSCAPE IN THE STYLE OF HUANG GONGWANG

Wang Shimin (1592–1680)
Dated 1666
Hanging scroll
Ink on paper. H 134.5 cm; W 56.5 cm
The Metropolitan Museum of Art
Gift of Douglas Dillon, 1980 (1980.426.2)

30

31

31. LANDSCAPES IN THE STYLES OF OLD MASTERS

Wang Jian (1598–1677)
Dated 1668
Album of ten paintings and two double-leaf
    frontispieces by Wang Shimin (1592–1680)
Ink and color on paper. H 25.7 cm; W 16.5 cm
The Metropolitan Museum of Art
Purchase, The Dillon Fund Gift, 1979 (1979.439)

32. The Sound of Spring in a Lonely Valley

Hongren (1610–1664)
Dated 1661
Hanging scroll
Ink on paper. H 103 cm; W 41.3 cm
The Metropolitan Museum of Art
Bequest of John M. Crawford Jr., 1988 (1989.363.133)

33. Wooded Mountains at Dusk

Kuncan (1612–1673)
Dated 1666
Hanging scroll
Ink and color on paper. H 126.2 cm; W 60.6 cm
The Metropolitan Museum of Art
Bequest of John M. Crawford Jr., 1988 (1989.363.129)

34

34. ALBUM OF LANDSCAPES

Fan Qi (1616 – after 1694)
Dated 1646
Album of eight paintings
Ink and color on paper. H 16.8 cm; W 20.3 cm
The Metropolitan Museum of Art
The Sackler Fund, 1969 (69.242.8–15)

35. SNOW CLEARING: LANDSCAPE
AFTER LI CHENG

Wang Hui (1632–1717)
Dated 1669
Hanging scroll
Ink and color on paper. H 110.8 cm; W 35.5 cm
The Metropolitan Museum of Art
Gift of Mr. and Mrs. Earl Morse, in honor of
    Professor Wen Fong, 1978 (1978.13)

35

因樹爲屋

印癡櫟園

元亮

陶菴

生還偶遂

吾師退谷老人

生長秦淮

周亮工印

周元亮珍藏書画印

讀画樓

敢園就園閩雪北雪

亮工櫟園

賴古堂

學陶

(not to scale)

Notes

NOTES TO INTRODUCTION

1. As recorded in Wang Shimin, *Wang Fengchang shu-hua tiba, xia*, p. 7.
2. *Yinren zhuan*, chapter 2, entry 1 (YRZ 2/1), and YRZ 2/20, respectively.

NOTES TO CHAPTER ONE

3. Information on Zhou's family background is provided by the following biographical sources in *Lai gu tang ji fu lu* (hereafter LGTJ/FL) in *Lai gu tang ji* (LGTJ), a collection of Zhou's writings published ca. 1678 by Zhou's eldest son, Zhou Zaijun (b. 1640); Huang Yuji (1629–1691), *Xing zhuang* (Accounts of Conduct [of Zhou Lianggong]); Zhou Zaijun, *Xing shu* (Records of Conduct [of Zhou Lianggong]); *Nian pu* (Chronological Biography [of Zhou Lianggong]); Qian Lucan, *Muzhi ming* (Tomb Inscription [of Zhou Lianggong]); Jiang Chenying (1628–1699), *Muzhi ming* (Tombstone Inscription). The *Nian pu* is hereafter referred to as LGTJ/FL, *Nian pu*, *Xing zhuang* as LGTJ/FL, *Xing zhuang*, and *Xing shu* as LGTJ/FL, *Xing shu*. The above primary sources are extensively utilized in the three biographies of Zhou by Lu Zengyu, Zheng Fangkun, and Lin Ji included in the *Beijuan ji*, 10/21–26. Huang Yuji, Zhou Lianggong's student, was a noted scholar and bibliophile active in Nanking. Jiang Chenying was also a famous scholar and author. For Huang and Jiang, see their biographies in Arthur W. Hummel, *Eminent Chinese of the Ch'ing Period* (hereafter ECCP), pp. 355–6. For Qian Lucan (also called Qian Xiangling), see *Du Hua Lu*.
4. According to the family genealogy in the *Xing zhuang* and *Xing shu* sections of the LGTJ, the founder of the Zhou clan was Zhou Guang of the Song dynasty, a *jin-shi* (metropolitan graduate) degree holder, who lived in Nanjing. Zhou Guang moved his family to Jinqi, Jiangxi, where he was sent as prefectural military administrator. His descendants thereafter remained in Jinqi at a place called Lixia for generations until the sixteenth century. Two of the best-known *hao* of Zhou Lianggong, Lixia and Li Yuan, refer to Lixia.
5. LGTJ/FL, *Nian pu*; LGTJ/FL, *Xing shu*, p. 39.
6. *Zhuji Xianzhi*, 26/22.
7. DHL 1/8 refers to *Du Hua Lu*, chapter 1, entry 8. This convention will be followed hereafter to refer to all *Du Hua Lu* entries.

8. Chen Danzhong (*jinshi* of 1643) was a teacher of the Nanjing painter Gao Cen (DHL 3/4). It can be assumed that Zhou Wenwei befriended Chen Hongshou while he was posted in Zhuji, Chen's hometown. Zhou Wenwei and Chen were both shengyuan degree holders, and it is reasonable to assume that the men would have met given the size of the small town and their common interest in art. We know that Zhou Lianggong met Chen while visiting his father at Zhuji. Since Zhou was only thirteen years old (in the Chinese calculation), and thus too young to initiate a friendship with Chen, who was thirteen years his senior, it is quite likely the two met through Zhou's father.
9. Zhou Lianggong mentions that one of the paintings in his father's collection was "Night Revels of Han Xizai" by Zhang Lu of the Ming dynasty; his seal carver friends and seal collection are mentioned in *Yinren zhuan* (YRZ), *zhuan* 1, entries 4 and 5.
10. LGTJ/FL, *Xing shu*, p. 53.
11. For a detailed discussion of Nanjing, see Frederick W. Mote, "The Transformation of Nanking 1350–1400," pp. 150–2, and Wang Huan-piao, et al., ed., *Shoudu zhi* (hereafter SDZ), vol. 1, pp. 436–437.
12. See de Bary, et al., *Sources of Chinese Tradition*, p. 24. Important studies on the Northern Song development include: James Cahill, "Confucian Elements in the Theory of Painting"; Susan Bush, *The Chinese Literati on Painting: Su Shih (1037–1101) to Tung Ch'i-ch'ang (1555–1636)*; Wm. T. de Bary, "Neo-Confucian Cultivation and Enlightenment."
13. Jiangnan refers to the rich region "south of the [Yangzi] river" within the Yangzi delta, including Nanjing, Suzhou, and Shanghai.
14. See the list of government offices in Nanjing during the Qing in SDZ, vol. 1, pp. 517–519.
15. William Atwell, "From Education to Politics: The Fu She," p. 354.
16. For a description of the Qinhuai district, see SDZ, vol. 1, pp. 422–438. Yu Huai, *Banchao zazhi*, trans. by Howard Levy under the title *A Feast of Mist and Flowers: The Gay Quarters of Nanking at the End of the Ming*; and Zhang Dai, *Taoan mengyi*.
17. For an extensive discussion of the Fushe and the importance of Nanjing in the Fushe movement, see Atwell, "From Education to Politics: The Fu She"; Wu Weiye, "Fu She Jishi"; and Lu Shiyi, "Fu She Jilie" in *Donglin yu Fu She*, pp. 33–116. Also see the Fushe founder Zhang Pu's biography in ECCP, pp. 52–53.
18. The Fang family included the high scholar-official Fang Gongqian and his son Fang Hengxian, a *jinshi* connoisseur-painter who is included in the *Du Hua Lu* as well

as the celebrated literatus Fang Wen. They were all relatives of the scholar-philosopher-painter Fang Yizhi. The two notorious powerbrokers of the Southern Ming court at Nanjing, Ruan Dacheng and Ma Shiying, were also refugees during this period.

19. See Frederic Wakeman, Jr., "The Shun Interregnum of 1644," pp. 47–49.

20. Biographies of Dong and Wang are included in Goodrich and Fang, *Dictionary of Ming Biographies* (hereafter DMB).

21. For a discussion of the cultural life of Nanjing during the 1620s and 1630s, see Willard J. Peterson, *Bitter Gourd: Fang I-chih and The Impetus for Intellectual Change* (hereafter *Bitter Gourd*), pp. 25–35.

22. All these men are included in ECCP.

23. Gongyuan was established during the Yongle reign (1403–1425) of the Ming. Jiuyuan, popularly called Chuzhong, was established by Emperor Taizi at the beginning of the Ming to house officially registered courtesans. During Taizi's day it was called Fuleyuan. Thereafter, the area around it became the most famous pleasure quarter in Jiangnan. See SDZ, vol. I, pp. 430–431.

24. LGTJ/FL, *Xing shu*.

25. Peterson, *Bitter Gourd*, p. 34.

26. See Ai's biography in ECCP, p. 4.

27. Zhou states in *Shu ying*, pp. 67, 113–153, that Ai's literary view was orthodox and should be followed. Zhou held on to this view even after he joined the Fushe, which was led by Chen Zilong and others who opposed Ai and followed the former and latter Seven Masters who advocated a direct return to the ancient literature, bypassing the Song masters. For the opposition between Ai and Chen, see Lu Shiyi, "Fu She Jilie" in *Donglin yu Fu She*, pp. 49–50; Peterson, *Bitter Gourd*, pp. 29–30; and Atwell, "Chen Tzu-lung (1608–1647): A Scholar-Official and the Late Ming Dynasty," ch. 2. For a further discussion on late Ming and early Qing literary movements, see R. John Lynn, "Orthodoxy and Enlightenment: Wang Shih-chen's Theory of Poetry and Its Antecedents." Zhou remained a close friend of Ai. His admiration for Ai is evidenced by the fact that more essays by Ai were included in his LGT *wen xuan* than by any other author. Ai joined the Ming resistance army in the South and died in 1646 in Fujian. When Zhou was posted in Fujian in 1647, he sent Ai's coffin back to his native place, Nanchang, Jiangxi, for burial. See LGTJ/FL, *Xing shu*, p. 54.

28. LGTJ 16/4–6.

29. See Gong's colophon in cat. no. 6 , Leaf FF.

30. This area was dotted with historical sites. According to tradition, during the Eastern Jin, the area was occupied by one of the period's most celebrated families, the Wang family from Shandong, which included Wang Xizhi and Wang Xianzhi. The Taoye Ferry was so named because it was where Wang Xianzhi once awaited the arrival of his new concubine from across the canal. See SDZ, p. 427.

31. Such studies as James Cahill's "Wu Pin and His Landscape Paintings" have brought to light some interesting painters active in Nanjing during the early seventeenth century. Yet we still have only a limited knowledge of Nanjing art during this formative period when the city was just beginning to emerge as an artistic center. Since an understanding of late Ming Nanjing art may further our understanding of artistic trends in the city during the early Qing, I have given a rather lengthy discussion on the city's artistic milieu in the 1620s.

32. The influence of artists from Suzhou on Nanjing was particularly strong. Suzhou was an important artistic center in its own right and, during the Ming-Qing transition period, was still under the dominant influence of Wen Zhengming. Many members of the Wen family stayed for extended periods of time in Nanjing and many Nanjing painters such as Jiang Qian (fl. 1540–1560), a son of the above-mentioned Zhe school painter Jiang Song, went to Suzhou to study with the Wen family.

33. For the study of Wu and Wang, see Elizabeth Fulder, "Professional Painters in Fukien and Nanking" in James Cahill, ed., *The Restless Landscape: Chinese Painting of the Late Ming Period*, pp. 103–114. Also see James Cahill, "Wu Pin and His Landscape Paintings."

34. For Zheng and Gao, see Fulder, "Professional Painters in Fukien and Nanking."

35. See Gu Qiyuan, *Kezi juiyu*, 10/8–10. Zhou basically repeats Gu's appraisal of Hu in Zhou Lianggong, *Lai gu tang shuhua ba* (hereafter LGTSHB), 22. Yao Lushi, a Han-lin scholar, was well known for his plum paintings and calligraphy. Yao was the father of the *Du Hua Lu* painter Yao Royi (DHL 4/6). For an example of Yao Lushi's painting, see *Bai mei ji*.

36. Zhou quotes the above passage by Gu twice in his own writings on Hu Zongren. See DHL 2/4 and LGTSHB, 22.

37. Despite the fact that Zhou owned some paintings by Gao Yang and Gao Yu, he never commented on them as far as I know.

38. DHL I/13.

39. Zhu was a descendant of Prince Qi (Zhu Fu, 1364–1428), the seventh son of Zhu Yuanzhang, the founder of the Ming. See Chen Rendao, *Jin kui [King Kwei] cang hua pingshi (Jin kui* THPS), pp. 185–189. The same source says he died at the age of sixty-seven. He was a member of the literary society in Nanjing called Lan She.

40. See DHL 3/15.

41. See DHL I/14.

42. Gao Fu, according to his letter to Zhou's third son, Zhou Zaiyan, became a *shengyuan* and a teacher of Zhou's sons. See Zhou Lianggong, *Lai gu tang chidu xin chao* (hereafter LGT, *Chidu*), II, 8/12. Le Yao stayed at Zhou's home for a prolonged period of time. Circumstantial evidence suggests that he might have been hired as a tutor for Zhou's sons.

43. DHL I/15.

44. See DHL I/15 and LGTSHB, 4 and 5.

45. He acquired seals by the member of the Qiulong society (of seal carvers) in Liangxi [Wuxi], including Qin Yu (YRZ 3/1) and Wang Ting (YRZ 3/6). These seals were brought to him in 1630 and 1631 by Gu Yinxi from Liangxi, who knew of Zhou's fondness for seals (YRZ 3/1).

46. LGTJ 20/13–14.

47. The three, which are all in hanging scroll format, include a painting of a tree in the collection of Wang Chi-ch'ien, New York; a landscape reproduced in *Shina nanga shusei,* III, 3 (listed in Osvald Sirén, *Chinese Painting*, VII, 318); and a bamboo painting in the photograph collection of the Art and Archaeology Department, Princeton University. The authenticity of these paintings remains to be studied.

48. Zhou's calligraphy in running script was classified in the *neng pin* (able class) category by the renowned calligraphy critic Bao Shichen (1775–1855) in his book *Yizhou shuangji,* p. 86. Also see Zhou's letter in LGTJ, 20/10 to Hu

Yukun in which he mentioned that he received many requests for calligraphy. Zhou's calligraphy has been published in Yujiro Nakata and Shen Fu's *Obei shuzo Chugoku hosho meisekishu*, vol. IV, fig. 21, and in the *Illustrated Catalogue of the Tokyo National Museum, Chinese Calligraphies*, p. 98.

49. See LGTJ/FL, *Nian pu*. Since no complete list of Fushe branches exists, it is often difficult to document whether local branches, which were given separate names, in fact belonged to Fushe. Since most of the members of the Xingshe, including Huang Zongxi, were clearly part of the Fushe, it seems reasonable to assume that it was a branch. Zhou was in close contact with Huang and many other Fushe members who were active in Nanjing at this date.

50. Huang was the son of the loyal member of the Donglin faction Huang Zunsu (1584–1626), who was executed four years earlier because of his opposition to the eunuch Wei Zhongxian (1568–1627). Wu was the maternal uncle of Fang Yizhi.

51. Wu Weiye placed first in the *jinshi* examination of the following year.

52. See Zhou's biography of Wan in YRZ 1/14.

53. For Chen's biography, see ECCP, pp. 102–103. The Shen brothers, both Fushe members, were natives of Xuancheng, Anhui. At least three of the men cited — Shen Shoumin, Chen Zilong, and Wan Shouqi — signed the famous manifesto, the "Liu du fang luan gong zhi," which was an open memorial drafted by Fushe members in 1638 impeaching Ruan Dacheng. Ruan was a former Donglin member who betrayed the "party" by becoming an adopted son of the notorious eunuch Wei Zhongxian, the leader of the opposing faction.

54. "From the time education [began to] decline, scholars have not understood the wisdom embodied in the classics. Instead they plagiarize what they have heard and seen and call it their own. Some have been lucky enough to become officials. [But] those at court are incapable of advising the emperor [and] those who are local officials do not know how to help the people. There are fewer and fewer talented men and the government gets worse every day. This is all because [of the decline in education]. I do not want [to attempt] to measure [my own] virtue nor calculate [my own] ability. I [only] hope to join with many scholars from all over the empire to revive the ancient teachings so that future generations will be able to provide useful service [for the country]. For this reason, [our group's] name is Fushe." Translated by W. Atwell in "From Education to Politics: The Fu She," p. 345. My discussion of the Fushe below is greatly indebted to Atwell's study.

55. The first project he carried out when he received his first government appointment as a magistrate in Shandong province in 1641 was to found a literary society. The society, which promoted education among poor students from the locality and prepared young scholars for the examination, was probably a branch of Fushe.

56. See LGTJ/FL, *Nian pu*, under 1631.

57. Zhou might have even joined his Fushe friends in the 1636 anti-Ruan Dacheng campaign and suffered the consequences when Ruan emerged as a powerful figure in the Nanjing court and took revenge on those who signed the memorial. See Atwell, p. 356; ECCP, p. 458.

58. Zhou's biography of Zhang is contained in LGTJ 18/1–4. Much of the discussion below is based on information contained in this biography.

59. Zhang was a key figure in maintaining the city's defenses under the five-month siege by Li's army in 1642. Zhang stayed on even after the local officials fled and died when the rebel army broke the dike of the Bian River, a tributary of the Yellow River, and flooded Xiangfu. It is quite probable that Zhang organized a local defense group in the years before 1642 to face the rebel uprising and rampant banditry which were commonplace throughout the north at this time.

60. See Sun's biography in ECCP, pp. 669–670. For a discussion of his catalogue, see Hsin-cheung Lovell, *An Annotated Bibliography of Chinese Painting Catalogues and Related Texts*, pp. 34–35, entry 46.

61. See LGTJ/FL, *Nian pu*, under 1635.

62. See YRZ 1/3.

63. Although we have no direct evidence from this period, later the two were involved in artistic activities together in Beijing.

64. Zhou remained a devoted disciple of Sun and in all his writings referred to Sun as *fuzi*, or teacher. The importance of the traditional examiner-examinee bond between them can be seen in the DHL 4/17–18. Zhou's deep gratitude to Zhang Minbiao is evident in his reaction to the tragic death of Zhang and his family in 1642 when the flood swept through Xiangfu. Zhou took Zhang's only surviving son into his home and brought him up. Zhou arranged the younger Zhang's wedding and bought back his original family estate for him. See LGTJ/FL, *Nian pu*, p. 4. Zhou also had Zhang's posthumous portrait painted and published in his writings. See DHL 1/4 and 3/9.

65. LGTJ/FL, *Nian pu* records this event under 1634. But since Sun did not take up his post until 1635, the date given by the *Nian pu* is incorrect and probably should read 1635. Also see LGTJ/FL, *Xing shu*, p. 40. Zhou later commemorated this event in a poem entitled, "Poem [to commemorate] a farm my teacher Beihai [Sun Chengze] bought for me." This poem is recorded in LGTJ 1/2. Other biographical material can be found in the *Xing shu* section of the LGTJ/FL.

66. See LGTJ/FL, *Nian pu* and *Xing zhuang*. Zhou is included in the list of *juren* degree holders in *Xiangfu xianzhi*, *zhuan* 11. Song Wan (1614–1673, *jinshi* 1647) from Shandong and Qian Lucan from Yushan notes that they also studied Zhou's provincial examination essay. See LGTJ *wen xuan*, 19/17; LGTJ/FL, *Muzhi ming*. For Song, see his biography in ECCP, p. 690.

67. The biographies of the four, all of whom were Zhou's friends, are located in ECCP.

68. All six have biographies in ECCP. By August 1639, Sun Chengze had been promoted as senior censor and placed in charge of the Kaifeng area tax administration with his office in Kuide, near Shangqiu. The Song family lived in Kuide. LGTJ/FL, *Xing zhuang*.

069. See DHL 2/2. In 1637, Zhou went to Kuide to visit Song Quan. See Zhou's poem entitled "Unable to Sleep at the Xueyuan," LGTJ 3/2. Song's son, Song Lao, also recalls Zhou's visit to his father in *Xipo leigao* (XPLG).

70. See LGTJ/FL, *Nian pu* under this year and LGTJ 9/12.

71. See Song Lao, XPLG, 13/6. Song records his gathering with Zhou and Zhou's circle at Qinhuai, Nanjing. See Song, XPLG 9/1. The intimate friendship between Zhou and Song Lao is evidenced by the many sorrowful poems Song composed in remembrance of Zhou for quite some time after Zhou's death. See Song, XPLG 3/7–8. He also recounted a dream he had after Zhou's death in which he

composed poems together with Zhou and Du Jun. See Song, XPLG 15/9.

72. See their biographies in ECCP. For a study of northern collectors, see Shen Fu, "Wang To and His Circle."

73. See Song Lao, *Man tang shuhua ba*, p. 83 and XPLG 4/15, 28/22. Song Lao notes that he met Wu Hong when the latter was a guest at the Xueyuan. Song also mentions that the two became friends and that Wu greatly benefited from studying the Song family collection of old paintings bestowed by the emperor (Shunzhi, r. 1644–1661) on his father Song Quan. Song points out that, through his family, Wu met the famous collector Liang Qingbiao, who commissioned Wu to copy some works from the Yuan dynasty. Zhou Lianggong introduced Wu to another eminent northern literatus and connoisseur, Song Wan (see DHL). These northern contacts developed by Wu Hong help explain his direct indebtedness to Northern Song landscape paintings, which were then largely in the collection of such famous northern collectors as Song Lao and Liang Qingbiao. They also explain Wu's popularity among the northern collectors and their frequent mention of his name in their writings. Song mentioned that he saw Wu in the autumn of 1679. The meeting probably took place in Nanjing. See Song, XPLG 3/15.

74. See DHL 3/13.

75. See LGTJ/FL, *Nian pu* under 1633.

76. LGTJ 3/13.

77. A list of *jinshi* degree recipients of the same year (who called each other *tongnian*) is found in *Ming-Qing jinshi timing beiming suoyin*, pp. 2616–2619.

NOTES TO CHAPTER TWO

78. For a description of their reunion, see Zhou's biography of Chen in DHL 1/15.

79. For detailed biographical information on Chen, see Huang Yongchuan, *Chen Hongshou Nian pu* and *Wangming bianxing juyi huajia zuopin zhan*.

80. Jin Bao, mentioned here, was Chen's close friend from Hangzhou. He received his *jinshi* in 1640 together with Zhou and was to live the life of a Ming loyalist and priest. See Jin's biography in ECCP, p. 166. Wu Ruijong was a *juren* of 1621 and a Fushe member. For Wu, see LGT, *Chidu*, vol. 1, ch. 7, and *Lidai huashi huizhuan*, ch. 45.

81. In 1640, when Fang and Zhou passed the metropolitan examination, the two became close friends. Strong bonds of friendship between *tongnian* were commonplace. As Miyazaki writes: "Those who became *jinshi* in the same year called each other 'classmate,' associated as comrades, and helped each other in times of need." See I. Miyazaki, *China's Examination Hell*, p. 89.

82. See Peterson, *Bitter Gourd*, pp. 115–116.

83. See *Yinshuwu Shuying*, pp. 116, 143, 144.

84. The seventh-rank post of magistrate was often given to those whose names appeared on the second and third lists of the metropolitan graduates. Zhou was on the third list. See Ch'u T'ung-tsu, *Local Government in China Under the Ch'ing*, p. 212, n. 26.

85. Zhou's poem is extant. See LGTJ 3/2. For more information, see Fang Yizhi's biography in DHL 2/7.

86. See LGTJ/FL, *Xingzhuang*, p. 27.

87. Zhou Lianggong, LGT, *wenxuan*, 19/17. Zhou Zaijun writes of his father's frugality: "During his 30-year-long government career, his property was not even comparable

to that of a middle-class family. He was content with a plain life and treated himself as if he was not an official, which was unbearable to some. . . . " See LGTJ/FL, *Xingzhuang*.

88. LGTJ/FL, *Nian pu* under 1641 and LGTJ/FL, *Xingzhuang*.

89. This is, however, difficult to prove since surviving Fushe records do not give a complete list of local branches.

90. Kojiro Yoshikawa, *An Introduction to Sung Poetry*, p. 98. "In traditional China, where formal schooling tended to be nominal and real learning was done at home under hired tutors, the relationship between teacher and disciple was less important than that between the students who took the civil service examination and the head of the examining committee, for those who passed the examination looked upon the head of the examining committee as the true teacher."

91. For a detailed discussion on local administration and the everyday official duties of a district magistrate, see Ch'u T'ung-tsu, *Local Government in China Under the Ch'ing* and John R. Watt, *The District Magistrate in Late Imperial China*, New York: Columbia University Press, 1972.

92. Quiet-sitting was an important means of spiritual cultivation which had as its ultimate goal "self-transcendency." For a full discussion of the Neo-Confucian practice of quiet-sitting and the concept of *wushi*, see de Bary, *Neo-Confucian Cultivation and Enlightenment*, pp. 17–172, 184–188.

93. After many years when Zhou heard that a magistrate ordered the removal of the placard because he felt that an official could not be in government service with no business to attend to, Zhou could not help but lament the ignorance of the man. See *Shuying*, 3/66, 5/135, 7/196.

94. de Bary, *Neo-Confucian Cultivation and Enlightenment*, p. 171.

95. Fang was probably on his way to see his father, who was in exile in Shaoxing, Zhejiang.

96. See DHL 2/5.

97. See Ho Ping-ti, *The Ladder of Success in Imperial China: Aspects of Social Mobility;* and Evelyn S. Rawski, *Education and Popular Literacy in Ch'ing China*.

98. This aspect of the seventeenth century has been marvelously explored in Peterson, *Bitter Gourd*, pp. 81–100. My discussion below is largely inspired by Peterson's book.

99. See Peterson, *Bitter Gourd*, pp. 81–84. Due to limited space, part of this passage has been eliminated.

100. See Peterson, *Bitter Gourd*, p. 92. Although Peterson does not identify Gu's nephew, he was probably Xu Qianxue. Gu at one time stayed with Xu and was disgusted by his many other "guests." See ECCP, pp. 421–426.

101. LGTJ 13/9.

102. See discussion on Nanjing art in the early seventeenth century on pp. 27–39.

103. For a discussion on Shen and Sheng, see Lucy Lohwa Yang, "The Wu School in the Late Ming, II: Innovative Masters," and Yoko Woodson, "The Sung-chiang (Yun-chien) Painters, 1: Sung Hsu and his Followers" in James Cahill, The Restless Landscape.

104. Letters to Hu from both Gong Xian and Cheng are found in LGT, *Chidu*, 1, 10/12.

105. See DHL 2/5.

106. See LGTSHB 22. In another letter Zhou admires Hu's understanding of color: "The ancients used colors to express plainness. Contemporaries use colors to show col-

orfulness. Only you, [Yukun] are able to discern the reason. Please instruct me." See LGT, *Chidu*, I, 12/8.

107. LGT, *Chidu*, I, 12/7.

108. YRZ 2/1.

109. Similar concepts frequently appear in late Ming and early Qing poetic theory. One example is Qian Qianyi's use of the word *xingling* (native sensibilities) and Wang Shizhen's *fenggu/qingxing* (personal temperament/intuitive power of discernment). See Richard J. Lynn, "Orthodoxy and Enlightenment: Wang Shizhen's Theory of Poetry and Its Antecedents," pp. 239, 243. For a discussion of the philosophical meaning of these terms, see Ku Hsiench'eng's essay cited in de Bary, *Neo-Confucian Cultivation and Enlightenment*, p. 181. This will be discussed further below.

110. LGTJ 13/4–5; the original statement is derived from the Tang poet Han Yu.

111. James Cahill, "Confucian Elements in the Theory of Chinese Painting" and Wright's introduction in Wright, ed. *The Confucian Persuasion*, p. 9.

112. LGTJ 14/19.

113. A close analysis of the descriptive words used by Zhou to express his approval or disapproval of paintings allows us to see what he meant by "scholarly spirit" in paintings. Paintings possessing scholarly spirit were described as "ancient," "hoary," "secluded," "tranquil," "deep," "simple," "lofty," "refined," "pure," "placid," "far-reaching," "resonant," "empty and vast," "serene," and "lonely and desolate." Vulgar works on the other hand were described as "sweet," "seductive," "voluptuous," "dazzling," "gorgeous," "crafty," "artificial," "incoherent," "obscure," "frigid," "insubstantial," "shallow," and "direct."

114. DHL 1/11.

115. *Shuying*, 6/158.

116. See DHL 1/2.

117. See DHL 4/11.

118. Wm. T. de Bary, p. 164. De Bary's summary of the Neo-Confucian concept of self-cultivation seems particularly apt: "As set forth in the *Chin-ssu lu*, the practice of sagehood is an all-embracing system of self cultivation. To integrate and maintain in balance different vital human activities, so that they foster and nourish each other, is of the essence."

119. The Manchus had been a formidable power north of the Great Wall since the end of the sixteenth century. By 1636 they had established the Qing dynasty with its capital at Shenyang and had subjugated the Korean peninsula.

120. In addition to whatever he learned from Zhang Minbiao while in Kaifeng, he studied Mao Yuanyi's (1594–ca. 1641, Guian, Zhejiang) *Wubei zhi* (self-preface dated 1621), an extensive military treatise of 240 *zhuan*. At the end of the Ming a large number of literati evidently were trained in martial arts and the military strategy. Qian Qianyi, for example, as a close friend of Mao Yuanyi, seems to have been well versed in military affairs. Mao Yuanyi, who lived in Nanjing, was a grandson of Mao Kun, who also wrote extensively on military matters. See *Shuying*, p. 110. For Mao's biography, see DMB, p. 1053. Many Fushe members such as Fang Yizhi and Chen Zilong also had military training. This aspect of late Ming is also discussed by Peterson, *Bitter Gourd*, pp. 88–96.

121. Zhou Lianggong, *Tongjin*, pp. 10–11.

122. See LGTJ/FL *Nian pu*; LGTJ/FL *Xingzhuang*; LGTJ /FL *Xingshu*. In memory of the Kaifeng people, Zhou had his family in Nanjing reprint the *Dongjing meng hua lu* (A

Journey in Memory to the Eastern Capital), an account of Kaifeng written by Meng Yuanlao of the Southern Song.

123. LGTJ/FL, Xingshu, p. 41. Zhou's friend Chen Zilong was also cited for his service in quelling a local uprising while working as magistrate of Shaoxing, Zhejiang. See Chen's biography in ECCP, pp. 102–103.

124. See LGTJ/FL, *Nian pu* under 1643. Zhou destroyed this shrine some twenty years later. See LGTJ 19/12–14.

125. See Frederic Wakeman, Jr., "The Shun Interregnum of 1644" for a vivid description of the capital city right before and immediately after its fall to Li Zicheng's army. I have drawn much information from Wakeman's study for the following discussion.

126. Angela Hsi, "Wu San-kuei in 1644: A Reappraisal."

127. YRZ 1/11–12.

128. The Ming commander Wu Sangui joined the Manchus in opposing Li after Li captured Beijing. See ECCP, p. 878.

129. See ECCP, pp. 587 for Ni and 229–230 for Fan.

130. For Zhou, see LGTJ/FL, *Nian pu* under 1644. For Sun, see ECCP, pp. 669–670.

131. See LGTJ/FL, *Nian pu* under 1644.

132. This account, titled "Guobian nanchen chao," is included in *Minzhong zhilie*, pp. 53–58.

133. Wakeman, "The Shun Interregnum of 1644," p. 67.

134. See LGTJ/FL, *Nian pu* under 1644.

135. The Prince of Fu was proclaimed emperor on the 19th of the 6th month of 1644. See the biographies of the Prince, Ma, Ruan, and Shi in ECCP.

136. Biographies of all these men are included in ECCP.

137. See Atwell, "The Fu She," p. 356.

138. LGTJ/FL, *Nian pu* under 1644.

139. See LGTJ/FL, *Nian pu* under 1644.

140. *Donghualu xuanji*, p. 17.

141. See *Qian Muzhai xiansheng nian pu*, p. 8.

142. *Donghualu xuanji*, p. 17.

143. *Donghualu xuanji*, pp. 16–17.

144. It is said that when Wang Duo called the roll, Zou Zhilin was unable to respond to Wang's call out of humiliation and that Qian Qianyi saved Zou from the situation. Zou reportedly later boasted that he therefore did not give in to the Manchus. See *Qingshi*, vol. 8, *zhuan* 530, p. 5825.

145. *Qingshi*, vol. 8, p. 5825.

146. See LGTJ/FL, *Nian pu* under 1645.

147. For an excellent discussion on the question of loyalty, see F. Mote, "Confucian Eremitism in the Yuan Period." Mote points out (p. 258) that the notion of *zhong*, or loyalty as a moral duty, theoretically binding on all servitors of a fallen dynasty only gained prominence under Neo-Confucian thought, which "promoted a new concept of loyalty consonant with its exultation of the ruler and the state." The roots of this interpretation of *zhong*, which was exploited by the holders of power, "do not go deeply into the thought of Confucius and Mencius, where in fact its ideological foundations are at least implicitly denied, but stems from Hsun-tzu and the Legalists."

Perhaps the most important point made by Mote is that "the workings of the loyalty concept varied with varying circumstances" (p. 288). The question of loyalty was a particularly emotional issue when the succeeding dynasty was an alien one. This posed serious problems for the Manchus who "were neither as confident in their military superiority, as willing to try to rule without integrating the Chinese into their administration, nor as insensitive to the feelings of their Chinese subjects, as were the Mongols" (p. 288).

The Manchu's recognition of the need to incorporate the Chinese into their administration in the early years of the dynasty and their attempt to preserve Chinese institutions, however, helped attract some scholar-officials into their service.

148. LGTJ/FL, *Xingzhuang*.

149. Zhang's letter is included in LGT *Chidu*, I, 9/2.

150. LGTJ 19/12–14.

151. YRZ 2/10.

152. YRZ 2/1.

NOTES TO CHAPTER THREE

153. Ding's home was a gathering place of Fushe members. See SDZ, p. 139.

154. See Qian Qianyi, *Yuxue ji*, 6/9

155. To raise Lu Yang's halberd alludes to the Ming restoration. Huainanzi narrates that during the battle of Hangou, when it was getting dark, Lu Yang raised the sun with his halberd. See Morohashi, *Dai kanwa jiten*, vol. 12, p. 728. Similar allusions appear constantly in Qian's poetry.

156. LGTJ/FL, *Xingzhuang*.

157. See LGTJ/FL, *Xingzhuang*. For a general discussion on the Lianghuai salt administration, see Jonathan Spence, *Tsao Yin and the K'ang-hsi Emperor*, pp. 166–200 and Ho Ping-ti, "The Salt Merchants of Yangchou: A Study of Commercial Capitalism in Eighteenth Century China."

158. See the list of books Zhou authored or compiled in Qian Lucan's *Muzhiming* in LGTJ/FL. Hereafter LGTJ/FL, *Muzhiming*.

159. YRZ 1/14.

160. See *Qingshi*, vol. 7, p. 5427.

161. LGTJ 7/15, 8/3.

162. Quoted from Gao's "A Poem on the Du Hua Pavilion," recorded in Liu Qunlin, *Qinghuajia shishi* (hereafter QHJSS), vol. 1, part 1, p. 56. Also see YRZ 1/15.

163. Zhu Ruiwu, who lived in Qinhuai when Zhou was growing up, became a monk just before 1644 and moved to the southern suburbs of Nanjing. Zou Zhe was still living in Qinhuai.

164. By 1668, Zhou owned some twenty seals carved by Cheng. See YRZ 1/14.

165. See DHL 2/15. Gong remained in Wucheng for about ten years.

166. YRZ 1/14.

167. YRZ 1/12.

168. Han was a concubine of the seal-carver Liang Qianqiu, a brother of Liang Danian. According to Zhou, Han's seals were valued by such famous contemporary scholars as He Cide and Du Jun.

169. YRZ 1/15.

170. YRZ 2/14.

171. Zhou's opposition to Zheng can be viewed in light of recent studies of the response of the Ming elite to the transition period. One study shows that the "gentry" of Tongcheng, Anhui, offered no strong resistance to alien rule and that they even made successful efforts to minimize the disruption during this traumatic period by cooperating with the new regime. See Hilary J. Beattie, "The Alternative to Resistance: The Case of T'ung-ch'eng," in Spence and Wills, ed. *From Ming to Ch'ing: Conquest, Region, and Continuity in Seventeenth-Century China*, pp. 239–276. Another study reveals that, even before the fall of the

Ming, a leading gentry member of Huizhou, Anhui, led the local militia in repelling a Ming army that was pillaging the area. See Jerry Dennerline, "Hsü-tu and the Lesson of Nanjing: Political Integration and the Local Defense in Chiang-nan, 1634–1645," in Spence and Wills, *From Ming to Ch'ing*, pp. 89–133. Another aspect that remains to be investigated in order to understand Zhou's military activities in Fujian is the contemporary view of Zheng Chenggong and his "Ming revival effort" and the ultimate reason for Zheng's failure.

172. Records of Zhou's activities in Fujian contain valuable information on Zheng Chenggong's army and the Fujian coastal problems of the mid-seventeenth century. See LGTJ/FL, Xingshu, *Xingzhuang*, and *Muzhiming*.

173. LGTJ/FL, *Xingshu* and *Xingzhuang*.

174. LGTJ/FL, *Xingshu*.

175. LGTJ/FL, *Xingshu*, pp. 45–46.

176. Excessive melting fees were often charged by officials involved in tax collection.

177. Xie Zhaozhe is best remembered for his book, *Wuza si*. Zhou befriended the Xie family in Fujian and acquired a portion of Xie's collection from Xie's son. See DMB, p. 550. The Huang family apparently moved to Nanjing from Fujian during Huang Zhuzhong's lifetime with their book collection. Huang was a close friend of Huang Zongxi and Qian Qianyi, both of whom often visited the family's library, Qianqing zhai, in Nanjing. Huang's son Huang Yuji became Zhou's student in the early 1660s and left an invaluable biography of Zhou and an account of Zhou's famous party at his Du Hua Pavilion in the winter of 1669. See DHL 4/19.

178. YRZ 3/21.

179. See LGTJ/FL, *Xingshu*. Shihualou probably refers to a collection of Yan Yu's poetry entitled *Canglang shihua*.

180. See LGTSHB, entry 25 and LGTJ 4/7.

181. LGTJ 3/12, 4/8, 5/1, 7/7.

182. YRZ 3/22.

183. See LGTJ 5/16, 7/6. Wu Weiye also refers to Zhou's Jimo in his poems recorded in *Jing huajia shishi, jia/shang*, 10. In his preface to these poems, Wu comments: "Zhou Liyuan has a habit of collecting ink-sticks (*mobi*), which at one time amounted to ten thousand specimens. He used to offer libation to these ink-sticks on New Year's Eve. . . ." Song Lao also mentions this custom in *Xipi Lei Kao*, 3/8, 18/4.

184. See LGTSHB, entry 25.

185. Zhou's friendship with Xu and their artistic activites were extensively documented in Xu's eleven letters to Zhou contained in LGT, *Chidu*, I, II, as well as in Zhou's own poems in LGTJ 9/18, 10/11, 12/2–3; YRZ 1/6; and LGTSHB, entries 3 and 15.

186. Zhou later introduced Xu's poetry to his eminent poet-critic friends, Qian Qianyi, Wang Shizhen, and Zhu Yizun, who highly esteemed it. See *Qingshi liezhuan*, 70/35.

187. Zhou described Xu You as follows: "He was the best in calligraphy, painting, poetry, and drinking. . . . He loved to paint small bamboos in imitation of Guan Zhongji [Guan Daosheng (1262–1319)]. With slender branches and tender leaves, they seem to naturally generate elegance. He carved his own seal which reads, 'Xu You huazhu' [Bamboo Painting of Xu You]. He impressed this seal whenever he painted bamboos." See LGTSHB, entry 3. Zhou also notes that Xu painted him against the background of his Jiaotang at Shaowu. See LGTSHB, entry 27.

188. Their jail experience together is vividly described in

Xu's biography in the *Du Hua Lu* and in Zhou's colophons to Xu's paintings recorded in the LGTSHB.

189. In 1648, upon Zhou's request, Guo painted "Jiaotang sezhutu," depicting Zhou at his Jiaotang studio at Shaowu. See LGTSHB, entry 25.

190. YRZ 2/9.

191. See Zhou's preface to this book titled *Guang jinshi yunfu*, recorded in LGTJ 15/12–15.

192. For other seal carvers Zhou met in Fujian, see YRZ 1/10, 3/15, 3/16, 3/18, 3/19, and 3/23.

193. YRZ 3/23.

194. YRZ 3/16.

195. YRZ 3/25.

196. He had a son named Xue Qian who earned a *shengyuan* degree, but was also forced to carve seals for a living.

197. YRZ 3/16. Xue Juxuan carved several dozen seals for Zhou.

198. YRZ 2/20.

199. DHL 2/1.

200. Friends who were not in government service frequently accompanied officials not only as companions, but also to avail themselves of the comfortable and speedy travel arrangements accorded officials.

201. See LGTSHB, entry 4.

202. DHL 1/15.

203. For example, he painted for the Hangzhou official Nan Shenglu (*jinshi* of 1637). See Chen's painting for Nan, titled "The Four Pleasures of Nan Shenglu," in the Drenowatz collection. See Chu-tsing Li, *A Thousand Peaks and Myriad Ravines: Chinese Paintings in the Charles A. Drenowatz Collection*, fig. 5. Also Huang Shu (*jinshi* of 1637), another Ming-Qing official, reports that he had a number of paintings by Chen and indicates that Nan had many of Chen's works. See DHL 1/15.

204. A poem Zhou composed in rhyme with Chen's welcoming poem is extant. See LGTJ 3/15. Although this poem is undated, we may assume it belongs to this period based on its content and its appearance in LGTJ, which I believe organized poems in chronological order.

205. Xu Bangda is said to have doubted the authenticity of this scroll (see Huang, *Chen Hongshou nian pu*, p. 127). Although I have not seen the original work, and its whereabouts is unknown, all stylistic and documentary evidence indicates that it is genuine. Formerly in Zhang Daqian's (1899–1983) collection, the work also bears two colophons by Zhang, one of which affirms that Zhou once owned the scroll.

206. For Lin Chong, who was renowned in Fujian as a calligrapher in standard script, see Zhou Lianggong, *Minxiao ji*, p. 13. Guo Dingjing's colophon is a transcription of Tao Qian's ode "Gui qu lai tu," and Lin Chong's is a transcription of Zhuge Liang's former and latter "Qushi biao" (Memorial on Sending Forth the Army). They are written in the small standard script for which the artists were famous in Fujian. We are informed by Lin and Guo that they transcribed these at Qianpu, Fujian, upon Zhou's request in the early summer of 1652.

207. An anonymous Song painting, "A Noble Scholar Under a Willow," in the collection of the National Palace Museum in Taipei and another anonymous Song dynasty handscroll in the Freer Gallery of Art entitled "Tao Yuanming Returning to Seclusion," are perhaps the earliest known paintings of Tao Qian. See *Chinese Art Treasures*, Geneva: Skira, pl. 26, and Thomas Lawton, *Chinese Figure Painting*, pl. 4. Qian Xuan of the Yuan dynasty, a Song loyalist painter, used Tao Qian symbolism to protest the political situation of his time. See Lee and Ho, *Chinese Art Under the Mongols: The Yüan Dynasty* (1279–1368), p. 184.

208. For the history of the Three Kingdoms period and the life of Zhuge Liang, see Achilles Fang, *The Cronicle of the Three Kingdoms*. Both memorials (the first written in 227 A.D., and the second written in 228) are translated in Fang's book, vol. 1, pp. 225–227 and 257–279.

209. As noted above, the painting Chen executed for Zhou as a farewell gift in 1641 took Tao Qian as the theme.

210. The painting, entitled "Yinjiu du Saotu," is cited in Huang, *Chen Hongshou nian pu*, p. 74.

211. See Zhang's letter in LGT, *Chidu*, 1, 9/2.

212. LGTJ/FL, *Xingshu*. Zhu Ruiwu in his 1646 painting for Zhou calls him Master Taoan in his dedicatory inscription.

213. DHL 3/19.

214. LGTJ 7/8.

215. See *Shuying*, p. 19.

216. Zhao served the Mongol court despite his Song imperial lineage.

217. This is a poetic inscription Zhao wrote on a painting, translated by Frederick W. Mote in "Confucian Eremitism in the Yüan Period," pp. 286–287. The title of Tao's ode "Returning Home" was originally translated as "On Returning" by Mote. I have kept the former translation for consistency. For further discussion on Zhao Mengfu's service under the Mongols, see Chu-tsing Li, "Zhao Mengfu shi Yuan de jizhong wenti."

218. DHL 3/4.

219. DHL 3/4.

220. One of the extant paintings by Zhang Feng now in a Japanese collection is a portrait of Zhuge Liang. Osvald Sirén, *Chinese Painting: Leading Masters and Principles*, vol. 6, pl. 371, B.

221. See LGTJ/FL, *Xingshu*, p. 54.

222. The question of whether or not Tao Qian himself was truly contented is irrelevant. We deal here only with the idealized image of Tao Qian which developed out of his writings after his death.

223. Wen Fong, "Archaism as a 'Primitive' Style," p. 106.

224. Fong, "Archaism," p. 108.

225. Political and social protest and "resistance" became the dominant artistic force. Even scholar-officials like Zhou Lianggong and those who actively sought government careers under the Qing invoked political symbolism in their own literary and artistic works and also sought this quality in others. Therefore almost every entry in the *Du Hua Lu* makes some political allusion to the fall of the Ming court or the Manchu conquest. This political sentiment is particularly evident in the biographies of Chen Hongshou, Kuncan (DHL 2/8), Fang Hengxian (DHL 2/12), Gong Xian (DHL 2/15), Xu You (DHL 3/3), Zhang Feng (DHL 3/4), and Yao Royi (DHL 4/6).

226. See LGTJ 8/8. The painting was certainly a political allusion and an expression of Chen's concern over Zhou's well-being. According to tradition, the phrase "Modoujian" appeared as an inscription on the abdomen of a stone statue outside the city wall of Gucheng, Xiangzhou, which read: "Just touch your helmet [instead]. Be careful not to talk." This must have become established as a political allusion by the early Tang, because it appears in the biography of Liu Ji, a prime minister during the reign of Taizong of the Tang. According to the story, Liu met an unusual per-

son when he was young who told him that "You are destined to help to bring peace [to this country]. You must strictly follow the 'modoujian' warning." See *Chogeng lu*, ch. 9 under Modoujian. Also see Morohashi, vol. 5, p. 367 and vol. 1, p. 1034. Chen apparently sought to apply the same warning to Zhou. A poem Zhou composed for Chen in response indicates that Chen must have written "Modoujian" on the abdomen of the statue in this painting. The painting seems to have been lost.

227. See Mao Qiling's preface to the *Du Hua Lu* and his letters to Zhou regarding the research on Chen in his *Xihe heji*, 56/7–10.

228. Zhou also wrote many moving colophons on Chen's paintings which he subsequently published. After Chen's death, Zhou secured a collection of Chen's poems which he planned to publish. During his six-year imprisonment, Zhou took special pains to safeguard Chen's paintings from falling into the hands of the vulgar men who would not understand his art.

229. DHL 2/15.

230. We have already encountered the term *xingqing* as applied to Zhou's discussion of Hu Yukun's painting in chapter 2.

231. LGTJ 13/11–12.

232. As for *gediao*, I have not yet found Zhou's use of this term in direct reference to painting, but the basic concept is nonetheless present in his discussion of painting as well as in that of other contemporaries. *Gediao* was the key critical term used by Li Dongyang (1447–1516), one of the former Seven Masters. For a discussion on this concept and other important contemporary concepts in literary theory and criticism, see Lynn, "Orthodoxy and Enlightenment," pp. 233–234. Also see Wai-kam Ho, "Tung Ch'i-ch'ang's New Orthodoxy."

233. The actual meaning of *gediao* is very complex in Chinese poetic theory, since it presupposes the long inherited stylistic tradition from the past. It is further complicated by the existence of the "orthodox" tradition founded by Yan Yu of the Song period, who not only held a belief in poetry as a means of self-cultivation and in poetic "enlightenment," but also advocated that a realization of poetic enlightenment can only come from a thorough assimilation of the stylistic tradition, centering around the enlightened poetry of the Han, Wei, Jin, and Tang with Du Fu as the supreme model. The *gediao* concept in the orthodox tradition of literature exerted a great influence on late Ming and early Qing painting theory, as evident in Dong Qichang's theory of bianhe (metamorphosis and inner correspondence) and of the Northern and Southern Schools. Since Zhou only really began to have an understanding and appreciation of the true value of *gediao* in the creative process of a painter through his meeting with Wang Hui, this aspect will be further discussed in Chapter 5.

234. Zhou even had seals carved reading "Budu Wang Li Zhong Tan zhishi" (Don't read the poems of Wang Shizhen, Li Panlong, Zhong Xing, and Tan Yuanqun). Zhong Xing (1574–1624) and Tan Yuanqun (1583–1637) were the founders of the Jinling school of poetry.

235. For Zhou's critical discussions on this subject, see LGTJ 13/12–13 and 20/8. Zhou repeats this view often, as seen in *Shuying*, p. 199: "Ancient poems are to express their sincere innermost feeling. . . ." For a discussion on poetry as social criticism, see Burton Watson, *Early Chinese Literature*, pp. 229–230.

236. See my discussion on this aspect of the *Du Hua Lu*

in the Introduction to my translation of the *Du Hua Lu* (forthcoming).

237. See LGTJ/FL, *Xingshu* and LGTJ/FL, *Muzhiming*.

238. DHL 2/5.

239. See the Shunzhi reign events recorded in *Qingshi*, *Tonghua lu xianji*, and all biographies of major political figures in ECCP.

240. See their biographies in ECCP.

241. See *Donghua lu xianji*, p. 143. Later in 1660, Cheng was impeached by an opponent, Wei Yijie (1616–1686), and subsequently dismissed. Listed among Cheng's offenses, cited by Wei, was his recommendation of Zhou.

242. For Chen Mingxia, see ECCP, p. 95.

243. See above note 241.

244. LGTJ/FL, *Nian pu*.

245. LGTJ/FL, *Xingshu*.

246. See Qian's preface to the anthology. Qian also contributed a preface to Zhou's collection of poems, *Laigutang shiji*, see LGTJ/FL.

247. Zhang and Zhou shared many mutual friends, including Sun Chengze, Gong Dingzi, and Cao Rong.

248. DHL 1/14.

249. At this time, Fang Yizhi lived at the Gaozuo temple in the city. See "Guobian nanchen chao," p. 56.

250. LGTJ, 5/2.

251. See Zhang Xun's colophon on a landscape scroll (Freer accession no. 80, 180–15) painted by Fang Hengxian, Cheng Sui, and Zhang Xun in collaboration.

252. See Sun's inscription written on a painting by the *Du Hua Lu* painter Shi Lin. Cited in DHL 4/17.

253. DHL 1/6.

254. LGTSHB, entry 1.

255. Yang Xin, "Cheng Zhengkui ji qi, 'Jiangshan woyu tu,'" p. 79.

256. See DHL 2/12.

NOTES TO CHAPTER FOUR

257. Qian Lucan and Huang Yuji strongly argue that these frequent transfers made it impossible for Zhou to exercise his talent and ability at the court. See LGTJ/FL, *Muzhiming* and *Xingzhuang*.

258. A detailed record of this imperial audience is found in LGTJ/FL, *Xingshu*, p. 47, and LGTJ/FL, *Muzhiming*, p. 14. According to Zhou's official biography in *Qingshi Liezhuan*, the proposals were supported by Zhou's ally, the Fujian governor Tong Guoqi.

259. *Erchenzhuan* in *Qingshi Liezhuan*.

260. The text goes on to explain that, "Later, the Fujian governor Tong Guoqi presented to the court the secret correspondence of [Zheng Chenggong's father] Zheng Zhilong and [his uncle] Honggui [d. 1657] with Zheng Chenggong. Zheng Zhilong was executed on November 24, 1661."

261. See Lin Zhi's biography in *Beizhuan zhi*, 10/21. The execution decision was made when a former brigade-general of Zheng Chenggong brought a similar charge against Zheng. See Zheng's biography in ECCP, pp. 110–112.

262. See Tong Dai's biography in *Qingshi*, vol. 5, p. 3752 (*zhuan* 241). For a more detailed discussion of the coastal removal proposal, see Zheng Chenggong's biography in ECCP, p. 109. The removal policy was later officially adopted when a similar proposal was submitted in 1657 by

Huang Wu (d. 1674), a former general of Zheng Chenggong.

263. The rehabilitation of the coastal area began in 1683 after the Qing conquest of Taiwan. See the biography of Du Zhen (*jinshi* of 1658) in ECCP, p. 777.

264. LGTJ 24/7–8.

265. LGTJ/FL, *Xingzhuang*, p. 29.

266. See *Jiangzhen nianbiao* under 1656 in *Qingshi*, vol. 4, p. 2853 (*zhuan* 189). The alternate name Duntai may be explained by his adoption of a Manchu name — not an uncommon practice among Chinese bannermen.

267. See the biography of Tong Guowei in ECCP, p. 795.

268. See Tong Yangxing's biography in ECCP, p. 797.

269. See Tong Guoqi's biography in ECCP, pp. 792–794. In the 1660s his son Shijing, a student at the Imperial Academy, married Zhou Lianggong's fourth daughter. See LGTJ/FL, *Xingzhuang*, pp. 58–59. For Zhou's friendship with Tong Guoqi while in Fujian, see Zhou's poem datable to 1650 in LGTJ 8/9.

270. LGTJ/FL, *Xingzhuang*, p. 29.

271. LGT *Chidu*, III, 9/12.

272. LGTJ/FL, *Xingshu*, p. 55.

273. LGT *Wenxuan*, 19/17–18.

274. See Gong Dingzi, *Dingshantang wenji*, 6/54.

275. LGTJ/FL, *Nian pu*.

276. LGTJ 8/13 and LGTSHB, entry 11.

277. LGTJ 21/6–7.

278. The verdict coincided with the coming of a long-awaited rain which ended a drought. According to LGTJ the local people sang a song, called "Rain of Ending the Case," in celebration of Zhou's acquittal. See LGTJ/FL, *Nian pu*, and LGTJ 24/1–13. For a list of the five judges, see LGTJ/FL, *Xingshu*, pp. 48–49.

279. LGTJ/FL, *Nian pu*.

280. This graphic, emotional account is recorded in LGTJ 21/11 and LGT *Wenxuan*, 16/5–7. Gao sent the work to Zhou in 1660 with an illustration by the Fujian painter Li Gen (DHL 4/3). See LGTJ 10/7. Gao also composed poems for two of the five judges and other friends, who accompanied Zhou to Beijing. Gao also compiled poems the Fujian people composed for Zhou and the provincial judge Cheng Zhixuan. Cheng died shortly after he was released. See DHL 4/14 and Zhou's sacrificial speech at Cheng's funeral ceremony in LGTJ 24/1–3.

281. The Fujian people built two *shengzi* (a temple in honor of one still living), which were probably converted to schools at Zhou's own request sometime before 1664. See LGTJ 19/12–14. In 1696, twenty-four years after Zhou's death, in gratitude to Zhou, retired scholar-officials of eight *jun* obtained government approval to enshrine Zhou's tablets in the Shrine of Famous Officials of all eight district *jun* schools. See Lin Ji's biography of Zhou in Beizhuanji, 10/21.

282. The Fujian local elders chose the *shengyuan* Zhe Ting to appeal to the court for Zhou's release. See *Shuying*, p. 42. Others who followed them were Hu Yukun, Wu Zongxin (*zi* Guanwu) from Anhui, and Hu Jie. Hu Jie, a famous Ming loyalist and friend of Xu You, Chen Hongshou, Gong Xian, and Gong Dingzi, had come down to Fujian sometime around 1656 and had been a constant companion of Zhou and Xu You. Although it is not clear whether or not he was implicated in Zhou's case, he did follow Zhou's group to the north at this time.

283. LGTJ 9/5.

284. LGTJ 9/5.

285. LGTJ/FL, *Nian pu* under 1659.

286. See Dirk Bodde and Clarence Morris, *Law in Imperial China*, p. 495.

287. LGTJ/FL, *Xingzhuang*, p. 30, and LGTJ/FL, *Nian pu* under 1660.

288. DHL 2/6.

289. See Wu's biography in ECCP, p. 882.

290. LGTJ/FL, *Xingshu*, p. 54. Another account in *Xingshu* notes that Zhou was absolutely against exacting unusual melting fees or taxes. This suggests that Zhou would not have had unusually large amounts of unofficial, irregular income, which was not uncommon for Qing officials. See Zhang Zhongli, *The Income of the Chinese* Gentry.

291. For a discussion on the economic aspect of art patronage see my conference paper, "Chou Liang-kung and his *Tu-hua-lu* Painters: Social and Economic Aspects of Mid-Seventeenth Century Chinese Painting."

292. Bodde and Morris, *Law in Imperial China*, p. 542.

293. See Song's colophon on an album for Zhou in LGT *Wenxuan*, 19/17–18.

294. See LGTJ 5/15–16 and LGTJ/FL, *Xingshu*.

295. See Song Wan's colophon in LGT *Wenxuan*, 19/17–18.

296. LGTSHB, entry 4.

297. In principle, all sentences involving officials as offenders, even if punishable by caning only, had to be ratified by the emperor before they could be carried out. Bodde and Morris, *Law in Imperial China*, p. 117.

298. LGTJ/FL, *Nian pu*; LGTJ 2/2.

299. LGTJ/FL, *Nian pu*, and Gao Fu's preface to *Shuying*.

300. See Gong's poem written on the 7th day of the 1st month in 1660 for Zhou in his *Dingshantang shiji*, 27/18, and Zhou's poem written on the same day in response in LGTJ 10/1. Their poems were relayed back and forth by Wu Zongxin, Zhou's student who followed him from Fujian to Beijing and stayed with him until his release. In a letter Zhou wrote to Gong in 1664 after his release, Zhou expressed his appreciation for Gong's unfailing friendship during his imprisonment: "Later when I was in trouble and had to stand on trial, you did whatever you could to extend your helping hands to rescue me from this calamity. You never hesitated to risk your own life to prove my innocence. Yet [at the time] I really did not know of your efforts, but only felt the affection and comfort hidden in your poems. Even this disaster did not prevent you from writing poems for me. Whenever you happened to read my poems you would always respond [with poems] in rhyme with them. During those three years you never failed to refer to my situation in your poems." See LGTJ 16/4–6. Also see Zhou's poems written for Gong from jail in LGTJ 9/18–19 and 10/1–2.

301. LGTJ 14/11–12. Also see my discussion on the literary style of the *Du Hua Lu* in the introduction to my translation of the work (forthcoming).

302. See the prefaces of Jiang Chenglie and Xu Fang (1622–94) to *Shuying*.

303. Zhou had his constant companion, Wu Zongxin, edit the collection of poems under the title *Laigutang shiji* and had his son Zaijun obtain a preface by Qian Qianyi and publish it in Nanjing in 1660. LGTJ/FL, *Nian pu*; Qian Qianyi's preface to *Laigutang shiji* in LGTJ/FL. The collection seems to have been later collapsed into a posthumous collection, *Laigutang ji*, which I have used extensively for this study.

304. During the Ming and Qing there was an abundance of *suibi*, or "random jottings" of men of letters on many different subjects. One well-known example is the work by Xie Zhaozhe called *Wuzazi* (Five Assorted Offerings).

305. See the entry for *Shuying* in *Siku chouhui shu tiyao-gao* by Wang Zhongmin, which contains an excerpt from the text, pp. 1–2. The title *Shuying* was chosen from a phrase (origin unknown): "[All that is] left is the shadow of what [this old man] has studied." According to Zhou Zaiyan's (b. 1653, Zhou's third son) preface to the book, it was first published in the winter of 1667 in Nanjing.

306. The deaths of his mother, née Feng (d. 1656), second son Zaiyang (1647–1656), and father Zhou Wenwei (d. 1658) while he was imprisoned, all seem to have been at least partially attributable to their worry over Zhou and must have made him feel responsible. The misery and anxiety Zhou felt over his failure to attend their funerals and his concern that he might never properly mourn the death of his parents as their eldest son are expressed in his poems. The coffins of his parents were to remain unburied at the Gaozuo temple in Nanjing until his final verdict was announced. See LGTJ/FL, *Nian pu*.

307. LGTJ 21/12–13.

308. LGTJ 21/6.

309. LGTJ 8/16, 9/2, 9/4.

310. LGTJ 8/17.

311. LGTJ 9/13–14.

312. The two Fujian scholar-artists Song Zijian and Xu You were involved in Zhou's case, and the seal carver-painter Huang Jing (b. ca. 1595 – d. 1663) was held under a separate charge in the same prison. A glimpse of their life in jail can be obtained through Zhou's biographies of Xu You and Huang Jing found in both the *Du Hua Lu* and the *Yinren zhuan*.

313. DHL 2/5.

314. According to Zhou, Xu followed Xu Wei and Chen Hongshou for his calligraphy. Xu's album of calligraphy in the Art Museum of Princeton University supports Zhou's judgment and esteem, while remarks made by such prominent poets of his time as Qian Qianyi, Wang Shizhen, and Gong Dingzi confirm Zhou's assessment of his accomplishment as a poet. Xu's poems are included in Qian's *Liechao shiji* and Wang's *Ganjiu ji*.

315. He occasionally also did landscape paintings as can be seen from the record of one painting he did sometime around 1648 for Zhou, depicting Zhou's Jiaotang studio in Shaowu, Fujian. See LGTSHB, entry 27.

316. See DHL 3/3 and Zhou's poem "Mourning the Death of Xu Yujie," LGTJ 10/15.

317. See LGTSHB, entry 21.

318. QHJSS, *jiashang*/16.

319. Zhou's poem is in the *yuefu* tradition, and is found in the DHL 3/3.

320. YRZ 2/2.

321. The censorship of Zhou's books in the eighteenth century confirms this. See the introduction to my translation of the *Du Hua Lu* (forthcoming).

322. DHL 2/5; DHL 3/1.

323. Contained in QHJSS, *jiashang*/16.

324. See Gong, *Dingshantang shiji*, 4/24.

325. LGTJ/FL, *Xingshu*.

326. LGTJ/FL, *Xingzhuang*.

327. See the biography of the Shunzhi emperor (Fulin) in ECCP, p. 258.

328. LGTJ/FL, *Xingzhuang* and *Xingshu*.

329. The emperor reduced Zhou's sentence from immediate execution by strangulation to death by decapitation after the Autumn assizes. The addendum "after the assizes," according to Bodde and Morris's study, often resulted in commutation during the Qing. See Bodde and Morris, *Law in Imperial China*, pp. 78, 99, 134–143.

330. LGTJ/FL, *Nian pu*.

331. See *Erchen zhuan* in *Qingshi Liezhuan*.

332. See Chen Weisong, "Zhou Liyuan xiansheng shu," in *Beijuanji*, 10/26–27. Chen's essay was written to celebrate Zhou's return when the two met in Yangzhou, and records what Zhou said during a gathering at the time.

333. His return was whole-heartedly celebrated by numerous friends including Mao Xiang, Wang Shizhen, Cheng Sui, Wu Qi, Wu Jiaji, Deng Hanyi, Lin Sihan, Huang Yun, Tang Yunjia, Mei Lei, Du Jun, Hu Jie, and Chen Weisong — many of whom wrote essays and poems to celebrate his return alive. The names of all those who wrote congratulatory writings for Zhou upon his return is listed in Mu Quansun, "Yunzuzai kan biji," 25–26. I would also like to express my thanks to Andrew Hsieh, who informed me of this list. Also see LGTSHB, entry 5 and GLTJ 10/8–9.

334. LGTJ/FL, *Nian pu*, and *Erchen zhuan* in *Qingshi Liezhuan*.

335. LGTJ 17/2.

336. See Qian's preface to *Laigutang shiji* in LGTJ.

337. LGTSHB, entry 11; LGTJ 21/6.

338. *Qian Muzhai xiansheng nian pu*, p. 12, ECCP, pp. 148–150.

339. See ECCP, p. 149; *Qian Muzhai xiansheng nian pu*, pp. 9–10.

340. While Qian was teaching the young Zheng in Nanjing, Qian named him Damu, which means the "great material." Qian reportedly used his concubine Liu Shi to transmit the funds to Zheng and went to Nanjing to welcome Zheng's army. *Qian Muzhai xiansheng nian pu*, pp. 9–10, 13, 15–17. Also see Chen Yinke, *Liu Rushi biezhuan*, 1980, chapter 5, "The Ming Restoration Movement."

341. LGT *Chidu*, III, 4/13.

342. LGT *Chidu*, I, 5/7.

343. They were lost in the fire set by the mob protesting his collaboration. For a more detailed account, see *Qian Muzhai xiansheng nian pu*, p. 12.

344. *Qian Muzhai xiansheng nian pu*, pp. 14–16.

345. Qian became an ardent Buddhist after suffering the 1650 burning of his Jiangyulou. The fire consumed much of his collection of invaluable rare books and art objects, as well as his numerous manuscripts on history and *guwen*, which were the result of years of work. In his preface to Zhou Lianggong's *Laigutang wenxuan* dated 1654, Qian vividly recounts this painful experience and his turning to Buddhism as a consequence. He called himself "Haiyin baiyi dizi" (Disciple of the White-robed Avalokitesvara from Haiyin [at Mount Pute]). See *Qian Muzhai xiansheng nian pu*, pp. 12, 17.

346. See Zhou Zaijun's description of his father in LGTJ/FL, *Xingshu*, and that by a Lisengren in a preface to *Laigutang shiji* in LGTJ. Yu Zhiding's (1647–1709) portrait of Zhou, probably posthumous, mildly reflects these descriptions.

347. LGTJ 10/15, 19/12–14.

348. Zhou in fact expressed his disapproval of the life style of Buddhist laymen like Jin Ding, who did not marry

or serve the government. This is probably why he avoided printing Jin's writings, which are filled with Buddhist sayings. See LGTJ 13/13–14.

349. This view is reflected in a colophon written on a painting owned by his friend Lin Sihuan, who served in Fujian with Zhou, and, like Zhou, was slandered and imprisoned from 1658 to 1660. See LGTSHB, entry 9.

350. de Bary, *Neo-Confucian Cultivation and Enlightenment*, p. 201.

NOTES TO CHAPTER FIVE

351. See ECCP, pp. 345–347.

352. Manchu rule in the south was not really consolidated until Kangxi crushed the Three Feudatories in 1681 and finally conquered Taiwan in 1683. But the Manchu administration over the Jiangnan area had already been well entrenched by the early 1660s.

353. YRZ 2/14.

354. Wang is better known as the editor of the *Mustard Seed Garden Painting Manual*.

355. Gong lived to be more than seventy years old and his long life no doubt contributed to his fame and influence.

356. Much to the regret of his brother Zhang Yi and Zhou, Zhang Feng died within ten days of meeting Zhou.

357. Zhou admired Hu's paintings of chrysanthemums for their nonchalant quality. Hu was active in the 1660s, and his two sons also had become painters.

358. YRZ 1/14.

359. YRZ 1/10.

360. The grouping currently used is Zhang Geng's list, which includes Gong Xian, Fan Qi, Gao Cen, Ye Xin, Hu Cao, Wu Hong, Zou Zhe, and Xie Sun. I have not found any reference by Zhou to the last painter. For a further discussion on the problem of the origins of this grouping, see William Wu, "Kung Hsien," pp. 161, 169, 276, n. 180. Two points should be added to Wu's discussion: 1) none of the artists and literary men who were in close contact with Zhou and Nanjing refer to such a grouping, except Song Lao who refers to the Eight Nanjing Masters in a poem composed for Liu Yu around 1689 without identifying its membership or its origin; 2) the uncertainty surrounding the grouping is evident from the fact that another account — the *Jiangning fuzhi* (revised edition) — which again attributes the grouping to Zhou, lists a different membership: Fan Qi, Gao Cen, Zou Zhe, Wu Hong, Chen Zhe, Wu Dan (Zhongbu), Cai Ze, and Li Yuli. The last four painters were relatively obscure in Zhou's time. Furthermore, I have not found references to the last three in Zhou's writings.

361. LGT, *Wenxuan*, 19/17.

362. DHL 3/19.

363. Le Mu was a close friend of Gu Dashen's. Zhou had known Gu from before 1645. LGTJ 6/18.

364. See Mei Qing's poem composed for Wang Hui in *Qinghui zengyen*, 2/8.

365. Daoji lived away from the Jiangnan area and was probably still too young to attract Zhou's attention. A hanging scroll painting by Kuncan dated 1669 for Zhou bears Daoji's colophon, but the authenticity of the painting is in doubt. See Sirén, *A History of Later Chinese Painting*, pl. 200.

366. *Shiqu baoji sanbian*, vol. 5, p. 2140.

367. Wang Shimin, *Wang Fengchang shuhua tiba, xia*, p. 7. The entry heading reads: "Colophon at the end of an album of paintings by contemporary artists dedicated to the honorable Zhou Liyuan [Zhou Lianggong]."

368. Wu Li, a native of Changshu, was a student of Wang Shimin and Wang Jian and a close friend of Wang Hui.

369. The relationship between the two Jiangnan centers and Zhou's role as an intermediary between the two will be closely examined below.

370. LGT, *Chidu*, II, 15/13.

371. This colophon is written on Wang Hui's painting presented to Zhou Lianggong, now in the collection of the Asian Art Museum, San Francisco.

372. See DHL 4/18. Gao Cen was ill and Gong Xian was in seclusion.

373. DHL 4/18.

374. DHL 1/12.

375. DHL 2/7.

376. LGT, *Chidu*, I, 5/3.

377. The anthology contains, for example, Gong Xian's letter criticizing Hu Yukun, Cheng Zhengkui's appreciating Hu Yukun, Zou Zhe's criticizing Chen Hongshou for his eroticism; also included are Zhang Feng's discussion on painting with his brother Zhang Yi, Gao Fu's discussion on painting with his brother Gao Cen, Zhang Feng's discussion on painting with Cheng Zhengkui, Tu Yanfen's detailed observation of Chen Hongshou's method of painting plums; more examples are Chen Danzhong's discussion on painting with Zong Hao, Kuncan's discussion on painting with Cai Longwen, Cheng Zhengkui's letter to Yun Xiang, and many others.

378. LGT, *Chidu*, III, 13/2.

379. DHL 4/18.

380. Wang Shimin's grandfather was Grand Secretary Wang Xijue (1534–1611), while Wang Jian's great-grandfather was Wang Shizhen (1526–1590), an eminent scholar-poet-connoisseur whose last government position was Minister of the Board of Punishments.

381. Wang Shimin and Wang Jian's biographies are not contained in the official histories of the Ming and Qing dynasties. The following conclusion on Wang Shimin's relationship with Wen Tiren and his anti-Fushe stance is largely drawn from reading Lu Shiyi, *Fushe Jilie* (4/99–102), and other writings of the period.

382. The Wang family in fact had several confrontations with their fellow townsmen Zhang Pu, who founded the Fushe in Taicang in 1627, and Zhang Cai, who was Zhang Pu's best friend.

383. Ma Shiying was also included among the total six "evil officials."

384. The degree to which political divisions were mirrored in the art world of the period and the possible impact of this division is an intriguing question that merits closer study.

385. The following observation on Wu Weiye is based on Wu's own account of the history of the Fushe, entitled *Fushe Jishi*, and his poems (see, for example, one poem dated 1647 Wu composed for Wang Shimin in QHJSS), and Lu, *Fushe Jilie*.

386. Wu included Wang Shimin and Wang Jian in his poem, titled "Huazhong jiuyou" (Nine Friends in Painting), probably written in the late 1650s. The other members of the Nine Friends are Dong Qichang, Bian Wenyu, Shao

Mi, Cheng Jiasui, Li Liufang, and Yang Wencong. This poem follows the tradition of the so-called "Lunhua jueju," a regulated verse which strings together names of famous figures in the art world and gives poetic descriptions of each man's personality, art, life, etc. The chosen ones are not necessarily related to each other as a group. It had become a popular poetry genre among connoisseurs and painters by Wu's time. Wu's "Huazhong jiuyu" reveals that his choice of the nine was a reflection of his personal esteem towards them. When written by such famous literary figures as Wu Weiye, such poems were widely circulated and gradually became established as a tradition. There is evidence that the eminent Qing poet-critic Wang Shizhen played a major role in the popularization of the grouping of his four friends, Wang Shimin, Wang Jian, Wang Hui, and Wang Yuanqi under the "Four Wangs."

387. See bibliography for books and articles on Dong Qichang's art and theory. I have drawn on the works of Wen Fong, Wai-kam Ho, and John Lynn and have adopted their translations and interpretations of some key critical terms and ideas, here and elsewhere.

388. In Fang Yizhi's critical terminology, this transition can be viewed as one from a stage "with method," a formally conscious stage, to one with "no method," where the artist goes beyond self-consciousness. See Fang's theoretical comment recorded in DHL 2/7.

389. The view of the two Wangs here was similar to that of Yan Yu (1180–1235), the Song founder of the orthodox literary tradition: "There is no need to argue about what is right and what is wrong in poetry. All one has to do is take his own poetry and place it among the poetry of the ancients. If, upon showing it to a connoisseur, he is unable to notice that it is any different, one is then a true man of antiquity." Yan Yu, Canglang shihua jiaoshi, p. 127, quoted in Lynn, pp. 222–223.

390. The two Wangs' interpretations of Dong Qichang's orthodox theory is closely akin to an elaboration of Yan Yu's poetics by the former Seven Masters of mid-Ming and to the formalistic emphasis of Ming literary criticism. Li Dongyang and Li Mengyang's theory of *gediao* (formal style), in which they advocated imitation as the way to become a master of poetry, seems to directly parallel the Taicang school's theory.

391. Dong's assertion was based upon his belief that the Four Great Masters' art was appropriate to study since it was "amenable to formal analysis" in contrast to Song art which was beyond rational analysis.

392. Marc Wilson, *Kung Hsien*.

393. Wilson, *Kung Hsien*, p. 21.

394. Sometimes in his study of Dong Yuan, Gong would refer to the works of Dong Yuan's student, the monk Juran, which he thought were the most reliable vestige of Dong's work. See Wu, "Kung Hsien," p. 117.

395. See the small landscape he painted for Zhou Lianggong fig. 50, cat. no. 26.

396. Sirén, *Leading Masters and Principles*, vol. v, pp. 103–104.

397. Wang utilized endorsements of recognized scholars and teachers such as Qian Qianyi and Wu Weiye, and they in turn took the opportunity to ask for his paintings in exchange. For example, Wang Hui asked Wu to write a colophon on another painting (no longer extant) he painted for Zhou. See Wang Hui, comp., *Qinghuige zengyi chidu* (hereafter QZC), *shang*/16. Several letters of the two elder Wangs reveal that this was a common practice of Wang

Hui. See, for example, Wang Jian's letter in QZC, *shang*/21.

398. Wang Shimin, *Wang Fengchang shuhuatiba*, 6/8.

399. QZC *xia*/11.

400. DHL 2/11.

401. In this point, I differ from Lynn's understanding of Qian Qianyi's literary theory. From my own readings of Qian's extant critical writings, I have reached the conclusion that Qian was never against the revival of ancient literature.

402. See those colophons recorded in Wang's collected works, *Yuyang shizhuan* and *Yuyang xu shizhuan*.

403. Lynn, "Orthodoxy and Enlightenment," p. 256.

404. For a discussion on this aspect, see my introduction to the *Du Hua Lu* (forthcoming).

405. See his preface to his book, *Guang jishi yunfu*, in LGTJ 15/14.

406. DHL 3/4.

407. Wang Shizhen maintained a close friendship with the two elder Wangs as well as Wang Hui and Wang Shimin's grandson, Wang Yuanqi, who have been grouped together as the "Four Wangs." Wang Shizhen, Wang Hui, and Wang Yuanqi dominated the art world of the Kangxi reign (1622–1722) after Zhou's death. John Lynn has pointed out in his study of Wang Shizhen's poetics a close affinity between Wang Shizhen and Wang Yuanqi in their orthodox view of art and illustrates his point with a long discussion the two had on "orthodoxy and intuitive control." See Lynn, pp. 243–244.

408. Wang Hui, comp., *Qinghui zengyan*, 4/22.

409. QZC *xia*/28.

410. Whitfield, *In pursuit of Antiquity*, p. 42.

411. Other examples include the two landscape paintings published in *Bunjinga Seihen*, Tokyo: Chuo koronsha, 1974, vol. 7, "Landscape after Kuan Tung" (colorplate) and p. 23.

412. See for example the album leaf in the Sackler collection reproduced in Fu, *Studies in Connoisseurship*, Cat. No. XV, Leaf G, "Peach Blossom Spring."

413. I hope to have another occasion to explore the personal and stylistic relationship between Wang Hui and the Nanjing artists in the 1660s.

414. See Wang Shimin's letters to a friend complaining that Wang Hui valued money over friendship, quoted in Contag, *Chinese Masters of the 17th Century*, pp. 13–14.

415. QZC *shang*/6.

416. QZC *shang*/16.

417. See the list of names of those who corresponded with Wang in *Qinghuige zengyi chidu* and *Qinghui zengyan*. For information on his work at court on the "Nanxuntu" (Pictorial Record of the Kangxi Emperor's Southern Tour) project, see Simon B. Heilesen, "Southern Journey," *Bulletin of the Museum of Far Eastern Antiquities*, 1980, no. 52. Also see Whitfield, *In Pursuit of Antiquity*, p. 45.

418. Several excellent studies on the subject of Confucian morality are available in Wright, ed., *The Confucian Persuasion and Confucianism in Action*.

419. According to the "law of avoidance," officials were forbidden from holding office in their native province or in neighboring provinces within a 500-*li* radius. Ch'u T'ung-tsu, *Local Government in China under the Ch'ing*, p. 320, n. 28.

420. In an inscription, Gong Xian expressed his high esteem for Ma's work. See Wu, "Kung Hsien," pp. 148–149.

421. Other examples of artists whose reputations suffered because of historical condemnation of their polit-

ical activity are legion. For example, Yang Xiong's literary reputation suffered due to his service in two ruling houses; the calligraphy of Li Si was not recognized because of his role as prime minister for the infamous First Emperor of the Qin (r. 221–208 B.C.), and Cai Jing's (1046–1125) calligraphy suffered a similar fate as Li Si's after he was labeled an evil minister. See Zhou's comments on Li Si's calligraphy in LGTSHB, entry 12, and Wang Shizhen's on Cai Jing in Ma's biography quoted below.

422. DHL 4/19.

423. Contradictory reports are found regarding which books were actually burnt. Zhou's eldest son, for example, reports that the *Du Hua Lu* was not one of the burnt books, while his younger brother says it was. It is generally agreed that Zhou did not burn the works of his friends.

424. LGTJ 20/16.

425. LGTJ 20/14.

426. LGTJ/FL. For Lu's biography, see ECCP, 551. Lu's preface was taken out of the book sometime after 1723 when Lu's anti-Manchu writings were proscribed. See Goodrich, *The Literary Inquisition*, pp. 22, 84–85. Fortunately the *Qingren bieji conggan* of LGTJ restored Lu's preface and put in the addendum.

427. Translated in Cyril Birch, ed., *Anthology of Chinese Literature*, vol. 2, p. 134.

428. For example, the famous loyalist recluse Hu Jie was constantly dependent on the financial help of Zhou Lianggong and Gong Dingzi. When he died, Zhou and Gong bought a burial site for him. See LGT, *Chidu*, I, 5/13–15, and II, 16/6. A countless number of loyalists depended on collaborator-scholar-officials for moral and financial support and for preservation of their names for posterity.

429. Wilson, *Kung Hsien*, 27.

430. I have adopted Silbergeld's translation of the colophon with only minor changes. See Silbergeld, "Political Symbolism," p. 273.

431. Gong Dingzi, *Dingshantang wenji*, 6/37.

432. LGT, *Chidu*, II, 11/8.

433. LGTJ 20/14.

434. One interesting new editorial principle he wanted to adopt in his compilation project was to eliminate the names of the authors. This once again reflects his contempt for ambition and fame. He wrote to a friend: "Nowadays, whenever a poet raises a banner [i.e., establishes himself with his own style], he makes one more enemy because he is known to others. However, the idea of raising a banner is not for the sake of the poetry, but for fame. The idea of fame is not suitable for [the art of poetry]. Aren't there any poets worthy of establishing a banner among those poets of the 300 poems in the *Shijing*? Yet there is not a single name in these poems. . . . " See LGTJ 19/9. In response to Zhou's new editorial approach, a friend of Zhou wrote to him advising against it: "I have heard that you would like to select a collection of poems by contemporary poets, but have decided not to put down the names of the authors. You think you can really concentrate on the quality of poems without being bothered by considerations of friendship, keeping people's face, and quenching complaints and quarrels afterwards, but . . . ." See LGTJ, *Chidu*, II, 11/12.

435. QZC, *shang*/15. This letter was written in response to Wang Hui's letter received on the 2nd day of the 2nd month of 1671.

436. Peterson, *Bitter Gourd*, p. 14.

437. See Yu Yingshi, *Fang Yizhi wanjiekao*, p. 189.

438. YRZ 3/10.

439. YRZ 1/6; DHL 3/3.

440. YRZ 1/9.

441. LGTJ/FL, *Xingzhuang*.

Chinese Glossary

Ai Nanying	艾南英	Dong Qichang	董其昌
An Qi	安歧	Donglin Shuyuan	東林書院
Bai Tao Fang	百陶舫	*Du Hua Lu*	讀畫錄
Ban Gu	班固	Du Jun	杜濬
Baoen Temple	報恩寺	Fa Ruozhen	法若真
Bao Shu Zi	抱蜀子	Fan Jingwen	范景文
Beixue ji	北雪集	Fan Qi	樊圻
Bian Wenjin	邊文進	Fang Hengxian	方亨咸
Bian Wenyu	卞文瑜	Fang Kongzhao	方孔炤
Cao Rong	曹溶	Fang Qiyi	方其義
Chen Danzhong	陳丹衷	Fang Yizhi	方以智
Chen Hongshou	陳洪綬	Feng Kezong	馮可宗
Chen Kaizhong	陳開仲	Feng Youjiang	馮幼將
Chen Mingxia	陳名夏	Fu Shan	傅山
Chen Shu	陳舒	Fu Wang	福王
Chen Taisun	陳台孫	Fushe	復社
Chen Zhenhui	陳貞慧	Ganyuan	敢園
Chen Zilong	陳子龍	Gao Cen	高岑
Cheng Jiasui	程嘉燧	Gao Fu	高阜
Cheng Lin	程林	Gao Jie	高傑
Cheng Sui	程邃	Gao Shiqi	高士奇
Cheng Zhengkui	程正揆	Gao Yang	高陽
Cui Zizhong	崔子忠	Gao Yu	高遇
Dai Benxiao	戴本孝	Gaozuo Temple	高座寺
Dai Mingyue	戴明説	*Gengzi Xiao Xia Ji*	庚子銷夏記
Daoji	道濟	Gong Dingzi	龔鼎孳
Ding Jizhi	丁繼之	Gong Xian	龔賢
Dongjing Menghua Lu	東京夢華錄	Gu Dashen	顧大申

Gu Kaizhi	顧愷之	Kuncan	髠殘
Gu Mengyu	顧夢與	*Laigutang shiji*	賴古堂詩集
Gu Qiyuan	顧起元	*Laigutang wenxuan*	賴古堂文選
Gu Yanwu	顧炎武	Lan Ying	藍瑛
Gu Yuanfang	顧元方	Li Gen	李根
Guan Xiu	貫休	Li Liufang	李流芳
Guiqulai Ci	歸去來辭	Li Xia	櫟下
Guo Dingjing	郭鼎京	Li Zicheng	李自成
Guo Gong	郭鞏	Liang Danian	梁大年
Han Yuesu	韓約素	Liang Qianqiu	梁千秋
He Faxiang	和發祥	Liang Qingbiao	梁清標
Hongren	弘仁	Lin Chong	林寵
Hou Fangxia	侯方夏	Lin Jin	林晉
Hou Fangyu	侯方域	Lin Xiong	林熊
Hou Ke	侯恪	Liu Du	劉度
Hu Cao	胡慥	Liu Jiu	劉酒
Hu Shikun	胡士昆	Liu Liangzuo	劉良佐
Hu Yukun	胡玉昆	Liu Yu	劉埥
Hu Zhengyan	胡正言	Liu Zongzhou	劉宗周
Hu Zongren	胡宗仁	Lu Wang	魯王
Huang Daozhou	黃道周	Luo Mu	羅牧
Huang Gongwang	黃公望	Luo Yao	羅耀
Huang Jing	黃經	Ma Shiying	馬士英
Huang Songsu	黃嵩素	Ma Shouzhen	馬守貞
Huang Yuji	黃虞稷	Mao Kun	茅坤
Huang Zongxi	黃宗羲	Mao Xiang	冒襄
Ji Dong	計東	Mao Yuanyi	茅元儀
Jiang Chengzong	姜承宗	Mei Qing	梅清
Jiang Haochen	江皡臣	Mi Wanzhong	米萬鍾
Jiang Song	蔣嵩	*Min Xiao Ji*	閩小記
Jianzhai	減齋	*Mo Dou Jian*	磨兜堅
Jiaotang	蕉堂	Nan Shenglu	南生魯
Jiaotangshi	蕉堂詩	Ni Can	倪燦
Jin Bao	金堡	Ni Yuanlu	倪元璐
Jiuyuan	就園	Ni Zan	倪瓚
Kong Shangren	孔尚任	Qi Biaojia	祁彪佳

Qi Xiongjia	祁熊佳	Wang Shizhen	王世貞
Qi Zhijia	祁豸佳	Wang Shizhen	王士禎
Qian Lucan	錢陸燦	*Wanshan zhongshi*	萬山中詩
Qian Qianyi	錢謙益	Wei Baizhi	魏百雉
Qinhuai	秦淮	Wei Zhongxian	魏忠賢
Qiu Min	丘旼	Wei Zhihuang	魏之璜
Ruan Dacheng	阮大鍼	Wei Zhike	魏之克
Shao Mi	邵彌	Weishe	濰社
Shen Hao	沈顥	Wen Zhengming	文征明
Shen Shichong	沈士充	Weng Ling	翁陵
Shen Shoumin	沈壽民	Wu Bin	吳彬
Shewu Pavilion	射烏樓	Wu Daoning	吳道凝
Shi Lin	施霖	Wu Di	吳弟
Shi Zhong	史忠	Wu Hong	吳宏
Shizhuzhai Hua Pu	十竹齋畫譜	Wu Jingzi	吳敬梓
Shihualou	詩話樓	Wu Qiyuan	吳期遠
Sima Qian	司馬遷	Wu Ruilong	伍瑞隆
Song Luo	宋犖	Wu Shiguan	吳士冠
Song Quan	宋權	Wu Wei	吳偉
Song Yu	宋玉	Wu Weiye	吳偉業
Sun Chengze	孫承澤	*Wu Za Zu*	五雜俎
Taicang	太倉	Xia Sen	夏森
Tao Hua Shan	桃花扇	Xiang Shengmo	項聖謨
Tao Qian	陶潛	Xiao Yuncong	蕭雲從
Tong Dai	佟岱	Xie Bin	謝彬
Tongshu	同書	Xie Cheng	謝成
Wan Shouqi	萬壽祺	Xie Daoling	謝道齡
Wang Duo	王鐸	Xie Zhaozhi	謝肇淛
Wang Gai	王概	*Xingshu*	行述
Wang Hui	王翬	Xingshe	星社
Wang Jian	王鑒	Xu Hongji	徐弘基
Wang Jianzhang	王建章	Xu Qianxue	徐乾學
Wang Meng	王蒙	Xu Yanshou	徐延壽
Wang Longqi	王隆起	Xu You	許友
Wang Shilu	王士祿	Xu Zhi	許豸
Wang Shimin	王時敏	Xue Wu	薛五

Xue Juxuan	薛居瑄	Zhang Xun	張恂
Xue Qian	薛錢	Zhang Yi	張怡
Xueyuan	雪苑	Zhao Bei	趙備
Yan Ermei	閻爾梅	Zhao Cheng	趙澄
Yan Yu	嚴羽	Zhao Zhilong	趙之龍
Yang Bu	楊補	Zhao Zuo	趙左
Yang Tingshu	楊廷樞	Zheng Chenggong	鄭成功
Yang Wencong	楊文驄	Zheng Hongkui	鄭鴻逵
Yao Lüshi	姚履施	Zheng Yuanxun	鄭元勳
Yao Ruoyi	姚若翼	Zheng Zhilong	鄭芝龍
Yao Yunzai	姚允在	Zheng Zhong	鄭重
Ye Xin	葉欣	Zhou Lianggong	周亮工
Yinren zhuan	印人傳	Zhou Liangjie	周亮節
Yinshuwu	因樹屋	Zhou Minqiu	周敏求
Yiyang	翼揚	Zhou Tinghuai	周庭槐
Yu Zhiding	禹之鼎	Zhou Wenwei	周文煒
Yun Shouping	惲壽平	Zhou Zaijun	周在浚
Yun Xiang	惲向	Zhu Da	朱耷
Zeng Qing	曾黥	Zhu Ruiwu	朱睿𥮎
Zha Shibiao	查士標	Zhu Shiwang	朱時望
Zhang Feng	張風	Zhu Yihai	朱以海
Zhang Gu	章谷	Zhu Yizun	朱彝尊
Zhang Hong	張宏	Zhu Yousong	朱由崧
Zhang Keda	張可大	Zhu Zhiqiao	朱智㰘
Zhang Lu	張路	Zhuang Jiongsheng	莊冏生
Zhang Minbiao	張民表	Zong Hao	宗灝
Zhang Pu	張浦	Zong Yuanding	宗元鼎
Zhang Ruitu	張瑞圖	Zou Dian	鄒典
Zhang Xianzhong	張獻忠	Zou Zhe	鄒喆
Zhang Xiu	張修	Zou Zhilin	鄒之麟
Zhang Xueceng	張學曾		

Bibliography

ABBREVIATIONS

BZZB: *Lidai mingren beizhuan nianli zongbiao*
CP: Sirén, *Chinese Painting: Leading Masters and Principles*
CPBio: Laing, *Chinese Paintings in Chinese Publications, 1958–1968*
CSJCCB: *Congshu jicheng chubian*
DHL/SL: "Supplementary List of Artist Names" in DHL
DHL: Zhou Lianggong, *Du Hua Lu*
DHZCS: *Duhua zhai congshu*
DMB: Goodrich and Fang, *Dictionary of Ming Biography*
ECCP: Hummel, *Eminent Chinese of the Ch'ing Period*
HSXGCS: *Haishan xianguan congshu*
HSCS: *Huashi congshu*
Jinkui CJ: Chen, *Jinkui canghua ji*
Jinkui CPS: Chen, *Jinkui canghua pingshi*
LGT Chidu: Zhou Lianggong, *Laigutang chidu xinchao*
LGT Shiji: Zhou Lianggong, *Laigutang shiji*
LGT Wenxuan: Zhou Lianggong, *Laigutang wenxuan*
LGTJ: Zhou Lianggong, *Laigutang ji*
LGTJ/FL: "Fulu" (Addendum) in LGTJ
LGTSHB: Zhou Lianggong, *Laigutang shuhuaba*
MQZJ: *Ming Qing zhi ji minghua tezhan*
PISCP: *Proceedings of the International Symposium of Chinese Painting*
QHGZYCD: Wang Hui, comp., *Qinghuige zengyi chidu*
QHJSS: *Qing huajia shishi*
QSJSCB: *Qingshi jishi chubian*
SDZ: *Shoudu zhi*
SHJNP: *Song Yuan Ming Qing shuhuajia nianpiao*
Shuying: Zhou Lianggong, *Yinshuwu shuying*
YRZ: Zhou Lianggong, *Yinren zhuan*
YSCB: *Yishu congbian*

WESTERN LANGUAGE SOURCES:

Acker, William. *Some T'ang and Pre-T'ang Texts on Painting.* Leiden: E.J. Brill, 1954.

An Album of the Ting-ching-tang Collection of Chinese Paintings and Calligraphy: Ming and Ch'ing Periods. Selected and compiled by Lin Tsung-i. Tokyo: Asuka Gallery, 1968.

Atwell, William S. "From Education to Politics: The Fu She." In de Bary, *The Unfolding of Neo-Confucianism,* pp. 333–367.

Bai Qianshen. "Fu Shan (1607–1684/85) and the Transformation of Chinese Calligraphy in the Seventeenth Century." Ph.D. dissertation, Yale University, 1996.

Barnhart, Richard. "Survivals, Revivals, and the Classical Tradition of Chinese Figure Painting." In PISCP.

Bodde, Derk and Clarence Morris. *Law in Imperial China.* Philadelphia: University of Pennsylvania Press, 1973.

Bush, Susan. *The Chinese Literati on Painting: Su Shih (1037–1101) to Tung Ch'i-ch'ang (1555–1636).* Cambridge: Harvard University Press, 1971.

Cahill, James. *The Distant Mountains: Chinese Painting of the Late Ming Dynasty, 1570–1644.* New York: Weatherhill, 1982.

———. *Fantastics and Eccentrics in Chinese Painting.* New York: The Asia Society, Inc. 1967.

———. "The Early Styles of Kung Hsien." *Oriental Art,* no. 5, vol. XVI (Spring 1970): 51–71.

———. "Confucian Elements in the Theory of Painting." In *The Confucian Persuasion,* ed. by Arthur F. Wright. Stanford: Stanford University Press, 1960.

Cahill, James, ed. *Shadows of Mt. Huang.* University Art Museum, Berkeley, 1981.

———. *The Restless Landscape: Chinese Painting of the Late Ming Period.* Berkeley: University Art Museum, 1971.

Ch'iu, A. K'ai-ming. "The Chieh Tzu Yuan Hua Chuan," in *Archives of the Chinese Art Society of America,* V (1961): 55–69.

Chang Chung-li. *The Chinese Gentry: Studies in Nineteenth-century Chinese Society.* Seattle: University of Washington Press, 1970.

Chin Shih Di Ming Pei Lu of Ch'ing Dynasty. Harvard-Yenching Institute Sinological Index Series, Supplement no. 19, Reprint, Taipei: Chengwen chubanshe, 1966.

Chou Ju-hsi. "In Quest of the Primordial Line: The Genesis and Content of Tao-chi's 'Hua-yu-lu.'" Ph.D dissertation, Princeton University, 1970.

Chu T'ung-tsu. *Local Government in China under the Ch'ing.* Stanford: Stanford University Press, 1969.

Contag, Victoria. *Chinese Masters of the Seventeenth Century.* Rutland, Vermont: Charles Tuttle, 1970.

Contag, Victoria and Wang Chi-ch'ien. *Seals of Chinese Painters and Collectors of the Ming and Ch'ing Periods.* Hong Kong: Hong Kong University Press, 1970.

Crawford, Robert B. "The Biography of Juan Ta-ch'eng," in *Chinese Culture,* 6.2 (1965), pp. 22–105.

de Bary, Wm. Theodore. "Neo-Confucian Cultivation and Enlightenment," in de Bary et al. *The Unfolding of Neo-Confucianism.*

de Bary, Wm. Theodore, et al. *The Unfolding of Neo-Confucianism.* New York: Columbia University Press, 1970.

———. *Sources of Chinese Tradition.* New York: Columbia University Press, 1960.

Fong, Wen C. "Orthodoxy and Change in Early Ch'ing Landscape Painting," in *Oriental Art,* no. 1, vol. XVI (Spring 1970).

———. Tung Ch'i-ch'ang and the Orthodox Theory of Painting," in *National Palace Museum Quarterly,* II:3 (January 1968).

———. "Wang Hui: The Great Synthesis," in *National Palace Museum Quarterly,* III:2 (October 1968).

Fong, Wen C. (Cont'd)."Archaism as a 'Primitive' Style," in Christian F. Murck, ed., *Artists and Traditions,* pp. 89–109.

Fong, Wen C., et al. *Images of the Mind: Selections from the Edward L. Elliott and John B. Elliott Collections of Chinese Calligraphy and Painting at The Art Museum, Princeton University.* Princeton: Princeton University Press, 1984.

Fu Shen, C. Y. "Wang To and His Circle: The Rise of Northern Connoisseur-Collectors," paper prepared for the symposium "Eight Dynasties of Chinese Painting," held at the Cleveland Museum of Art, 1981.

———. "An Aspect of Mid-Seventeenth Century Chinese Painting: The 'Dry Linear' Style and the Early Work of Tao-chi," in *Proceedings of the "Symposium on Paintings and Calligraphy by Ming I-min,"* held at The Chinese University of Hong Kong, 1975, pp. 579–618, Cheng Te-k'un et al., eds., in *The Journal of the Institute of Chinese Studies* of The Chinese University of Hong Kong, no. 2, vol. VIII (December 1976).

———. "A Study of the Authorship of the Hua-shuo," in PISCP: 85–140.

Fu, Marilyn W., and Fu Shen, C. Y. *Studies in Connoisseurship: Chinese Paintings from the Arthur M. Sackler Collection, New York and Princeton.* Princeton: Princeton University Press, 1973.

Fu, Marilyn W., and Fu Shen, C. Y., et al. *Traces of the Brush: Studies in Chinese Calligraphy.* New Haven: Yale University Press, 1977.

Goodrich, L. Carrington. *The Literary Inquisition of Ch'ien-lung.* Baltimore: Waverly Press, 1935.

Goodrich, L. Carrington, and Fang Chao-ying, eds. *Dictionary of Ming Biography.* 2 vols. New York: Columbia University Press, 1976.

Hay, John A. "Huang Kung-wang." Ph.D. dissertation, Princeton University, 1978.

Ho, Ping-ti. *The Ladder of Success in Imperial China: Aspects of Social Mobility.* New York: Columbia University Press, 1962.

———. "The Salt Merchants of Yang-chou: A Study of Commercial Capitalism in Eighteenth Century China," in *Harvard Journal of Asiatic Studies,* no. 17 (1954): 130–168.

Ho, Tseng-yu. "A Report on Ch'en Hung-shou," in *Archives of the Chinese Art Society of America,* vol. VIII (1959).

Ho, Wai-kam. "Nan-Ch'en bei-Ts'ui: Ch'en of the South and Ts'ui of the North," in *The Bulletin of the Cleveland Museum of Art,* vol. 49, no. 1 (January 1962): 2–11.

———. "Tung Ch'i-ch'ang's New Orthodoxy and the Southern School Theory," in *Artists and Traditions,* edited by Christian Murck, pp. 113–130.

Hummel, Arthur W., ed. *Eminent Chinese of the Ch'ing Period.* 2 vols. Washington, D.C.: United States Government Printing Office, 1943–1944.

Kim, Hongnam. "Chou Liang-kung and his *Tu-hua-lu* Painters: Social and Economic Aspects of Mid-Seventeenth Century Chinese Painting," in Li, Chu-tsing, et al., eds. *Artists and Patrons: Some Social and Economic Aspects of Chinese Painting.* The Kress Foundation of Art History, University of Kansas, The Nelson-Atkins Museum of Art, and the University of Washington Press, 1989.

Kung Hsien and the Nanking School: Some Chinese Paintings of the 17th Century. Introduction by Aschwin Lippe. Exhibition catalogue: China House Gallery. New York, 1955.

Kuo Chi-sheng. "The Paintings of Hung-jen." Ph.D. dissertation, The University of Michigan, 1980.

Laing, Ellen J. *Chinese Paintings in Chinese Publications, 1958–1968: An Annotated Bibliography and an Index to the Paintings.* Michigan Papers in Chinese Studies, no. 6. Ann Arbor, 1968.

Lee, Sherman E., et al. *Eight Dynasties of Chinese Painting: The Collections of the Nelson Gallery-Atkins Museum, Kansas City, and the Cleveland Museum of Art.* Cleveland: The Cleveland Museum of Art and Indiana University Press, 1980.

Levy, Howard, trans. *A Feast of Mist and Flowers: The Gay Quarters of Nanking at the End of the Ming.* Yokohama: published privately, 1966.

Li Chi. "The Changing Concept of the Recluse in Chinese Literature," in *Harvard Journal of Asiatic Studies* XXIV (1962–1963): 235–247.

Li, Chu-tsing. *A Thousand Peaks and Myriad Ravines: Chinese Paintings in the Charles A. Drenowatz Collection.* 2 vols. Ascona: Artibus Asiae, 1974.

Lippe, Aschwin. "Kung Hsien and the Nanking School," in *Oriental Art,* n.s. II (Spring 1956), 21–29; n.s. IV (Winter 1958): 159–170.

Liu, James T. C. *Reform in Sung China: Wang An-shih (1021–1086) and His New Policies.* Cambridge: Harvard University Press, 1968.

Lovell, Hsin-cheung. *An Annotated Bibliography of Chinese Painting Catalogues and Related Texts.* Ann Arbor: The University of Michigan Center for Chinese Studies, 1973.

Lynn, R. John. "Orthodoxy and Enlightenment: Wang Shih-chen's Theory of Poetry and Its Antecedents," in de Bary, Wm T., et al. *The Unfolding of Neo-Confucianism.*

March, Andrew. "Landscape in the Thought of Su Shih (1036–1101)." Ph.D. dissertation, University of Washington, 1964.

Miyazaki, Ichisada. *China's Examination Hell: The Civil Service Examinations of Imperial China.* Trans. by Conrad Schirokaufer. New Haven: Yale University Press, 1981.

Mote, Frederick W. "The Transformation of Nanking, 1350–1400," in *The Cities of Imperial China,* ed. by G. William Skinner. Stanford: Stanford University Press, 1977.

Murck, Christian F., ed. *Artists and Traditions.* Princeton: Princeton University Press, 1976.

Peterson, Willard J. *Bitter Gourd: Fang I-chih and the Impetus for Intellectual Change.* new Haven: Yale University Press, 1979.

Proceedings of the International Symposium on Chinese Painting. Taipei: National Palace Museum, 1970.

Rao Zongyi. "Painting and the Literati in the Late Ming," in *Journal of the Institute of Chinese Studies of The Chinese University of Hong Kong,* vol. VIII, no. 2: 391–409.

Rawski, Evelyn S. *Education and Popular Literacy in Ch'ing China.* Ann Arbor: The University of Michigan Press, 1979.

Riely, Celia C. "Tung Ch'i-ch'ang's Ownership of Huang Kung-wang's 'Dwelling in the Fu-ch'un Mountains,'" in *Archives of Asian Art,* no. 28 (1974–1975): 57–76.

Rolex, Robert A. "'Setting Out at Dawn on an Autumn River': A Painting by Wang Hui," in *Artibus Asiae,* vol. XLI, no. 1.

Ruhlmann, Robert. "Traditional Heroes in Chinese Popular Fiction," in *The Confucian Persuasion,* edited by Arthur F. Wright. Stanford: Stanford University Press, 1960, pp. 141–176.

Silbergeld, Jerome L. "Kung Hsien's Self Portrait in Willows with Notes on the Willow in Chinese Painting and Literature," in *Artibus Asiae,* vol. XXXXII (1980), no. 1: 5–38.

——. "Political Symbolism in the Landscape Painting and Poetry of Kung Hsien (c. 1620–1689)." Ph.D. dissertation, Stanford University, 1974.

Sirén, Osvald. *A History of Later Chinese Painting.* 2 vols. New York: Hacker Art Books, 1978.

——. *The Chinese on the Art of Painting.* New York: Stocken Books, 1969.

——. *Chinese Painting: Leading Masters and Principles.* London: Percy Lund, Humpheries and Co. Ltd., 1958.

Sources of Chinese Tradition. Comp. by Wm T. de Bary et al. New York: Columbia University Press, 1960.

Spence, Jonathan D. *The Emperor of China: Self-portrait of K'ang-hsi.* Princeton: Princeton University Press, 1974.

——. *Ts'ao Yin and the K'ang-hsi Emperor.* New Haven: Yale University Press, 1966.

Spence, Jonathan D., and John E. Wills, Jr., eds. *From Ming to Ch'ing: Conquest, Region, and Continuity in Seventeenth-Century China.* New Haven: Yale University Press, 1979.

Strassberg, Richard E. *The World of K'ung Shang-jen.* New York: Columbia University Press, 1983.

The Painting of Tao-chi. A catalogue of an exhibition, August 13—September 17, 1967. Held at the Museum of Art, University of Michigan, ed. by Richard Edwards. Ann Arbor, 1967.

Tomita, Kojira, and Kaiming A. Chiu. "Album of Six Chinese Paintings Dated 1618," in *Bulletin of the Museum of Fine Arts,* XLVIII (Boston, 1950), p. 26.

Wakeman, Frederic, Jr. "The Shun Interregnum of 1644," in Spence and Wills, eds., *From Ming to Ch'ing,* pp. 41–87.

Wang Xiuchu. "Yangzhou shiri ji" (A Memoir of the Ten Days' Massacre in Yangchow). Trans. by Lucien Mao. In *Tian Xia Monthly,* vol. IV (1937): 515–537.

Watson, Burton. *Early Chinese Literature.* New York: Columbia University Press, 1962.

——. *Records of the Grand Historian of China.* 2 vols. New York: Columbia University Press, 1961.

Wenley, A. "A Note on the So-called Sung Academy of Painting," in *Harvard Journal of Asiatic Studies,* 1942.

Whitfield, Roderick, et al. *In Pursuit of Antiquity.* Rutland: Turtle Co., 1969.

Wilson, Marc. "Kung Hsien: Theoretist and Technician in Painting," in *The Nelson Gallery and Atkins Museum Bulletin,* Kansas City, 1969.

Woodson, Yoko. "The Sung-chiang (Yun-chien) Painters, I: Sung Hsu and His Followers," in James Cahill, ed. *Restless Landscape.*

Wu, Nelson. "The Evolution of Tung Ch'i-ch'ang's Landscape Style as Revealed by His Works in the National Palace Museum," in PISCP: 1–84.

——. "Tung Ch'i-ch'ang (1555–1636): Apathy in Government and Fervor in Art," in *Confucian Personalities,* A. F. Wright and D. C. Twitchett, eds. Stanford: Stanford University Press, 1962.

Wu, William D. Y. "Kung Hsien." Ph.D. dissertation, Princeton University, 1979.

———. "Kung Hsien's Style and His Sketchbooks," in *Oriental Art,* no. XVI (Spring 1970): 72–81.

Yang Xianyi and Yang, Galys, trans. *The Scholars* (Rulin waishi) by Wu Jingzi (1701–1754). New York: The University Library, 1972.

———. *Li Sao and Other Poems of Chu Yuan.* Beijing: Foreign Language Press, 1953.

Yang, Lucy Lo-hwa. "The Wu School in Late Ming, II: Innovative Masters," in James Cahill, ed. *Restless Landscape.*

Zheng Dekun. "Twenty Ming Yimin Painters in the Mufei Collection," in *The Journal of the Institute of Chinese Studies of the Chinese University of Hong Kong,* vol. VIII: 223–256.

ASIAN LANGUAGE SOURCES:

Baimei ji 白梅集. Shanghai: Shangwu yinshuguan, 1927.

Bao Shichen 包世臣. *Yizhou shuangji* 藝舟雙楫, in YSCB, IV.

Beizhuanji 碑傳集. Comp. by Qian Yiji 錢儀吉. n.p. Jiangsu shuju, 1983.

Chen Jiru 陳其儒 (1558–1639). *Baoyantang biji* 寶顏堂筆記. Shanghai: Wenming shuju, 1922.

Chen Rendao 宸仁禱. *Jinkui* [King Kwei] *canghua ji* 金匱藏畫集. Kyoto: Benrido, 1956.

———. *Jinkui* [King Kwei] *canghua pingshi* 金匱藏畫評史. Hong Kong: Dongnan shuju, 1956.

Chen Wannai 陳萬氖. *Kong Dongtang* [Kong Shangren] *xiansheng nianpu* 孔東塘先生年譜. Taipei: Shangwu yinshuguan, 1970.

Chen Yuan. "Siku tiyao zhong zhi Zhou Lianggong," 四庫提要中之周亮工 in *Wenxian luncong* 文獻論叢. Beijing: Gugong Bowuyuan, 1936.

Congshu jicheng chubian 叢書集成初編. Comp. by Wang Yunwu 王雲五. Shanghai: Shangwu yinshuguan, 1936.

Deng Shi 鄧實. *Tanyi lu* 談藝錄, in YSCB, vol. XXIX.

Dong Qichang 董其昌 (1555–1636). *Huayan* 畫眼, in YSCB, vol. XII.

Duhua zhai congshu 讀畫齋叢書. Published in 1799.

Fuzhou fuzhi 福洲府志. Taipei, 1967 (reprint of 1754 edition). In the collection of the Library of Congress.

Gong Dingzi 龔鼎孳. *Dingshan tang shiji* 定山堂詩集. 43 *juan* with *Shiyu* 詩餘, 4 *juan.* 1883 edition.

———. *Dingshan tang wenji* 定山堂文集. 6 *juan.* Taipei, 1924.

Gong Xian 龔賢. *Chaizhangren huajue* 柴丈人畫訣, in *Huayuan biji* 畫苑秘笈, ed. by Wu Bijiang. Reprint, Taipei, 1959.

Gu Ningyuan 顧凝遠 (fl. ca. early 17th c.). *Huayin* 畫引, in YSCB, vol. XII.

Gu Qiyuan 顧起元. *Kezuo zhuiyu* 客座語. An edition with a postscript dated 1618 in the Library of Congress Rare Books Collection.

Gugong minghua 故宮名畫, ed. by Wang Shijie 王士節. Taipei, 1966–1969.

Gugong shuhua lu. 故宮書畫錄. Taipei: National Palace Museum, 1956.

Guotai meishuguan xuanji: Ming-Qing mingjia shuhua jicui 國泰美術館選集明清名家書畫集淬. Taipei: Guotai meishuguan, 1978, vol. 6.

"Guobian nanchen chao" 國變難臣鈔, an addendum to *Minzhong jilüe* 閩中記略. In *Taiwan wenxian congkan,* 1968, Taipei: Zhonghua shuju, 1968.

Haishan xianguan congshu 海山仙館叢書. Comp. by Pan Shicheng 潘仕成. Printed in 1849.

Huang Yongquan 黃湧泉. *Chen Hongshou* 陳洪綬. Shanghai, 1958. In *Zhongguo huajia congshu* 中國畫家叢書. Hong Kong: Zhongguo shuhua yanzhou hui, 1970.

——. *Chen Hongshou nianpu* 陳洪綬年譜. Beijing: Renmin meishu chubanshe, 1960.

——. *Chen Laolian banhua xuanji* 陳老蓮版畫選集. Beijing, 1957.

Huashi congshu 畫史叢書, 10 vols. Comp. by Yu Anlan 于安畕. Shanghai, 1962.

Ji Yingzhong 紀映鐘 (1609–1689). *Zhuangsou shichao, fu buyi* 戇溲詩鈔附補遺. Shanghai: Shanghai yinshuguan, 1937.

Jiang Shaoshu 姜紹書. *Wusheng shishi* 無聲詩史. Postscript dated 1720. In HSZS, vol. IV.

Jiangning fuzhi 江寧府志. Comp. by Yao Nai 姚氖. Jiaqing (1796–1820) edition.

Jinling fuzhi 金陵府志. Comp. by Chen Kaiyu 陳開虞 (fl. late 17th c.). A 1668 edition in the Library of Congress Rare Books Collection.

Jinling gujin tukao 金陵古今圖考. Comp. by Zhu Zhifan 朱之蕃 (b. 1654). In *Jinling tu sanzhong* 金陵圖三種.

Jinling suoshi 金陵瑣事. A Wanli (1573–1620) edition in the Library of Congress Rare Books Collection.

Jinling suozhi 金陵瑣志. A 1900 edition in the Library of Congress collection.

Jinling tongzhuan 金陵通傳. Comp. by Chen Boyu 陳伯雨. Reprint of 1904 edition, in *Zhongguo fangzhi congshu* 中國方志叢書, vol. XXXVIII (Huazhong difang).

Jinling tu sanzhong 金陵圖三種, 4 vols. Comp. by Zhu Zhifan 朱之蕃 (b. 1654). An edition in the Library of Congress Rare Books Collection.

Jinling tuyong 金陵圖詠. 1 *juan*. Comp. by Zhu Zhifan 朱之蕃 (b. 1654). An edition in the Library of Congress Rare Books Collection.

Jinshu 晉書. Comp. by Fang Xuanling 防玄齡. Beijing: Zhonghua shuju, 1924.

Kaifeng fuzhi 開封府志. Comp. by Zhang Mu et al. 40 *juan*. 1695 edition.

Kong Shangren 孔尚任. *Taohuashan* 桃花扇, completed in 1699. Translated by Chen Shih-hsien and Harold Acton, with the collaboration of Cyril Birch. Berkeley: University of California Press, 1976.

Lao Tianbi 勞天比, ed. *Zhile lou suocang Ming yimin shuhua lu* 至樂樓所藏明遺民書畫錄. Hong Kong: Dongnan yinwu chubanshe, 1962.

Li Changheng [Li Liufang] *shanshui* 李長蘅山水. Shanghai: Shangwu yinshuguan, 1929.

Li Rihua 李日華. *Zhulan huasheng* 竹懶畫勝, in YSCB, vol. XIII.

Lianghuai yanfa zhi 兩淮鹽法志. 4 vols., ed. by Xian Gaichong (written in 1693). Taipei: n.p., 1966.

Liangshu 梁書. Comp. by Yao Silian 姚思廉. Beijing: Zhonghua shuju, 1973.

Liu Tiren 劉體仁. *Qisong tang shi xiaolu* 七頌堂識小錄, in YSCB, vol. XXIX.

Liu Yiqing 劉義慶. *Shishuo xinyu* 世説新語. Hong Kong: Yang Yong, 1969.

Longyou [Yang Wencong] *momiao ce* 龍友墨妙冊. Osaka: Hakubundo, 1917.

Lu Xinyuan 陸心源. *Rangliguan guoyan lu* 穰黎館過眼錄, 1891.

Mao Qiling 毛奇齡 (1623–1716). *Xihe heji* 西河合集. 493 *juan*. (First printed in 1699.) 1770 edition.

Miao Quansun 繆荃孫. "Yunzizai kan biji" 雲自在堪鼻記. In *Guocui xuebao* ed., *Guxue huikan* 古學彙刊. Taipei: Lixingshuju, vol. III.

Ming-Qing jinshi timingbei suoyin 明清進士題名碑索引, in *Lidai jinshi timing lu* 歷代進士題名錄. Taipei, 1970.

Ming-Qing zhiji minghua tezhan 明清之際名畫特展. Exhibition catalogue, National Palace Museum, Taipei, 1970.

Mingshi 明石. Comp. by Zhang Tingyu 長廷玉 (1672–1755) et al. Reprint, Taipei: Zhonghua shuju.

Pang Yuanji 龐元濟. *Xuzhai minghua xulu* 虛齋名畫續錄. Shanghai, 1924; Addendum, 1925.

——. *Xuzhai minghua lu* 虛齋名畫錄. Shenjiang: Wuxing pangshi, 1909.

Qian Mu 錢穆. *Zhuangzi zuanjian* 莊子纂箋. Hong Kong: Dongnan yinwu, 1962.

Qian Muzhai [Qian Qianyi] *xiansheng nianpu* 錢牧齋先生年譜. Comp. by Jin Hezhong 金鶴仲. Taipei, 1932.

Qian Qianyi 錢謙益. *Youxue ji* 有學裻, in *Muzhai quanji* 牧齋全集. Published by Suihanzhai, 1910.

Qin Zuyong 秦租永 (1825–1884). *Tongyin lunhua* 桐陰論畫, in YSCB, vol. XVI.

Qinghua jia shishi 清畫家詩史. Comp. by Li Junzhi 李濬之. Beijing: National Library of Peiping [Beijing], 1930.

Qingshi 清史. 550 *juan* in 8 vols. Taipei: Guofang yanjiuyuan, 1961.

Qingshi jishi chubian 清史紀事初編. Comp. by Deng Wencheng 鄧文成. Taipei: Zhonghua shuju, 1970.

Qingshi liezhuan 清史列傳. 80 *juan*. Shanghai: Zhonghua shuju, 1928.

Rao Zongyi 饒宗頤. "Zhang Dafeng jiqi jiashi," 張大風及其家世, in *Journal of the Institute of Chinese Studies* of The University of Hong Kong, vol. VIII, no. 1 (1976), pp. 51–70.

——. "Fang Yizhi zhi hualun," 方以智之畫論 in *Journal of the Institute of Chinese Studies*, no. 7 (1974), pp. 170–175.

Shao Sengmi [Shao Mi] *shanshui ce* 邵僧彌山水冊. Shanghai: Shangwu yinshuguan, 1939.

Shaoxing fuzhi 紹興府志. A 1792 edition. In the Library of Congres Rare Books Collection.

Shen Hao 沈顥 (1586–after 1661). *Huachen* 畫辰 (a Ming edition). In *Guang Baichuan xuehai* 廣百川學海. Comp. by Feng Kebin 馮可賓.

Shenzhou daguan 神州大觀. 16 vols. Shanghai, 1912–1921.

Shi Runzhang 施閏章 (1619–1683). *Shi Yushan xiansheng quanji* 施愚山先生全集. 24 *juan*. 1765 edition.

Shicheng shan zhi 石城善志, an appendium to *Jinling suozhi* (1900 edition). Library of Congress collection.

Shiqu baoji sanbian 石渠寶笈三編. Comp. by Hu Jing et al., commissioned by the Qianlong
    Emperor (r. 1736–1795). Completed 1816. Facsimile reprint, Taipei, 1969, vol. 5.

Shoudu zhi 首都志. Comp. by Wang Huanbiao 王煥鑣 et al. 2 vols. Taipei: Zhengzhong shuju,
    1966 (first edition, n.p., pub. in 1935).

Sima Qian 司馬遷. *Shiji* 史記 (completed in 91 B.C.). 10 vols. Reprint, Beijing: Zhonghua
    shuju, 1959.

Song Lao. *Mantang shuhuaba* 漫堂書畫跋, in YSCB, vol. XXV.

Song Luo 宋犖 (1634–1713). Xipo Leigao 西坡類槁, 1711 edition.

Su Shi 蘇軾 (1036–1101). *Dongpo tiba* 東坡題跋, in YSCB, vol. XXII.

Sun Chengze 孫承澤. *Gengzi xiaoxia ji* 庚子銷夏記 (written in 1660). In *Zhibuzu zhai congshu*
    知不足齋叢書, comp. by Bao Tingbo (1728–1814).

Sun Shaoyuan 孫紹遠. *Shenghua ji* 聲畫集. In *Linting shi'erzhong* 林亭十二種, comp. by Cao Yin
    曹寅, 1706. Shanghai: Gushu liutong chu, 1921.

Tang Hou 湯垕 (fl. early 14th c.). *Hualun* 畫論, in *Meishu congshu* 美術叢書, III, 7.

Tang shu 唐書. Comp. by Ouyang Xiu 歐陽修. A 1644 edition. In the Library of Congress
    collection.

Wang Duo 王鐸 (1592–1652). *Nishanyuan xuanji* 擬山園選集. 54 *juan*. First printed in 1653.

Wang Hui 王翬 (1632–1717), comp. *Qinghui zengyan* 清暉贈言. Published by Fengyu lou (Deng
    Shi 鄧實) in 1911, based on the original edition.

——. comp. *Qinghui ge zengyi chidu* 清暉閣贈貽尺牘. In the collection of the Harvard-
    Yenching Library.

Wang Hui huapu 王翬畫譜. Taipei: National Palace Museum, 1970.

Wang Shimin 王時敏 (1592–1680). *Wang Fengchang shuhua tiba* 王奉常書畫題跋. Reprint of
    1909 edition.

Wang Shiqing 汪世清. "Gong Xian de *Caoxiang tang ji*" 龔賢的草香堂集, in *Wenwu* 文勿,
    no. 5, 1978.

Wang Shiqing et al. *Jianjiang ziliao ji* 漸江資料集. Hefei: Anhui renmin chubanshe, 1984.

Wang Shizhen 王士禛 (1632–1711). *Daijing tang quanji* 帶經堂全集. 72 *juan*. 1684 edition.

——. *Yuyang shanren ganjiu ji* 漁洋山人感舊集, with biographies provided by Lu Jianzeng
    盧見曾. 16 *juan*. 1752 edition.

Wu Mingdao 吳銘道. "Fushe xingshi bulu," 復社姓氏補錄, in *Guichi xiansheng zhe yishu* 貴池先生
    哲遺書, vol. V, Taipei: Yiwen yinshuguan, 1962.

Wu Yingji 吳應箕. "Fushe xingshi," 復社姓氏 ("Qianjuan" 前卷, "Houjuan" 後卷, and "Fulu" 附
    錄). In *Guichi xiansheng zhe yishu* 貴池先生哲遺書, Taipei: Yiwen yinshuguan, 1920.

——. "Liudu fangluan gongjie xingshi," 留都防亂公揭姓氏 in *Guichi xiansheng zhe yishu* 貴池先生
    哲遺書. Taipei: Yiwen yinshuguan, 1920.

Xiangfu xian zhi 祥符縣志. Comp. by Lu Zengyu 魯曾煜, 1739 edition.

Xiangfu xian zhi 祥符縣志, 24 *juan*; Addendum 1 *juan*, 1898 edition.

Xu Jinling suozhi 續金陵瑣志. Comp. by Wang Guandao.

Xuanhe huapu 宣和畫譜 (written ca. 12th century), in YSCB, vol. IX.

Yan Yu (1180–1235) 嚴羽. *Canglang shihua* 滄浪詩話. In *Jindai bishu* 津逮秘書, comp. by Mao Jin 毛晉 (1599–1659).

Yang Xin 揚新. "Cheng Zhengkui jiqi 'Jiangshan woyou tu,'" 程正揆及其江山臥遊圖 in *Wenwu* 文勿, no. 12, 1981.

Ye Xia'an [Gongchuo] 葉遐庵. *Xia'an tanyilu* 遐庵談藝錄, no publisher, no date.

Yishu congbian 藝術叢編. Comp. by Yang Jialuo 楊家駱, 24 vols. Shanghai: Shijie shuju, 1906–1910. Preface 1962.

Yong Rong 永瑢 et al. *Lidai zhiguanbiao* 歷代職官表. Taipei: Zhonghua shuju, 1677.

Yu Huai 余懷 (1616–1696). *Banqiao zaji* 板橋雜記. Collated edition, privately published by Howard S. Levy, Yokohama, 1966.

Yu Yi 余毅, ed. *Ming Chen Hongshou huaji* 明陳洪綬畫集. Taipei: Zhonghua shuhua chubanshe, 1974.

Yu Yingshi 余英時. *Fang Yizhi wanjie kao* 方以智晚節考. Hong Kong: Xin ya yanjiusuo, 1972.

Zhang Dai 張岱. *Tao'an mengyi* 陶庵夢憶. Reprint, Taipei: Kaiming, 1957.

Zhang Geng 張庚 (1686–1760). *Guochao huazheng lu* 國朝畫徵錄. Jiangdu: Liushi, 1895.

Zhang Huaiguan 張懷瓘 (fl. 713–741). *Shuduan* 書斷. In Zhang Yanyuan 張彥遠 (ca. 810–880), *Fashu yaolu* 法書要錄, in YSCB, vol. I.

Zhang Yanyuan 張彥遠. *Lidai minghua ji* 歷代名畫記 (completed in 847). In YSCB, vol. VII.

Zhao Wendu [Zhao Zuo] *shanshui ce*. 趙文度山水冊. Shanghai, 1929.

Zhao Xuejiang [Zhao Cheng] *fanggu shanshui ce* 趙雪江仿古山水冊. Hakubundo, Osaka: Hakubundo, 1919.

Zheng Xizhen 鄭錫珍. *Hongren Kuncan* 弘仁髡殘. Shanghai renmin meishu chubanshe, 1963.

Zhile lou cang Ming yimin shuhua 至樂樓藏明藝民書畫. The Art Gallery, Institute of Chinese Studies, The Chinese University of Hong Kong, 1975.

Zhou Lianggong 周亮工 (1612–1672). *Laigutang ji* 賴古堂集. In *Qingren bieji congkan* 清人別集叢刊. Shanghai: Shanghai guji chubanshe, 1978.

———. *Tongjin* 通燼, completed in ca. 1641. Taipei: Guangwen shuju, 1976.

———. *Min xiaoji* 閩小記. Taipei: Chengwen chubanshe, 1975.

———. *Laigutang chidu xinchao* 賴古堂尺牘新鈔. 3 vols. Taipei: Zhonghua shuju, 1972.

———. *Yinshuwu shuying* 因樹屋書影. Originally printed in 1667. Beijing: Zhonghua shuju, 1958.

———. *Yinren zhuan* 印人傳. 1910 edition. In *Cuilangganguan congshu* 翠琅玕館叢書, XXXIV.

———. *Du Hua Lu* 讀畫录. 4 *juan* (first printed in ca. 1673).

This book is included in the following *congshu*:

1. *Duhuazhai congshu* 讀畫齋叢書 (DHZCS), pub. in 1799.

2. *Haishan xianguan congshu* 海山仙館叢書 (HSXGCS). Comp. by Pan Shicheng 潘仕成 and pub. in 1849.

3. *Fengyulou congshu* 風雨樓叢書 (FYLCS). Comp. by Deng Shi.

4. *Congshu jicheng chubian* 叢書集成初編 (CSJCCB). Comp. by Wang Yunwu 王雲五 and pub. in 1936.

5. *Yishu congbian* 藝術叢編 (YSCB). Comp. by Yang Jialuo (preface 1962).

6. *Huashi congshu* 畫史叢書 (HSCS), pub. in 1963.

——. *Laigutang ji* 賴古堂集. Includes *Laigutang wenji* 賴古堂文集, *Laigutang shiji* 賴古堂時集, and *Laigutang shuhuaba* 賴古堂書畫跋, with original prefaces and 1 *juan* of "fulu." 24 *juan*. A 1675 edition in the Library of Congress Rare Books Collection.

——. *Laigutang shuhuaba* 賴古堂書畫跋. In YSCB, vol. XXV.

Zhou Lianggong, comp. *Laigutang wenxuan* 賴古堂文選. 20 *juan*. Kangxi reign (1662–1722) edition.

Zhou Liyuan [Zhou Lianggong] *Du hua lou shuhua jicui* 周亮工讀畫樓書畫裒淬. Special supplement to *Gugong zhoukan*. Beijing: Gugong bowuyuan, 1931.

Zhou Liyuan [Zhou Lianggong] *shouji mingren huace* 周亮工手集名人畫冊. *Shenzhou guoguang ji*, a special issue. Shanghai: Shenzhou guoguang she, 1966.

Zhou Wenwei 周文煒 (d. 1659). "Guanzhai sishi jixiang xiang," 觀宅四十吉祥相. In *Zhaodai congshu* 昭代叢書, a "bieji" 別集. 1849 edition (based on the Shikai tang collection).

Zhu Huiliang 朱惠良. *Zhao Zuo yanjiu* 趙左研究. Taipei: National Palace Museum, 1579.

Zhu Jingxuan 朱景玄. *Tang chao minghua lu* 唐朝名畫錄, completed early 840s. In YSCB, vol. VIII.